Lecture Notes in Computer Science

16696

Founding Editors

Gerhard Goos
Juris Hartmanis

The series Lecture Notes in Computer Science (LNCS), including its subseries Lecture Notes in Artificial Intelligence (LNAI) and Lecture Notes in Bioinformatics (LNBI), has established itself as a medium for the publication of new developments in computer science and information technology research, teaching, and education.

LNCS enjoys close cooperation with the computer science R & D community, the series counts many renowned academics among its volume editors and paper authors, and collaborates with prestigious societies. Its mission is to serve this international community by providing an invaluable service, mainly focused on the publication of conference and workshop proceedings and postproceedings. LNCS commenced publication in 1973.

Elena Cabrio · Eric Monteiro
Editors

Natural Language Processing and Information Systems

31st International Conference on Applications
of Natural Language to Information Systems, NLDB 2026
Trondheim, Norway, June 17–19, 2026
Proceedings

 Springer

Editors
Elena Cabrio
Université Côte d'Azur
Nice, France

Eric Monteiro
Norwegian University of Science
and Technology
Trondheim, Norway

ISSN 0302-9743   ISSN 1611-3349 (electronic)
Lecture Notes in Computer Science
ISBN 978-3-032-29531-6   ISBN 978-3-032-29532-3 (eBook)
https://doi.org/10.1007/978-3-032-29532-3

This Springer imprint is published by the registered company Springer Nature Switzerland AG
The registered company address is: Gewerbestrasse 11, 6330 Cham, Switzerland

If disposing of this product, please recycle the paper.

Preface

We are delighted to present the proceedings of the 31st International Conference on Natural Language and Information Systems (NLDB 2026), held in Trondheim, Norway, June 17–19, 2026.

Recent advances in AI have increased the expectations of users when it comes to information access systems. With powerful LLMs, users engage with information using natural language instead of artificial query languages. At the same time, this raises not only technical but also ethical concerns, such as sustainability, reliability, and privacy. NLDB has established itself as a venue to discuss precisely the intersection of natural language and information systems. The NLDB conference brings together researchers, practitioners, and industry professionals to share, explore and critically assess advances in our field. The fact that it has run for more than three decades speaks to the relevance and significance of such a meeting point across domains and institutions. Consistent with tradition, also this year's NLDB spanned from foundational research to innovative applications across a range of domains.

This year's conference received 46 submissions. All submissions were rigorously single-blind peer reviewed by 2-3 reviewers (including meta-reviews). As a result, 22 papers were accepted for publication and are included in the proceedings. Such papers describe research contributions addressing theoretical aspects, algorithms, applications, architectures, resources, and other aspects of NLP, as well as survey and discussion papers. More specifically, the following topics were mainly addressed: Generative Models and Large Language Models (five papers), Social Media and Web Data (three papers), AI Safety and Ethics (three papers), Efficient/Low-Resource Methods in NLP (three papers), Information Retrieval and Text Mining (three papers), Explainable AI (three papers) and Interpretability and Model Analysis in NLP (two papers).

We sincerely thank all authors for their contributions and the reviewers and Program Committee members for their thoughtful evaluations and dedication to the conference. We also acknowledge the invited speakers, whose keynotes enriched the program by highlighting emerging trends and open challenges in the field.

Finally, we extend our deepest appreciation to the Organizing Committee, Local Chairs, volunteers, and sponsors whose support made NLDB 2026 possible. We hope that these proceedings will serve as a valuable resource and inspiration for future research in natural language and information systems.

May 2026Elena Cabrio
Eric Monteiro

Organization

General Chairs

Jon Atle Gulla	Norwegian University of Science and Technology, Norway
Kerstin Bach	Norwegian University of Science and Technology, Norway
Farid Meziane	University of Derby, UK
Vijayan Sugumaran	Oakland University, USA

Program Chairs

Elena Cabrio	Université Côte d'Azur, France
Eric Monteiro	Norwegian University of Science and Technology, Norway

Local Organization

Benjamin Kille (Chair)
Karolina Storesund (Administration)
Vandana Yadav (Local Organizer)
Abdul Kazeem Shamba (Local Organizer)
Christoph Eder (Communication and Publicity)

Program Committee

Ahsaas Bajaj	Instacart, USA
Davide Audrito	University of Turin, Italy
Davide Buscaldi	Université Sorbonne Paris Nord, France
Dittaya Wanvarie	Chulalongkorn University, Thailand
Ekaterina Sviridova	Université Côte d'Azur, France
Emilio Sulis	University of Turin, Italy
Epaminondas Kapetanios	University of Hertfordshire, UK
Flavius Frasincar	Erasmus University Rotterdam, Netherlands
Giancarlo Sperlì	University of Naples Federico II, Italy

Helmut Horacek	German Research Center for AI, Germany
Irene Siragusa	University of Palermo, Italy
Isabelle Comyn-Wattiau	ESSEC Business School, France
Katarina Laken	Fondazione Bruno Kessler, Italy
Lucia Cascone	University of Salerno, Italy
Luigi Lomasto	University of Salerno, Italy
Luisa Mich	University of Trento, Italy
Maguelonne Teisseire	INRAE - UMR Tetis, France
Manjula D.	Anna University, India
Mauro Dragoni	Fondazione Bruno Kessler, Italy
Mathieu Roche	CIRAD – TETIS, France
Mithun Balakrishna	Lymba Corporation, USA
Nada Mimouni	CNAM, France
Natalia Loukachevitch	Lomonosov Moscow State University, Russia
Nicolò Penzo	Fondazione Bruno Kessler, Italy
Patrizio Bellan	Fondazione Bruno Kessler, Free University of Bozen-Bolzano, Italy
Philipp Cimiano	Bielefeld University, Germany
Roberto Nai	University of Turin, Italy
Ryutaro Ichise	Tokyo Institute of Technology, Japan
Sebastiano Vecellio Salto	Fondazione Bruno Kessler, Italy
Somnath Banerjee	Tartu Ülikool, Estonia
Soto Montalvo	Universidad Rey Juan Carlos, Spain
Stephan Reiff-Marganiec	University of Derby, UK
Sunil Vadera	University of Salford, UK
Thanapon Noraset	Mahidol University, Thailand
Valerio Basile	University of Turin, Italy
Valeriya Goloviznina	European University at St. Petersburg, Russia
Yasir Arfat	University of Derby, UK
Zoubida Kedad	Universite de Versailles-St-Quentin, France

Sponsor

Research Council of Norway.

Contents

Generative and Large Language Models

Social Media and Web Data

Explainable AI

Interpretability and Models Analysis in NLP

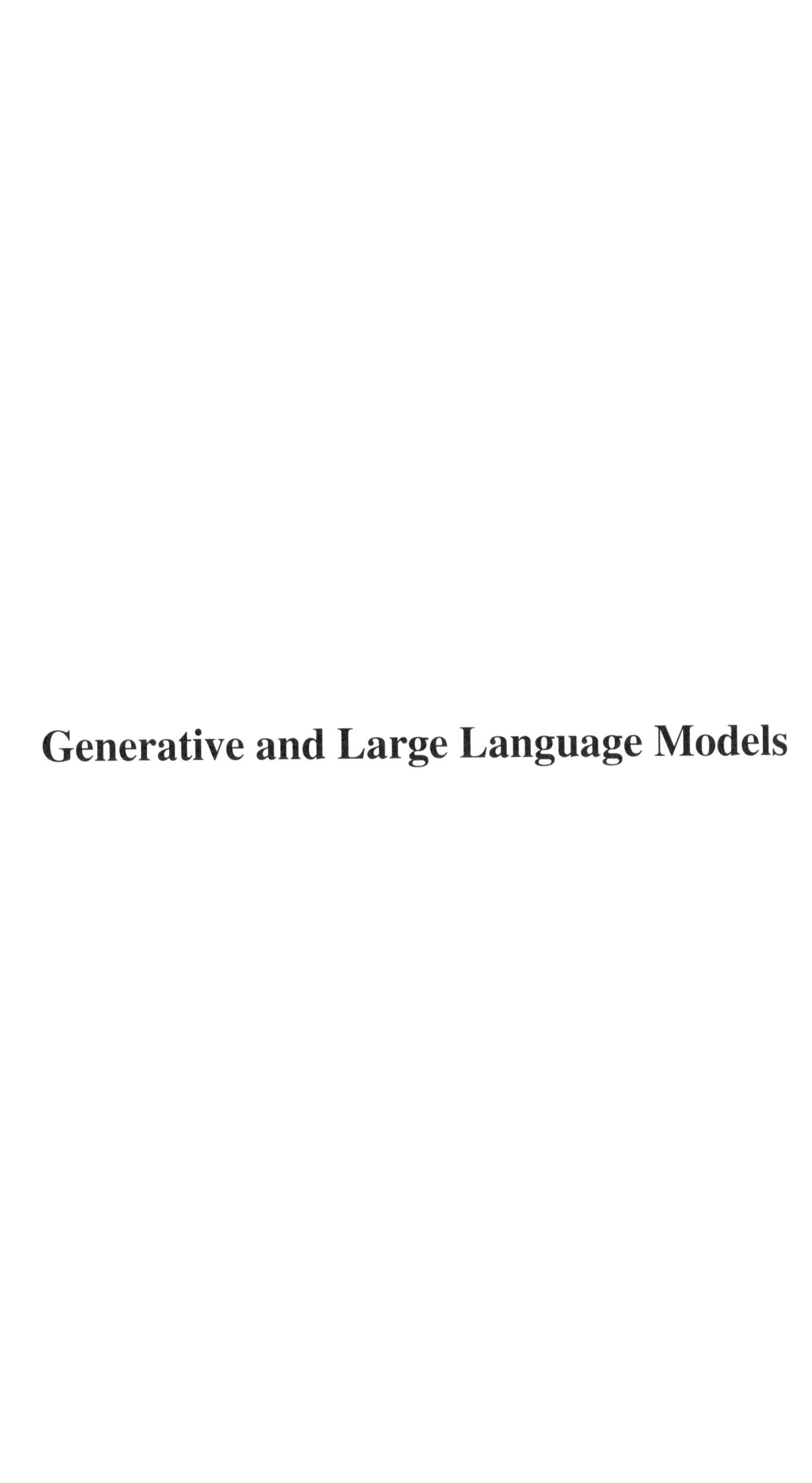

Generative and Large Language Models

Summarising Regulations: an Empirical Study of Long-Document Summarisation Methods Under Extreme Compression

Tuba Gokhan[1]([✉]) [iD], Mubashir Ali[2] [iD], and Mark Lee[2] [iD]

[1] Mohamed bin Zayed University of Artificial Intelligence, Abu Dhabi, UAE
`tuba.gokhan@mbzuai.ac.ae`
[2] University of Birmingham, Birmingham, UK
`{m.ali.16,m.g.lee}@bham.ac.uk`

Abstract. Regulatory documents are extreme in length, structurally heterogeneous, and linguistically technical, yet they must be summarised with high precision because omissions or distortions can materially change compliance meaning. We introduce *ReguSum*, a dataset of U.S. agency regulatory documents from the Securities and Exchange Commission (SEC) and the Internal Revenue Service (IRS) (2020–2024), paired with agency-provided abstracts that we treat as gold reference summaries. Compared to widely used long-document summarisation benchmarks, ReguSum operates in a long-input with extreme compression ratios exceeding 200:1 that stresses content selection and length budgeting under practical context limits.

Using ReguSum, we evaluate three families of methods under a unified pipeline: (i) internal input structuring with length control (whole-document truncation, dynamic chunking, and section-aware hierarchical summarisation); (ii) seven retrieval-augmented summarisation variants that differ in query formulation and context construction; and (iii) clustering-based semantic chunking with HDBSCAN, evaluated with global versus document-specific parameterisation and combined with hierarchical decoding. Overall, retrieval-augmented variants do not surpass strong internal-structuring baselines in this setting, whereas semantic chunking is most effective when paired with hierarchical summarisation.

Keywords: Regulatory document summarisation · Long-document summarisation · Extreme compression · Retrieval-augmented summarisation · Hierarchical summarisation · Semantic chunking

1 Introduction

Regulatory documents are a demanding testbed for long-document summarisation. They are typically *extreme in length, structurally heterogeneous,* and *linguistically technical,* and they encode compliance-critical details such as numerical thresholds, deadlines, exceptions, cross-references, and procedural conditions.

E. Cabrio and E. Monteiro (Eds.): NLDB 2026, LNCS 16696, pp. 3–17, 2027.
https://doi.org/10.1007/978-3-032-29532-3_1

These properties collide with practical model constraints: standard encoder–decoder summarisation models cannot ingest full regulations, while truncation and fixed-size chunking can systematically omit or fragment legally salient content. This motivates structured long-input processing and evidence selection mechanisms, including long-context modelling and retrieval-augmented generation [2,12,23].

From a legal perspective, *regulations* also differ from statutes and case law in ways that directly affect summarisation. Statutes are enacted by legislatures and often state high-level requirements, whereas regulations are issued by agencies under delegated authority and operationalise compliance through prescriptive, implementation-level rules. For example, a statute may mandate financial transparency broadly, while an agency such as the U.S. Securities and Exchange Commission (SEC) specifies concrete reporting formats, timelines, definitions, exemptions, and enforcement procedures. As a result, regulatory summaries must be concise *without losing constraints* a difficult balance when the source text is very long and the reference abstract is short.

To support research on summarising *extreme-length* regulatory text, we introduce *ReguSum*[1], a dataset of U.S. regulatory documents collected from https://www.regulations.gov/. ReguSum focuses on two agencies(the SEC and the Internal Revenue Service (IRS))and covers documents from 2020–2024. Each document is paired with an agency-provided abstract, which we treat as the gold reference summary. In contrast to widely used long-document summarisation datasets (e.g., BillSum and GovReport), ReguSum exhibits substantially longer inputs paired with short abstracts, yielding very high compression ratios and placing strong pressure on content selection, length budgeting, and faithful abstraction.

We study three complementary strategies for handling these constraints under a unified experimental pipeline. First, we benchmark *internal input-structuring* baselines (whole-document truncation, dynamic chunking, and section-aware hierarchical summarisation) while keeping preprocessing, generators, and decoding fixed. Second, we evaluate *retrieval-augmented summarisation* variants that condition generation on a compact set of retrieved text fragments rather than the full document [12], analysing the effect of query construction and context assembly. Third, we investigate *semantic chunking* via HDBSCAN clustering to form topic-coherent segments prior to generation [14], and integrate these segments with hierarchical decoding to better preserve dispersed requirements and exceptions. We evaluate all approaches using ROUGE and BERTScore [13,25].

Our contributions are:

- We introduce *ReguSum*, a large and publicly available dataset of SEC and IRS regulatory documents (2020–2024) paired with agency-provided abstracts, and release it publicly.
- We provide a controlled comparison of input-structuring baselines, retrieval-augmented summarisation variants, and HDBSCAN-based semantic chunking under strict long-input constraints.

---

[1] https://github.com/RegNLP/ReguSum.

– We present empirical evidence on the trade-offs among these strategies for extreme-length regulatory summarisation, highlighting the conditions under which structure-aware and semantic segmentation approaches outperform retrieval-based alternatives.

2   Related Work

Long-document summarisation has expanded beyond news into public-sector and legal genres. BillSum [10] covers U.S. legislative bills, while GovReport [8] targets substantially longer government reports. In the legal domain, EUR-Lex-Sum [1] provides EU legal acts with curated summaries across multiple languages, and Multi-LexSum [20] introduces expert-written multi-granularity summaries for civil rights litigation cases. Despite this progress, agency-issued regulations remain comparatively underrepresented in summarisation benchmarks. ReguSum complements existing resources by focusing on U.S. regulations paired with agency-provided abstracts as gold reference summaries, and by emphasising a high-compression regime that stresses input budgeting and content selection.

RAG conditions generation on retrieved evidence rather than the full input [12]. For long-document summarisation, this "retrieve-then-summarise" paradigm can reduce effective context length, but outcomes depend on system-level choices such as retriever design, query formulation, and context integration [21]. Recent work further shows that chunking decisions materially affect retrieval quality and end-to-end performance [22], and that hierarchical indexing can help retrieve at an appropriate granularity for summarisation [7]. These findings are directly relevant to ReguSum: regulatory requirements and exceptions are often dispersed across distant sections, so retrieval must balance focus with coverage under strict budgets. We therefore benchmark seven RAG variants as a controlled study of query construction and context integration for regulatory summarisation.

Text segmentation has long been used to improve processing of long documents, from lexical cohesion methods such as TextTiling [6] to statistical and topic-model-based approaches [3,15,19]. Recent summarisation work revisits semantic segmentation as an explicit component of long-document pipelines, for example via semantic self-segmentation [16] or divide-and-conquer summarisation [4]. This line of work motivates our hypothesis that topic-coherent segmentation can mitigate the shortcomings of fixed-size chunking on regulatory documents. We adopt clustering-based semantic chunking using HDBSCAN [14], which supports variable-sized clusters without requiring a fixed number of segments, and evaluate both global and document-specific clustering parameterisation, including hierarchical decoding over semantic chunks, within the ReguSum setting.

3   ReguSum: Regulatory Summarisation Dataset

We introduce *ReguSum*, a dataset of U.S. agency-issued regulatory documents for long-document summarisation. The corpus is collected from https://www.

regulations.gov/ and focuses on SEC and IRS documents from 2020–2024. Regulations operationalise delegated statutory authority through prescriptive procedures, thresholds, deadlines, and exceptions, making summarisation sensitive to omissions and to fragmented conditions.

Data Acquisition and Preprocessing. We download the source HTML documents, remove boilerplate while preserving the regulatory text, and segment each document into an ordered sequence of sections using regex markers aligned with surface cues (e.g., headings and amendment blocks). We retain only documents with an agency-provided abstract in the `SUMMARY:` block, which we use as the gold reference summary (`gold_summary`).

Dataset Format. ReguSum is released as JSON. Each entry includes gold_summary, Agency ID (SEC/IRS), Title, Topics (when available), original_content, and Sections (a list of header/text pairs). This supports both flat summarisation (via original_content) and structure-aware methods (via Sections).

Table 1. Comparison of long-document summarisation datasets. BillSum and GovReport statistics are from [9]. ReguSum statistics are computed on our corpus.

Feature	BillSum	GovReport	ReguSum
# doc-summ.	21.3K	19.5K	354
doc tokens	1,686	9,409	**42,795**
doc sents	42	300	**1,106**
summ tokens	243	607	158
summ sents	7.1	21.4	5.9
Compression$_{tokens}$	12.2	18.7	**270.9**
Compression$_{sents}$	9.7	18.1	**188.9**
Coverage	0.913	0.942	0.878
Density	6.600	7.700	5.304
Redundancy	0.163	0.124	0.106
Uniformity	0.903	0.932	0.884
Sections per doc	–	–	7.1

Long-Input, Extreme-Compression Regime. Table 1 contrasts ReguSum with BillSum and GovReport. ReguSum documents are substantially longer: **4.5×** longer than GovReport (42,795 vs. 9,409 tokens) and **25.4×** longer than BillSum (42,795 vs. 1,686). At the same time, reference summaries are shorter (158 tokens), yielding an unusually high compression setting: token compression is **270.9** (**14.5×** and **22.2×** higher than GovReport and BillSum), with similarly elevated sentence compression (**188.9**). This regime makes full-document encoding typically infeasible and motivates structure-aware approaches such as section-aware chunking and hierarchical summarisation.

Section Structure and Summary Properties. Table 2 summarises additional corpus characteristics. ReguSum exhibits heterogeneous section granularity: while the mean document contains 7.13 sections, section length is highly

Table 2. Additional ReguSum characteristics (computed on our corpus). Novel n-gram percentages measure the proportion of summary n-grams not present in the source document.

Statistic	Mean	Median	P90
Sections per document	7.13	6	16
Tokens per section	5,996	710	15,946
Sentences per section	154.8	25	413
Numeric token rate (document)	0.058	0.050	0.105
Numeric token rate (summary)	0.058	0.055	0.100
Legal-reference rate (document)	0.018	0.013	0.041
Legal-reference rate (summary)	0.006	0.004	0.017
Novel 1-gram (%)	12.2	3.5	40.8
Novel 2-gram (%)	39.4	30.1	79.9
Novel 3-gram (%)	59.5	54.9	90.5
Novel 4-gram (%)	72.0	71.8	95.9

skewed (median 710 tokens vs. P90 15,946), reinforcing the need for adaptive chunking and section-aware hierarchical summarisation. Numeric-token rates indicate a consistent prevalence of dates, thresholds, and amounts in both documents and abstracts. Legal-reference rates are higher in documents than in summaries, suggesting that agency abstracts often compress or paraphrase citation-heavy clauses rather than copying them verbatim. Finally, the novel n-gram rates show that reference abstracts are not purely extractive (e.g., 39.4% novel 2-grams; 72.0% novel 4-grams), underscoring the need for faithful abstraction rather than sentence copying.

We release ReguSum to support future work on summarisation methods that remain robust under long inputs, heterogeneous structural cues, and highly compressed reference abstracts.

4   Methods

We evaluate three complementary strategies for summarising regulatory documents under standard encoder–decoder context constraints: (i) **baseline long-input handling** via truncation, dynamic chunking, and section-aware hierarchical summarisation; (ii) **retrieval-augmented summarisation (RAG)** that conditions generation on a compact set of retrieved regulatory fragments; and (iii) **semantic chunking with HDBSCAN**, which forms topic-coherent segments prior to generation. Across all methods, we apply the same document normalisation, generator checkpoints, decoding defaults, and evaluation protocol unless explicitly noted.

4.1   Baseline Methods

We benchmark long regulatory document summarisation using a unified framework in which we vary only the *input structuring strategy* and keep the generator family, preprocessing, decoding configuration, and postprocessing fixed. For each strategy, we evaluate the same encoder–decoder models in two settings: (i) *pre-trained* (off-the-shelf), and (ii) *fine-tuned* on ReguSum to quantify domain-adaptation effects (Fig. 1).

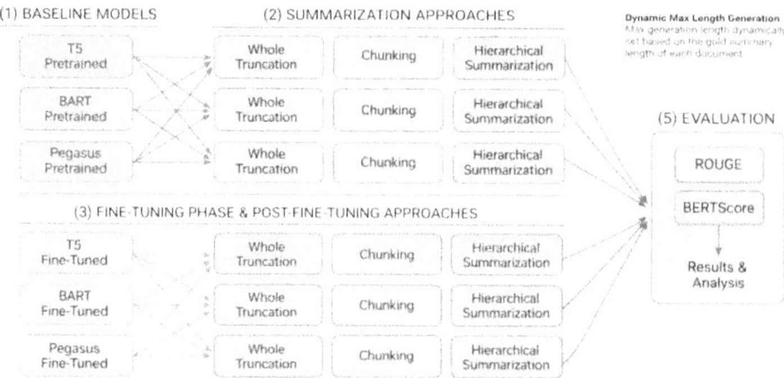

Fig. 1. Baseline framework: summarisation models (pre-trained vs. fine-tuned), input structuring strategies (truncation, dynamic chunking, and section-aware hierarchical summarisation), and a shared evaluation protocol.

Models: We evaluate three encoder–decoder summarisation families: T5 [5], BART [11], and PEGASUS [24]. Concretely, we use `t5-large`, facebook/bart-large-cnn, and google/pegasus-xsum. Unless otherwise stated, we use each checkpoint's default summarisation decoding configuration and apply identical cleaning and postprocessing across methods.

Input Structuring Strategies: ReguSum documents typically exceed the maximum input length of standard encoder–decoder models. We therefore compare three baselines that differ only in how they expose document content to the generator:

- **Whole-Document Truncation:** The model receives the longest prefix that fits its maximum input length. This baseline is simple but can omit later passages that contain exceptions, thresholds, and amendment language.
- **Dynamic Chunking:** Each document is split into overlapping chunks, and each chunk is summarised independently. Chunk length is chosen *per document* to respect the model's input limit while covering the full document with a manageable number of chunks; consecutive chunks share a fixed overlap (200 tokens) to reduce boundary effects. Chunk-level summaries are then aggregated into a document summary using the same generator (concatenation followed by a final summarisation pass).
- **Section-Sware Hierarchical Summarisation:** We leverage the section structure released with ReguSum. Each section is summarised independently, and the resulting section summaries are concatenated and summarised again

to produce a document-level summary. This preserves high-level organisation and reduces the risk of mixing distant procedural or amendment blocks.

Length Control: Agency abstracts are short relative to their source documents, and multi-stage strategies can otherwise produce overly verbose outputs. To stabilise generation and keep outputs comparable across strategies, we guide output length using the reference abstract length. For strategies with intermediate units (chunks or sections), we allocate a per-unit target length as $L_{\text{unit}} = L_{\text{gold}}/N_{\text{units}}$, where N_{units} is the number of chunks or sections, and apply the same document-level target at the final aggregation step.

Finally, dynamic chunking is our standard chunking baseline throughout. Retrieval-augmented summarisation and HDBSCAN-based semantic chunking are evaluated as extensions built on top of this framework (Sects. 4.2 and 4.3).

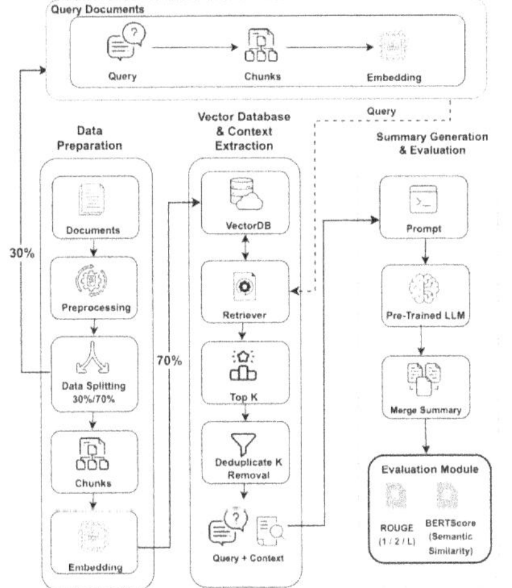

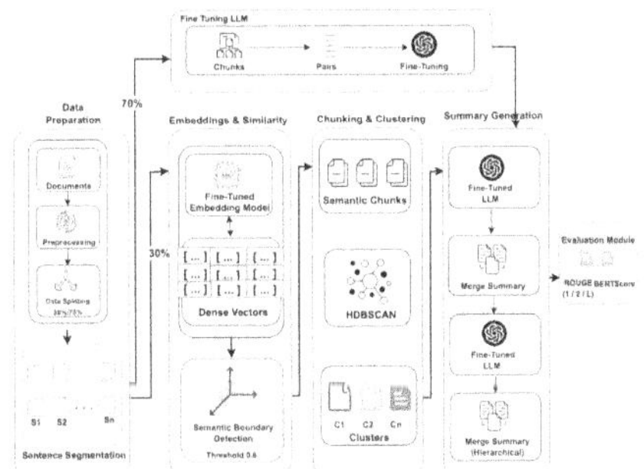

(a) Retrieval-augmented summarisation (Query + Retrieved Context): documents are chunked and embedded, Top-K chunks are retrieved from a vector store, deduplicated, and provided to the generator.

(b) HDBSCAN-based semantic chunking: sentence segmentation and embedding, semantic boundary detection to form variable-length chunks, HDBSCAN clustering of chunk vectors, and cluster-wise (optionally hierarchical) summarisation.

Fig. 2. Pipelines for retrieval-augmented summarisation and clustering-based semantic chunking.

4.2 Retrieval-Augmented Summarisation

Retrieval-augmented summarisation follows a query-conditioned generation framework in which the generator produces the final abstract from a compact set of retrieved regulatory fragments rather than from the full document. The pipeline is illustrated in Fig. 2a; additional variant-specific diagrams are provided in Appendix A (Fig. 3).

Preprocessing and Split: Raw documents are normalised by removing URLs, newline artefacts, redundant punctuation, excess whitespace, and non-informative symbols. We divide the corpus into two disjoint subsets: **70%** to build the retrieval index (and to fine-tune models where applicable) and **30%** for evaluation.

Index Construction and Retrieval: The index subset is segmented into fixed-length chunks to respect the embedding model's maximum input length. Dense vector representations are computed for each chunk using a pre-trained embedding encoder and stored in a Chroma vector database[2]. For each evaluation instance, the corresponding document is similarly chunked and embedded, and the retriever queries the database to return the Top-K most similar chunks; duplicate chunks are removed to reduce redundancy.

Conditioning Modes and RAG Variants: We evaluate two conditioning modes that align with the method labels reported in Table 3:

- **Retrieved Context only (Context-only).** The generator receives only the retrieved chunks.
- **Query + Retrieved Context (Query+Context).** A query string is prepended to the retrieved chunks to form the model input.

Within this framework, we report seven RAG variants (RAG-1 to RAG-7), which differ in whether the generator is pre-trained vs. fine-tuned, whether the input is Context-only vs. Query+Context, and whether the query is the original prompt, a shortened query derived by average pooling, or a query derived from an intermediate summary (*Query(summary)*). We use the same generator families as in the baselines (T5/BART/PEGASUS; pre-trained or fine-tuned per variant), ensuring that differences are attributable to retrieval and query design rather than to changes in the underlying model family.

4.3 HDBSCAN-Based Semantic Chunking

We propose an HDBSCAN-based semantic chunking framework that replaces fixed-size chunking with content-driven segmentation prior to generation. The pipeline is shown in Fig. 2b.

Sentence Segmentation and Embeddings: Each document is segmented into sentences using Stanza [17], retaining sentence identifiers to preserve traceability. Each sentence is encoded using a Sentence-BERT (SBERT) encoder [18].

---

[2] https://github.com/chroma-core/chroma.

Semantic Boundaries and Semantic Chunks: We compute cosine similarity between consecutive sentence embeddings and mark a boundary when similarity falls below a tuned threshold (0.6). Sentences between successive boundaries are grouped into variable-length semantic chunks, with minimum and maximum size constraints enforced for stability.

Chunk Clustering and Variants: Each semantic chunk is represented via mean pooling over its sentence embeddings and clustered using HDBSCAN. We evaluate two parameterisation regimes, corresponding to Table 3: (i) **Global parameters**, where a single HDBSCAN configuration is applied to all evaluation documents; and (ii) **Document-based parameters**, where parameters are selected per document from a fixed candidate set.

Cluster-Wise Summarisation and Hierarchical Compression: Chunks within each cluster are concatenate.

5   Results

Evaluation Split: For RAG and HDBSCAN-based methods, we use a 70/30 split, where 70% of documents are used for index construction and parameter selection (and for model fine-tuning when applicable), and 30% are used for evaluation. Baseline methods are evaluated on the same evaluation split to ensure comparability across settings.

Evaluation Metrics: We report results using both lexical and semantic metrics. We compute ROUGE-1, ROUGE-2, and ROUGE-L F1 scores with `rouge-score` `0.1.2`[3] and BERTScore F1 with `bert-score` `0.3.13`[4]. All metrics are evaluated through the Hugging Face `evaluate` `0.4.5`[5] framework to ensure consistent and reproducible scoring.

Table 3 summarises ROUGE-1/2/L and BERTScore-F1 across three method families: (i) internal input structuring baselines (truncation, dynamic chunking, section-aware hierarchy) for pre-trained and fine-tuned generators, (ii) seven retrieval-augmented summarisation (RAG) variants, and (iii) HDBSCAN-based semantic chunking with global versus document-specific parameters. Four findings are consistent across metrics.

Across all architectures, fine-tuning on ReguSum yields substantial gains over pre-trained checkpoints. Under extreme compression, methods that explicitly manage the input—via dynamic chunking or hierarchical aggregation—are consistently strong, indicating that budgeting and structured conditioning matter more than exposing the model to longer raw text.

---

[3] https://pypi.org/project/rouge-score/.
[4] https://pypi.org/project/bert-score/.
[5] https://pypi.org/project/evaluate/.

Table 3. ReguSum results (ROUGE-1/2/L, BERTScore-F1) across baselines, seven RAG variants, and HDBSCAN semantic chunking (global vs document-specific). Underline = block best; bold-underline = overall best.

Model	Method	ROUGE-1	ROUGE-2	ROUGE-L	BERTScore-F1
Baseline-1: Pre-trained					
BART-Pretrained	Whole-Doc (Truncate)	0.334	0.124	0.213	0.832
BART-Pretrained	Dynamic Chunking	0.354	0.121	0.209	0.828
BART-Pretrained	Section-Aware Hierarchical	0.310	0.102	0.194	0.828
Pegasus-Pretrained	Whole-Doc (Truncate)	0.246	0.096	0.179	0.831
Pegasus-Pretrained	Dynamic Chunking	0.270	0.092	0.178	0.814
Pegasus-Pretrained	Section-Aware Hierarchical	0.184	0.053	0.138	0.811
T5-Pretrained	Whole-Doc (Truncate)	0.289	0.097	0.190	0.828
T5-Pretrained	Dynamic Chunking	0.318	0.100	0.180	0.818
T5-Pretrained	Section-Aware Hierarchical	0.253	0.076	0.162	0.819
Baseline-2: Fine-tuned					
BART-Finetuned	Whole-Doc (Truncate)	0.381	0.154	0.250	0.845
BART-Finetuned	Dynamic Chunking	0.392	0.214	0.294	0.861
BART-Finetuned	Section-Aware Hierarchical	0.451	0.237	0.337	0.876
Pegasus-Finetuned	Whole-Doc (Truncate)	0.302	0.131	0.222	0.839
Pegasus-Finetuned	Dynamic Chunking	0.309	0.174	0.236	0.838
Pegasus-Finetuned	Section-Aware Hierarchical	0.429	0.242	0.330	0.857
T5-Finetuned	Whole-Doc (Truncate)	0.284	0.098	0.192	0.830
T5-Finetuned	Dynamic Chunking	0.310	0.182	0.243	0.842
T5-Finetuned	Section-Aware Hierarchical	0.420	0.218	0.313	0.857
RAG-1: Pretrained + RAG (Retrieved Context only)					
BART-Pretrained	Summary based on Retrieved Context	0.266	0.075	0.155	0.813
Pegasus-Pretrained	Summary based on Retrieved Context	0.233	0.070	0.156	0.824
T5-Pretrained	Summary based on Retrieved Context	0.259	0.060	0.154	0.817
RAG-2: Pretrained + RAG (Query + Retrieved Context)					
BART-Pretrained	Summary based on Query+Retrieved Context	0.206	0.081	0.124	0.810
Pegasus-Pretrained	Summary based on Query+Retrieved Context	0.200	0.078	0.134	0.823
T5-Pretrained	Summary based on Query+Retrieved Context	0.181	0.067	0.109	0.809
RAG-3: Fine-tuned + RAG (Retrieved Context only)					
BART-Finetuned	Summary based on Retrieved Context	0.328	0.161	0.245	0.845
Pegasus-Finetuned	Summary based on Retrieved Context	0.320	0.160	0.244	0.842
T5-Finetuned	Summary based on Retrieved Context	0.346	0.171	0.267	0.847
RAG-4: Fine-tuned + RAG (Query + Retrieved Context)					
BART-Finetuned	Summary based on Query+Retrieved Context	0.215	0.127	0.163	0.856
Pegasus-Finetuned	Summary based on Query+Retrieved Context	0.207	0.111	0.153	0.834
T5-Finetuned	Summary based on Query+Retrieved Context	0.199	0.110	0.147	0.837
RAG-5: Fine-tuned + RAG (avg pooling query shortening; Retrieved Context only)					
BART-Finetuned	Summary based on Retrieved Context	0.370	0.169	0.254	0.855
Pegasus-Finetuned	Summary based on Retrieved Context	0.385	0.197	0.281	0.848
T5-Finetuned	Summary based on Retrieved Context	0.373	0.185	0.275	0.849
RAG-6: Query(summary) → Fine-tuned + RAG (Retrieved Context only)					
BART-Finetuned	Summary based on Retrieved Context	0.357	0.180	0.277	0.863
Pegasus-Finetuned	Summary based on Retrieved Context	0.383	0.175	0.273	0.846
T5-Finetuned	Summary based on Retrieved Context	0.345	0.171	0.266	0.847
RAG-7: Query(summary) → Fine-tuned + RAG (Query + Retrieved Context)					
BART-Finetuned	Summary based on Query+Retrieved Context	0.386	0.192	0.281	0.857
Pegasus-Finetuned	Summary based on Query+Retrieved Context	0.414	0.206	0.317	0.846
T5-Finetuned	Summary based on Query+Retrieved Context	0.431	0.233	0.327	0.855
Clustering-1: HDBSCAN (Global parameters)					
BART-Finetuned	Chunking with Clustering	0.371	0.220	0.281	0.866
BART-Finetuned	Chunking with Clustering + Hierarchical	**0.469**	0.266	0.363	**0.877**
Pegasus-Finetuned	Chunking with Clustering	0.324	0.193	0.258	0.847
Pegasus-Finetuned	Chunking with Clustering + Hierarchical	0.408	0.247	0.343	0.869
T5-Finetuned	Chunking with Clustering	0.289	0.180	0.232	0.842
T5-Finetuned	Hierarchical Clustering	0.467	**0.289**	**0.388**	0.863

(continued)

Table 3. (*continued*)

Model	Method	ROUGE-1	ROUGE-2	ROUGE-L	BERTScore-F1
Clustering-2: HDBSCAN (Document-based parameters)					
BART-Finetuned	Chunking with Clustering	0.344	0.200	0.255	0.863
BART-Finetuned	Hierarchical Clustering	<u>0.466</u>	0.255	0.349	<u>0.871</u>
Pegasus-Finetuned	Chunking with Clustering	0.321	0.189	0.258	0.847
Pegasus-Finetuned	Hierarchical Clustering	0.424	<u>0.258</u>	<u>0.358</u>	<u>0.871</u>
T5-Finetuned	Chunking with Clustering	0.298	0.179	0.238	0.844
T5-Finetuned	Hierarchical Clustering	0.401	0.253	0.343	0.867

For pre-trained models, dynamic chunking is the most reliable alternative to whole-document truncation. In contrast, section-aware hierarchical summarisation tends to underperform without domain adaptation, suggesting that off-the-shelf generators do not consistently exploit regulatory section structure when operating under tight context constraints.

Naïve cross-document retrieval augmentation (retrieved context only, or query + retrieved context) underperforms strong internal-structuring baselines, particularly with pre-trained generators. With fine-tuned generators, RAG improves, but the gain depends strongly on how the retrieval query and context are constructed. Query shortening (avg pooling) and the two-stage *Query(summary)* strategy (RAG-6/7) produce the strongest RAG results; nevertheless, even the best RAG configuration remains below the best within-document structuring and clustering-based approaches, consistent with retrieval introducing topical drift or missing document-specific requirements.

HDBSCAN-based semantic chunking achieves the strongest overall performance when paired with hierarchical summarisation. Global clustering parameters yield the best peak scores (best ROUGE-1 and BERTScore-F1), while document-specific parameterisation remains competitive but slightly weaker at the top end. Overall, these results indicate that *semantic structuring within the target document*, followed by *hierarchical aggregation*, is the most effective strategy for regulatory long-document summarisation under extreme compression.

6 Discussion, Conclusions and Future Work

We introduced *ReguSum*, a long-document summarisation dataset for U.S. regulatory texts from the SEC and IRS (2020–2024), paired with agency-provided abstracts as reference summaries. ReguSum operates under extreme input length and compression, making performance highly sensitive to input budgeting, fragmentation, and the omission of compliance-critical details. We benchmarked three families of approaches in a unified pipeline: within-document input structuring (truncation, dynamic chunking, section-aware hierarchical summarisation), retrieval-augmented summarisation (seven variants), and HDBSCAN-based semantic chunking with global versus document-specific parameterisation.

Our results suggest that strong structure-aware baselines provide a robust foundation under extreme compression: explicitly organising the target document and aggregating information hierarchically is consistently effective. In contrast, simple cross-document retrieval augmentation does not reliably outperform these baselines, and can introduce topical drift when superficially similar regulatory language appears in unrelated contexts. The best overall performance is achieved by semantic chunking via HDBSCAN when paired with hierarchical decoding, highlighting segmentation and aggregation—rather than additional external context—as the most promising levers for this regime.

Limitations. ReguSum currently comprises 354 document–summary pairs, which is sufficient for controlled benchmarking but may be limited for training larger models; we therefore release the full data collection and preprocessing pipeline to enable dataset expansion. Our RAG setting uses cross-document retrieval (indexing only a knowledge subset), which may disadvantage weaker variants by retrieving context that is not tightly aligned with the target document. Moreover, agency abstracts reflect communication choices and may not fully represent an "ideal" compliance-oriented summary that preserves every constraint and exception, and ROUGE/BERTScore do not directly measure factual consistency or regulatory constraint preservation. Finally, we focus on three encoder–decoder families (T5, BART, PEGASUS) and do not evaluate long-context LLMs or specialised long-document architectures.

Future work includes (i) stronger evaluation of *regulatory faithfulness* beyond ROUGE/BERTScore, emphasising obligations, thresholds, dates, and exceptions; (ii) improved retrieval under strict budgets via domain-tuned retrievers, hierarchical/section-aware indexing, and redundancy-aware selection; and (iii) broader coverage by extending ReguSum to additional agencies and regulatory domains.

Disclosure of Interests. All documents in the ReguSum dataset were obtained from https://www.regulations.gov/, the official U.S. federal rulemaking portal. Regulatory texts issued by government agencies are in the public domain under 17 U.S.C. § 105. We include only agency-issued documents (e.g., SEC and IRS rules) and exclude public comments or third-party attachments. The dataset is released for academic research in NLP; generated summaries are not a substitute for legal advice and should be used with caution in compliance-sensitive contexts.

Appendix

A   Retrieval-Augmented Summarisation (RAG): Variant Diagrams

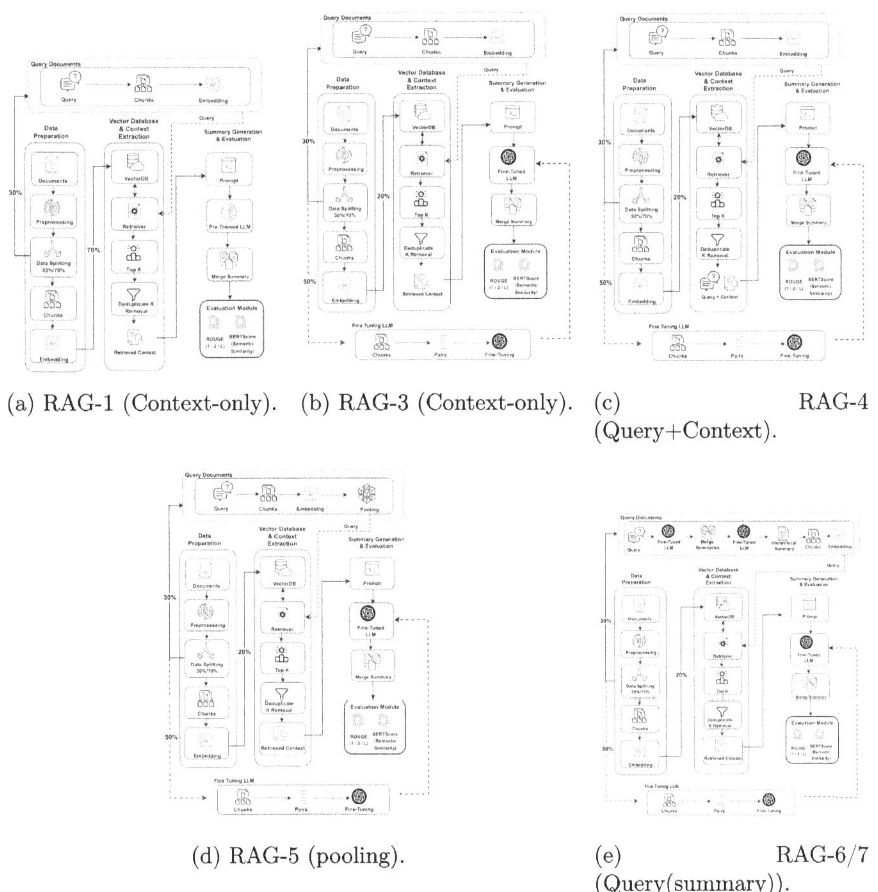

(a) RAG-1 (Context-only).   (b) RAG-3 (Context-only).   (c) RAG-4 (Query+Context).

(d) RAG-5 (pooling).   (e) RAG-6/7 (Query(summary)).

Fig. 3. RAG variant diagrams used in our unified evaluation pipeline.

References

1. Aumiller, D., Chouhan, A., Gertz, M.: EUR-Lex-Sum: a multi- and cross-lingual dataset for long-form summarization in the legal domain. In: Goldberg, Y., Kozareva, Z., Zhang, Y. (eds.) Proceedings of the 2022 Conference on Empirical Methods in Natural Language Processing, pp. 7626–7639. Association for Computational Linguistics, Abu Dhabi, United Arab Emirates (2022). https://doi.org/10.18653/v1/2022.emnlp-main.519

2. Beltagy, I., Peters, M.E., Cohan, A.: LongFormer: the long-document transformer (2020). https://arxiv.org/abs/2004.05150
3. Choi, F.Y.Y.: Advances in domain independent linear text segmentation. In: 1st Meeting of the North American Chapter of the Association for Computational Linguistics (2000). https://aclanthology.org/A00-2004/
4. Gidiotis, A., Tsoumakas, G.: A divide-and-conquer approach to the summarization of long documents. IEEE/ACM Trans. Audio, Speech and Lang. Proc. **28**, 3029–3040 (2020). https://doi.org/10.1109/TASLP.2020.3037401
5. Guo, M., Ainslie, J., Uthus, D., Ontanon, S., Ni, J., Sung, Y.H., Yang, Y.: LongT5: efficient text-to-text transformer for long sequences. In: Carpuat, M., de Marneffe, M.C., Meza Ruiz, I.V. (eds.) Findings of the Association for Computational Linguistics: NAACL 2022, pp. 724–736. Association for Computational Linguistics, Seattle, United States (2022). https://doi.org/10.18653/v1/2022.findings-naacl.55
6. Hearst, M.A.: TextTiling: segmenting text into multi-paragraph subtopic passages. Comput. Linguist. **23**(1), 33–64 (1997)
7. Hosking, T., Tang, H., Lapata, M.: Hierarchical indexing for retrieval-augmented opinion summarization. Trans. Assoc. Comput. Ling. **12**, 1533–1555 (2024). https://doi.org/10.1162/tacl_a_00703, https://aclanthology.org/2024.tacl-1.84/
8. Huang, L., Cao, S., Parulian, N., Ji, H., Wang, L.: Efficient attentions for long document summarization. In: Toutanova, K., et al. (eds.) Proceedings of the 2021 Conference of the North American Chapter of the Association for Computational Linguistics: Human Language Technologies, pp. 1419–1436. Association for Computational Linguistics, Online (2021). https://doi.org/10.18653/v1/2021.naacl-main.112
9. Koh, H.Y., Ju, J., Liu, M., Pan, S.: An empirical survey on long document summarization: datasets, models, and metrics. ACM Comput. Surv. **55**(8) (2022). https://doi.org/10.1145/3545176
10. Kornilova, A., Eidelman, V.: BillSum: a corpus for automatic summarization of US legislation. In: Wang, L., Cheung, J.C.K., Carenini, G., Liu, F. (eds.) Proceedings of the 2nd Workshop on New Frontiers in Summarization, pp. 48–56. Association for Computational Linguistics, Hong Kong, China (2019). https://doi.org/10.18653/v1/D19-5406, https://aclanthology.org/D19-5406/
11. Lewis, M., et al.: BART: denoising sequence-to-sequence pre-training for natural language generation, translation, and comprehension. In: Jurafsky, D., Chai, J., Schluter, N., Tetreault, J. (eds.) Proceedings of the 58th Annual Meeting of the Association for Computational Linguistics, pp. 7871–7880. Association for Computational Linguistics, Online (2020). https://doi.org/10.18653/v1/2020.acl-main.703
12. Lewis, P., et al.: Retrieval-augmented generation for knowledge-intensive NLP tasks. In: Proceedings of the 34th International Conference on Neural Information Processing Systems. NIPS '20, Curran Associates Inc., Red Hook, NY, USA (2020)
13. Lin, C.Y.: ROUGE: a package for automatic evaluation of summaries. In: Text Summarization Branches Out. pp. 74–81. Association for Computational Linguistics, Barcelona, Spain (2004). https://aclanthology.org/W04-1013/
14. McInnes, L., Healy, J., Astels, S., et al.: HDBSCAN: hierarchical density based clustering. J. Open Source Softw. **2**(11), 205 (2017)
15. Misra, H., Yvon, F., Jose, J.M., Cappe, O.: Text segmentation via topic modeling: an analytical study. In: Proceedings of the 18th ACM Conference on Information and Knowledge Management. p. 1553–1556. CIKM '09, Association for Computing Machinery, New York, NY, USA (2009). https://doi.org/10.1145/1645953.1646170

16. Moro, G., Ragazzi, L.: Semantic self-segmentation for abstractive summarization of long documents in low-resource regimes. Proc. AAAI Conf. Artif. Intell. **36**(10), 11085–11093 (2022). https://doi.org/10.1609/aaai.v36i10.21357, https://ojs.aaai.org/index.php/AAAI/article/view/21357

17. Qi, P., Zhang, Y., Zhang, Y., Bolton, J., Manning, C.D.: Stanza: a Python natural language processing toolkit for many human languages. In: Proceedings of the 58th Annual Meeting of the Association for Computational Linguistics: System Demonstrations (2020). https://nlp.stanford.edu/pubs/qi2020stanza.pdf

18. Reimers, N., Gurevych, I.: Sentence-BERT: sentence embeddings using Siamese BERT-networks. In: Inui, K., Jiang, J., Ng, V., Wan, X. (eds.) Proceedings of the 2019 Conference on Empirical Methods in Natural Language Processing and the 9th International Joint Conference on Natural Language Processing (EMNLP-IJCNLP), pp. 3982–3992. Association for Computational Linguistics, Hong Kong, China (2019). https://doi.org/10.18653/v1/D19-1410, https://aclanthology.org/D19-1410/

19. Riedl, M., Biemann, C.: Topictiling: a text segmentation algorithm based on LDA. In: Proceedings of ACL 2012 Student Research Workshop, pp. 37–42. ACL '12, Association for Computational Linguistics, USA (2012)

20. Shen, Z., Lo, K., Yu, L., Dahlberg, N., Schlanger, M., Downey, D.: Multi-LexSum: real-world summaries of civil rights lawsuits at multiple granularities. In: Proceedings of the 36th International Conference on Neural Information Processing Systems. NIPS '22, Curran Associates Inc, Red Hook, NY, USA (2022)

21. Wang, X., et al.: Searching for best practices in retrieval-augmented generation. In: Al-Onaizan, Y., Bansal, M., Chen, Y.N. (eds.) Proceedings of the 2024 Conference on Empirical Methods in Natural Language Processing, pp. 17716–17736. Association for Computational Linguistics, Miami, Florida, USA (Nov 2024). https://doi.org/10.18653/v1/2024.emnlp-main.981

22. Wang, Z., et al.: Document segmentation matters for retrieval-augmented generation. In: Che, W., Nabende, J., Shutova, E., Pilehvar, M.T. (eds.) Findings of the Association for Computational Linguistics: ACL 2025, pp. 8063–8075. Association for Computational Linguistics, Vienna, Austria (Jul 2025). https://doi.org/10.18653/v1/2025.findings-acl.422

23. Zaheer, M., et al.: Big Bird: transformers for longer sequences. In: Proceedings of the 34th International Conference on Neural Information Processing Systems. NIPS '20, Curran Associates Inc, Red Hook, NY, USA (2020)

24. Zhang, J., Zhao, Y., Saleh, M., Liu, P.J.: PEGASUS: pre-training with extracted gap-sentences for abstractive summarization. In: Proceedings of the 37th International Conference on Machine Learning. ICML'20, JMLR.org (2020)

25. Zhang, T., Kishore, V., Wu, F., Weinberger, K.Q., Artzi, Y.: BERTScore: evaluating text generation with BERT (2020). https://arxiv.org/abs/1904.09675

ThinknCheck: Grounded Claim Verification with Compact, Reasoning-Driven, and Interpretable Models

Delip Rao[ID], Feijiang Han[ID], and Chris Callison-Burch[(✉)][ID]

University of Pennsylvania, Philadelphia, PA, USA
{delip,feijhan,ccb}@seas.upenn.edu

Abstract. We present ThinknCheck, a 1B-parameter verifier for grounded claim verification that first produces a short, structured rationale and then a binary verdict. We construct LLMAggreFact-Think, a 24.1k reasoning-augmented training set derived from LLMAggreFact, and fine-tune a 4-bit Gemma3 model to follow this format. On LLMAggreFact, ThinknCheck attains 78.1 balanced accuracy (BAcc), surpassing MiniCheck-7B (77.4) with 7x fewer parameters; removing the reasoning step reduces BAcc to 57.5. On SciFact, ThinknCheck reaches 64.7 BAcc, a +14.7 absolute gain over MiniCheck-7B. By contrast, zero-shot chain-of-thought on the base Gemma3-1B harms accuracy relative to direct answers, and preference optimization with a simple format+accuracy reward underperforms supervised reasoning. To probe the latter, we introduce GSMClaims and a domain-specialized variant, ThinknCheck-Science, which improves across benchmarks, including 61.0% accuracy on GSMClaims. Overall, explicit, supervised reasoning enables compact verifiers that are competitive while remaining resource-efficient and interpretable.

Keywords: Claim verification · Reasoning · Language models · Natural language inference

1 Introduction

Large Language Models (LLMs) are increasingly pivotal in modern AI-driven workflows involving natural language claim verification [31], yet their propensity for hallucinations [40], reasoning errors [3], and their opaque nature limit broader deployment, particularly in high-stakes domains like healthcare and scientific innovation.

Current claim verification approaches, while evolving, often face challenges. Some methods can be computationally intensive, requiring multiple LLM calls for a single verification [11,22]. Verification using large, closed-source models also raises concerns regarding cost, privacy, and data security. While the trend

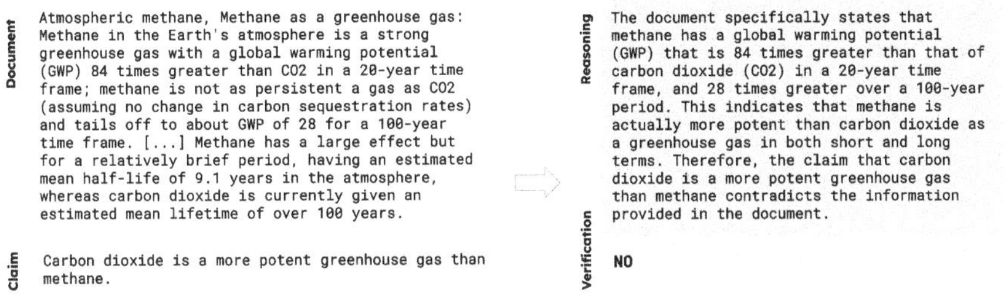

Fig. 1. A sample from the LLMAggreFact-Think dataset, which also illustrates our formulation of the claim verification task: Given a pair of claim and document, our goal is to produce cogent reasoning in addition to the verification label. The [...] represents parts of the reasoning tokens that we elided to accommodate the example in this figure.

in general reasoning models has seen the development of very large systems, such as OpenAI's o-series and DeepSeek's R1 [5], which aim for broad reasoning capabilities, there is a concurrent need for smaller, more specialized models [30] that can perform robustly on specific tasks like claim verification, especially in resource-constrained environments. Our work aligns with this latter direction, focusing on creating efficient yet powerful verification models.

To address these challenges, we introduce ThinknCheck, a suite of novel low-footprint claim verification models that explicitly generate structured reasoning chains *before* rendering a verification decision. Specifically ThinknCheck is a 4-bit quantized 1B parameter Gemma3 [8] model, fine-tuned on our newly createdLLMAggreFact-Think dataset—a version of theLLMAggreFact benchmark [30] that we augmented with explicit reasoning traces. As illustrated in Fig. 1, explicitly generating reasoning allows ThinknCheck to handle claims that require multi-step inference, a common scenario where prior models falter. Our contributions are as follows:

- Introduce THINKNCHECK, a **reasoning-optimized document-grounded claim verifier** that reasons before verifying, improving accuracy and interpretability by producing a concise rationale before the decision.
- Demonstrate ThinknCheck's explicit reasoning significantly **boosts verification accuracy** (+20.6 points over non-reasoning ablation) and **substantially improves out-of-domain generalization** (+14.7 points on scientific claims).
- Create and release GSMClaims, a novel benchmark from reformulated grade school math problems, to **evaluate arithmetic reasoning capabilities in claim verification systems**.
- Develop ThinknCheck-Science, a specialized variant **optimized for scientific and mathematical verification**, achieving significant performance improvements across relevant benchmarks.
- Answer how much "thinking" is optimal for small models: To demystify this, we empirically relate rationale length to verification accuracy. We observe an

inverted-U pattern: mid-length reasoning performs best, while **very short and very long chains degrade performance in distinct ways** (See Fig. 2).
- **Open source all** created datasets and models under an Apache 2.0 license[1].

2   Related Work

Our work connects four threads: (i) claim verification and benchmarks, (ii) reasoning in LMs, (iii) lightweight verifiers, and (iv) supervision for reasoning.

Claim Verification and Benchmarks. Early resources such as FEVER and SCI-FACT established document-grounded claim verification as a supervised classification task mapping a (claim, document) pair to a support decision [30–32]. Hallucination and opacity concerns with LLMs motivate verifiers that are both accurate and interpretable [3,40]. LLMAGGREFACT aggregates nine sources to test diverse scenarios [10,14,17,21,23,24,29,34,42], while domain-specific suites such as SCIFACT probe scientific claims and GSM8K targets math reasoning [4,32]. To directly assess numerical reasoning in verification, we reformulate GSM8K into GSMCLAIMS.

Reasoning-Augmented Verification. Reasoning traces (e.g., Chain-of-Thought) can help models explain intermediate steps [35] and have been adapted via verifiable-CoT and ReAct to interleave reasoning with actions [12,38]. While very large models (e.g., DeepSeek R1) aim for broad reasoning [5], multiple studies find that vanilla CoT can underperform at small scales [16,18]. We fine-tune a compact model to produce structured, pre-decision rationales specific to claim verification, and observe that preference-optimization methods such as GRPO—which have shown promise at larger scales [20,27,41]—do not help at 1B parameters.

Lightweight and Specialized Verifiers. There is growing interest in small, efficient models for deployment [1]. `MiniCheck` (7B) demonstrated the value of a purpose-built verifier trained on synthetic data and outperformed `AlignScore` on LLMAggreFact [30,39]. However, `MiniCheck` struggles on multi-step cases and does not produce explanations that are important for trust [2,7,13]. ThinknCheck is a 1B model that *reasons before deciding,* yielding concise rationales with lower footprint.

Supervising Reasoning. We supervise rationales via SFT on synthetic traces (knowledge distillation) [37]. Although preference optimization (e.g., GRPO) is another path [20,28,41], in our 1B setting SFT on structured reasoning yields better outcomes. We use a standard TRL stack for reproducibility [36].

---

[1] URL withheld for blind-review.

3   Problem Formulation

The standard formulation of document-grounded claim verification, as used by previous research [30] and predecessors, is a classification task: a discriminator $\mathcal{M}$ maps a claim (from space $\mathcal{C}$) and document (from space $\mathcal{D}$) to a discrete label in $\{0,1\}$ (1 for supported, 0 otherwise): $\mathcal{M} : \mathcal{C} \times \mathcal{D} \rightarrow \{0,1\}$

Our work extends this by incorporating explicit reasoning. We define this task with a reasoner $\mathcal{R}$ that maps the input claim-document pair to a reasoning trace $\mathcal{T}$ and a boolean verification label: $\mathcal{R} : \mathcal{C} \times \mathcal{D} \rightarrow \mathcal{T} \times \{0,1\}$ This richer output format enhances interpretability and aims to improve accuracy by requiring the model to articulate its reasoning. We adopt the binary labels SUPPORTED (1) and NOTSUPPORTED (0) from prior work, treating "REFUTES" and "NOTSUPPORTED" identically[2].

4   Dataset and Model Development

This section details the creation of our training dataset LLMAggreFact-Think and the model training procedures for ThinknCheck.

4.1   LLMAggreFact-Think Dataset Construction

To train our reasoning-based verifier, we created LLMAggreFact-Think by augmenting the 30.4K examples in the LLMAggreFact development set with reasoning chains. Using zero-shot prompting, GPT-4o-mini[3] generated a step-by-step reasoning process and a YES/NO verification label for each (document, claim) pair—see Fig. 1; prompt in Appendix A. For high-quality reasoning, we filtered instances where GPT-4o-mini's generated label mismatched the original LLMAggreFact label, reducing the dataset from 30.4K to 24.1K examples[1]. This filtered set, LLMAggreFact-Think, contains 4-tuples: (claim, document, verification label, reasoning). We opted against using reasoning traces from `Deepseek R1` [5] due to their verbosity and token inefficiency. To ensure quality, we randomly sampled 100 samples across all 9 datasets in LLMAggreFact and manually inspected the reasoning traces derived from GPT-4o and found them to be accurate.

---

[2] We concur with previous research [30] that "REFUTES", common in general NLI problems, is rare in claim verification.

[3] Accessed on March 4, 2025. We did not use the o-series models for this as it does not provide access to raw reasoning tokens.

[4] Notably, ~21% of LLMAggreFact dev set labels differed from GPT-4o-mini's predictions; analyzing this discrepancy is beyond this paper's scope. Hence we chose to only train on examples with agreement.

4.2   ThinknCheck-1B Model Training

We implemented ThinknCheck-1B by fine-tuning a 4-bit quantized Gemma3 1B model on LLMAggreFact-Think (training details in Appendix B). Our choice of Gemma3 was inspired by its size, recency, and its overall performance across diverse LLM benchmarks [8]. The fine-tuning prompt (Appendix C) mirrored the LLMAggreFact-Think data structure, constraining the model to output both reasoning and the final verification solution.[5] For finetuning we used the 24.1K examples constructed as reported in Sect. 4.1 and retained 20% of that as a development set.

4.3   Ablation Model Variants: Base Model, Non-Thinking, CoT, and GRPO

To isolate the reasoning step's impact, we trained an ablation model, ThinknCheck-nothink-1B. It shares ThinknCheck-1B's architecture, data, and hyperparameters but was trained with a prompt (Appendix D) requesting only the final solution, omitting reasoning generation. This ablation ensures that observed performance gains are not solely due to our choice of Gemma3 as the backbone. For context, we also evaluate the Gemma3-1B base model without fine-tuning (direct YES/NO) and with a Chain-of-Thought (CoT) prompt [35] at inference time using the same decoding settings; these rows appear in Table 1. Beyond SFT, we train a preference-optimized variant using the Dr. GRPO variant with GSPO enabled in HuggingFace's TRL library [36]. We experimented with LoRA adapters initialized with and without SFT warm start, each jointly optimizing a two-term reward: (i) a *format-adherence* bonus that requires the model to emit both <REASONING> and <SOLUTION> in order; and (ii) a *class-weighted accuracy* term that upweights the minority class to counter label imbalance.[6] Full reward definitions, numeric weights, sampling limits, logging/checkpointing, and other reproducibility details are provided in Appendix E; empirical results are reported in Sect. 5.3.

4.4   GSMClaims Dataset for Arithmetic Reasoning

We construct **GSMClaims** from the GSM8K test set [4] by reframing each problem into *two* claim-verification instances using GPT-4o: (1) convert the problem context into a reference document; (2) generate a *positive* claim whose answer is the correct computed value; and (3) generate a *negative* claim with a plausible but incorrect value reflecting common calculation errors. This 3-step process yields **2,634** balanced items in which verification hinges on performing

---

[5] Inference uses parameters recommended by the Gemma3 paper: temperature=1.0, top_p=0.95, and top_k=64.

[6] We keep 4-bit loading and the same LoRA configuration as in Sect. 4.2, generate 5 candidates per prompt, and train for a single epoch (400 steps) with fused AdamW (5×10^{-6} LR), warmup ratio 0.1, per-device batch size 4 and gradient accumulation 4.

the arithmetic grounded in the document. We manually inspected a subset of 100 positive and negative claims and found them to be near-perfectly accurate; the prompt template is provided in Appendix F.

4.5   ThinknCheck-Science: Specializing for Complex Claims

To better handle quantitative and scientific claims, we train **ThinknCheck-Science**, a targeted variant of ThinknCheck-1B. We augment the LLMAggreFact-Think training data with **614** reasoning-enhanced examples from SciFact [32] and **398** from GSMClaims, emphasizing specialized knowledge and arithmetic calculation. ThinknCheck-Science retains the base architecture, quantization, and training procedure of ThinknCheck-1B, differing only in the enriched supervision set aimed at strengthening numerical and domain-specific reasoning.

5   Experiments

Research Questions. We structure the evaluation around three questions: **RQ1**. Do explicit, supervised rationales help at 1B scale? **RQ2**. Do they improve out-of-domain generalization (SCIFACT) over specialized baselines? **RQ3**. Do coarse preference rewards (GRPO) help or hurt?

5.1   Evaluation Metrics

Following prior work [6,15,29,30], we adopt Balanced Accuracy (BAcc) as our primary metric for evaluating potentially imbalanced datasets like LLMAggreFact and SciFact.[7] For the balanced GSMClaims dataset, we report standard accuracy, so our results are interpretable with previous works.

5.2   Baselines

We compare ThinknCheck against three categories of baselines: (1) closed LLMs in zero-shot settings (GPT-4, GPT-4o, Claude-Sonnet-3.5) as reported by [30]. All significance statements use 10k bootstrap resamples over the 29.3k LLMAggreFact test instances with paired resampling across models. Our goal is not to compete with these private and massive foundation models, but to provide context., (2) specialized verification models (AlignScore, MiniCheck-7B), and (3) ThinknCheck variants (ThinknCheck-nothink, ThinknCheck, ThinknCheck-Science) to isolate the impact of reasoning and data augmentation components.

---

[7]

$$\mathrm{BAcc} = \frac{1}{2}\left(\frac{\mathrm{TP}}{\mathrm{TP} + \mathrm{FN}} + \frac{\mathrm{TN}}{\mathrm{TN} + \mathrm{FP}}\right),$$

where TP, TN, FP, and FN represent true positives, true negatives, false positives, and false negatives, respectively.

Table 1. Balanced accuracy (BAcc) on the LLMAGGREFACT test set (29.3k examples) and SCIFACT development set. The 1B *reasoning-supervised* ThinknCheck model attains 78.1 BAcc on LLMAggreFact, exceeding the specialized 7B MiniCheck (77.4), and reaches 64.7 on SciFact (+14.7 over MiniCheck). Chain-of-Thought on the non-fine-tuned base reduces performance (55.7 → 51.4), while answer-only SFT yields only a small gain (57.5). The ThinknCheck-nothink ablation scores 21.7 on SciFact, confirming that reasoning drives generalization. Significance: paired bootstrap, $p < 0.05$.

Model	LLMAggreFact BAcc	SciFact BAcc
GPT-4 (zero-shot)	75.3	–
GPT-4o (zero-shot)	75.9	–
Claude-Sonnet-3.5 (zero-shot)	77.2	–
AlignScore (355M/fp16)	70.4	–
MiniCheck (7B/fp16)	77.4	50.0
Gemma3 (1B/fp4) ("base")	55.7	–
Gemma3 + CoT (1B/fp4)	51.4	–
ThinknCheck-nothink (1B/fp4)	57.5	21.7
ThinknCheck (1B/fp4)	**78.1**	**64.7**

5.3   Core Verification Performance and Generalization

Table 1 summarizes results on LLMAggreFact and SciFact. The reasoning-supervised **ThinknCheck-1B** (4-bit) attains **78.1** BAcc on LLMAggreFact, surpassing MiniCheck-7B (77.4) despite using ∼7× fewer parameters, and matching or exceeding zero-shot closed models (GPT-4: 75.3; GPT-4o: 75.9; Claude Sonnet 3.5: 77.2). Reasoning is essential: removing it (*ThinknCheck-nothink*) drops BAcc to 57.5, a −20.6 point decline. On the 1B base, zero-shot CoT hurts relative to direct answers (55.7 → 51.4), whereas supervised reasoning reverses the pattern and yields the best 1B result. All deltas are significant under paired bootstrap ($p < 0.05$).

On SciFact, ThinknCheck-1B achieves 64.7 BAcc, a substantial +14.7 absolute point improvement over MiniCheck-7B (50.0 BAcc). The ThinknCheck-nothink ablation performs poorly (21.7 BAcc), confirming that reasoning drives this enhanced generalization. These results demonstrate that ThinknCheck handles claims requiring deeper understanding more effectively, with important implications for deployment in domain-shifting scenarios.

Preference Optimization. Preference optimization with a simple two-term reward (format + class-weighted accuracy) underperforms supervised reasoning: GRPO from base yields 52.6 BAcc (below 55.7), and GRPO from an SFT warm start reaches 74.2 (below 78.1). A manual audit indicates GRPO gravitates toward a lexical-overlap shortcut (predicting YES when the claim reuses document phrasing). At 1B scale, explicit reasoning supervision is a more reliable path than zero-shot CoT or coarse preference rewards for grounded verification. Full GRPO details are in Appendix E.

5.4 Cross-Benchmark Performance: GSMClaims and ThinknCheck-Science

Table 2. Performance across all benchmarks. ThinknCheck-Science, trained with additional scientific and arithmetic data, achieves the best performance on all three evaluations, including 61.0% accuracy on GSMClaims (17% relative improvement over ThinknCheck-1B).

Model	LLMAggreFact BAcc	SciFact BAcc	GSMClaims Acc
MiniCheck-7B	77.4	50.0	51.3
ThinknCheck-nothink-1B	57.5	21.7	49.4
ThinknCheck-1B	78.1	64.7	52.2
ThinknCheck-Science-1B	**79.2**	**66.4**	**61.0**

We used the GSMClaims dataset (Sect. 4.4) to evaluate arithmetic reasoning. As expected, both ThinknCheck-1B (52.2%) and MiniCheck-7B (51.3%) find this task challenging, confirming that current datasets relying heavily on textual entailment are insufficient for numerical reasoning. ThinknCheck-Science (Table 2), trained with additional scientific and arithmetic data, achieves 61.0% on GSMClaims—a 17% relative improvement. It also improves on LLMAggreFact (79.2) and SciFact (66.4), indicating that specialized training enhances rather than compromises general verification.

5.5 How Much Reasoning Is Enough? Reasoning Length Vs. Accuracy

We study ThinknCheck-1B on the LLMAggreFact test set to relate the amount of generated reasoning to correctness: we tokenize the `<REASONING>` span with the Gemma3 tokenizer, bucket examples into ten equal-sized deciles by token length, and compute BAcc per decile (Fig. 2). Accuracy follows an inverted-U: mid-length rationales yield the best BAcc, whereas very short and very long chains underperform. Short chains exhibit recall exceeding precision, consistent with liberal "YES" predictions triggered by shallow matches; at the longest lengths, recall drops below precision, reflecting conservative behavior and more false negatives. Length is not causal—longer chains co-vary with instance difficulty and the need to aggregate more evidence—but the pattern aligns with our error taxonomy (Sect. 6): terse chains co-occur with lexical-overlap false positives, and very long chains with over-cautiousness and insufficient aggregation.

Together with the ablations in Sect. 5.3, the takeaway is that focused, succinct-but-substantive reasoning, rather than maximal length, is most reliable at 1B scale.

6   Error Analysis

We analyzed ThinknCheck-1B errors on LLMAggreFact, SciFact, and GSM-Claims using a unified taxonomy (Fig. 3). **Lexical Overlap Bias** was most prevalent in LLMAggreFact (5.3%) but lower in GSMClaims (3.9%). In GSM-Claims, **Arithmetic Reasoning** errors dominated (43.2% of errors). **Over-cautiousness**, the leading error in SciFact (41.4% of errors), reflects difficulty confirming complex scientific assertions. **Negation/Temporal** errors were significant in SciFact (32.8%) but rare in GSMClaims (0.9%). **Insufficient Aggregation** was critical in LLMAggreFact (4.6%) where multi-hop synthesis is key.

GRPO optimization increased the share of lexical-overlap false positives: the policy frequently predicted YES when the claim reused document phrases without verifying entailment. Consistent with Sect. 5.5, terse rationales coincide with lexical-overlap false positives, while very long rationales correlate with over-cautiousness and insufficient aggregation. These domain-specific error profiles suggest that no single mitigation strategy suffices; targeted approaches such as adversarial data mining and domain-specific prompting are needed.

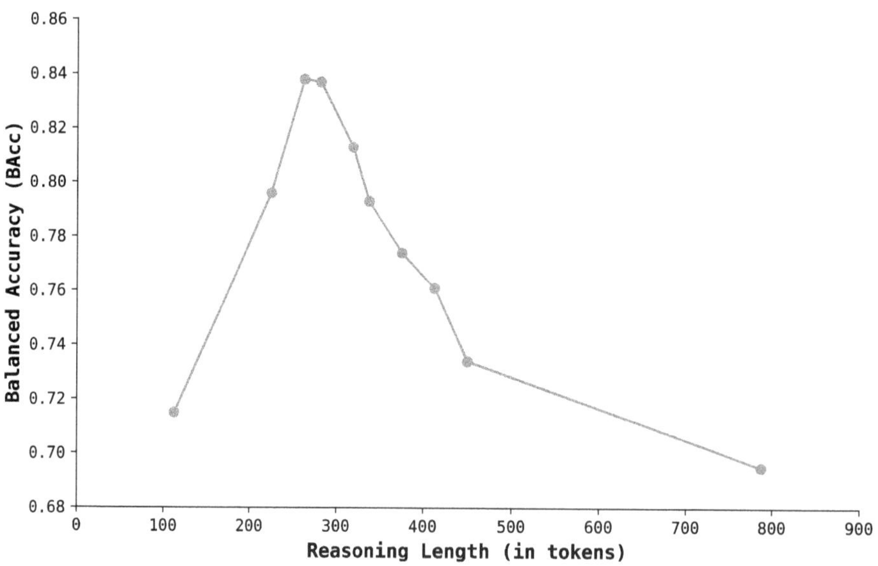

Fig. 2. Reasoning length vs. balanced accuracy (LLMAggreFact). ThinknCheck-1B outputs are grouped into deciles by the token length of the <REASONING> span (Gemma tokenizer). BAcc peaks for mid-length rationales and drops for very short and very long chains. Short chains show recall > precision; very long chains show the opposite trend.

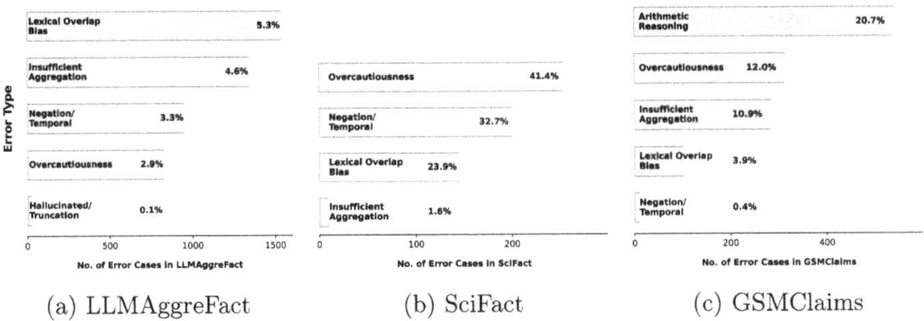

(a) LLMAggreFact   (b) SciFact   (c) GSMClaims

Fig. 3. Distribution of error types on (a) LLMAggreFact, (b) SciFact, and (c) GSM-Claims. Error profiles vary dramatically by domain: general claims are dominated by lexical overlap and aggregation failures; scientific claims by overcautiousness; mathematical claims by arithmetic reasoning errors.

7   Conclusion

We introduced ThinknCheck, a compact verifier trained to reason before deciding. At 1B parameters, supervised rationales raise performance on LLMAggreFact to 78.1 BAcc and improve out-of-domain generalization on SciFact (64.7 BAcc vs. 50.0 for MiniCheck-7B). Removing the reasoning step lowers BAcc by 20.6 points, and both zero-shot chain-of-thought on the base model and GRPO with a simple reward degrade accuracy under our setup. Analysis of model traces suggests that widely used verification datasets emphasize surface matching while under-testing evidence synthesis and arithmetic. Our GSMClaims benchmark and the domain-adapted ThinknCheck-Science address these gaps and yield gains across tasks, including 61.0% accuracy on GSMClaims. A reasoning length study further indicates that mid-length rationales are most reliable for this setting, though length likely correlates with instance difficulty rather than causing accuracy changes. In sum, the results support small, reasoning-supervised verifiers as practical building blocks for grounded verification when compute, privacy, or latency constrain model size. Immediate next steps include constructing harder, balanced datasets that require multi-sentence synthesis and numerical reasoning, adding lightweight tool use for arithmetic, and learning adaptive reasoning budgets that keep rationales concise without sacrificing correctness.

8   Limitations

ThinknCheck advances claim verification, and we identify several promising directions for future development. Our CoT result reflects a single prompt and decoding setup; while consistent with recent reports that CoT can hurt small models without adaptation, we did not exhaustively analyze all CoT prompt variations. Our GRPO setup uses a concise, two-term reward and a short training horizon (400 steps); alternative rewards (e.g., evidence-aware or contrastive), stronger KL or behavior-cloning constraints to the SFT policy, or longer training may change outcomes. We therefore interpret the GRPO results as a negative finding under a transparent, reproducible configuration rather than a general indictment of preference optimization. While the Gemma3-1B backbone supports a 32k-token context window, our experiments do not stress this limit: we evaluate single-document verification with relatively short inputs – a limitation of current claim verification benchmarks. Extending ThinknCheck to truly long-context settings (multi-document packs [26,33], $\geq$10k tokens) is left for future work. We also used a fixed maximum decoding budget for the <REASONING> span; making this budget adaptive could reduce both under- and over-thinking. Furthermore, performance on tasks like GSMClaims suggests that integrating external tools (e.g., calculators) [25] is a key step for complex arithmetic reasoning. Finally, aligning with challenges in prior work [30,39], calibrating output logits to serve as reliable confidence scores [19] remains an important area for ongoing investigation and future refinement of ThinknCheck.

All created datasets and models will be released under an Apache 2.0 license[8].

Acknowledgments. This research was developed with funding from the Defense Advanced Research Projects Agency's (DARPA) SciFy program (Agreement No. HR00112520300). The views expressed are those of the author and do not reflect the official policy or position of the Department of Defense or the U.S. Government.

A   Prompt for Generating LLMAggreFact-Think

```
You are expert fact checker with a strong attention to detail and access to
a wealth of information. Given a document and a claim, determine if the
claim is entailed by the document, only using the facts in the document.
Respond in the following format:

<reasoning>
... // clear, but short description of your step by step
   // thinking to arrive at the entailment
   // keep the reasoning sentences separated by a newline.
</reasoning>
<entailment>
... // This is always a single word, either "YES" or "NO"
</entailment>
```

B   Hyperparameter Details

For fine-tuning, we used LoRA [9] with rank=64, lora_alpha=64, and a learning rate of 2e-4 scheduled linearly. We updated the query, key, value, and output projection layers, as well as MLP gate, up, and down projections. The fine-tuning was performed on an A100 GPU for 1 epoch, with 5 warmup steps, a

---

[8] URL withheld for blind review.

batch size of 4 with 4 accumulated steps, and an 8bit-AdamW optimizer with a weight decay of 0.01.

C Finetuning Prompt for ThinknCheck

You are given a document and a claim. The document is enclosed between <DOCUMENT> and </DOCUMENT>. The claim is between <CLAIM> and </CLAIM>. Determine if the claim is entailed by the document. Think about the problem and provide your reasoning. Place the reasoning between <REASONING> and </REASONING>. Then, provide your entailment solution between <SOLUTION> and </SOLUTION>. The entailment should be either a YES or a NO.

```
<DOCUMENT>
{document}
</DOCUMENT>
<CLAIM>
{claim}
</CLAIM>
<REASONING>
{reasoning}
</REASONING>
<SOLUTION>
{solution}
</SOLUTION>
```

D Finetuning Prompt for ThinknCheck-Nothink

You are given a document and a claim. The document is enclosed between <DOCUMENT> and </DOCUMENT>. The claim is between <CLAIM> and </CLAIM>. Determine if the claim is entailed by the document. Provide your entailment solution between <SOLUTION> and </SOLUTION>. The entailment should be either a YES or a NO.

```
<DOCUMENT>
{document}
</DOCUMENT>
<CLAIM>
{claim}
</CLAIM>
<SOLUTION>
{solution}
</SOLUTION>
```

E   GRPO Details

We use TRL's `GRPOTrainer` with the Dr. GRPO loss and GSPO. The reward is $R = 0.5 \cdot R_{\text{fmt}} + 1.0 \cdot R_{\text{acc}}$, where $R_{\text{fmt}} \in \{+1, -1\}$ checks for both <REASONING> and <SOLUTION> tags, and R_{acc} applies class-weighted accuracy ($w_{\text{YES}}{=}0.6356$, $w_{\text{NO}}{=}2.3435$, scale ±4.0). We draw 5 completions per prompt, cap prompts at 4,306 tokens and completions at 378 tokens, and train for one epoch (400 steps) with `adamw_torch_fused` (LR $5{\times}10^{-6}$, warmup 0.1, batch 4, gradient accumulation 4). LoRA adapters are initialized from an SFT-400 checkpoint. GRPO variants use the same I/O format and decoding defaults as SFT.

F   Prompt to Generate GSMClaims

Given an arithmetic problem and a solution, rewrite them as a document and a a pair of positive and negative claims such the positive claim is entailed by the document (after solving some arithmetic) and the negative claim is not entailed by the document (after solving some arithmetic). Produce your answer only as a JSON. Do not add anything before and after the JSON.

References

1. Allal, L.B., et al.: SmolLM2: when Smol goes big–data-centric training of a small language model. arXiv preprint arXiv:2502.02737 (2025)
2. Bansal, G., et al.: Does the whole exceed its parts? The effect of AI explanations on complementary team performance. In: Proceedings of the 2021 CHI Conference on Human Factors in Computing Systems (2020). https://api.semanticscholar.org/CorpusID:220128138
3. Chen, H.T., Xu, F., Arora, S.A., Choi, E.: Understanding retrieval augmentation for long-form question answering. arXiv preprint arXiv:2310.12150 (2023)
4. Cobbe, K., et al.: Training verifiers to solve math word problems (2021). https://arxiv.org/abs/2110.14168
5. Guo, D., et al.: Deepseek-R1: incentivizing reasoning capability in LLMs via reinforcement learning (2025). https://arxiv.org/abs/2501.12948
6. Fabbri, A.R., Wu, C.S., Liu, W., Xiong, C.: QaFactEval: improved QA-based factual consistency evaluation for summarization. arXiv preprint arXiv:2112.08542 (2021)
7. Fan, M., Yang, X., Yu, T.T., Liao, V.Q., Zhao, J.: Human-AI collaboration for UX evaluation: effects of explanation and synchronization. ArXiv **abs/2112.12387** (2021). https://api.semanticscholar.org/CorpusID:260496371
8. GemmaTeam, Kamath, A., et al.: Gemma 3 technical report (2025). https://arxiv.org/abs/2503.19786
9. Hu, E.J., et al.: LORA: low-rank adaptation of large language models (2021). https://arxiv.org/abs/2106.09685
10. Hu, Y., Ganter, T., Deilamsalehy, H., Dernoncourt, F., Foroosh, H., Liu, F.: MeetingBank: a benchmark dataset for meeting summarization. arXiv preprint arXiv:2305.17529 (2023)

11. Jacovi, A., et al.: A chain-of-thought is as strong as its weakest link: a benchmark for verifiers of reasoning chains (2024)

12. Jacovi, A., et al.: A chain-of-thought is as strong as its weakest link: a benchmark for verifiers of reasoning chains. arXiv preprint arXiv:2402.00559 (2024)

13. Javaid, M., Estivill-Castro, V.: Explanations from a robotic partner build trust on the robot's decisions for collaborative human-humanoid interaction. Robotics **10**, 51 (2021). https://api.semanticscholar.org/CorpusID:233627254

14. Kamoi, R., Goyal, T., Rodriguez, J.D., Durrett, G.: WICE: real-world entailment for claims in Wikipedia. arXiv preprint arXiv:2303.01432 (2023)

15. Laban, P., Schnabel, T., Bennett, P.N., Hearst, M.A.: SummAC: Re-Visiting NLI-based models for inconsistency detection in summarization. Trans. Assoc. Comput. Ling. **10**, 163–177 (2022)

16. Li, Y., et al.: Small models struggle to learn from strong reasoners (2025). https://arxiv.org/abs/2502.12143

17. Liu, N.F., Zhang, T., Liang, P.: Evaluating verifiability in generative search engines. arXiv preprint arXiv:2304.09848 (2023)

18. Liu, R., Geng, J., Wu, A.J., Sucholutsky, I., Lombrozo, T., Griffiths, T.L.: Mind your step (by step): chain-of-thought can reduce performance on tasks where thinking makes humans worse (2025). https://arxiv.org/abs/2410.21333

19. Liu, X., Chen, T., Da, L., Chen, C., Lin, Z., Wei, H.: Uncertainty quantification and confidence calibration in large language models: a survey. arXiv preprint arXiv:2503.15850 (2025)

20. Liu, Z., et al.: Understanding R1-zero-like training: a critical perspective (2025). https://arxiv.org/abs/2503.20783

21. Malaviya, C., Lee, S., Chen, S., Sieber, E., Yatskar, M., Roth, D.: ExpertQA: expert-curated questions and attributed answers. arXiv preprint arXiv:2309.07852 (2023)

22. Malaviya, C., Lee, S., Chen, S., Sieber, E., Yatskar, M., Roth, D.: ExpertQA: expert-curated questions and attributed answers. In: 2024 Annual Conference of the North American Chapter of the Association for Computational Linguistics (2024). https://openreview.net/forum?id=hhC3nTgfOv

23. Nallapati, R., Zhou, B., Gulcehre, C., Xiang, B., et al.: Abstractive text summarization using sequence-to-sequence RNNs and beyond. arXiv preprint arXiv:1602.06023 (2016)

24. Narayan, S., Cohen, S.B., Lapata, M.: Don't give me the details, just the summary! topic-aware convolutional neural networks for extreme summarization. arXiv preprint arXiv:1808.08745 (2018)

25. Patil, S.G., Zhang, T., Wang, X., Gonzalez, J.E.: Gorilla: large language model connected with massive APIS. Adv. Neural. Inf. Process. Syst. **37**, 126544–126565 (2024)

26. Poli, M., et al.: Hyena Hierarchy: towards larger convolutional language models. In: International Conference on Machine Learning, pp. 28043–28078. PMLR (2023)

27. Shao, Z., et al.: DeepSeekMath: pushing the limits of mathematical reasoning in open language models (2024). https://arxiv.org/abs/2402.03300

28. Shao, Z., et al.: DeepSeekMath: pushing the limits of mathematical reasoning in open language models. arXiv preprint arXiv:2402.03300 (2024)

29. Tang, L., et al.: Understanding factual errors in summarization: errors, summarizers, datasets, error detectors. arXiv preprint arXiv:2205.12854 (2022)

30. Tang, L., Laban, P., Durrett, G.: MiniCheck: efficient fact-checking of LLMs on grounding documents (2024). https://arxiv.org/abs/2404.10774

31. Thorne, J., Vlachos, A., Christodoulopoulos, C., Mittal, A.: Fever: a large-scale dataset for fact extraction and verification. arXiv preprint arXiv:1803.05355 (2018)
32. Wadden, D., Lin, S., Lo, K., Wang, L.L., van Zuylen, M., Cohan, A., Hajishirzi, H.: Fact or Fiction: verifying scientific claims. In: Webber, B., Cohn, T., He, Y., Liu, Y. (eds.) Proceedings of the 2020 Conference on Empirical Methods in Natural Language Processing (EMNLP), pp. 7534–7550. Association for Computational Linguistics, Online (2020). https://doi.org/10.18653/v1/2020.emnlp-main.609
33. Waleffe, R., et al.: An empirical study of mamba-based language models. arXiv preprint arXiv:2406.07887 (2024)
34. Wang, Y., et al.: FactCheck-Bench: fine-grained evaluation benchmark for automatic fact-checkers. arXiv preprint arXiv:2311.09000 (2023)
35. Wei, J., et al.: Chain-of-thought prompting elicits reasoning in large language models. Adv. Neural. Inf. Process. Syst. **35**, 24824–24837 (2022)
36. von Werra, L., et al.: TRL: transformer reinforcement learning. https://github.com/huggingface/trl (2020)
37. Xu, X., et al.: A survey on knowledge distillation of large language models. arXiv preprint arXiv:2402.13116 (2024)
38. Yao, S., et al.: React: synergizing reasoning and acting in language models. In: International Conference on Learning Representations (ICLR) (2023)
39. Zha, Y., Yang, Y., Li, R., Hu, Z.: AlignScore: evaluating factual consistency with a unified alignment function (2023). https://arxiv.org/abs/2305.16739
40. Zhang, M., Press, O., Merrill, W., Liu, A., Smith, N.A.: How language model hallucinations can snowball. arXiv preprint arXiv:2305.13534 (2023)
41. Zheng, C., et al.: Group sequence policy optimization (2025). https://arxiv.org/abs/2507.18071
42. Zhu, C., Liu, Y., Mei, J., Zeng, M.: MediaSum: a large-scale media interview dataset for dialogue summarization. arXiv preprint arXiv:2103.06410 (2021)

What Do Claim Verification Datasets Actually Test? A Reasoning Trace Analysis

Delip Rao[ID] and Chris Callison-Burch[(✉)][ID]

University of Pennsylvania, Philadelphia, PA, USA
{delip,ccb}@seas.upenn.edu

Abstract. Despite rapid progress in claim verification, we lack a systematic understanding of what reasoning these benchmarks actually exercise. We generate structured reasoning traces for 24K claim-verification examples across 9 datasets using GPT-4o-mini and find that direct evidence extraction dominates, while multi-sentence synthesis and numerical reasoning are severely under-represented. A dataset-level breakdown reveals stark biases: some datasets almost exclusively test lexical matching, while others require information synthesis in roughly half of cases. Using a compact 1B-parameter reasoning verifier, we further characterize five error types and show that error profiles vary dramatically by domain – general-domain verification is dominated by lexical overlap bias, scientific verification by overcautiousness, and mathematical verification by arithmetic reasoning failures. Our findings suggest that high benchmark scores primarily reflect retrieval-plus-entailment ability. We outline recommendations for building more challenging evaluation suites that better test the reasoning capabilities verification systems need.

Keywords: Claim verification · Benchmark analysis · Reasoning traces

1 Introduction

Claim verification benchmarks such as LLMAggreFact [13], SciFact [15], and FEVER [14] are widely used to evaluate factual grounding models. Recent systems report near-human balanced accuracies on these benchmarks, yet practical deployment reveals persistent failures on claims requiring multi-step reasoning, numerical computation, or evidence synthesis across sentences (see Fig. 1 for a simple illustration). This gap raises a question: what kinds of reasoning do current benchmarks actually exercise?

To answer this question, we generate structured reasoning traces for 30.4K examples from the LLMAggreFact benchmark – which aggregates nine widely-used claim-verification datasets – using GPT-4o-mini in a zero-shot setting. After filtering for label agreement with ground truth, we retain 24.1K traces and systematically analyze the reasoning strategies they reveal. We complement this

E. Cabrio and E. Monteiro (Eds.): NLDB 2026, LNCS 16696, pp. 33–43, 2027.
https://doi.org/10.1007/978-3-032-29532-3_4

Claim: Water boils at 100C.
Document: The temperature at which water boils is 212F.

....

MiniCheck-7B verification result:
```
DOES NOT SUPPORT
```

....

Compact reasoning verifier (1B) result:
```
SUPPORTS
```
Reasoning trace:
The document states that the temperature at which water boils is 212F. The claim states that water boils at 100C, which is equivalent to 100F. To determine if the claim is true, I need to convert 100C to Fahrenheit. 100C is equal to 212F, which is the same as the boiling point of water. Thus, the claim is supported by the information in the document.

Fig. 1. Surface matching fails on claims requiring reasoning. A state-of-the-art 7B verifier [13] rejects the claim because $100°C$ does not appear in the document, even though $100°C = 212°F$. A compact reasoning verifier that generates an explicit reasoning trace before deciding correctly handles the unit conversion. This example motivates our analysis: if benchmarks primarily reward surface matching, high scores may not reflect genuine verification ability.

with an error analysis using a compact 1B-parameter reasoning verifier that we train on these traces, which allows us to characterize failure modes across general, scientific, and mathematical domains.

Our contributions are:

- A taxonomy of six reasoning patterns observed in claim verification, based on manual review of 1,000 stratified samples.
- Quantitative evidence that direct evidence extraction (surface matching) accounts for the majority of verification reasoning, while multi-sentence synthesis and step-by-step verification are rare.
- A dataset-level analysis revealing significant variation in reasoning demands across the nine constituent datasets in LLMAggreFact.
- An error taxonomy from a compact verifier identifying five domain-dependent error types, showing that error profiles differ dramatically between general, scientific, and mathematical claims.
- Concrete recommendations for constructing more challenging claim verification benchmarks.

2   Related Work

Dataset Bias and Annotation artifacts. Studies in NLI have shown that benchmarks can contain systematic biases that allow models to achieve high accuracy without genuine understanding [20]. Similar concerns apply to claim verification, where surface-level cues may substitute for deeper reasoning.

Claim Verification Benchmarks. LLMAggreFact [13] aggregates nine sources spanning news, science, and dialogue domains [5,7–12,16,21]. SciFact [15] and FEVER [14] target scientific and Wikipedia claims. While these benchmarks have driven progress, the reasoning complexity they demand has not been systematically characterized.

Reasoning in NLP Evaluation. Chain-of-thought prompting [17] has enabled analysis of model reasoning processes. Recent work on verifiable CoT [6] and reasoning-augmented verification [18] provides tools for inspecting what reasoning models actually perform. Large reasoning models such as DeepSeek R1 [2] generate verbose traces, while distilled approaches can produce more concise rationales suitable for systematic analysis.

Lightweight Verifiers. Compact verification models such as MiniCheck [13] and AlignScore [19] have shown that specialized training can match larger models. We use a compact reasoning verifier as an analysis tool to characterize error patterns across domains.

3 Reasoning Trace Generation

To systematically analyze the reasoning demands of claim verification benchmarks, we generated structured reasoning traces for all 30.4K examples in the LLMAggreFact development set. Using zero-shot prompting, GPT-4o-mini generated a step-by-step reasoning process and a YES/NO verification label for each (document, claim) pair. To ensure trace quality, we filtered instances where the generated label mismatched the original LLMAggreFact label, reducing the dataset from 30.4K to 24.1K examples.[1] This filtered set contains traces across all nine constituent datasets in LLMAggreFact. We randomly sampled 100 traces across all 9 datasets and manually verified their accuracy. We opted against DeepSeek R1 [2] traces due to their verbosity and token inefficiency, which would complicate systematic analysis.

4 Reasoning Pattern Taxonomy

4.1 Methodology

We sampled 1,000 instances with stratified sampling over the dataset source, then manually reviewed the generated rationales for each (document, claim) pair. For every instance, annotators identified the primary reasoning strategy used to justify the predicted label. Through an iterative pass, we consolidated categories, recorded recurring patterns, and selected representative examples (Sect. 5).

---

[1] Approximately 21% of LLMAggreFact dev set labels differed from GPT-4o-mini's predictions; analyzing this discrepancy is beyond this paper's scope.

4.2   Reasoning Patterns

We observe six recurring strategies: (A) *Direct evidence extraction and matching* (quoting or paraphrasing spans that explicitly support/contradict the claim); (B) *Handling nuance and implication* (contextual or partial support without verbatim statements); (C) *Absence of evidence identification* (stating that the document lacks the requisite information); (D) *Synthesis of multiple information points* (integrating evidence across sentences/sections); (E) *Addressing scope/specificity mismatches* (claim broader/narrower or adding elements absent from the source); and (F) *Step-by-step verification* (checking procedural or sequential claims).

4.3   Overall Distribution

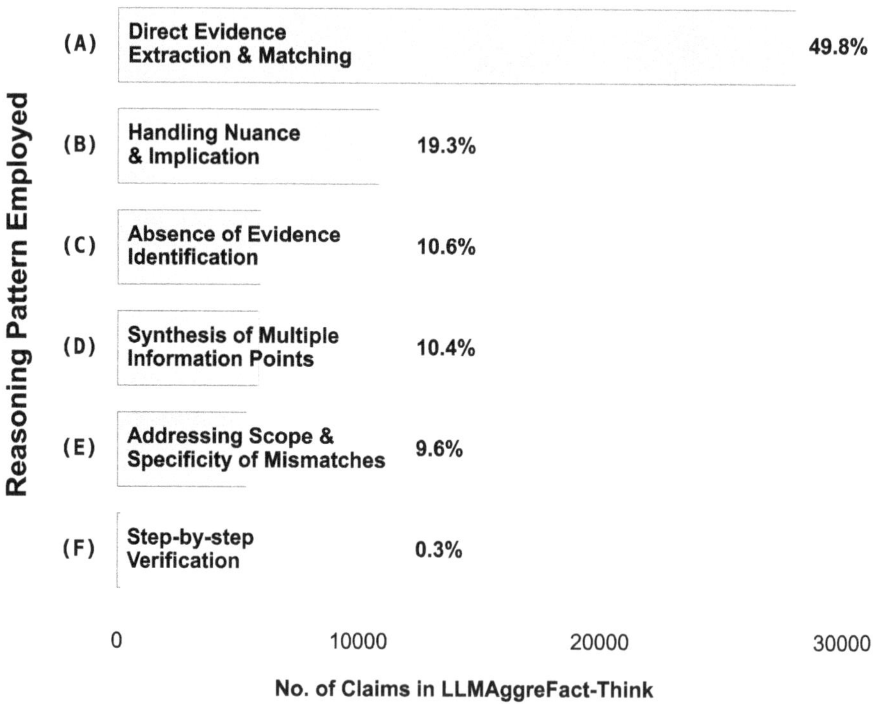

Fig. 2. Distribution of reasoning patterns across 24.1K claim verification traces. Direct evidence extraction (A) dominates the verification strategies (27,988 instances), followed by other reasoning strategies. See Sect. 4.2 for pattern definitions.

Overall distribution (Fig. 2) shows a strong dominance of direct extraction (A), with substantially smaller shares for nuance (B), absence identification (C), and multi-sentence synthesis (D); step-by-step verification (F) is rare. This indicates that the majority of verification reasoning in LLMAggreFact reduces to locating and matching relevant text spans.

4.4 Dataset-Level Analysis

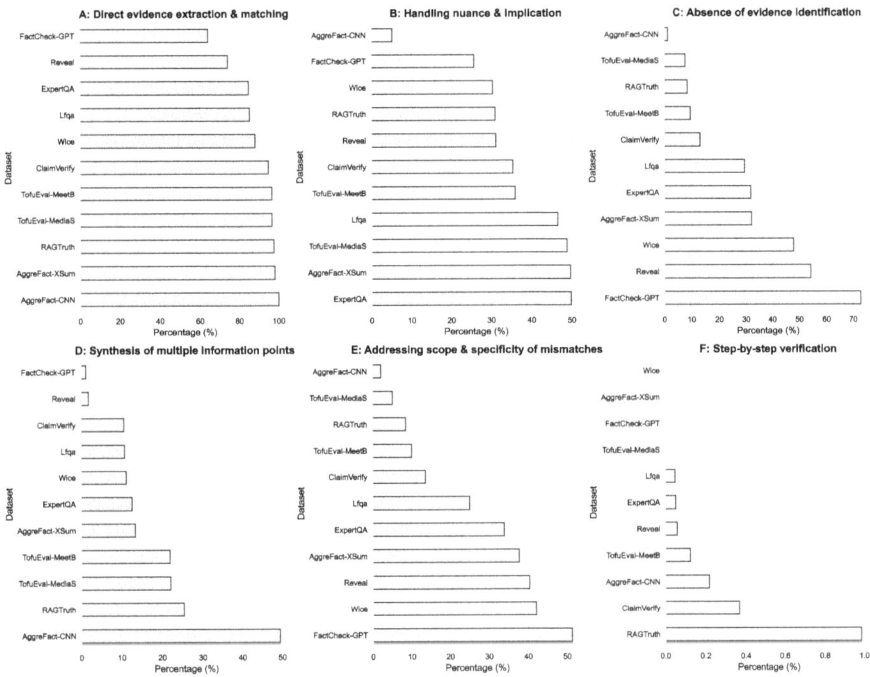

Fig. 3. Distribution of reasoning strategies across the nine source datasets in LLMAggreFact. Each subplot (A–F) corresponds to a reasoning pattern: (A) Direct evidence extraction and matching, (B) Handling nuance and implication, (C) Absence of evidence identification, (D) Synthesis of multiple information points, (E) Addressing scope and specificity mismatches, and (F) Step-by-step verification. Different datasets elicit markedly different reasoning patterns.

The dataset-level breakdown (Fig. 3) reveals clear biases: e.g., AggreFact-CNN requires information synthesis in roughly half of cases, whereas even the dataset with the highest rate of multi-step verification (RAGTruth) exhibits it in only ~0.9% of instances. We also observe complementarity between patterns: sources with very high direct extraction (A) tend to have low synthesis (D). Scope/nuance phenomena (E/B) are more prominent in FactCheck-GPT and Wice, while absence identification (C) varies drastically by formulation (from < 1% in AggreFact-CNN to > 70% in FactCheck-GPT).

5   Representative Examples

We present one example for each identified reasoning pattern, drawn from the generated traces.

Direct Evidence Extraction and Matching:

> ***Claim:*** "Proper clean-up prior to insertion of the vaginoscope is essential."
> ***Reasoning:*** "The document contains a sentence that explicitly states 'Proper clean-up prior to insertion of the vaginoscope is essential.' This directly matches the claim made..."

Absence of Evidence Identification:

> ***Claim:*** "A star's temperature is determined by the amount of mass and energy it has."
> ***Reasoning:*** "The document discusses determining the effective temperature of a star from its spectrum but does not mention the relationship between a star's mass, energy, and temperature... Therefore, the claim is not backed by the facts in the document..."

Synthesis of Multiple Information Points:

> ***Claim:*** "However, according to customer reviews, the quality of the food served at the restaurant is subpar."
> ***Reasoning:*** "The document contains multiple customer reviews expressing dissatisfaction... One review explicitly states that the food was 'horrible,'... Another review criticizes the broth as 'least flavorful'... Together, these reviews confirm that the quality of food... is indeed regarded as subpar by customers."

Addressing Scope and Specificity Mismatches:

> ***Claim:*** "Thermodynamics provides the fundamental laws of energy conservation, mass conservation, and chemical equilibrium that govern the behavior of chemical systems."
> ***Reasoning:*** "The document discusses the first law of thermodynamics, which addresses energy conservation, aligning with part of the claim. However, it does not support the components of mass conservation and chemical equilibrium... Therefore, the claim goes beyond what is explicitly stated... and is only partially supported."

Handling Nuance and Implication:

> ***Claim:*** "The restaurant's use of fresh and high-quality ingredients, such as shrimp and pork belly, has also been commended by reviewers."
> ***Reasoning:*** "...One review even states that 'the shrimp you could really sink your teeth into,' suggesting that the shrimp is fresh and of high quality. The combination of positive comments about these specific ingredients supports the claim."

Step-by-Step Verification:

> **Claim:** "Return beef and any accumulated juices to the pan, along with tomato sauce, liver spread, and bay leaves."
> **Reasoning:** "...passage 3 explicitly states to 'Return beef and accumulated juices to pan' and also adds 'Add water, tomato sauce, liver spread and bay leaf.' Therefore, all elements of the claim are present in the passage..."

6 Error Analysis from a Compact Verifier

6.1 Approach

To characterize where current verification systems fail, we trained ClaimTrace, a compact reasoning verifier, on the generated traces. ClaimTrace is a 4-bit quantized Gemma3 1B model [3] fine-tuned with LoRA [4] to produce structured reasoning followed by a verification decision. We evaluate ClaimTrace on held-out data from three domains: general claims (LLMAggreFact), scientific claims (SciFact [15]), and mathematical claims (a math-reasoning benchmark derived from GSM8K [1]), and systematically categorize its errors.

6.2 Error Taxonomy

Through systematic analysis of ClaimTrace predictions across all three domains, we identified five primary error categories (six for mathematical claims): **Lexical Overlap Bias**: incorrectly predicting support based on surface-level lexical similarity without proper semantic entailment. **Insufficient Aggregation**: failure to synthesize information distributed across multiple sentences. **Negation/Temporal Confusion**: mishandling negations or temporal relationships. **Overcautiousness**: requiring complete explicit evidence for all components of a claim, defaulting to rejection even when most sub-claims are supported. **Hallucinated Justification**: generating confident reasoning unsupported by the document. For mathematical claims, we add **Arithmetic Reasoning**: failure to execute correct computation despite understanding the problem structure.

6.3 Error Distribution Across Domains

Error profiles vary dramatically by domain (Fig. 4). In LLMAggreFact, **Lexical Overlap Bias** is the most prevalent error (5.3% of all examples), followed by **Insufficient Aggregation** (4.6%) – reflecting the dominance of direct evidence extraction in these datasets. In SciFact, **Overcautiousness** dominates (41.4% of errors), with the verifier predicting "not supported" unless every component of a scientific claim is explicitly stated; **Negation/Temporal** errors are also substantial (32.8%). In the mathematical domain, **Arithmetic Reasoning** errors are most common (43.2% of errors), followed by **Overcautiousness** (25.0%) and **Insufficient Aggregation** (22.7%).

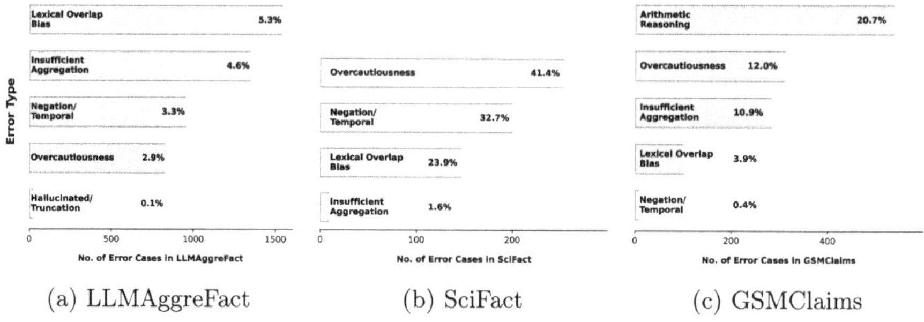

(a) LLMAggreFact   (b) SciFact   (c) GSMClaims

Fig. 4. Distribution of error types on (a) LLMAggreFact, (b) SciFact, and (c) a math-reasoning benchmark derived from GSM8K. Error profiles vary dramatically across domains: general-domain verification is dominated by lexical overlap bias, scientific verification by overcautiousness, and mathematical verification by arithmetic reasoning failures.

6.4   Key Error Examples

Lexical Overlap Bias (General Domain):

Claim: Roberto Martinez felt Seamus Coleman should have been awarded a free-kick before the defender conceded the penalty that allowed Swansea to pinch a 1-1 draw at the Liberty Stadium.
Ground Truth: NO   **Predicted:** YES
Analysis: ClaimTrace matches surface phrases without verifying true entailment.

Overcautiousness (Scientific Domain):

Claim: 1,000 genomes project enables mapping of genetic sequence variation consisting of rare variants with larger penetrance effects than common variants.
Ground Truth: YES   **Predicted:** NO
Analysis: The document discusses the identification of common variants and implications of rare variants, but ClaimTrace rejects the claim because the specific number of genomes is not mentioned.

Arithmetic Reasoning (mathematical domain):

Claim: Janet makes $18 every day at the farmers' market.
Ground Truth: YES   **Predicted:** NO
Analysis: The document provides the information needed to calculate the earnings, but ClaimTrace fails to execute the computation correctly.

7   Findings and Implications

Our analysis yields three key findings with direct implications for benchmark design.

Finding 1: High Scores Primarily Reflect Retrieval and Entailment. The dominance of direct evidence extraction (Pattern A) across LLMAggreFact means that a model achieving high balanced accuracy on this benchmark is primarily demonstrating its ability to locate and match relevant text spans. While this is a necessary component of verification, it is not sufficient for claims requiring deeper reasoning. The strong correlation between benchmark performance and Pattern A prevalence suggests that current metrics overestimate general verification ability.

Finding 2: Multi-sentence Synthesis and Numerical Reasoning are Under-Tested. Patterns D (synthesis) and F (step-by-step verification) together account for a small fraction of the reasoning demands in LLMAggreFact. This means that verification systems can achieve competitive scores while having weak capabilities in exactly the reasoning types needed for complex, real-world claims. The near-random performance of both a 7B specialized verifier and our compact model on mathematical claims further demonstrates this gap.

Finding 3: Error Profiles are Domain-Specific. The dramatic variation in error distributions across general, scientific, and mathematical domains shows that no single mitigation strategy suffices. Improving lexical overlap handling (the dominant general-domain error) would have minimal impact on scientific claim verification, where overcautiousness is the primary issue.

Recommendations. Based on these findings, we suggest the following directions for benchmark development: (1) adversarial data mining that specifically targets lexical overlap to reduce surface-matching shortcuts; (2) inclusion of more multi-hop claims requiring evidence synthesis across sentences; (3) dedicated numerical reasoning components, since current benchmarks almost entirely lack such demands; (4) domain-stratified evaluation that reports per-domain performance rather than single aggregate scores; and (5) finer-grained labels such as PARTIAL support to capture the nuanced nature of real-world claim verification.

8   Conclusion and Limitations

We presented a systematic analysis of the reasoning demands in claim verification benchmarks, generating and analyzing 24.1K structured reasoning traces across nine datasets. Our taxonomy reveals that direct evidence extraction dominates current benchmarks, while multi-sentence synthesis and numerical reasoning are severely under-represented. Domain-specific error analysis using a compact verifier shows that failure modes vary dramatically across general, scientific, and mathematical claims. These findings suggest that current high benchmark scores primarily reflect retrieval-plus-entailment ability rather than robust verification reasoning.

Limitations. Our analysis relies on reasoning traces from a single generator (GPT-4o-mini); different models may produce traces emphasizing different strategies. The analysis is limited to the nine datasets aggregated in LLMAggreFact. Manual coding of reasoning patterns, while conducted with stratified sampling and iterative consolidation, involves subjective judgment. The compact verifier used for error analysis has limited capacity, and a larger model might exhibit different error patterns.

Acknowledgments. This research was developed with funding from the Defense Advanced Research Projects Agency's (DARPA) SciFy program (Agreement No. HR00112520300). The views expressed are those of the author and do not reflect the official policy or position of the Department of Defense or the U.S. Government.

References

1. Cobbe, K., et al.: Training verifiers to solve math word problems (2021). https://arxiv.org/abs/2110.14168
2. DeepSeek-AI, Guo, D., et al.: DeepSeek-R1: incentivizing reasoning capability in LLMs via reinforcement learning (2025). https://arxiv.org/abs/2501.12948
3. GemmaTeam, Kamath, A., et al.: Gemma 3 technical report (2025). https://arxiv.org/abs/2503.19786
4. Hu, E.J., et al.: LORA: low-rank adaptation of large language models (2021). https://arxiv.org/abs/2106.09685
5. Hu, Y., Ganter, T., Deilamsalehy, H., Dernoncourt, F., Foroosh, H., Liu, F.: MeetingBank: a benchmark dataset for meeting summarization. arXiv preprint arXiv:2305.17529 (2023)
6. Jacovi, A., et al.: A chain-of-thought is as strong as its weakest link: a benchmark for verifiers of reasoning chains. arXiv preprint arXiv:2402.00559 (2024)
7. Kamoi, R., Goyal, T., Rodriguez, J.D., Durrett, G.: WICE: real-world entailment for claims in Wikipedia. arXiv preprint arXiv:2303.01432 (2023)
8. Liu, N.F., Zhang, T., Liang, P.: Evaluating verifiability in generative search engines. arXiv preprint arXiv:2304.09848 (2023)
9. Malaviya, C., Lee, S., Chen, S., Sieber, E., Yatskar, M., Roth, D.: ExpertQA: expert-curated questions and attributed answers. arXiv preprint arXiv:2309.07852 (2023)
10. Nallapati, R., Zhou, B., Gulcehre, C., Xiang, B., et al.: Abstractive text summarization using sequence-to-sequence RNNs and beyond. arXiv preprint arXiv:1602.06023 (2016)
11. Narayan, S., Cohen, S.B., Lapata, M.: Don't give me the details, just the summary! topic-aware convolutional neural networks for extreme summarization. arXiv preprint arXiv:1808.08745 (2018)
12. Tang, L., et al.: Understanding factual errors in summarization: errors, summarizers, datasets, error detectors. arXiv preprint arXiv:2205.12854 (2022)
13. Tang, L., Laban, P., Durrett, G.: MiniCheck: efficient fact-checking of LLMs on grounding documents (2024). https://arxiv.org/abs/2404.10774
14. Thorne, J., Vlachos, A., Christodoulopoulos, C., Mittal, A.: Fever: a large-scale dataset for fact extraction and verification. arXiv preprint arXiv:1803.05355 (2018)

15. Wadden, D., et al.: Fact or Fiction: verifying scientific claims. In: Webber, B., Cohn, T., He, Y., Liu, Y. (eds.) Proceedings of the 2020 Conference on Empirical Methods in Natural Language Processing (EMNLP), pp. 7534–7550. Association for Computational Linguistics, Online (Nov 2020). https://doi.org/10.18653/v1/2020.emnlp-main.609
16. Wang, Y., et al.: FactCheck-Bench: fine-grained evaluation benchmark for automatic fact-checkers. arXiv preprint arXiv:2311.09000 (2023)
17. Wei, J., et al.: Chain-of-thought prompting elicits reasoning in large language models. Adv. Neural. Inf. Process. Syst. **35**, 24824–24837 (2022)
18. Yao, S., et al.: React: synergizing reasoning and acting in language models. In: International Conference on Learning Representations (ICLR) (2023)
19. Zha, Y., Yang, Y., Li, R., Hu, Z.: AlignScore: evaluating factual consistency with a unified alignment function (2023). https://arxiv.org/abs/2305.16739
20. Zhao, Z., Wallace, E., Feng, S., Klein, D., Singh, S.: Calibrate Before Use: improving few-shot performance of language models. In: Meila, M., Zhang, T. (eds.) Proceedings of the 38th International Conference on Machine Learning. Proceedings of Machine Learning Research, vol. 139, pp. 12697–12706. PMLR (2021). https://proceedings.mlr.press/v139/zhao21c.html
21. Zhu, C., Liu, Y., Mei, J., Zeng, M.: MediaSum: a large-scale media interview dataset for dialogue summarization. arXiv preprint arXiv:2103.06410 (2021)

Using Text Simplification in Norwegian News Summarization

Vandana Yadav$^{(\boxtimes)}$ ⓘ, Jon Atle Gulla ⓘ, Özlem Özgöbek ⓘ, and Lemei Zhang ⓘ

Norwegian University of Science and Technology, Trondheim, Norway
{vandana.yadav,jon.atle.gulla,ozlem.ozgobek,lemei.zhang}@ntnu.no

Abstract. This paper explores the automated generation of Norwegian news summaries tailored for children aged 6 to 12, a task representing a unique convergence of text summarization and text simplification. While traditional summarization focuses on condensing information, child-centric summaries require reframing content through reduced linguistic complexity, positive orientation and narrative-driven discourse. Leveraging the NorwAI-Qwen3-8B-reasoning model, we evaluate two prompting strategies across the NorSumm and PersonalSum datasets. We utilize the Läsbarhetsindex (LIX) and Kolmogorov-Smirnov (K-S) tests as primary metrics to assess lexical complexity shifts. Our results demonstrate that highly prescriptive prompts (Prompt 2) are significantly more effective at creating a complexity gap between adult and child-oriented content. Notably, the NorwAI-Qwen3 model outperformed previous benchmarks in semantic alignment (BERTScore), though a gap remains in structural lexical overlap compared to top-performing models. This work establishes a foundation for accessible digital news for younger Norwegian audiences while identifying critical needs for multi-dimensional evaluation frameworks and parallel corpora.

Keywords: Text Simplification · News Summarization · Readability Score

1 Introduction

Automatic text summarization aims to generate a summary for a document or multiple documents by condensing the contents of the document(s) while maintaining the structure, semantic, and context of the document(s). Most of the summarization methods are focused on preserving the contents' original structure and meaning. Summarization methods may produce summaries with either same level or lower level of complexity in the text/document(s). In some cases, summaries are targeted to generate less complex content. Although, these summaries are simplified for the readers (adults), it may not highly conform to news summaries for children of age group 6 to 12 years old. Children and adult news summaries differ in various aspects. First, children news summaries need to have simple/easy to read text and avoid high level related topics of the news

E. Cabrio and E. Monteiro (Eds.): NLDB 2026, LNCS 16696, pp. 44–58, 2027.
https://doi.org/10.1007/978-3-032-29532-3_5

article. Second, it can differ in discourse style: children may prefer news summaries in story-like format, whereas adults would prefer in more scientific way (Introduction, Events, Conclusions). Third, in news summaries for children, it is important to avoid upsetting/harsh parts of the articles or have news summaries in upbeat tune. So, positively orient the articles for children. Fourth, shorter news summaries than longer adult summaries would help keep younger audiences more engaged on news platform and updated with current affairs. In conclusion, summary of the news article for children should incorporate the following components: easy to read text, text that has similar meaning to the news article, optimistic sentences, upbeat discourse style (interesting for children), and avoid upsetting words/phrases. To obtain simpler text in news summaries meant for children, Text Simplification task can be considered. Text Simplification is an evolving field within Natural Language Processing that seeks to lower the linguistic complexity of content (unlike summarization methods where complexity maybe of same level, lower or higher depending user's needs) while preserving its core meaning. Readability/Complexity of the text can be estimated on following aspects of simplification of the text: lexical (vocabulary), semantic (meaning), and syntactic (structure of the text such as word order and sentence composition). Therefore, summarizing news for children is considered a unique convergence of Text Simplification and Text Summarization. This hybrid task requires more than just condensing information and simplifying text but it involves reframing content through positive orientation and adopting narrative-driven discourse (story-like language). Since text simplification doesn't necessarily generate simplified text with positive orientation or narrative-based discourse style, evaluating these simplified summaries for children requires a holistic approach that measures linguistic complexity, orientation, discourse, and story structure, all while ensuring the core factual integrity of the original article is preserved. We cannot just use standard ROUGE scores which looks at overlapping words between two texts. It would require tools that measure lexical (SARI and readability index like Läsbarhetsindex (LIX)), syntactic (like LENS model-based metrics measuring meaning preservation and grammaticality) and tone.

1.1 Motivation for News Summaries for Children

In an era of quick digital access, the challenge is no longer to find information, but make it accessible for younger audiences (such as 6 to 12 years old). Engaging children in current affairs requires a delicate balance: providing factual updates on the world while ensuring the format is child-friendly and age-appropriate. Beyond engagement of children, text simplification serves as a vital tool for mental health assessments and educational equality. As noted in recent research on lemma-based metrics, substituting complex terminology with simpler lexical variants can significantly improve the accuracy of assessment questionnaires and the efficacy of educational software [5]. This can be particularly crucial for young students developing core literacy skills and non-native speakers navigating a new language. Despite its importance, there is a notable gap in research regarding text simplification and summarization for children within the Norwegian linguistic context. This paper aims to address this void by exploring how automated systems can adapt adult-centric news into digestible content for younger minds.

To investigate the current landscape of Norwegian automated summarization, this study addresses the following questions:

- RQ 1: How do existing Norwegian language models perform in summarization task for adults and children using zero-shot prompting Large Language Models capabilities?
- RQ 2: To what extent do traditional Scandinavian readability metrics, specifically the Läsbarhetsindex (LIX), effectively differentiate the lexical complexity across standard news articles, adult-centric summaries, and child-oriented summaries?

This paper provides an evaluation of Norwegian Large Language Models for adult-centric and child-centric news summarization. The key contributions of the paper are as follows:

1. We demonstrate that while Norwegian LLMs (specifically NorwAI-Qwen3-8B-reasoning) are capable of text simplification, their effectiveness is highly sensitive to prompt structure. Our findings show that standard prompts often fail to create a sufficient complexity gap for younger audiences. However, with refined instructions, the model successfully reduced the LIX readability score, effectively shifting content from standard news to reduced lexical complexity appropriate for child's level.
2. By applying the Kolmogorov-Smirnov (K-S) test to LIX score distributions, we provide statistical evidence that LLM-generated summaries for children are not just shorter, but represent a fundamentally different linguistic distribution ($p < 0.001$).
3. We show that the prescriptive prompting is the effective strategy for the NorwAI-Qwen3-8B-reasoning model, providing superior semantic alignment (BERTScore) and structural coherence (ROUGE-LSum). Additionally, we show that NorwAI-Qwen3-8B-reasoning model outperforms previous benchmarks on Norwegian adult-centric news summarization in semantic similarity (BertScore) though a gap remains in lexical overlap (ROUGE-L and ROUGE-LSum) compared to top-performing models.

2   Related Works

The task of generating news summaries for children requires a unique combination of text simplification and text summarization (text condensation) [9]. While traditional summarization focuses on removing redundancy to produce overview of the article, child-centric methods must ensure generated text aligns with the cognitive and developmental needs of younger audiences [1,2].

Foundations of Child-Specific News Processing. Early research in this field was often motivated by manual news services like the BBC's Newsround which simplified adult news by shortening articles using an upbeat tone and removing upsetting content [2]. One of the extractive approaches combined statistical ratings for importance, positive sentiment, and readability [2]. It adapted the inverted pyramid structure of journalism by doubling the importance weights of the lead sentences to ensure core information was preserved. Prior to this, a study explored an approach for children that emphasized on sentence splitting and replacing difficult terms with easier synonyms [3].

Document-Level Studies. Current research has transitioned from sentence-level analysis to document-level simplification that seeks to simplify an entire document while maintaining overall logical/thematic consistency. One of the recent studies identified that current Large Language Models (LLMs) often default to mere summarization when tasked with document simplification, resulting in a significant loss of information [7]. To resolve this, it proposed ProgDS, a progressive framework that decomposes the task into discourse-level (organization), topic-level (paragraph structures), and lexical-level (vocabulary) simplification utilizing in-context learning [7]. Similarly, in a comparable study, abstractive summarization as a proxy for gold-standard simplification was evaluated. The findings indicated that paragraph-by-paragraph summarization outperformed document-wide methods though still served better as a preparatory step than a complete substitute for human experts [10].

Specialized LLMs and Educational Safety. The development of child-specific language models such as KidLM addresses the limitations of generic LLMs, which are often trained on unscreened/unverified internet data that may include stereotypes or inappropriate content [6]. By introducing a user-centric pipeline to curate a high-quality corpus specifically for children and proposed stratified masking to prioritize kid-specific vocabulary during training. Additionally, a study evaluated the most advance model (GPT-4o) against human baselines using zero-shot prompting strategies for Newsela corpus (matching 100 grade 12 (original) texts with their corresponding grade 4 versions) [4]. It concluded that while LLMs reduce lexical complexity, they still produce text with more syntactic complexity than of human baselines thereby inhibiting the access for children.

As per our knowledge, there are no studies in news summarization for children. However, there are studies which analyzes lexical complexity using four corpus [5]. It proposes a lemma-level measure based on Läsbarhetsindex (LIX) index testing its application on mental assessment questionnaire-based datasets to substitute complex terms to meet different language requirements of the candidate taking the assessment. In Scandinavia, LIX (Läsbarhetsindex) is the gold standard developed by Swedish scholar Carl-Hugo Björnsson for measuring text difficulty because it handles the unique nature of Norwegian and Swedish (such as long compound words) better than English-centric formulas like Flesch-Kincaid Grade Level (FKGL) [18].

3   Experiment Setup

To evaluate the news summarization capabilities of LLMs within a Norwegian linguistic context, we established a comparative framework focusing on two distinct target audiences: general adults and children (ages 6–12).

3.1   Datasets

The evaluation is conducted using the following news summarization datasets in Norwegian:

1. **NorSumm.** [8] is a high-quality benchmark dataset designed to evaluate the abstractive summarization capabilities of Large Language Models (LLMs) in Norwegian. It has 378 total summaries derived from 63 news articles. Each article is paired with 3 unique human summaries written by three native Norwegian speakers. Each summary has both language variant (Bokmål and Nynorsk, 6 summaries total per article).
2. **PersonalSum.** [16] is a high-quality, human-annotated Norwegian dataset designed for personalized text summarization. Unlike traditional datasets (Norwegian CNN DailyMail dataset [21]) which aim for a single gold standard summary, PersonalSum provides multiple summaries for an article based on different user profiles. It includes about 1100 personalized summaries derived from 442 news articles.

Currently, there is a lack of available corpora containing paired examples of complex and simplified text.

3.2   Prompting Strategy

In this study, we leverage the prompting capabilities of LLMs to generate Norwegian news summaries tailored for both adult and child audiences. The summarization process employs two distinct prompting strategies derived from the NorEval benchmark [8] (see Table 1). For each target audience, the first prompt is designed to be concise, while the second provides more elaborate instructions to guide the model's output. Child-centric prompts are highly prescriptive, emphasizing positive tone, specific sentence length constraints (max 15 words), and explicit vocabulary substitution (e.g., swapping "strategi" for "plan"). Adult-centric prompts focus on structural completeness and character limits (700 characters) rather than specific linguistic constraints [8].

3.3   Model Selection

We employ NorwAI-Qwen3-8B-reasoning [21] as our primary model. This choice is motivated by its reasoning capabilities and specialized adaptation to the Norwegian language. While previous benchmarks particularly NorSumm [8]

Table 1. Prompts used in the evaluation of summarization for adults and children across NorSumm and PersonalSum datasets.

Prompts in Norwegian:

s **Generation of Children News Summaries:**

Prompt 1: Oppsummer den gitte nyhetsartikkelen i fire eller fem setninger på norsk for barn i alderen 6 til 12 år.

Prompt 2: Skriv en nyhetssammendrag av følgende artikkel for barn 6-12 år. Bruk: Korte setninger (max 15 ord), Enkle ord (ikke bruk: kompleks, implementere, strategi → bruk: vanskelig, gjøre, plan), Positiv tone.

Generation of Adults News Summaries:

Prompt 1: Skriv en oppsummering av følgende artikkel med kun noen få punkter

Prompt 2: Skriv en kort og presis oppsummering av teksten over. Språket må være klart og lett å forstå. Sørg for å ikke introdusere feil. Oppsummeringa må dekkje følgande spørsmål: kven, kva, kor, når, og kvifor er denne saka viktig å vite om. Oppsummeringa må vere engasjerande og framheve nøkkelinformasjon fra artikkelen. Oppsummeringa skal innehalde maksimalt 700 tegn, inkludert mellomrom.

Prompts in English:

Generation of Children News Summaries:

Prompt 1: Summarize the given news article in four or five sentences in English for children aged 6 to 12.

Prompt 2: Write a news summary of the following article for children 6-12 years old. Use: Short sentences (max 15 words), Simple words (do not use: complex, implement, strategy → use: difficult, do, plan), Positive tone.

Generation of Adults News Summaries:

Prompt 1: Write a summary of the following article using only a few bullet points.

Prompt 2: Write a short and precise summary of the text above. The language must be clear and easy to understand. Ensure no errors are introduced. The summary must cover the following questions: who, what, where, when, and why this case is important to know about. The summary must be engaging and highlight key information from the article. The summary shall contain a maximum of 700 characters, including spaces.

---

established baselines based on Mistral and Llama, more recent evaluations demonstrate that Qwen3-based models provide significantly improved reasoning because of having different thinking modes [20]. Additionally, Qwen3 often uses a Mixture-of-Experts (MoE) architecture (such as Qwen3-Coder-Next), which allows it to have the brain of a large model but the speed of a small one [19]. Additionally, as the NorSumm [8] study specifically evaluated models using zero-shot prompting, adopting the same strategy for NorwAI-Qwen3-8B allows for a direct comparison.

3.4   Evaluation Metrics

The generation of news summaries for children is a combination of text simplification and text summarization methods, so metrics revolving around both tasks can be considered for evaluating them. Evaluation metrics typically involves SARI (sentence-level) [12], SARI-D (document-level) [13] for simplification quality, LENS (Learnable Evaluation metric for Natural language Summarization) [11] for alignment with reference, Flesch-Kincaid Grade Level (FKGL) (English) [18] and Läsbarhetsindex (LIX) (Norwegian) for readability, and BERTScore [15] for semantic similarity [7]. Each has a focus on a different aspect of the text (Table 2). In the Norwegian context, there are no available corpora consisting of pairs of complex and simple texts, or pair of human authored child-centric news summary and adult-centric news summary. The datasets available (Nor-Summ and PersonalSum) have news articles and summaries for general audience. Thus, we don't have human authored (gold-standard) news summaries for children which can be used as reference summaries (ground-truth) for evaluating the generated news summaries for children. Hence, we are unable to compare the child and adult-centric news summaries with the automatic metrics namely LENS, SARI, BertScore, ROUGE [14] that evaluate simplification quality and semantic similarity with the reference summaries. Although SAMSA is designed to be reference-free and it specifically rewards structural simplification by utilizing Abstract Meaning Representation (semantic graph) that represents who is doing what in a sentence, it is not language-agnostic. It would require a semantic parser to understand the meaning of the Norwegian text before it can score it. BLEU is increasingly discouraged for simplification because it penalizes valid deletions and simple word swaps [17].

Table 2. Comprehensive overview of metrics that looks into lexical similarity, structure, and semantic alignment.

Metric	Focus	Comparison	Key Strength
LENS	Human Alignment(Neural-based)	Output vs Source+Reference	Current SOTA; highest correlation with human judgment.
SALSA	Semantic Error	Output vs Source	Identifies specific simplification errors (meaning loss).
SARI	Simplicity (Edit Operations)	Output vs Source+Reference	Rewards adding simple words and deleting jargon.
SAMSA	Structural (Sentence Splitting)	Output vs Source	Ideal for evaluating sentence splitting in news.
BERTScore	Semantic Similarity	Output vs Reference	Ensures factual accuracy is preserved in summaries.
LIX/FKGL	Shallow complexity (Readability Scores)	Output alone	**LIX** is the standard for Norwegian; FKGL is for English.
BLEU/ROUGE	Lexical Similarity (N-gram Overlap)	Output vs Reference	Traditionally used; now considered secondary in TS research.
Compression Ratio	Information Density (Statistical)	Output vs Source	Measures text reduction, essential for targeting specific age groups.

Evaluation Metrics Employed. Due to the absence of human-authored (gold-standard) summaries for children in the Norwegian language, evaluating structural and semantic similarity for child-centric summaries remains a significant challenge. The LIX (Läsbarhetsindex) readability score becomes our primary metric to assess the lexical complexity across both adult-centric and child-centric news summaries. For adult-centric summaries, where reference texts are available, we further evaluate lexical and semantic similarity using ROUGE-L and BERTScore, respectively.

Lexical Complexity for Adult and Child-centric News Summaries. LIX readability score helps in analyzing the length of sentences and the frequency of long words (defined as words with more than 6 letters). While LIX focuses on word length (character count), FKGL (English readability score) relies on syllable counts to estimate the U.S. school grade level required to understand the text [18]. A LIX score 20–30 (very easy) and 30–40 (medium difficulty) is typically targeted. Scores above 40 are often considered too academic [5]. A recent study [5] showed that the document-level complexity, LIX, can segment texts of different levels of complexity (four corpora: Children's books, News articles, Encyclopedia entries, & Legislative texts from the Norwegian parliament) into categories that match their assumed complexity. As the LIX score can separate the corpus into their known complexity level, the LIX score has some information on the complexity of individual words within these documents. Further, statistical testing known as the Kolmogorov-Smirnov test (K-S test) was used to confirm that the LIX index successfully separated these four corpora into distinct complexity classes. Therefore, to assess readability shifts across the entire text, we employed the LIX index in conjunction with two-sample Kolmogorov-Smirnov (K-S) tests. LIX scores were calculated as in the mentioned study [5] for the original news articles, the generated adult-centric summaries, and the child-centric summaries. We then performed pairwise K-S tests across these groups including an adult reference summary to determine if their complexity distributions were statistically distinct.

Lexical Overlap and Semantic Similarity for Adult-centric News Summaries. For the evaluation of lexical overlap between reference adult-centric news summary and generated adult-centric news summary, the ROUGE-L and ROUGE-Lsum frameworks were employed. ROUGE-L and ROUGE-LSum both use the Longest Common Subsequence to calculate scores but they are applied at different granularities [14]. ROUGE-L calculates LCS by considering the entire summary as one continuous string, while ROUGE-Lsum calculates the LCS for each individual sentence in the summary and then aggregates them (usually via a weighted average). Additionally, BertScore was employed to check whether the meaning of the source article is preserved or not in the generated adult-centric summary. It uses embeddings from BERT to measure semantic similarity between the output (generated adult-centric summaries) and the reference summaries of the source (news articles). NorSumm provides three references, comparing the generated summary to just one might result in a low score if the human and model focused on different key points. So, similar to NorSumm evaluation [8], we calculate the three scores (ROUGE-L. ROUGE-Lsum, and BertScore) against all three human summaries. Then choose the highest of the three scores for that specific prompt. Each news article in PersonalSum have reference summaries ranging from 1 to 6. As the number of reference summaries is not same, we considered the first reference summary of each news article.

4 Results

4.1 Lexical Complexity for Adult and Child-Centric News Summaries

NorSumm: Prompt 1. (Tables 3 and 5) The generated adult-centric summaries ($\mu = 43.01$) showed a slight increase in complexity compared to the original articles ($\mu = 40.45$), but this change was not statistically significant ($p = 0.056$). The generated child-centric summaries ($\mu = 35.96$) were significantly simpler than both the original articles ($p = 0.0017$) and the adult-centric summaries ($p < 0.001$). The high standard deviation in case of adult-centric summaries (8.9) means the model is inconsistent and some adult summaries are likely very dense ($\mu = 50+$) while others are standard.

Table 3. Descriptive statistics of LIX distributions for the **NorSumm** dataset.

Category	Mean (μ)	Variance (σ^2)	Std. Dev (σ)
Original Articles	40.45	38.05	6.17
Prompt 1			
Adult-centric Summary	43.01	79.72	8.93
Child-centric Summary	35.96	52.12	7.22
Prompt 2			
Adult-centric Summary	44.30	87.41	9.35
Child-centric Summary	28.61	66.32	8.14

Table 4. Descriptive statistics of LIX distributions for the **PersonalSum** dataset.

Category	Mean (μ)	Variance (σ^2)	Std. Dev (σ)
Original Articles	40.20	42.02	6.48
Prompt 1			
Adult-centric Summary	42.50	68.50	8.28
Child-centric Summary	36.18	52.28	7.23
Prompt 2			
Adult-centric Summary	44.11	59.76	7.73
Child-centric Summary	30.73	66.97	8.18

NorSumm: Prompt 2. (Tables 3 and 5) The generated adult-centric summaries ($\mu = 44.30$) were significantly more complex than the original articles ($p = 0.0033$). The child-centric summaries ($\mu = 28.61$) achieved a much lower LIX score, indicating a highly significant reduction in complexity compared to

Table 5. Kolmogorov-Smirnov (K-S) test results for **NorSumm's** reading complexity. Statistics & P-Values compares the LIX distributions between the original Articles and the generated summaries.

Prompt	Comparison	D-Statistic	P-Value	Significant?
Prompt 1	Articles vs. Adults	0.2381	0.0559	No
	Articles vs. Kids	0.3333	0.0017	Yes
	Adults vs. Kids	0.4286	< 0.001	Yes
Prompt 2	Articles vs. Adults	0.3175	0.0033	Yes
	Articles vs. Kids	0.6984	< 0.001	Yes
	Adults vs. Kids	0.7143	< 0.001	Yes

both articles and adult summaries ($p < 0.001$). Prompt 2 was much more effective at differentiating between the two target audiences, creating a complexity gap of approximately 15.7 LIX points, compared to the 7.0 point gap in Prompt 1.

PersonalSum: Prompt 1. (Tables 4 and 6) The generated adult Summaries ($\mu = 42.50$) are slightly more complex than the original articles ($\mu = 40.20$). The D-statistic of 0.1538 indicates a small but measurable shift toward a more sophisticated vocabulary or longer sentence structure. The model reduced the LIX score of child summaries ($\mu = 36.18$) by roughly 4 points compared to the articles. The complexity gap between adult summaries and child summaries is 6.3 LIX points. While significant, this is a relatively conservative adjustment.

PersonalSum: Prompt 2 (Tables 4 and 6) The D-statistic for articles and child summaries jumped from 0.267 (P1) to 0.5136 (P2). A D-statistic above 0.5 is considered a very large effect size in K-S tests, meaning the distributions of the two text types have very little overlap. The child Summaries ($\mu = 30.73$) achieved a dramatic drop in complexity. The complexity gap between adult-centric and child-centric summaries expanded to 13.4 LIX points.

Table 6. K-S Test results for **PersonalSum's** reading complexity. Statistics and P-Values compares the LIX distributions between the original Articles and the generated summaries.

Prompt	Comparison	D-Statistic	P-Value	Significant?
Prompt 1	Articles vs. Adults	0.1538	5.56e-05	Yes
	Articles vs. Kids	0.2670	2.94e-14	Yes
	Adults vs. Kids	0.3371	1.20e-22	Yes
Prompt 2	Articles vs. Adults	0.2534	7.16e-13	Yes
	Articles vs. Kids	0.5136	1.72e-53	Yes
	Adults vs. Kids	0.6131	7.27e-78	Yes

4.2   Lexical Overlap and Semantic Similarity for Adult-Centric News Summaries

In NorSumm, we see the most significant jump for P2 in ROUGE-LSum (from 33.3 to 35.5). The BERTScore also improves in both datasets when using P2, suggesting that P2 encourages the model to generate summaries that are not just lexically similar, but semantically closer to the reference. NorSumm and PersonalSum have a noticeable performance gap between them. NorSumm scores are generally higher across all metrics (ROUGE-L $\approx$ 27, BERTScore $\approx$ 75). PersonalSum scores are lower (ROUGE-L $\approx$ 24, BERTScore $\approx$ 73). PersonalSum appears to be a more challenging task for the model. In NorSumm, there is a wide gap between ROUGE-L and ROUGE-LSum (27 vs 35). This suggests that the model is performing significantly better when the ROUGE metric considers the overall structure and sentence breaks of the summary. In PersonalSum, ROUGE-L and ROUGE-LSum are almost identical ($\approx$ 24). This indicates that the summaries in PersonalSum are likely shorter or more flat in structure, providing less opportunity for the LSum variant to capture structural advantages.

Table 7 compares the performance of the NorwAI-Qwen3-8B-reasoning model across two datasets (NorSumm and PersonalSum) using two different prompting strategies (P1 and P2)

Table 7. NorwAI-Qwen3-8B-reasoning model results for **NorSumm** and **PersonalSum** datasets with 2 prompts.

	NorSumm			PersonalSum		
	ROUGE-L	**ROUGE-LSum**	**BERTScore**	**ROUGE-L**	**ROUGE-LSum**	**BERTScore**
P1	27.166	33.370	74.384	23.997	24.047	73.261
P2	27.428	35.500	75.395	24.256	24.075	73.676
Average	27.297	34.435	77.889	24.126	24.061	73.468

5   Discussions

The evaluation of the NorwAI-Qwen3-8B-reasoning model across the NorSumm and PersonalSum datasets reveals insights into the influence of prompting strategies on linguistic complexity (via LIX readability score) of both adult and child-centric news summaries. In addition to this, provides insights into the model's capacity (via ROUGE and BERTScore) for adult-centric news summarization. A primary finding of this study is the superior performance of Prompt 2 over Prompt 1 in achieving distinct stylistic goals. In both datasets, Prompt 2 facilitated a much wider complexity gap between adult and child-centric summaries. For NorSumm, this gap reached 15.7 LIX points, compared to only 7.0 in Prompt 1. Despite this progress, the LIX distribution suggest that further lexical reduction is required to reach the target zone (20–30) for children's news as LIX readability score with K-S test helps to understand surface level lexical complexity gap between the generated news summaries. While the Kolmogorov-Smirnov (K-S) test effectively confirms surface-level lexical shifts, comprehensive evaluation of child-friendly properties would require additional metrics focusing on semantic density, positive orientation, and discourse structure. Furthermore, current research suggests that morphological complexity does not inherently hinder comprehension of the text [5]. In languages like Norwegian, long compound words such as bokhylleseksjon (book (bok) + shelf (hylle) + section (seksjon)) exceeds six characters yet remain intuitively accessible because their meaning is a transparent sum of their parts. In the context of news articles and summaries, a word's length may not strictly dictate its cognitive load. Analyzing the complexity of content words through a morphological lens rather than solely rely on character counts, would provide a much deeper understanding of how information is processed by the reader. A more granular understanding of readability could be achieved through a lemma-based complexity measure, which assigns a complexity score to individual content words based on their distribution across documents of varying difficulty [5]. It can be interesting to analyze complexity of content words within news articles and their summaries.

In case of adult-centric news summarization performance, the results indicate that Prompt 2 is the more effective strategy for the NorwAI-Qwen3-8B-reasoning model, providing superior semantic alignment (BERTScore) and structural coherence (ROUGE-LSum). Furthermore, the lower performance on the PersonalSum dataset highlights a potential difficulty in adapting to personalized summarization styles, whereas the model shows robust performance on the more conventional NorSumm task. A comparative analysis against the NorSumm benchmarking study [8] (its results shown in Table 8) reveals significant advantages. Following their methodology of averaging metrics across prompts, the NorwAI-Qwen3-8B-reasoning model achieves an average BERTScore of 77.88 on the Bokmål portion of the NorSumm dataset. This significantly outperforms the Viking-13B model, which previously held the benchmark with an average of 70.9. However, the ROUGE-L metrics present a different hierarchy: while the NorwAI-Qwen3-8B-reasoning model does not surpass the Viking-13B (33.76), its performance remains competitive, closely trailing the Viking-7B (30.56) and normistral-7b-scratch (25.32). These results indicate that while the model excels at capturing the underlying semantic meaning of adult-centric news, there remains a slight gap in structural lexical overlap compared to the top-performing Viking models. Finally, due to the current absence of reference sum-

Table 8. Shows top three results from NorSumm study for Bokmål used in their zero-shot evaluation experiments [8].

Model	ROUGE-L	BERTScore
Viking-13B	33.76	70.90
Viking-7B	30.56	69.65
normistral-7b-scratch	25.32	58.25

maries for children's news, quantitative evaluation remains restricted to adult-centric datasets.

6   Future Work

The findings of this study establish a foundation for automated generation of age-appropriate Norwegian news summaries, while simultaneously identifying critical gaps in current evaluation frameworks. To address these limitations, we propose the following directions for future research:

1. Multi-Dimensional Evaluation Frameworks. While this study utilized LIX as a proxy for readability, it fails to capture the different aspects of child-friendliness. Future work should move beyond word counts to incorporate a holistic evaluation of structural and discourse analysis, semantic density, and sentiment. Structural and discourse analysis involves examining sentence complexity and logical flow to ensure the narrative structure aligns with children's cognitive development. Semantic density measures the ratio of information to word count to prevent over-simplification that leads to loss of essential meaning. Developing specialized metrics to evaluate positive orientation and encouraging tones, which are essential for presenting sensitive news to younger audiences.
2. LLM-as Judge and Human evaluation. To bridge the gap between automated scores and human perception for new summaries, a two-tiered validation strategy can assist in readability and comprehesion of news summaries for children. Leveraging advanced LLMs to act as judges specifically tasked with identifying shifts in tone, positive framing, and discourse style. However, this
3. Development of Parallel Norwegian Corpora. A significant hurdle in this field is the absence of high-quality, human-authored "gold" summaries for children. We aim to develop a Parallel Multi-Level Corpus for Norwegian news. This dataset would include source articles paired with summaries across varying difficulty levels, enabling more robust supervised training and benchmarking of simplification models.
4. Advanced Morphological Analysis. By analyzing the distributional frequency of lemmas, we can better understand whether long Norwegian compound words (e.g., ') actually hinder child comprehension or if they function as accessible, transparent building blocks in long texts such as news articles.

While the NorwAI-Qwen3-8B-reasoning model simplifies Norwegian news at the lexical level via prescriptive prompting (Prompt 2), bridging the gap in positive framing and structural discourse remains a challenge. Future work should evaluate whether more sophisticated summarization architectures such as Fine-Tuning or Reinforcement Learning from Human Feedback (RLHF) can outperform or complement varied prompting strategies in capturing these qualitative child-friendly properties.

7   Conclusion

In conclusion, it was confirmed that Large Language Models can effectively adapt adult-centric Norwegian news into simpler formats when guided by detailed, prescriptive prompting (Prompt 2). While the LIX index successfully validates surface-level lexical reductions, it is insufficient for capturing the child-friendly properties such as upbeat tone or narrative structure. The NorwAI-Qwen3-8B-reasoning model demonstrated superior performance in capturing semantic meaning, significantly outperforming previous benchmarks like Viking-13B in BERTScore. However, the research highlights a persistent challenge: the lack of human-authored reference summaries for children's news in Norwegian, which restricts quantitative evaluation. We think that future efforts must prioritize the development of parallel multi-level corpora and more sophisticated metrics such as lemma-based complexity and sentiment analysis to ensure automated news summaries truly align with the cognitive needs of young readers.

References

1. Cohen, E., et al.: Simplify-This: a comparative analysis of prompt-based and fine-tuned LLMs (2026). https://arxiv.org/abs/2601.05794
2. Macdonald, I., Siddharthan, A.: Summarising news stories for children. In: Proceedings of the 9th International Natural Language Generation Conference, pp. 1–10 (2016). https://doi.org/10.18653/v1/W16-6601
3. De Belder, J., Moens, M.F.: Text simplification for children. In: Proceedings of the SIGIR Workshop on Accessible Search Systems, pp. 19–26. ACM, Geneva (2010). https://doi.org/10.1145/1835941.1835947
4. Smirnova, A., et al.: Text simplification for children: evaluating LLMs vis-'à'-vis human experts. In: Proceedings of the Extended Abstracts of the CHI Conference on Human Factors in Computing Systems, p. 512 (2025). https://doi.org/10.1145/3706599.3719889
5. Wold, S., Mæhlum, P., Hove, O.: Estimating lexical complexity from document-level distributions. In: Calzolari, N., Kan, M.-Y., Hoste, V., Lenci, A., Sakti, S., Xue, N. (eds.) Proceedings of the 2024 Joint International Conference on Computational Linguistics, Language Resources and Evaluation (LREC-COLING 2024), pp. 6309–6318. ELRA and ICCL, Torino, Italia (2024). https://aclanthology.org/2024.lrec-main.558
6. Nayeem, M.T., Rafiei, D.: KidLM: Advancing language models for children – early insights and future directions. In: Al-Onaizan, Y., Bansal, M., Chen, Y.-N. (eds.) Proceedings of the 2024 Conference on Empirical Methods in Natural Language Processing (EMNLP 2024), pp. 4813–4836. Association for Computational Linguistics, Miami, Florida (2024). https://aclanthology.org/2024.emnlp-main.277
7. Fang, D., Qiang, J., Zhu, Y., Yuan, Y., Li, W., Liu, Y.: Progressive document-level text simplification via large language models. arXiv preprint arXiv:2501.03857 (2025). https://arxiv.org/abs/2501.03857
8. Touileb, S., Mikhailov, V., Kroka, M., Øvrelid, L., Velldal, E.: Benchmarking abstractive summarisation: a dataset of human-authored summaries of Norwegian news articles. arXiv preprint arXiv:2501.07718 (2025). https://arxiv.org/abs/2501.07718

9. Sikka, P., Mago, V.: A survey on text simplification. arXiv preprint arXiv:2008.08612 (2020). https://arxiv.org/abs/2008.08612v2

10. Magnifico, G., Barbu, E.: Can summarization approximate simplification? A gold standard comparison. In: Johansson, R., Stymne, S. (eds.) Proc. NoDaLiDa/Baltic-HLT 2025, pp. 383–389. University of Tartu Library (2025). https://aclanthology.org/2025.nodalida-1.41

11. Maddela, M., Dou, Y., Heineman, D., Xu, W.: LENS: a learnable evaluation metric for text simplification. arXiv preprint arXiv:2212.09739 (2023). https://arxiv.org/abs/2212.09739

12. Xu, W., Napoles, C., Pavlick, E., Chen, Q., Callison-Burch, C.: Optimizing statistical machine translation for text simplification. Trans. Assoc. Comput. Linguist. 4, 401–415 (2016). https://doi.org/10.1162/tacl_a_00107

13. Sun, R., Jin, H., Wan, X.: Document-level text simplification: dataset, criteria and baseline. arXiv preprint arXiv:2110.05071 (2021). https://arxiv.org/abs/2110.05071

14. Lin, C.-Y.: ROUGE: a package for automatic evaluation of summaries. In: Text Summarization Branches Out: Proceedings of the ACL-04 Workshop, pp. 74–81. Association for Computational Linguistics, Barcelona (2004). https://aclanthology.org/W04-1013

15. Zhang, T., Kishore, V., Wu, F., Weinberger, K.Q., Artzi, Y.: BERTScore: evaluating text generation with BERT. In: Proceedings of the 8th International Conference on Learning Representations (ICLR 2020), Addis Ababa (2020). https://arxiv.org/abs/1904.09675

16. Zhang, L., Liu, P., Henriksboe, M.T.O., Lauvrak, E.W., Gulla, J.A., Ramampiaro, H.: PersonalSum: a user-subjective guided personalized summarization dataset for large language models. In: Proceedings of the 2024 Conference on Empirical Methods in Natural Language Processing (EMNLP 2024). LNCS. Springer, Cham (2024). https://doi.org/10.48550/arXiv.2410.03905

17. Sulem, E., Abend, O., Rappoport, A.: BLEU is not suitable for the evaluation of text simplification. In: Riloff, E., Chiang, D., Hockenmaier, J., Tsujii, J. (eds.) Proceedings of the 2018 Conference on Empirical Methods in Natural Language Processing, pp. 738–744. Association for Computational Linguistics, Brussels, Belgium (2018). https://doi.org/10.18653/v1/D18-1081

18. Kincaid, J.P., Fishburne Jr., R.P., Rogers, R.L., Chissom, B.S.: Derivation of New Readability Formulas (Automated Readability Index, Fog Count and Flesch Reading Ease Formula) for Navy Enlisted Personnel. Technical Report, Naval Technical Training Command, Millington, TN (1975). https://apps.dtic.mil/sti/citations/ADA006655

19. Snyder, B.: I Finally Found a Local LLM I Actually Want to Use for Coding. XDA Developers (2026). https://www.xda-developers.com/finally-found-local-llm-want-use-coding/

20. Qwen Team: Qwen3 Technical Report: Advancing Frontier Intelligence with Thinking Modes. arXiv preprint arXiv:2505.09388 (2025). https://arxiv.org/abs/2505.09388

21. Gulla, J.A., Liu, P., Zhang, L.: NorwAI's Large Language Models: Technical Report. arXiv preprint arXiv:2601.03034 (2026). https://arxiv.org/abs/2601.03034

If I Could Turn Back Time: Temporal Reframing as a Historical Reasoning Task for Large Language Models

Lars Bungum[1(✉)], Charles Yijia Huang[2], and Abeer Kashar[2]

[1] NTNU, Trondheim, Norway
lars.bungum@ntnu.no
[2] University of Waterloo, Waterloo, Canada
{charles.huang1,akashar}@uwaterloo.ca

Abstract. This study leverages an 85-year-old quiz book as a resource. Prompting LLMs to answer the questions as if it were 1940 poses a difficult Historical Reasoning task. Results show that scaling increases accuracy (85% for the top model), and that English system prompts are better for most model families. Because the correct answers in the book are given in free-form language, we employ an LLM-as-judge. A native speaker has still done systematic checks of the quality of the judge and analyzed the questions all models got wrong. We also surveyed models with continued training with additional Norwegian text, which increased performance. While the overall task is framed as temporal reframing, some of the discovered errors stem from general semantic shift or ambiguity that persist beyond 1940.

Keywords: Question-answering · Temporal Reframing

1 Introduction

Temporal Reframing (TR) is a challenging cognitive task for humans and machines alike, as what was correct in 1940, may no longer be in 2025. In this work, we leverage a quiz book from 1940, "Vet De Det", pseudonymously published by Hugin Ravn, henceforth called "The Book" as a question-answering resource for Large Language Model (LLM) evaluation. It is used to evaluate how well LLMs are able to answer questions as temporally reframed to the year 1940. The Book consisted of 1000 questions in 25 categories in Norwegian, whose labels were sometimes indicative of their content (*"Around the World"*), and other times not (*"First Round"*).

To illustrate how challenging the task is, consider the question *"What country has an area that exceeds that of the United States of America and Canada together?"*, which in 1940 was true for the Soviet Union ($\sim$22 Mkm^2 $>\sim$19 Mkm^2) but not for Russia ($\tilde{\ }$17Mkm^2). The task of imagining that it is some arbitrary time period for an LLM, requires what for human

E. Cabrio and E. Monteiro (Eds.): NLDB 2026, LNCS 16696, pp. 59–75, 2027.
https://doi.org/10.1007/978-3-032-29532-3_6

participants would be described as reasoning. Without full knowledge of how openly available but commercial models are trained, we consider it unlikely that they have been explicitly trained for TR, and even more unlikely for the specific year 1940.

Logical tasks are often divided into a) inductive, b) deductive, or c) abductive reasoning tasks [1]. They denote reasoning tasks that identify patterns from observations, reach conclusions based on premises with certainty, and forming the most likely explanation without certainty, respectively. The task at hand is primarily deductive, but also enlists abductive reasoning for cases where relevant information of internal facts in the model are incomplete. Such a condition could arise for some questions in The Book.

Cao *et al.* [2] note that it is hard to design datasets that do not simply measure language proficiency or shallow pattern matching. Regarding the discussion of whether LLMs at all reason (or think), we consider in the following that LLMs are reasoning when they simulate behavior that would require reasoning on the part of humans, despite that they are constructed from simpler building blocks without explicit logical rules.

Due to the historical reasoning element, TR stands out from traditional Question-Answering tasks, which use LLMs as knowledge bases. For each question, the LLMs must consider the premise that questions should be answered as if we were in 1940. While LLMs could be trained on a dataset as our 1940 instance, it is inconceivable that such instruction-datasets could exist for all periods, as questions could be posed for events from geological time and beyond. Thus, what we define as reasoning abilities is necessary to find the right answer.

Our study investigates two main Research Questions for both international and Norwegian models:

- **RQ1**: How does performance scale with parameter size?
- **RQ2**: What is the effect of prompting in English and Norwegian?

We conducted experiments on the DeepSeek-R1 [3], Gemma3 [4], Llama3.1 [5], and Qwen3 [6] LLM families for the scaling experiments, as well as running the experiments on three different models developed especially for Norwegian. Those were two models from the Mimir project [7], and the NorwAI-Magistral-24B-reasoning (henceforth: NorMagistral24B) model[1].

1.1   Contributions

This paper makes the following contributions:

- Temporal Reframing framed as a Historical Reasoning task, which is a novel task for Norwegian.
- Analysis of LLM mistakes that stem from general semantic shift or ambiguity that persist beyond 1940.
- Investigation of scaling effects on four families of LLMs.

---

[1] https://huggingface.co/NorwAI/NorwAI-Magistral-24B-reasoning.

- Application and basic evaluation of LLM-as-judge scoring.
- Evaluation of NorMagistral24B with dedicated reasoning capabilities on the task.
- Thorough error evaluation that examines the difficulty of the task.
- Demonstration that English system prompts can give better results for a Norwegian downstream task (true for most models).

2 Related Work

This work falls within the scope of overall evaluation of LLMs, but more specifically addresses evaluation of historical reasoning capabilities. Evaluation of LLMs is a broad topic, which is important for academia and industry actors alike. As an example, DeepSeek-R1 models are presented on their Huggingface[2] page with their performance on the datasets AIME 2024[3], Codeforces[4], GPQA-Diamond [8], Math-500 [9], MMLU [10], and SWE-Bench [11] verified. Additionally, many independent *leaderboards* exist, which combine performance on many evaluation dimensions and present an overall ranking. Examples are the *Open Large Norwegian Model Leaderboard*[5] at Huggingface, or the *Norwegian Model Evaluation Harness* by EleutherAI [12], or the Euroeval[6] framework [13]. The leaderboards focus on different tasks, and subdivisions thereof. Euroeval, for instance, divides subtasks into Natural Language Generation and Understanding.

LLM evaluation has been surveyed extensively, e.g., in the influential but dated survey by Chang *et al.* [14], which analyzed what to evaluate, where to evaluate it, and how to evaluate it. Also, the above-mentioned survey by Cao *et al.* [2] aims to go beyond benchmarks to core capabilities they exemplify as knowledge, reasoning, instruction following, multi-modal understanding, and safety, as well as highlighting LLM-as-judge approaches to answer the need for automated evaluation. Peng *et al.* [15] looked beyond core capabilities and argue that LLMs have to be evaluated as agents to be useful.

Wang *et al.* [16] built the BiTimeBERT model to incorporate temporal knowledge through time-aware masked language modeling, and citing promising results on tasks like Named Entity Disambiguation, for which reasoning in time could be useful. Uddin *et al.* [17] created the UnSeenTimeQA dataset, a Time Sensitive Question Answering (TSQA) benchmark. It is comprised of questions of what some person was doing in a given year, or reasoning about time intervals. The authors are concerned with the abilities of present datasets to measure temporal reasoning as opposed to recalling memorized knowledge like *"Where did Diego Maradona play in 1987?"*, and address this by avoiding web-searchable

---

[2] https://huggingface.co/deepseek-ai/DeepSeek-R1.
[3] https://artofproblemsolving.com/wiki/index.php/2024_AIME_I_Problems.
[4] https://codeforces.com.
[5] https://huggingface.co/organizations/open-llm-leaderboard/.
[6] Formerly known as ScandEval.

questions. Other TR datasets exist, such as Time-Sensitive-QA [18] and TempReason [19] that were based on mining Wikipedia for questions. Tan et al. outline three levels of temporal reasoning; time-time relations (*What is the year after 2010?*), time-event relations (as the Maradona question above), and event-event reasoning (*What team did Pelé play for after Santos?*) Published in the early stages of the Generative AI avalanche, these datasets were vulnerable to data leakage.

Existing TSQA benchmarks focus on retrieving or reasoning about specific temporal facts (often with context or post-cutoff events) and counterfactual tasks explore hypothetical alternate timelines. Our TR task, in contrast, is distinct in that it forces the model to adopt a single fixed historical viewpoint (1940) using only parametric knowledge and without any external context. Furthermore, the use of a real 1940 Norwegian quiz book changes the setup by emphasising historical reasoning and long-term semantic shifts as opposed to freshness or timeline ordering.

More recently, Pham *et al.* [20] launched SealQA, a benchmark based on constantly mining fresh questions, that would be able to test the reasoning capabilities of LLMs when the answer to the questions were given as context, and could not be found in the training material. Also, Wei *et al.* [21][7] launched the Time dataset, consisting of 38,522 QA pairs across eleven subtasks spanning three levels: basic temporal understanding (e.g., *"What happened first?"*), temporal expression reasoning (e.g., *"What happened between two dates in 2011?"*), and complex temporal relationship reasoning, including counterfactual and timeline ordering tasks. A counterfactual time reasoning question could be asking how old the Berlin Wall would have been had it fallen 8 years later.

Our work also relates to testing LLMs for higher-order theories of mind [22, 23] because it tests the ability of LLMs to recursively imagine the perspectives of others. In our work, the LLMs have to imagine the perspective of another time, given the knowledge until its cutoff, but not the perspective of a specific person.

3   Method

The method can be described in three steps. 1) creating a dataset from the 1940 book, 2) querying LLMs on these questions, and 3) evaluating the answers with a different LLM.

3.1   Dataset Creation

The Book was scanned and read with Optical Character Recognition (OCR). The structure of the book was to have questions in the first part and answers in the back, which meant that questions and answers needed to be paired in the

---

[7] Accepted to NeurIPS according to the authors' website, last visited on October 24, 2025.

```
{
  "qa_pairs": [
    {
      "question": "Hvilken fastlandsstat er stoerre enn U.S.A. og Canada
↪   tilsammen?",
      "answer": "Sovjet-Samveldet (21.6 mill. km2, 15 % av
↪ jordoverflaten)."
    }
  ]
}
```

Fig. 1. Example JSON payload for the example question in Sect. 1.

resulting JSON file. The resulting text was also manually checked for errors in OCR. The Python package `pytesseract`[8] was used for the OCR, and a custom script was created to connect questions with answers to produce the final JSON output exemplified in Fig. 1.

3.2 Querying Models

In the second phase, Ollama[9] servers were instantiated on the HPC cluster IDUN [24] for interaction with the models. With the exception of the largest DeepSeek-R1 model, all models could fit on one GPU. The largest model required three H200 GPUs, and Ollama conveniently handles the distribution of the model to more GPUs.

The models were provided with a system prompt, either in English and Norwegian in separate instances, instructing them to only apply knowledge prior to 1940 in their answers. Subsequently, the models were posed the questions from the dataset in the user prompt separately. The output was stored to file.

3.3 LLM-as-Judge Evaluation

Because of the nature of the dataset, where answers were provided as explanations, grading the LLM output was a challenge. With separate experiments for two languages for 20 models, each generating 1000 answers, some automatic solution was required. We considered converting the dataset to a multiple choice format, but opted for an LLM-as-judge [25] solution.

We appointed gpt-oss:120B [26] as judge. The model was presented with the suggested answer from an LLM agent and the correct answer from the book. Based on this answer, it was instructed to determine whether the answers were true or false using one-shot prompting. Questions are always posed in Norwegian, but the prompts are also presented in English for comparison. The prompts used both for querying models and grading are presented below.

---

[8] https://github.com/madmaze/pytesseract.
[9] https://ollama.com/.

3.4 Prompts Used

System Prompt: All evaluated models were prompted with this system prompt in English or Norwegian before receiving questions from the dataset:

> *You are an expert in answering history quizzes using only knowledge from up to 1940. Answer in one or two sentences, using only knowledge up to 1940."*

> *Du er ekspert på norsk språk og verdenshistorie før 1940. Svar kort (1–2 setninger) og bruk kun kunnskap før 1940. Svar på norsk.*

Grader Prompt: The grader was initialized with this system prompt before being presented with the LLM agent answer and the correct answer from the book:

> *"You are an expert in grading history quizzes using only knowledge from up to 1940. Given a question, a test answer, and the correct answer, output T if the test answer is essentially correct, or F if it is wrong. OUTPUT EXACTLY 1 CHARACTER AND NOTHING ELSE. example: question: What's the capital of Egypt? Model Answer: Paris Correct answer: Cairo Your output: F"*

Table 1[10] shows eight answers that would likely have been graded as correct by a human, despite some superfluous information. Two stemmed from mistakes in the correct answer section of The Book. This amounts to <1% of the questions, which means that the reported scores should have been a percentage point higher for the strongest model. For the correct answers, 150 samples were inspected and no mistakes were found. We therefore assume that such errors are less frequent.

Table 2 contrasts the previous table with three selected examples of difficult questions that were answered correctly.

3.5 Model Selection

For our experiments, we selected two groups of Model families, henceforth, Groups A and B. The models in Group A were chosen because they were offered multiple data points, that they were easily available through Ollama's library, and also that they are widely known and recognized as well-performing on reasoning tasks. As mentioned in Sect. 1, the model families were DeepSeek-R1,Gemma3, Llama3.1, and Qwen3.

Group B comprised the NorMagistral24B model, the corresponding Magistral24B model (the former received continued training with Norwegian text), two 7B Mimir models, and also the gpt-oss model used as a judge. The difference between the Scratch and Core models that the latter use pretrained weights from

---

[10] Translations are provided by one of the authors who is a native speaker. Norwegian originals are omitted for brevity.

Table 1. Manually identified grading mistakes in the questions considered wrong for DeepSeek-R1:671B. The abbreviation BA is used to denote the "correct" Book Answers.

Question (in English)	Answer (abbreviated)	Explanation
Who invented the execution machinery used during the French revolution?	It was requested by Dr. Guillotin, but designed by Dr. Louis and prototyped by Tobias Schmidt.	Since Guillotin (BA) was mentioned first, and the others named thereafter, this should arguably count as correct.
How long has England (sic) owned Gibraltar?	227 years.	The BA was 250 years, but 1940–1704 = 236, so the model's answer was actually closer. It is unclear whether this is due to the "wrong" correct answer in The Book, or the grader's inability to see how close the answer was to the correct.
What was the full name of Charles XIV John?	Jean-Baptiste Jules Bernadotte.	The BA is Jean Baptiste Bernadotte (1763–1844) and the answer should clearly have been graded as correct.
What is the population of the United States?	123 million.	The BA is 130 million, which is close enough. It is unclear whether the grader gets it wrong due to superfluous and erroneous reasoning in the candidate answer, or if it does understand how close the numbers are.
What does the hedgehog mostly eat?	Insects, beetles, and worms. It can also eat frogs, toads, and rodents.	The BA is "insects and sometimes worm and snails", which is very close, and should have been graded as correct. Possibly, the mention of rodents made the grader too strict.
What are the "headhunters" on Borneo called?	Dayaks, including the Iban, Bidayuh and Kayan peoples.	The BA is Dayaks with a different spelling ("Dajaker"). The extra information may have nudged the grader to a false verdict.
What job did Alexander Kielland have when he died?	Amtmann i Romsdals Amt.	The BA is Amtmann in Møre, which is incorrect. The Amt was actually called Romsdals Amt. However, the model's answer incorrectly added that he had the position from 1891 (1902 was correct), which could have confused the grader further. As a consequence, this is more of a dataset error than a grader error.
What living Russian emigrant author received the Nobel Prize?	Ivan Bunin.	The BA is "Ivar Bunin". This was again a dataset error, more than a grader error.

Table 2. Selected successful answers by DeepSeek-R1:671B that demonstrate strong TR. The abbreviation BA is used to denote the "correct" Book Answers.

Question (in English)	Answer (abbreviated)	Explanation
What is the name of the national association that most Norwegian cooperatives are affiliated with?	Norges Kooperative Landsforening (NKL), founded in Oslo on 28 December 1906.	NKL was renamed to Coop in the year 2000.
What is India's largest city?	Calcutta (now Kolkata) was generally considered the largest city in British India by population.	The model avoids answering Mumbai, which is widely recognized as the largest city today.
Which country currently has the highest standard of living in the world?	The United States (De Forente Stater) was generally considered the country with the highest standard of living.	The model correctly answered USA while appropriately framing the answer with interwar industrial strength and relative prosperity, despite that other countries are usually recognized as having higher standards of living today.

Mistral 7B v0.1 [7]. Finally, we ran the same experiments on the two available versions of the gpt-oss model, mostly out of curiosity of how it would perform on a task it graded itself.

All models were quantized with the default Q4_K_M scheme, except for the NorMagistral24B model, which was downloaded directly from Huggingface and quantized with Q8_K[11]. The numbers 4 and 8 represent the number of bits used to represent each weight, which means that a higher number represents the weight with higher precision.

4 Experiments and Results

All our experiments follow the same trajectory as described in Sect. 3. For each LLM, we pose the questions in English and Norwegian, to be graded by our evaluation script. The Group A experiments were designed to investigate the scaling effect on TR and Group B was to sample the performance on Norwegian-focused LLMs primarily, with the less relevant performance on the grader model as an addition (Fig. 2).

Table 3 gives an overview of the LLMs in Group A. Subfigures a and c have six (twelve) data points, which intimate fitted curves with a maximum not far after the largest models. Especially for the DeepSeek-R1 models, the incline gradually reduces (after 7B). However, one should be careful with this interpretation, as

---

[11] Some details on the differenes between the quantizations schemes are contained here
https://github.com/ggml-org/llama.cpp.

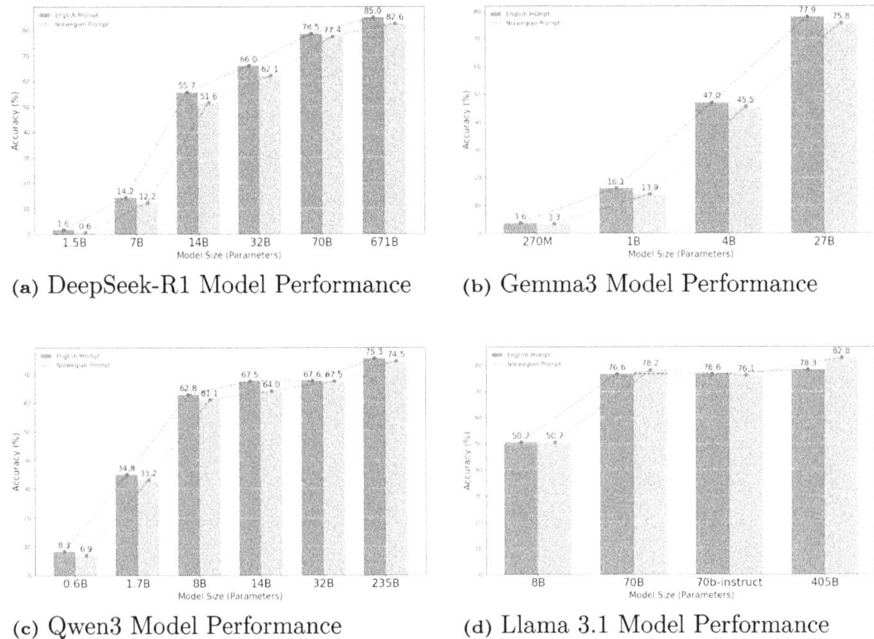

(a) DeepSeek-R1 Model Performance   (b) Gemma3 Model Performance

(c) Qwen3 Model Performance   (d) Llama 3.1 Model Performance

Fig. 2. Group A Model Performance

some qualities can appear in LLMs only after an unknown parameter size. Such emergent properties are implied to come without specific training and appear as a qualitative changes in behavior emerge as a consequence of quantitative changes in the system [27]. While there could be further jumps in performance, the Figure suggests a correlation between model size and performance on the TR task with diminishing returns.

Subtables 3a and 3b complete the picture. For Group B, a graphical representation would have offered little and was omitted. It should be pointed out that the NorMagistral24B model was quantized with higher precision than the other models. However, the parameter size lies between the models of the other LLM families. The limited performance for the 7B models (for Mimir-7B-Scratch-Instruct and DeepSeek-R1 especially, performance for smaller Qwen3 and Gemma3 models was better) could indicate that the capability emerges only beyond this size.

With regards to our second RQ on prompting language, we see that the English prompts are consistently better for all LLM families with the exception of Llama3.1, where the performance is on par until the largest 405B model, where Norwegian prompts are doing better by a margin of four percentage points. It is also the case for the NorMagistral24B model's only data point, but not for the Mimir-Mistral models of smaller size. All experiments were run only once out of concern for resource use. Since the Llama3.1 405B model was an anomaly with regard to prompting language, however, the experiment was run twice and the average of the two runs is presented in the results.

Table 3. Accuracy results for Model Groups A and B.

(a) Model Group A

Family	Model/Size	EN (%)	NO (%)
DeepSeek-R1	671B	85.0	82.7
	70B	78.6	77.5
	32B	66.1	62.2
	14B	55.8	51.7
	7B	14.2	12.2
	1.5B	1.6	0.6
Llama 3.1	405B	78.3	82.8
	70B	76.6	78.2
	70B-Instruct	76.6	76.1
	8B	50.7	50.7
Gemma3	27B	78.0	75.9
	4B	47.2	45.7
	1B	16.2	14.1
	270M	3.6	3.3
Qwen3	235B	75.3	74.5
	32B	67.7	67.6
	14B	67.6	64.1
	8B	62.8	61.1
	1.7B	35.0	33.3
	0.6B	8.3	6.9

(b) Model Group B

Family	Model/Size	EN (%)	NO (%)
gpt-oss	120B	80.6	79.0
	20B	66.7	65.6
NorMagistral24B	24B	75.5	76.2
magistral24B	24B	69.7	70.4
Mimir-Mistral	7B-Scratch-Instruct	7.9	6.5
	7B-Core-Instruct	31.1	29.5

We also note that the NorMagistral model did significantly better regardless for both prompting languages, and that the Core version of the smaller Mimir-Mistral model was modest, while still much better than the struggling Scratch version.

To determine the amount of random noise in our results, we run McNemar's test on paired outcomes (correct/incorrect per question). For each comparison we form a 2×2 table with a = both correct, b = model 1 correct and model 2 wrong, c = model 1 wrong and model 2 correct, and d = both wrong. We report two-sided p-values.

Table 4. McNemar paired significance test.

Comparison	a	b	c	d	χ^2	p-value
DeepSeek-R1: English vs. Norwegian	2527	464	323	2650	24.905	0.0000 (sig.)
Gemma3: English vs. Norwegian	1162	276	215	2323	7.332	0.0068 (sig.)
Qwen3: English vs. Norwegian	2706	439	350	2469	9.815	0.0017 (sig.)
Llama 3.1 (405B): English vs. Norwegian	730	48	93	123	13.730	0.0002 (sig.)
Magistral-24B vs. NorMagistral24B (grouped)	1209	298	180	301	28.638	0.0000 (sig.)
Llama 3.1 (8-70B): English vs. Norwegian	1773	264	253	692	0.193	0.6601 (n.s.)
NorMagistral24B: English vs. Norwegian	681	69	76	168	0.248	0.6183 (n.s.)

Table 4 reports McNemar paired significance tests for the main comparisons. Prompting language has a statistically significant effect for the international model families DeepSeek-R1, Gemma3, and Qwen3, with English prompts outperforming Norwegian, while Llama 3.1 shows a significant advantage for Norwegian prompts. In contrast, no significant language effect is observed for Nor-Magistral24B or Magistral-24B models. NorMagistral24B significantly outperforms Magistral-24B in direct paired comparison, whereas the difference between the Llama 3.1 70B Base and Instruct variants is not statistically significant.

Figure 3 plots all models tested on the benchmark to plot the Pareto frontier. For both languages, the models that cluster around the top-left knee-region (where the trade-off is optimal include the Llama-3.1:70b model, but also the smaller NorMagistral. The largest Llama and DeepSeek models find themselves far from the knee.

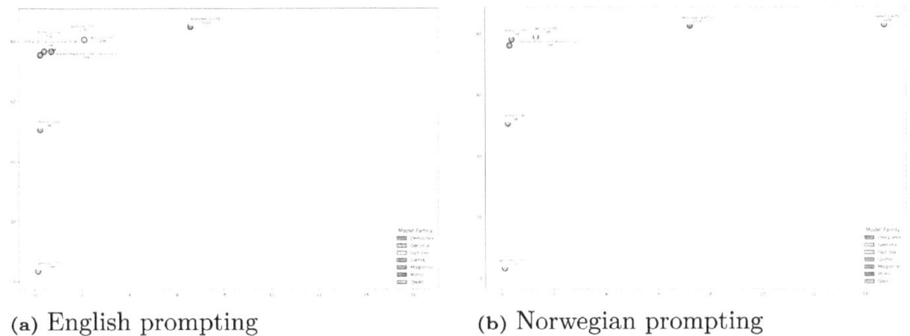

(a) English prompting   (b) Norwegian prompting

Fig. 3. Pareto Frontier of Model Performance: Accuracy versus Total GPU Hours (Larger points indicate Pareto-optimal models; dashed line approximates the frontier.) Total GPU hours across all evaluations: 108.2 h. Model families colour-coded as per legend.

Table 5. Examples of wrong answers from the 21 questions on which all models failed.

Question (in English)	Answer (abbreviated)	Explanation
Where does the term "lotter" come from?	The Norse word "lotr", meaning a slob.	The term refers to Lotta Svärd from *The Tales of Ensign Stål* by J. L. Runeberg.
What is the biggest name in Norwegian speed walking?	Sonja Henie	Old term "gangsport" confused with figure skating.
What was the name of the last Swedish "stattholder" in Norway?	Severin Løvenskiold	Model misses that he was Norwegian.
What is Norway's strongest lighthouse?	Strongman Jo Visdal (1871–1923)	Homonym "fyr" (lighthouse/guy).
What is Norway's largest dam?	Lake Mjøsa	Model confuses natural lake with artificial dam.

4.1 Error Analysis

21 questions were answered incorrectly by all models. We considered them the most difficult, and extracted them for qualitative evaluation and used the answers from the strongest model, DeepSeek-R1:671B to illustrate. Table 5[12] shows a selection of wrong answers with an explanation. After perusal, it is clear that the models struggle with ambiguous words where the intended meaning is no longer used frequently or obsolete terms. This is true for the speed walking term, *"gangsport"*, *"Kristian Kvint"*, who now is usually referred to as Christian V, and also the word for "dam", which in present Norwegian usually references an artificial lake, but more rarely a reservoir. Otherwise, it is clear that the models confidently provide answers even when misunderstanding the questions completely. Such unsubstantiated answers are often termed hallucinations. [28].

5 Discussion

Temporal Reframing is a complicated cognitive task. As reflected in Sect. 2, it can be difficult to separate fact retrieval from reasoning in the behavior exhibited by the LLMs. Table 5 reflects that the models struggle with ambiguous words, especially when there have been semantic shifts for terms over time. In addition to this list, the strongest DeepSeek-R1 model gave an insightful incorrect answer for the following question: *What were the names of the most famous writers in German literature at the start of the last century?*, which it answers with Rainer Maria Rilke and Stefan George, who were writers active in the beginning of the 20th century. This means that the model could not reason that it had to pick the most famous writers from at the start of the 19th century, where Goethe and Schiller should have been easy answers.

A key question in interpreting the results is to what extent performance reflects factual recall versus genuine temporal reasoning. Many failures reported in Table 5 (e.g., ambiguous terms such as "gangsport", "fyr", or "dam") stem from general semantic shifts and lexical ambiguity that would challenge models even without any TR. That said, these word senses were likely more prevalent in 1940, which means the reframing is a hint. In contrast, successful cases such as those in Table 2 demonstrate the models' ability to enforce a 1940 knowledge cutoff and adopt the historical perspective. While the task is framed as TR, a substantial portion of both errors and correct answers arise from general reasoning capabilities—semantic understanding, perspective-taking, and constraint adherence—rather than pure fact retrieval from the training corpus.

Overall, the performance of the strongest models is very good, and we expect that it would be better than many, if not most, Norwegians living today. However, the performance is not stellar, even for a straight-forward question-answering test, only obscured by the temporal reframing. Because the test year was 1940, the information needed to answer the questions correctly should be present in

---

[12] Translations are provided by one of the authors who is a native speaker. Norwegian originals are omitted for brevity.

the training material at the cut-off dates for all models. We note that there are mistakes both in the corpus and the grader, which preclude perfect scores. We did, however, look into the mistakes, and found that they do not explain the majority of model mistakes.

We also note that gpt-oss was used as the evaluator, its scores could have been inflated when it was also doing the grading. We were simply curious about how it would do when it was "marking its own papers", if it could somehow tell that the answers it graded came from querying the same model. We interpret these results with caution (no manual grading or alternative LLM-as-judge were used), we present the results as the experiments were run. Our results do not seem unreasonable, however, given the reported performance of gpt-oss on other tasks.

While The Book is an obscure Norwegian trivia book from 1940, it is publicly available, and we cannot rule out that it has formed, or will form, part of the training material for either pre- or post-training of LLMs. We have, however, not seen any indication that this has been the case.

The Llama3.1 405B showed better performance for the Norwegian prompting, as opposed to the other models in Group A. We also experimented with both the 70B and 70B-Instruct models in this family, but saw little difference. The same score for English prompting and slightly worse for the instruct-tuned version for Norwegian. When we pooled the Llama models to 70B, the differences in prompting languages were not significant. For the 405B model, in contrast, it was. Possible explanations are a) heavily English-skewed instruction-tuning datasets, b) predominantly English pre-training data, and c) minor word-choice effects when translating the prompt. The Llama 3.1 family claims improved multilingual support [5], which is reiterated in the model cards, stating that the instruction-tuned models are optimized for multilingual dialog cases. It is our conjecture that better multilingual support made Llama 3.1 stand out from the other families.

Despite that inference is not resource-demanding compared to training and tuning models, we plotted the Pareto Frontier to assess the sweet-spot with regards to model size. Although this temporal reframing task has not been solved, even the best models received far from perfect scores, thus, the pursuit of these reasoning capabilities is legitimate. However, the plots show a very modest jump in performance from the size of 70B.

All results in this paper were produced with standard single-pass inference (system prompt + one Norwegian question → one answer) using Ollama. Also the largest model (DeepSeek-R1 671B) generated 1000 answers in 7910 s on 3xH200 GPUs ($\approx$240 GB total VRAM), which is not a large resource requirement. Smaller models (8B–70B) complete a query even faster, as the quantized models fit on a single GPU. As a consequence, a production server would deliver answers to questions with sub-second to few-second latency for typical users.

Our approach does not test the breadth of TR as in the related work, but offers an in-depth insight into how well LLMs do on time-travel to 1940, without being provided any other context. As such, all of the questions are time-event reasoning, and some require event-event reasoning, as the question on land area (see Sect. 1). Furthermore, our foray into TR for Norwegian offers a narrow, but deep account of state-of-the-art models' performance on questions from 1940. To the best of our knowledge, no TR research has been published for Norwegian.

Finally, we note that our prompts could have been phrased more precisely, as one question had an answer from the winter from March 1940, which means that the cut-off date should have been set to that month at the earliest. We do not, however, consider that this imprecision affected our results.

6   Conclusions and Future Work

We examined two main research questions. First, performance on the temporal-reframing task scales reliably with parameter size across all families, though even the strongest models reach only the mid-eighties. Second, English system prompts improved results for most international families, with the notable exception of the largest Llama 3.1 models.

6.1   Future Work

We would like to expand on this work by further analyzing the effects of different levels of quantization on TR. The present work only used one quantization size for each model, and knowing the effects of increasing the bits per weight (as well as no quantization) would be interesting. It is reasonable to assume better performance, but the magnitude is unclear.

We would like to investigate further whether NorMagistral24B's good results came as a consequence of increased parameter size or the reasoning capabilities. It should also be pointed out that there were 180 questions answered correctly by the magistral24B model and incorrectly by NorMagistral24B. A deeper dive into the nature of these questions could inform adverse effects of continued training.

Expanding on this work on TR by using other old trivia books in other non-English languages is another ambition. It is also possible that the LLMs would do better on this task by means of Retrieval-Augmented Generation (RAG) solutions that could, for instance retrieve articles on the history of countries.

In related work on testing LLMs for higher-order theories of mind [22,23], the authors found that LLMs excelled at higher-order perspectives. For our specific task (where TR as a second-order theory of mind forms only part), we believe that few randomly chosen Norwegians would match the performance of the best LLMs. Testing this empirically would be interesting (but costly).

Finally, we would also like to experiment with creating instruction-data from books of this type (as long as the copyright is expired), either directly or synthetically, e.g., by multiplying them with paraphrasing, to experiment with the effect on other TR tasks and datasets.

7   Limitations

Because The Book is under copyright protection, the corpus we used for querying the LLMs cannot be published without permission, as this would be equivalent to sharing the book. However, we consider presenting the results and quoting from the book to be fair use. The book is publicly available in Norwegian libraries. All translations into English are done by the authors.

Acknowledgments. The computations were performed on resources provided by Sigma2 - the National Infrastructure for High-Performance Computing and Data Storage in Norway. We would also like to thank Dhruv Gupta, Pauline Haddow, and Zhirong Zhang for valuable feedback on the manuscript.

Ethics Statement. Since this book was published in 1940, when Norway was under Nazi occupation, The Book had passed through the censorship regime in place. As a consequence, some questions could potentially contain offensive wording or other problematic bias. However, The Book was designed as a trivia book with the purpose of testing easily looked-up tidbits of information. A native speaker examined the questions and found four questions using the Norwegian term for Jews, of which none contained derogatory wording. (An example translates to *"What does the first part of the Old Testament contain, which according to Jewish partitioning is called 'The Law'?"*) As a consequence, they were kept in the presented scores. Three questions referenced the Norwegian term for "negro", but were not derogatory outside the use of the term itself. Because the term is considered offensive in 2025, however, we removed the questions from the scores. The stronger models answered the questions correctly (and without objection), which would have increased their scores by 3‰.

Furthermore, we acknowledge that we do not fully know how the models we have used in these experiments are trained, especially with regards to instruction-data. Finally, we address the environmental impact of HPC use by presenting Pareto Frontiers of our experiments to inform on the potential gains for this application.

References

1. Xu, F., et al.: Toward large reasoning models: a survey of reinforced reasoning with large language models. Patterns **6**(10), 101370 (2025)
2. Cao, Y., et al.: Toward Generalizable Evaluation in the LLM Era: A Survey Beyond Benchmarks (2025). arXiv:2504.18838 [cs.CL]
3. DeepSeek-AI: DeepSeek-R1: Incentivizing Reasoning Capability in LLMs via Reinforcement Learning (2025). arXiv:2501.12948 [cs.CL]
4. Team, G.: DeepMind, G.: Gemma 3 Technical report (2025). arXiv:2503.19786 [cs.CL]
5. Grattafiori, A., et al.: The Llama 3 Herd of Models (2024). arXiv:2407.21783 [cs.AI]
6. Yang, A., et al.: Qwen3 Technical report (2025). arXiv:2505.09388 [cs.CL]
7. de la Rosa, J., et al.: The Impact of Copyrighted Material on Large Language Models: A Norwegian Perspective (2025). arXiv:2412.09460 [cs.CL]

8. Rein, D., et al.: GPQA: a graduate-level Google-proof Q&A benchmark. In: First Conference on Language Modeling (2024)

9. Lightman, H., et al.: Let's verify step by step. In: Proceedings of the 12th International Conference on Learning Representations (ICLR) (2024)

10. Hendrycks, D., et al.: Measuring massive multitask language understanding. In: Proceedings of the 9th International Conference on Learning Representations (ICLR) (2021)

11. Jimenez, C.E., et al.: SWE-bench: can language models resolve real-world Github issues? In: The Twelfth International Conference on Learning Representations (2024)

12. Gao, L., et al.: A framework for few-shot language model evaluation, version v0.4.0 (2023)

13. Nielsen, D.S.: ScandEval: a benchmark for scandinavian natural language processing. In: Proceedings of the 24th Nordic Conference on Computational Linguistics (NoDaLiDa), pp. 185–201. University of Tartu Library, Tórshavn, Faroe Islands (2023)

14. Chang, Y., et al.: A Survey on Evaluation of Large Language Models (2023). arXiv:2307.03109 [cs.CL]

15. Peng, J.-L., et al.: A Survey of Useful LLM Evaluation (2024). arXiv:2406.00936 [cs.CL]

16. Wang, J., Jatowt, A., Cai, Y.: Towards Effective Time-Aware Language Representation: Exploring Enhanced Temporal Understanding in Language Models (2025). arXiv:2406.01863 [cs.CL]

17. Uddin, M.N., et al.: UnSeenTimeQA: Time-Sensitive Question-Answering Beyond LLMs' Memorization (2025). arXiv:2407.03525 [cs.CL]

18. Chen, W., Wang, X., Wang, W.Y.: A Dataset for Answering Time-Sensitive Questions (2021). arXiv:2108.06314 [cs.CL]

19. Tan, Q., Ng, H.T., Bing, L.: Towards Benchmarking and Improving the Temporal Reasoning Capability of Large Language Models (2023). arXiv: 2306.08952 [cs.CL]

20. Pham, T., et al.: SealQA: Raising the Bar for Reasoning in Search-Augmented Language Models (2025). arXiv:2506.01062 [cs.CL]

21. Wei, S., et al.: TIME: A Multi-level Benchmark for Temporal Reasoning of LLMs in Real-World Scenarios. arXiv preprint arXiv:2505.12891 (2025)

22. Chen, R., et al.: Theory of mind in large language models: assessment and enhancement. In: Che, W. (ed.) Proceedings of the 63rd Annual Meeting of the Association for Computational Linguistics (Volume 1: Long Papers), pp. 31539–31558. Association for Computational Linguistics, Vienna, Austria (2025)

23. Street, W., et al.: LLMs achieve adult human performance on higher-order theory of mind tasks. Front. Hum. Neurosci. **19 - 2025** (2026)

24. Själander, M., et al.: EPIC: An Energy-Efficient, High-Performance GPGPU Computing Research Infrastructure (2019). arXiv:1912.05848 [cs.DC]

25. Li, H., et al.: LLMs-as-Judges: A Comprehensive Survey on LLM-based Evaluation Methods (2024). arXiv:2412.05579 [cs.CL]

26. OpenAI, et al.: gpt-oss-120b & gpt-oss-20b Model Card (2025). arXiv: 2508.10925 [cs.CL]

27. Lu, S., et al.: Are emergent abilities in large language models just in-context learning? In: Ku, L.-W., Martins, A., Srikumar, V. (eds.) Proceedings of the 62nd Annual Meeting of the Association for Computational Linguistics (Volume 1: Long Papers), pp. 5098–5139. Association for Computational Linguistics, Bangkok, Thailand (2024)
28. Farquhar, S., et al.: Detecting hallucinations in large language models using semantic entropy. Nature **630**(8017), 625–630 (2024)

Social Media and Web Data

Ontology-Augmented Prompt Engineering for Aspect-Based Sentiment Classification

Quinten van de Vijver, Emma van Breukelen, Arjan Noordermeer, Anastasia Glebova, and Flavius Frasincar$^{(\boxtimes)}$

Erasmus University Rotterdam, PO Box 1738, 3000 DR Rotterdam, The Netherlands
`{559692qv,559643eb,564798an,557570ag}@student.eur.nl`,
`frasincar@ese.eur.nl`

Abstract. While reviews offer valuable insights into customer satisfaction, their large volume makes it challenging to identify sentiment on specific aspects. Large Language Models (LLMs) can help automate this process. A key subtask is Aspect-Based Sentiment Classification (ABSC), which identifies sentiment toward specific product or service aspects. In this paper, we evaluate the extent to which the performance of ABSC can be enhanced by integrating domain ontologies into LLMs. More specifically, two approaches to ontology prompt injection are investigated: full ontology injection and aspect-specific ontology injection. We test these strategies on four state-of-the-art LLMs and benchmark ABSC datasets from SemEval. The results show that the incorporation of domain ontologies, especially through full ontology injection, significantly improves ABSC accuracy. These findings highlight the value of domain knowledge in improving LLM-based sentiment classification.

Keywords: ABSC · Domain Ontology · Prompt Injection

1 Introduction

The increasing use of Large Language Models (LLMs) in recent years has significantly changed the landscape of Natural Language Processing (NLP), allowing for more cost-efficient solutions for various applications. One of these applications is Aspect-Based Sentiment Analysis (ABSA), which enables organizations and companies to gain valuable insights into customer sentiment [18,22]. By analyzing opinions on specific aspects of their businesses, companies can improve customer experience, develop targeted marketing strategies, or fine-tune products, ultimately boosting customer loyalty and revenue. Consequently, much research has been conducted in the field of ABSA, focusing on improving accuracy, efficiency, and scalability [22].

While general-purpose LLMs have demonstrated impressive performance in ABSA tasks without task-specific training, the potential for even better accuracy remains underinvestigated. For instance, ChatABSA–ChatGPT configured for

E. Cabrio and E. Monteiro (Eds.): NLDB 2026, LNCS 16696, pp. 79–93, 2027.
https://doi.org/10.1007/978-3-032-29532-3_7

ABSA–offers good results on ABSA, and even outperforms few-shot supervised models [1]. This suggests that LLMs encode substantial linguistic and semantic knowledge, beneficial for ABSA. However, LLMs trained on open-domain text may still lack domain-specific knowledge needed for expert-level sentiment understanding in specialized contexts. Recent industry perspectives highlight that domain ontologies can be used to boost domain knowledge of LLMs when generating outputs [3]. Integrating explicit domain knowledge–such as a domain ontology of product attributes–into LLM-based ABSA systems is therefore a promising direction.

This paper focuses on a specific task of ABSA, Aspect-Based Sentiment Classification (ABSC), which is responsible for detecting the sentiment of given aspects [2]. The central research question of this study is as follows:

How can the performance of ABSC be improved by integrating domain ontologies into LLMs?

To answer this question, four state-of-the-art LLMs are leveraged, extensive datasets containing laptop and restaurant reviews, and two new approaches to specialize the LLMs for ABSC are investigated. More specifically, this research explores full ontology prompt injection as well as aspect-specific ontology prompt injection. Using these new approaches, this study aims to enhance the ABSC performance of the LLMs. We find that while relatively simpler ABSC datasets tend to benefit from aspect-based ontology injection, relatively more complex datasets tend to benefit more from full ontology injection. The Python code is made freely available at: https://github.com/QuintenvdVijver/Ontology-Augmented-Prompt-Engineering.

The rest of the paper is structured as follows. In Sect. 2, a comprehensive review of related work in ABSA and domain-specific adaptation of LLMs is discussed. Section 3 describes the data used in this research and the data pre-processing steps. Then in Sect. 4, we present the methodology, where the two proposed approaches are discussed. Section 5 presents the results of this research and discusses their implications. Last, Sect. 6 concludes the paper, summarizing the key findings and suggesting directions for future research.

2   Related Work

Integrating Ontologies with LLMs. Research directly integrating ontologies with large-scale language models is still in its infancy, with only limited studies exploring this synergy. LLMs are powerful at capturing general linguistic patterns, but they do not inherently understand formal domain ontologies or hierarchical taxonomies [9]. To bridge this gap, some early studies have begun injecting ontological knowledge into LLM architectures or prompts. For example, design domain knowledge is introduced into an LLM-based sentiment model by modifying the transformer's positional encoding to emphasize ontology terms [6]. By encoding known design concepts and their relations, this method guides the model's attention to more relevant features, addressing LLM limitations in capturing domain-specific cues.

In the medical domain, OntoTune, an ontology-driven self-training framework, is presented to align LLMs with a formal ontology [8]. By using an existing ontology–SNOMED CT–as a scaffold for continual learning, this approach yields state-of-the-art performance on medical ontology tasks and domain-specific question answering, outperforming a direct ontology injection baseline–TaxoLLaMA– while better preserving the LLM's original knowledge. These examples, though from specialized domains, demonstrate the potential gains of integrating ontologies with LLMs–improved factual accuracy, better handling of domain jargon, and more logical consistent outputs.

Nonetheless, work on integrating ontologies with LLMs remains quite sparse. There is a clear need for further study on ontologyLLM integration, especially for ABSA tasks. To date, no extensive research has focused on injecting domain ontologies into LLMs for ABSA, making this an open area our work aims to address. The promise shown by initial efforts in related domains provides motivation to explore ontology-informed LLMs for ABSA.

Integrating Ontologies with Neural Networks. While ontologyLLM integration is nascent, there is a broader body of research on using ontologies or structured knowledge with neural non-LLM models (e.g., RNNs, CNNs, and transformer-based models) for ABSA and related tasks. Early approaches often combined knowledge-based components with machine learning classifiers. For instance, a hybrid approach using both ontology reasoning and statistical learning was demonstrated to outperform purely data-driven methods on ABSC [19]. In this hybrid method, a lexicalized domain ontology was used to predict the sentiment for a given aspect as a first step, and then an SVM model handled cases where the ontology was insufficient. This two-stage system achieved higher accuracy than baseline machine learning models alone–on SemEval ABSA benchmarks–illustrating that ontology features can significantly enhance performance.

Subsequent studies replaced SVM models with neural models in hybrid approaches. An approach called Hybrid Approach for ABSA (HAABSA) was developed, which used a neural attention model in the hybrid solution [21]. The model applied a pre-specified restaurant ontology to infer sentiment when possible, falling back on a neural model with a rotational attention mechanism for context understanding. This hybrid neural model slightly, but consistently, outperformed single-method baselines, confirming that even relatively simple ontology integration yields measurable gains.

More recent neural approaches integrate knowledge in more fine-grained ways. Some leverage knowledge graphs or ontologies to create extra inputs or attention signals for deep neural models. A neural architecture that combines BERT embeddings with an external knowledge graph of synonyms is proposed to improve ABSC [20]. In this design, words in a sentence are enriched with related concepts from a domain knowledge graph, and a dynamic attention mechanism then learns a knowledge-driven representation that highlights sentiment cues relevant to each aspect. This knowledge-enriched representation, processed through recurrent and attention layers, led to superior performance on multiple ABSA datasets compared to standard BERT fine-tuning. Other work has explored injecting sentiment lexicon or ontology features into neural models through additional input channels or loss functions. For example, an ontology-driven sentiment analysis was applied in the health domain, showing that an infectious diseases ontology could guide a neural classifier to better interpret domain-specific sentiment expressions [5].

Overall, integrating ontologies with neural networks is a well-established idea. Numerous studies confirm that neuro-symbolic approaches, which blend learned representations with symbolically encoded knowledge, can improve the accuracy and robustness of sentiment analysis systems. However, these efforts largely predate the era of generative LLMs and were often limited to relatively small networks or task-specific architectures. There remains a gap in translating these ontology integration successes into the LLM context, which our research aims to fill. We build on this foundation by focusing specifically on LLMs, unlike earlier approaches, leveraging LLMs' superior language understanding and exploring how ontological context can be integrated through prompt injection, without model fine-tuning. This is a shift from earlier work centered on internal model modifications. Furthermore our paper introduces and compares two prompt-based ontology injection strategies: full ontology injection and aspect-specific ontology injection. Unlike prior work that used a single integration strategy, we assess both techniques across multiple state-of-the-art LLMs and real-world ABSA datasets. Our study shows how these strategies affect performance, particularly across datasets of varying complexity.

3   Data

This section first describes our training, testing, and ontology data. Second, it outlines our data pre-processing.

3.1   Data Description

To conduct our research, we leverage the datasets of SemEval 2014 [16], SemEval 2015 [15], and SemEval 2016 [14]. These datasets contain reviews on specific domains, and are already split in training and testing parts. Our research focuses on the laptop and restaurant domains in English, as these domains have been most prominent in previous works in ABSC. This allows for better comparison between our research and existing research.

In the datasets, each review consists of one or more sentences, where each sentence expresses an opinion about one or more aspects related to the corresponding domain. In each opinion, the aspects are given together with their respective category, polarity–positive, negative, or neutral–, and target positions.

Figure 1 provides an example in which there are two aspects, 'food' and 'interior', of which the first is assigned a positive polarity and the second is assigned a negative polarity. The polarity frequencies, together with the total number of reviews for each dataset, are displayed in Table 1.

Additional to the SemEval datasets, we leverage domain ontologies for the laptop [24] and restaurant [19] domains, each containing structured, domain-specific knowledge. Using these ontologies we aim to increase the ABSC performance of the LLMs through prompt injection.

The domain ontologies are organized as a hierarchical network of classes, each representing an aspect (e.g., PriceMention), a sentiment (e.g., Negative), or both (e.g., PriceNegativePropertyMention). Classes relating to both an aspect and sentiment are always subclasses of the corresponding sentiment class (e.g., PriceNegativePropertyMention is a subclass of Negative). Each class may include two types of annotation properties: aspect annotations and lexical annotations. Aspect annotations connect a class, and hence also its subclasses, to a broader category which typically aligns with one of the category annotations in the SemEval dataset. Lexical annotations verbalize classes by associating them with words (e.g., PriceNegativePropertyMention has lexical annotations 'expensive', 'overpriced', and 'pricey'). The laptop ontology comprises 229 classes, 521 lexical annotations, and a depth of four. The restaurant ontology contains 386 classes, 749 lexical annotations, and a depth of five.

```
▾ <Review rid="Z#3">
  ▾ <sentences>
    ▾ <sentence id="Z#3:0">
        <text>Excellent food, although the interior could use some help.</text>
      ▾ <Opinions>
          <Opinion target="food" category="FOOD#QUALITY" polarity="positive" from="10" to="14"/>
          <Opinion target="interior" category="AMBIENCE#GENERAL" polarity="negative" from="29" to="37"/>
        </Opinions>
      </sentence>
```

Fig. 1. Example of a restaurant review from SemEval 2015 dataset.

Table 1. Polarity frequencies of SemEval datasets for restaurant (R) and laptop (L) domains.

	Training data			Test data			
	Positive	Negative	Neutral	Positive	Negative	Neutral	Total
SemEval 2014 (L)	42.20%	37.59%	20.20%	59.18%	32.65%	8.16%	2326
SemEval 2014 (R)	42.69%	37.46%	19.85%	53.45%	20.06%	26.49%	2950
SemEval 2015 (R)	75.29%	21.89%	2.81%	59.13%	34.67%	6.20%	1876
SemEval 2016 (R)	70.14%	26.02%	3.83%	74.31%	20.77%	4.92%	2529

3.2 Data Pre-processing

Before usage, the data needs to be pre-processed as follows. We start by restructuring the SemEval 2014 data as it has a different XML structure than the SemEval 2015 and 2016 data. In this process, we map the information contained in the 2014 SemEval data to an XML structure that is conform with the XML structure used in the 2015 and 2016 SemEval data.

Second, we delete sentences from the dataset that have no opinion, and opinions that have an implicit aspect (target = "NULL") or an indefinite polarity (polarity = "conflict"). Provided that our research focuses on ABSC, we need at least one opinion which the LLMs can process in a given sentence and an explicit aspect term for the LLMs to assign a polarity to. Opinions with indefinite polarities are removed as our research focuses on definite polarities–positive, negative or, neutral.

Third and last, to account for information leakage from the training data to the test data we remove all sentences from the training data which are also in the corresponding test data. This is especially relevant for the SemEval 2014 laptop data as 39 of the 49 sentences in the test data were also present in the training data.

4 Methodology

This section describes the methodological approach adopted in this research. First, it outlines our task and LLM selection. Second, it describes our ontology prompt injection approach, including prompt design, demonstration selection, ontology verbalization, and full and aspect-based ontology injection. Third and last, this section discusses the implementation details and the evaluation measures used to assess the effectiveness of our approaches.

4.1 Task and Model Selection

As previously introduced, this research focuses on ABSC, a subtask within ABSA where the goal is to determine the sentiment polarity (positive, neutral, or negative) of a given aspect within a given sentence. Due to its relative simplicity and structured nature, ABSC offers an effective entry point for integrating formal ontologies into LLM-based sentiment analysis.

In our implementation, we focus on the following state-of-the-art LLMs: GPT-4o mini [13], Llama-4-Scout-17B-16E Instruct (Llama-4-17B Instruct) [11], Llama-3-70B Instruct [10], and GPT-3.5 Turbo [12]. We selected these models based on their prominence in existing ABSA research for comparability [23], and on their instruction-following capabilities, which are crucial for processing ontology-augmented prompts. Moreover, we selected these models based on their different model sizes, which allows us to assess the scalability of our approaches. A technical overview of these models, including model size, context window, and release date is provided in Table 2.

Table 2. Comparison of LLMs by size (parameters), context window (tokens), and release date (month and year).

Model Name	Model Size	Context Window	Release Date
GPT-4o mini	8B	128K	July 2024
Llama-4-17B Instruct	17B	131K	April 2025
Llama-3-70B Instruct	70B	128K	April 2024
GPT-3.5 Turbo	175B	16K	August 2023

4.2 Ontology Prompt Injection

Ontology prompt injection involves modifying the model's input prompts without changing its internal weights. We employ two injection strategies, full ontology injection and aspect-based ontology injection. To establish a baseline for assessing these approaches, we also evaluate our models with no ontology injection. All approaches are tested in zero-shot and three-shot settings, where the three-shot setting is chosen for comparability with existing research, specifically the baseline in [23].

Prompt Design and Demonstration Selection. To ensure optimal understanding of the input prompt by the LLMs, we use the prompt design described in [23] and add a part for the domain ontology content to facilitate the ontology injection. The resulting design consists of four parts, as shown in Fig. 2. To evaluate the few-shot abilities for ABSC, we leverage keyword-based demonstration selection (BM25) [17] and semantic-based demonstration selection (SimCSE) [4] as these methods have been shown to outperform random demonstration selection in ABSA contexts [23]. BM25 selects demonstration sentences based on term frequency and relevance, while SimCSE selects based on overlapping meaning in sentences.

Ontology Verbalization. Before injection, we verbalize the domain ontology to account for the token limit of our selected LLMs' context windows. The raw RDF/XML ontology is syntax-heavy given that it includes the namespace declarations and makes extensive use of tags. Hence, this can lead to exceeding the token limit of models with smaller context windows when fully injected. Figure 3 provides a snippet of the raw restaurant ontology for the 'Accommodate' class, clearly showing the inefficient nature of the raw ontology for prompt injection.

We initiate the verbalization by identifying the root classes, i.e., those without parent classes and hence are highest in the network hierarchy. Afterwards, we filter these root classes for classes that are not sentiment related and hence are only aspect related. This filtering process is done to avoid repetition in the verbalization as sentiment-related information will be incorporated in a later step. Next, for each root class we extract all subclasses and their corresponding

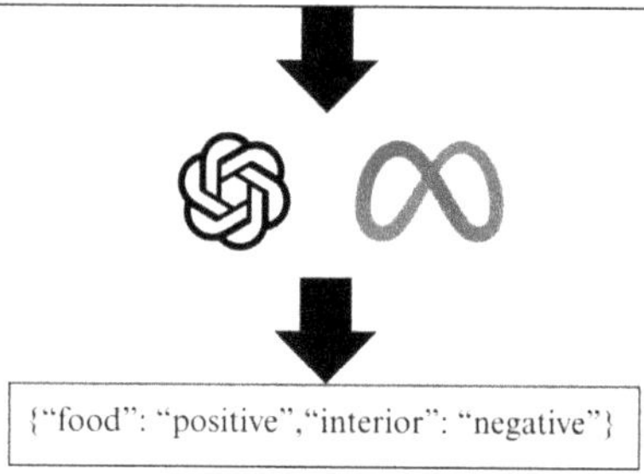

Fig. 2. Prompt design for ontology prompt injection.

lexical annotations. This includes the subclasses of subclasses and so on, such that we capture the whole domain ontology depth and not merely the layer that is one level below the root classes in the hierarchical structure. Additionally, for each subclass that has a sentiment class as superclass we add the sentiment relation, reintroducing all sentiment-related information that was filtered out previously. In the verbalization process, we preserve the hierarchical structure by using indentations. Moreover, we ignore the aspect annotations of the classes for efficiency. We assume that these general aspect annotations do not add significant domain knowledge to the ontology verbalization, given that the whole superstructure of each class is already included in the verbalization. Figure 4 provides a snippet of the verbalized restaurant ontology in which the 'Accommodate' class from Fig. 3 is integrated, which shows the token efficiency gain. More specifically, through this verbalization process we decrease the number of tokens for the restaurant ontology by 85% and for the laptop ontology by 92%. The exact tokens counts of the raw and verbalized ontologies are detailed Table 3.

```
<!-- http://www.kimschouten.com/sentiment/restaurant#Accommodate -->

<owl:Class rdf:about="http://www.kimschouten.com/sentiment/restaurant#Accommodate">
    <rdfs:subClassOf rdf:resource="http://www.kimschouten.com/sentiment/restaurant#ServicePositiveAction"/>
    <restaurant:lex>accommodate</restaurant:lex>
    <restaurant:lex>accomodate</restaurant:lex>
    <restaurant:lex>accomodating</restaurant:lex>
</owl:Class>
```

Fig. 3. Snippet of the raw restaurant ontology.

```
Domain_ontology:
    Class: Mention
      Subclass: ActionMention
        Subclass: ServicePositiveAction
          Sentiment Relation: Positive
          Subclass: Accommodate
            Lexical Forms: accommodate, accomodate, accomodating
        Subclass: GenericNegativeAction
          Sentiment Relation: Negative
          Subclass: Disappoint
            Lexical Forms: disappoint, disappointed, disappointing, dissappointed
```

Fig. 4. Snippet of the verbalized restaurant ontology.

Ontology Prompt Injection. We perform ontology prompt injection using two approaches, full ontology injection and aspect-based ontology injection. With full ontology prompt injection we provide extensive contextual information to the LLMs for ABSC by injecting the full verbalized domain ontology into the input prompt. We evaluate this approach for all SemEval datasets. With aspect-based ontology prompt injection, we aim for a more focused and efficient guidance of the LLMs by only injecting the branches of the domain ontology that are relevant to the given aspect. We extract the relevant branches from the ontology by using the category attributes in the SemEval datasets. More specifically, we filter the ontology for the classes that have a lexical form that matches the first part of the aspect category (e.g., 'food' in the category FOOD#QUALITY) as this part provides a general description of the aspect term. Subsequently, we extract the entire ontology branch for the previously determined classes and inject it in the input prompt. Given that the category attribute is only provided in the 2015 and 2016 SemEval datasets, we only evaluate this approach for those datasets.

Table 3. Token count for raw and verbalized domain ontologies, for the laptop and restaurant domain.

	Raw ontology	Verbalized ontology
Laptop	33821 tokens	2594 tokens
Restaurant	40174 tokens	6074 tokens

4.3   Implementation

Our implementation is done in Python. To run our models, we use two distinct API's. For LLaMA-4-17B Instruct and LLaMA-3-70B Instruct we use Deep Infra, and for GPT-4o-mini and GPT-3.5-Turbo we use the OpenAI Platform. For the implementation of the demonstration selection techniques, we use the *rank_bm25* for BM25 and *sup-simcse-roberta-large* for SimCSE from Hugging Face. To verbalize the domain ontologies, we use the *owlready2* library.

4.4   Evaluation

To assess the effectiveness of our proposed methods, we use the F1 score. While accuracy only focuses on precision, the F1 score balances precision and recall, providing a more robust measure than accuracy for ABSC. Moreover, by choosing the F1 score we ensure the comparability of our research with existing ABSC research, such as [23], as this evaluation measure has been most prominent in those works.

5   Results

This section analyses the results for all ontology prompt injection approaches, comparing the different approaches along the way. The full baseline and full ontology injection results are displayed in Table 4. The results for aspect-based ontology injection are presented in Table 5.

5.1   Baseline

The average baseline results in Table 4 show that GPT-4o mini and Llama-4-17B Instruct generally outperform Llama-3-70B Instruct and GPT-3.5 Turbo, respectively, in ABSC, despite the larger sizes of the latter models. This can be explained by the more recent launch of the former models. More recent models like GPT-4o mini and Llama-4-17B Instruct leverage more advanced transformer architectures, task-specific fine-tuning, and higher quality datasets, enabling them to outperform larger, older models like Llama-3-70B Instruct and GPT-3.5 Turbo in simple reasoning tasks. This is reflected in several leaderboards, such as the HELM core scenarios leaderboard from Stanford University [7].

Moreover, the results show that on average demonstration selection techniques BM25 and SimCSE increase ABSC performance in most cases, consistent with existing research [23]. However, contrary to this existing research, which evaluates BM25 and SimCSE on eight ABSA subtasks rather than on ABSC alone, we find that BM25 consistently outperforms SimCSE. This reflects the reliance of ABSC on explicit sentiment cues and aspect terms, rather than on broader semantic cues.

Furthermore, Table 4 shows that on average, ABSC performance is highest for the SemEval 2014 laptop reviews, followed by the SemEval 2016, SemEval 2015, and SemEval 2014 restaurant reviews, respectively. This indicates the relative ABSC complexity across datasets, which aligns with the existing research [23] except for the SemEval 2014 laptop data due to the more limited related test data in this research.

Table 4. F1 score for no ontology injection and full ontology injection for SemEval 2014 (L14, R14), SemEval 2015 (R15) and SemEval 2016 (R16). The averages and highest percentage point gains are given in bold.

	No injection					Full injection				
	L14	R14	R15	R16	**AVG**	L14	R14	R15	R16	**AVG**
GPT-4o mini	97.8	79.2	89.9	93.8	**90.2**	93.9	**83.3**	90.4	92.5	**90.0**
+ BM25	100.0	80.4	89.3	93.7	**90.8**	92.2	**82.7**	89.2	92.4	**89.1**
+ SimCSE	95.7	81.5	90.1	93.2	**90.1**	95.7	**84.4**	89.4	92.2	**90.4**
Llama 4 17B Instruct	91.8	79.6	88.4	94.1	**88.5**	91.9	79.3	**89.3**	94.3	**88.7**
+ BM25	95.1	82.5	88.8	93.7	**90.0**	95.7	81.3	**89.9**	93.8	**90.2**
+ SimCSE	95.1	82.9	88.3	93.1	**89.8**	91.5	81.8	**90.6**	93.1	**86.8**
Llama 3 70B Instruct	95.3	76.3	89.7	94.3	**88.9**	92.2	**80.4**	89.6	94.7	**89.2**
+ BM25	95.3	78.5	91.3	94.1	**89.8**	92.2	**80.0**	90.1	94.5	**89.2**
+ SimCSE	92.2	78.3	89.4	94.3	**88.5**	95.3	**81.9**	90.6	94.0	**90.4**
GPT-3.5 Turbo	90.6	74.3	87.7	92.3	**86.2**	93.3	**79.9**	87.2	91.8	**88.0**
+ BM25	95.8	76.2	88.8	90.2	**87.7**	97.6	**79.2**	88.5	92.1	**89.3**
+ SimCSE	91.5	77.1	88.1	89.8	**86.6**	93.2	**80.9**	87.7	90.1	**88.0**

5.2   Full Ontology Injection

Table 4 shows that, on average, full ontology injection is more effective for larger models than for smaller ones. Full ontology injection improves the average performance of GPT-4o mini with SimCSE by 0.3% points, while it improves the average performance of Llama-4-17B with no demonstrations and BM25 by 0.2% points. Similarly, full ontology injection improves the performance of Llama-3-70B Instruct with no demonstrations and SimCSE by 0.3 and 1.9% points respectively. Moreover, it improves the average performance of GPT-3.5 Turbo for all combinations, with a 1.8% point increase with no demonstrations, 1.6% points increase with BM25 and 1.4% points increase with SimCSE. This observation can be explained by the larger model size of Llama-3-70B Instruct and GPT-3.5 Turbo, which allows for better interpretation of the injected ontology, despite their less sophisticated architecture.

Second, the results demonstrate that generally the effectiveness of full ontology prompt injection increases with the relative complexity of datasets for ABSC as the highest percentage point gains are made consistently with the SemEval 2014 and SemEval 2015 restaurant data, which we concluded to be the most complex based on the baseline results. Typically, more complex datasets for ABSC feature more implicit sentiment cues. Hence, these results indicate that the structured domain ontology knowledge enables the LLMs to disambiguate nuanced expressions, leading to significant gains in terms of ABSC performance. However, for the less complex SemEval 2014 Laptop and SemEval 2016 Restaurant datasets, full ontology injection decreases the performance in five of the 12 instances. This indicates that for simpler, more straightforward sentiment classifications, the added complexity of the full ontology hinders performance by overcomplicating the input prompt.

Overall, our results indicate that full ontology prompt injection can be an effective strategy to enhance ABSC performance, depending on the model size and dataset complexity. There does not seem to be any significant correlation between the effectiveness of different demonstration selection techniques and full ontology injection.

Table 5. Standard F1 score of aspect-based and no ontology prompt injection for SemEval 2015 (R15) and SemEval 2016 (R16). The averages and highest percentage point gains are given in bold.

	No injection					Aspect-based injection				
	L14	R14	R15	R16	AVG	L14	R14	R15	R16	AVG
GPT-4o mini	-	-	89.9	93.8	**91.9**	-	-	**90.1**	93.4	**91.8**
+ BM25	-	-	89.3	93.7	**91.5**	-	-	88.9	**93.8**	**91.4**
+ SimCSE	-	-	90.1	93.2	**91.7**	-	-	89.2	**93.3**	**91.3**
Llama 4 17B Instruct	-	-	88.4	94.1	**91.2**	-	-	**89.1**	94.1	**91.6**
+ BM25	-	-	88.8	93.7	**91.3**	-	-	88.6	93.5	**91.1**
+ SimCSE	-	-	88.3	93.1	**90.7**	-	-	**88.5**	92.9	**90.7**
LLaMA 3 70B Instruct	-	-	89.7	94.3	**92.0**	-	-	88.3	**95.5**	**91.9**
+ BM25	-	-	91.3	94.1	**92.7**	-	-	88.0	**96.7**	**92.4**
+ SimCSE	-	-	89.4	94.3	**91.9**	-	-	88.2	92.7	**90.5**
GPT-3.5 Turbo	-	-	87.7	92.3	**90.0**	-	-	87.3	**93.7**	**90.5**
+ BM25	-	-	88.8	90.2	**89.5**	-	-	88.7	**92.3**	**90.5**
+ SimCSE	-	-	88.1	89.8	**89.0**	-	-	88.0	**93.3**	**90.7**

5.3 Aspect-Based Ontology Injection

The results for aspect-based ontology injection, presented in Table 5, show that overall, aspect-based ontology injection has a limited effect on the average baseline performance overall, with an equal distribution of instances where it improves, reduces, or maintains (no or 0.1% point change) performance relative to the baseline averages. However, for the 2016 SemEval data aspect-based ontology injection improves the ABSC performance in the majority of cases, while for the 2015 SemEval data it decreases the performance in most cases. This indicates that, despite the limited overall effectiveness of ABSC, it can be beneficial for relatively less complex datasets for ABSC which typically feature more explicit sentiment cues. While full ontology injection tends to hinder performance for simpler tasks by overcomplication the input prompt, aspect-based ontology injection avoids this by providing more focused and efficient guidance, which can explain the higher ABSC performance for these datasets.

5.4   Method Comparison

The observations made for full and aspect-based ontology injection expose a clear relationship between the relative data complexity for ABSC of the datasets that benefit from ontology injection, and the extensiveness of the ontology injected. The more extensive the ontology injected, the more complex the datasets for ABSC are most likely to benefit from the ontology injection, and vice versa. While relatively simpler datasets for ABSC tend to benefit from aspect-based ontology injection, relatively more complex datasets for ABSC tend to benefit from full ontology injection. Conversely, aspect-based ontology injection tends to decrease the ABSC performance of relatively more complex datasets, while full ontology injection tends to decrease the ABSC performance of relatively simpler datasets.

6   Conclusion

In this paper, we examined the impact of ontology injection on ABSC of an LLM using the SemEval 2014, 2015, and 2016 datasets for laptop and restaurant domains. Our research addressed the gap in ontologyLLM integration for ABSA by applying full and aspect-based ontology prompt injection strategies with models GPT-4o mini, LLaMA-3-70B Instruct, LLaMA-4-17B Instruct, and GPT-3.5 Turbo. The results reveal a clear relationship between the relative data complexity for ABSC of the datasets that benefit from ontology injection, and the extensiveness of the ontology injected. For full ontology injection, we find an increase in performance for relatively complex datasets while finding a decrease in performance for relatively simpler datasets for ABSC. Conversely, for aspect-based ontology injection, we find an increase in performance for relatively simpler datasets while finding a decrease in performance for relatively more complex datasets for ABSC. Overall, these results show that ontology prompt injection can be beneficial for ABSC when taking into account the extensiveness of the ontology injected and the complexity of the test datasets for ABSC.

Future research could extend this work by employing more LLMs and datasets. Moreover, it could explore different ontology structures, optimized verbalization techniques, and the integration of ontology injection with fine-tuning to boost performance.

References

1. Bai, Y., et al.: Is compound aspect-based sentiment analysis addressed by LLMs? In: Findings of the Association for Computational Linguistics: EMNLP 2024 (Findings EMNLP 2024), pp. 7836–7861. ACL (2024)
2. Brauwers, G., Frasincar, F.: A survey on aspect-based sentiment classification. ACM Comput. Surv. **54**(4), Article 85 (2021)
3. EK Team: The role of ontologies with LLMs. https://enterprise-knowledge.com/the-role-of-ontologies-with-llms/ (2024). Blog post
4. Gao, T., Yao, X., Chen, D.: SimCSE: simple contrastive learning of sentence embeddings. In: Empirical Methods in Natural Language Processing (EMNLP, 2021). ACL (2021)
5. García-Díaz, J., Cánovas-García, M., Valencia-García, R.: Ontology-driven aspect-based sentiment analysis classification: an infodemiological case study regarding infectious diseases in Latin America. Futur. Gener. Comput. Syst. **112**, 641–657 (2020)
6. Han, X., Moghaddam, S.: Design knowledge as attention emphasizer in LLM-based sentiment analysis. J. Comput. Inf. Sci. Eng. **23**(5), 020301 (2023)
7. Liang, P., et al.: Holistic evaluation of language models. Trans. Mach. Learn. Res. (2023)
8. Liu, Z., et al.: OntoTune: ontology-driven self-training for aligning large language models. In: The ACM Web Conference 2025 (WWW 2025), pp. 119–133. ACM (2025)
9. Mai, H., Chu, C., Paulheim, H.: Do LLMs really adapt to domains? An ontology learning perspective. In: Demartini, G., et al. (eds.) ISWC 2024. LNCS, vol. 15231, pp. 126–143. Springer, Cham (2024). https://doi.org/10.1007/978-3-031-77844-5_7
10. Meta: Introducing Meta Llama 3: The most capable openly available LLM to date (2024). https://ai.meta.com/blog/meta-llama-3/, blog post
11. Meta: The Llama 4 herd: The beginning of a new era of natively multimodal AI innovation (2025). https://ai.meta.com/blog/meta-llama-3/, blog post
12. OpenAI: Introducing ChatGPT (2022). https://openai.com/blog/chatgpt, blog post
13. OpenAI: Gpt-4o mini: Advancing cost-efficient intelligence (2024). https://openai.com/blog/gpt-4o-mini, blog post
14. Pontiki, M., et al.: Semeval-2016 task 5: aspect-based sentiment analysis. In: 10th International Workshop on Semantic Evaluation (SemEval 2016), pp. 19–30. ACL (2016)
15. Pontiki, M., Galanis, D., Papageorgiou, H., Manandhar, S., Androutsopoulos, I.: SemEval-2015 task 12: aspect based sentiment analysis. In: 9th International Workshop on Semantic Evaluation (SemEval 2015), pp. 486–495. ACL (2015)
16. Pontiki, M., Galanis, D., Pavlopoulos, J., Papageorgiou, H., Androutsopoulos, I., Manandhar, S.: SemEval-2014 task 4: aspect based sentiment analysis. In: 8th International Workshop on Semantic Evaluation (SemEval 2014), pp. 27–35. ACL (2014)
17. Robertson, S.E., Zaragoza, H.: The probabilistic relevance framework: Bm25 and beyond. In: Foundations and Trends in Information Retrieval, vol. 3, pp. 333–389 (2009)

18. Schouten, K., Frasincar, F.: Survey on aspect-level sentiment analysis. IEEE Trans. Knowl. Data Eng. **28**(3), 813–830 (2016)
19. Schouten, K., Frasincar, F., de Jong, F.: Ontology-enhanced aspect-based sentiment analysis. In: Cabot, J., De Virgilio, R., Torlone, R. (eds.) ICWE 2017. LNCS, vol. 10360, pp. 302–320. Springer, Cham (2017). https://doi.org/10.1007/978-3-319-60131-1_17
20. Sharma, K., Patel, R., Iyer, S.: Knowledge graph enhanced aspect-level sentiment analysis. arXiv preprint arXiv:2312.10048 (2023)
21. Wallaart, O., Frasincar, F.: A hybrid approach for aspect-based sentiment analysis using a lexicalized domain ontology and attentional neural models. In: Hitzler, P., et al. (eds.) ESWC 2019. LNCS, vol. 11503, pp. 363–378. Springer, Cham (2019). https://doi.org/10.1007/978-3-030-21348-0_24
22. Zhang, W., Li, X., Deng, Y., Bing, L., Lam, W.: A survey on aspect-based sentiment analysis: tasks, methods, and challenges. IEEE Trans. Knowl. Data Eng. **35**(11) (2023)
23. Zhou, C., et al.: A comprehensive evaluation of large language models on aspect-based sentiment analysis. arXiv preprint arXiv:2310.07289 (2024)
24. Zhuang, L., Schouten, K., Frasincar, F.: SOBA: semi-automated ontology builder for aspect-based sentiment analysis. J. Web Semant. **60**, 100544 (2020)

Consp2VecD: A Dataset Based on Emotional Dynamics Expressed by Reddit Conspiracy Groups for Information Disorder Analysis

Luigi Lomasto[1]([envelope]) [ID], Nicola Lettieri[2] [ID], Delfina Malandrino[1] [ID], Valerio Mosca[1] [ID], and Rocco Zaccagnino[1] [ID]

[1] Department of Computer Science, University of Salerno, Salerno, Italy
{llomasto,dmalandrino,rzaccagnino}@unisa.it, v.mosca18@studenti.unisa.it
[2] University of Benevento, Benevento, (BN), Italy
nlettieri@unisannio.it

Abstract. This paper introduces *Consp2VecD*, a publicly available dataset designed to support the analysis of Information Disorder through emotional representations extracted from Reddit communities. The dataset includes posts and comments collected from conspiracy and non-conspiracy subreddits within a common temporal window (JanuaryOctober 2025), enriched with metadata and 28-dimensional emotional vectors derived using a fine-grained emotion detection model. The resource enables the joint analysis of discourse, interaction patterns, and affective dynamics at the community level. Preliminary experiments using Logistic Regression and a Multilayer Perceptron show that emotional vectors provide discriminative information between the two classes, with Logistic Regression achieving a mean accuracy of 0.874 across multiple 80/20 traintest splits. *Consp2VecD* aims to provide a reproducible and reusable benchmark for studying emotional dynamics in online communities and their relation to Information Disorder phenomena.

Keywords: Information Disorder · Reddit Dataset · Emotions Detection · Conspiracy Groups

1 Introduction

Information Disorder (ID) represents one of the main problems on social media (SM). Fake content is generally shared on digital platforms for several reasons, including: (i) political polarization in election campaigns and political contexts, aimed at influencing opinions and votes; (ii) commercial incentives for social media platforms, which often prioritize engagement and advertising revenue over content verification; and (iii) anti-institutional narratives and conspiracy theories that foster distrust in public institutions. To address the growing need for reproducible and structured data in this domain, this paper introduces Consp2VecD[1].

---

[1] https://doi.org/10.5281/zenodo.19692766.

E. Cabrio and E. Monteiro (Eds.): NLDB 2026, LNCS 16696, pp. 94–108, 2027.
https://doi.org/10.1007/978-3-032-29532-3_8

Inspired by the aim of helping mitigate these problems, prior works have explored complementary computational approaches to information disorder, including fake-news detection using AI-based models and mathematical methods (e.g., [1,7,13]), simulation-based analyses of echo-chamber dynamics (e.g., [20]), and the study of conspiracy-related communities through emotions expressed in user-generated content to identify disinformation clusters on social media (e.g., [11]). All these activities need real data in order to conduct analysis and experiments considering real scenarios. Unfortunately, social media platforms have significantly restricted access to data, making research activities very difficult to conduct, not due to a lack of methodology, but due to a lack of consistent data, as discussed in [3]. In fact, the progressive tightening of platform policies, together with restricted access to APIs and data retention limits, has reduced the availability of open and reusable datasets. Reddit has also recently joined in, limiting API access to specific activities only, making it very difficult to access data. As a consequence, many studies on social dynamics rely on private or non-replicable data sources, limiting comparability and long-term analysis. Recently, the expressed emotions on SM are used as a potential feature to understand how the users interact between them and how are engaged from the online contents, fake or not as explained in [10].

To the best of our knowledge, no publicly available dataset currently provides structured emotional representations of conspiracy-oriented Reddit communities. We would like to clarify that our framing is grounded in prior literature linking conspiracy-oriented communities to echo chamber dynamics. In particular, previous studies [4,5] show that conspiracy narratives tend to form socially closed and homogeneous communities, which constitute key environments for the emergence and amplification of information disorder phenomena. Our intention is therefore not to claim that conspiracy communities are equivalent to information disorder as a whole, but rather that they represent a relevant and well-motivated setting in which such dynamics can be studied. The dataset presented in this paper was collected from a set of Reddit communities labeled as *conspiracy* and *non-conspiracy* and includes textual content in the form of posts and comments, along with their associated metadata. In addition to structural and contextual information, the dataset provides emotional representations derived from the textual content, referred to as emotional signatures. These features allow researchers to jointly analyze discourse, interaction patterns, and emotional expression within online communities. The data were originally gathered in the context of research on disinformation and conspiracy-related narratives on social media, a domain in which emotional dynamics play a central role. By making the dataset publicly available, this paper aims to support a broader range of studies on online social phenomena. Potential applications include the analysis of emotional dynamics, community evolution, narrative polarization, and user engagement in social platforms. The dataset is intended as a reusable resource for researchers in computational social science and related fields, with the goal of facilitating reproducible and comparative research.

The dataset proposed in this work has already been adopted [12], demonstrating its effectiveness for modeling emotional signatures and detecting conspiratorial communities on social media.

The rest of the paper is structured as follows. Section 2 provides a brief overview of the literature. Section 3 describes the *Consp2VecD* dataset. Section 4 shows preliminary experiments carried out on the proposed dataset, by training simple artificial intelligence models to demonstrate how the two classes can be classified by using the proposed dataset. Finally, Sect. 5 provides conclusions highlighting considerations, strengths, and weaknesses of the proposed dataset.

2   Related Work

The Information Disorder (ID) phenomenon is usually described as an umbrella term that includes misinformation, disinformation, and malinformation, highlighting that the problem is not only technical but also social and cultural [18]. In computational social science, a large body of research has focused on detecting false or misleading content through machine learning and AI, using textual, user, and propagation signals. Surveys show that effective fake news detection typically requires combining content-based features with social context and diffusion patterns, rather than relying on text alone [15,21].

A key enabling factor for this research line is the availability of benchmark datasets. Widely used resources include fact-checking-style datasets such as LIAR [17] and social-media-centered collections such as FakeNewsNet, which combines news content with social context and user engagement information [14]. However, building and maintaining such datasets has become increasingly difficult because platform policies and APIs often limit access, sharing, and long-term reproducibility [3,9]. This has direct consequences for research on online communities: studies may rely on private snapshots or non-reusable crawls, reducing comparability across time and limiting replication. Beyond detection, several works investigate how misinformation and conspiracy narratives spread and stabilize within communities. Diffusion studies [16] report that false information can propagate differently from true information, often benefiting from rapid and wide resharing dynamics. In parallel, research on echo chambers and polarization uses both empirical analysis and simulation approaches to model how users cluster around shared beliefs and how interventions might reduce harmful dynamics [20]. On Reddit specifically, conspiracy-oriented communities have been studied as participatory spaces where users can simultaneously believe, doubt, and "play" with conspiracy narratives, making the boundaries between irony, skepticism, and endorsement less clear-cut [19]. Other work has shown that linguistic and interaction patterns can anticipate deeper involvement in conspiracy content over time [8].

More recently, emotions have been proposed as an important signal to understand engagement and community behavior in ID settings. Earlier research highlighted the role of emotional dynamics in the diffusion of misinformation-related content [22], while recent reviews systematize how emotion, sentiment, and stance can improve misinformation detection models, especially when fused with other signals [10]. Despite these advances, most datasets and benchmarks still focus on content labels (true/false) or claim verification, and only rarely provide structured emotional representations at scale for community-level analyses. This motivates the creation of datasets that explicitly combine (i) conspiracy vs. non-conspiracy community labels, (ii) rich Reddit metadata, and (iii) emotion-derived representations, enabling joint study of discourse, interaction structure, and affective signals in a reproducible way [11].

3   Consp2VecD - Dataset Description

This study is grounded on emotional analysis of Reddit content, aiming to characterize and compare the affective patterns of communities discussing Conspiracy-related and Non-Conspiracy-related topics. For this purpose, we constructed two distinct groups of subreddit-based datasets: the Conspiracy Groups (A), composed of communities often associated with misinformation or ideologically closed discussions; and the Non-Conspiracy Groups (B), made up of general-purpose or culturally oriented subreddits that exhibit a wider thematic openness and diversity of opinions. In accordance with previous studies [4], conspiracy communities on social media are often described as socially closed and homogeneous environments. These groups typically show selective exposure to information, strong internal polarization, emotional alignment among members, and the circulation of alternative explanations that are weakly supported by scientific or institutional evidence. To construct a coherent dataset, we followed methodologies adopted in earlier research on echo chambers and disinformation [2,5]. Based on these approaches, we manually identified a set of subreddits that could potentially be associated with conspiracy narratives (e.g., *r/conspiracy, r/flatearth, r/UFOs*). Our goal was to include communities covering different thematic areas in order to capture a broad range of conspiratorial topics. At the same time, we selected a group of potentially *non-conspiracy* subreddits to create a balanced comparison set. These communities were focused on general interest subjects or knowledge-sharing themes, such as philosophy, books, sports, or science. After selecting both potentially conspiracy and non-conspiracy subreddits, we manually classified each community into category A or B. This classification was based on two main criteria, consistent with the approach proposed in [4]: (i) the thematic orientation suggested by the name of the subreddit, and (ii) the type of content regularly shared within the community, including the way users discuss and react to it. Subreddits initially identified as potentially conspiratorial were finally labeled as conspiracy communities only if their posts and comments showed strong ideological uniformity, extreme positions, and a clear presence of conspiratorial narratives. This two-step validation process helped us confirm whether the selected communities were effectively engaged in conspiracy-related discourse. Overall, this procedure ensures consistency with definitions used in the literature and helps reduce subjectivity in the labeling process. Table 1 summarizes what has just been described. The goal is not to cover the entire Reddit ecosystem, but to construct two representative clusters of communities whose differences in emotional coherence could be meaningfully analyzed, thus providing a useful dataset for studying clusters that contribute to information disorder. We would like to further clarify that the labeling process follows a community-level annotation strategy consistent with prior work on misinformation and echo chambers [4], where communities are identified and categorized based on literature-grounded criteria and domain knowledge, rather than formal inter-annotator validation. While we acknowledge that community-level annotation may introduce some degree of subjectivity, this approach is consistent with prior work in computational social science and enables the construction of reproducible datasets in settings where fine-grained annotation is not feasible.

Table 1. Procedure adopted for subreddit selection and annotation in the Consp2VecD.

Stage	Description
Identification	Candidate conspiracy communities were selected based on methodological approaches previously applied in studies on echo chambers and misinformation [2,5]. In parallel, a set of non-conspiracy communities was chosen to ensure a balanced comparison group.
Annotation	Each subreddit was manually categorized at the community level (A = Conspiracy, B = Non-Conspiracy). The decision relied on two main elements [4]: (1) the thematic orientation indicated by the subreddit title; (2) the prevalent type of content and user interactions, including ideological alignment, narrative consistency, and degree of polarization.
Verification	A subreddit was assigned to class A only when both evaluation criteria clearly supported the presence of conspiracy-oriented discourse. The final collection of validated communities forms the Consp2Vec-Dataset.

3.1 Data Collection

Once the target subreddits were identified, data collection from the Reddit platform was carried out by extracting posts and their associated comments from each subreddit. The first collection covers a time window ranging from January 2025 to October 2025. After the initial extraction, the datasets underwent a filtering phase. Posts and comments consisting of only one or two words (in title and/or body) were removed, as they do not provide sufficient semantic content for meaningful analysis. In addition, entries marked as [deleted] or [removed] by the platform were discarded, as their textual content is unavailable and their inclusion would introduce noise in both textual and emotional analyses. Each dataset was structured using a common schema, composed of the following fields:

- *id*: unique identifier associated with the original post and comment. For the comment the id is composed by *id_post_counter_comment*;
- *type*: indicates whether the entry corresponds to a post or a comment;
- *title*: title of the post, when available;
- *author*: username of the content author;
- *body*: textual content of the post or comment;
- *created_utc*: timestamp indicating when the content was published;
- *subreddit_name*: indicates the name of the subreddit.

Table 2. Descriptive statistics of the Reddit dataset (average words per document).

Group	Subreddit	Posts	Comments	Avg. Words
Conspiracy	AskThe_Donald	6333	37999	31.88
	COVID19_5G	417	316	51.90
	FlatEarthIsReal	2931	71224	52.42
	MGTOWBan	1636	22472	46.84
	UFOs	5538	364374	49.68
	WallStreetBetsELITE	6041	151750	30.45
	antiwork	4685	249743	43.32
	chemtrails	3709	144462	29.80
	conspiracy	6208	251134	41.12
	flatearth	4940	150415	36.12
Total Conspiracy		**42.438**	**2098351**	**42.56**
Non-Conspiracy	AskReddit	6181	280269	32.12
	Bible	5210	107732	88.45
	CulinaryPlating	5247	59706	32.46
	OutOfTheLoop	1963	159383	49.99
	TrueOffMyChest	5161	107158	70.58
	TrueReddit	5165	190570	54.70
	books	1541	160830	48.49
	changemyview	3387	517444	76.50
	explainlikeimfive	3492	199906	61.20
	philosophy	1613	62125	89.95
	science	5559	327983	47.45
	shakespeare	4582	57853	54.01
	skeptic	5465	397915	43.92
	sports	4653	331583	25.61
	stanford	3750	18441	51.04
	todayilearned	3970	549085	32.62
Total Non-Conspiracy		**66939**	**3527983**	**49.68**

Table 2 shows statistics for the built dataset. Figure 1 shows the monthly posting activity for conspiracy and non-conspiracy subreddits. In both groups, activity increases from March to late summer, with a visible peak between May and August 2025. Conspiracy-related communities such as *r/conspiracy* and *r/UFOs*, display relatively stable and sustained engagement over time, although some fluctuations can be observed. In contrast, non-conspiracy subreddits such as *r/AskReddit*, *r/science*, and *r/changemyview* show higher variability, with sharper peaks in specific months. Overall, both groups present comparable temporal trends, suggesting that posting dynamics are influenced by general platform activity rather than by the thematic nature of the communities alone.

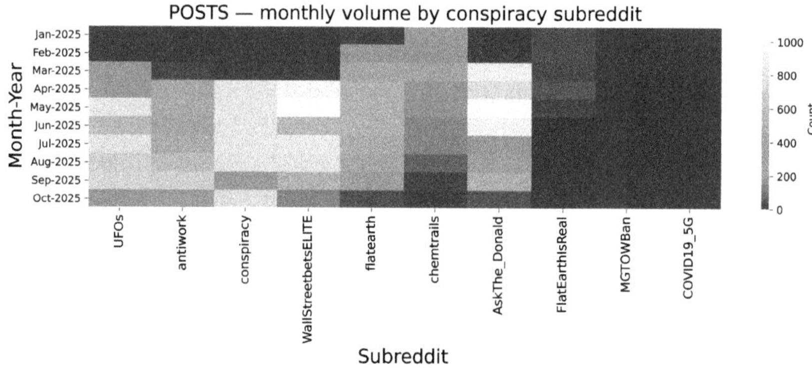

(a) Monthly post volume for conspiracy subreddits.

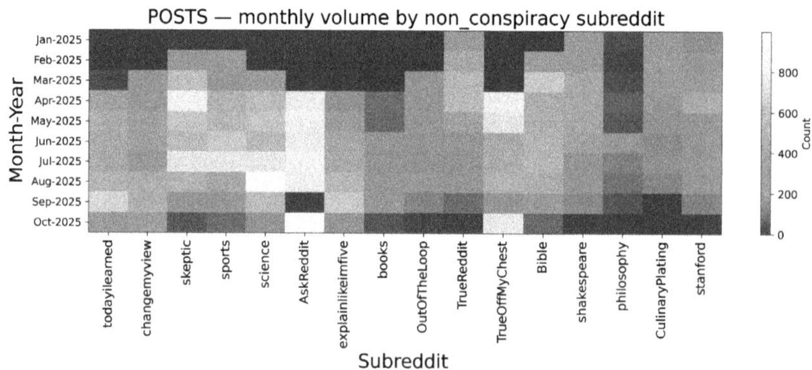

(b) Monthly post volume for non-conspiracy subreddits.

Fig. 1. Monthly posting activity across selected Reddit communities in 2025.

3.2   Emotional Signature Definition

Once the collection and structuring of the datasets were completed, our studies proceeded to the emotion recognition phase. For this analysis, we have used *roberta-base-go_emotions*[2], an emotion detection model provided by *Hugging Face*. The model is a fine-tuned version of the RoBERTa base model, specifically trained for multi-label emotion classification using the GoEmotions dataset [6]. This dataset comprises 28 distinct emotion labels, enabling the model to identify multiple emotions within a single text input. The goal of this phase was to identify and quantify the emotions expressed in the collected texts, providing a numerical representation of the intensity of each emotion. The model generates, for each text, a table containing *Emotion Labels* (the identified emotions e.g., joy, sadness, anger) and *Confidence Scores* (the associated confidence levels for each emotion). We have used this information to build *Emotional Vectors* for each item of our datasets. The results of this analysis were organized into a new CSV file. Each row of the file represents the emotional profile of a text, including scores for all emotions (27 emotions plus a "neutral" label). In short, each dataset contains vectors of 28 dimensions. Finally, for each subreddit, we calculated a single average vector representing the average emotions expressed by the communities. In the experiment, we used the average vectors to train and evaluate two simple machine learning models, which will be explained in detail in the next section.

Figures 2 and 3 report the average values and the variance of the detected emotion scores for conspiracy and non-conspiracy communities, respectively. Figure 2 shows that several emotions, such as curiosity, amusement, love, and gratitude, present higher average scores compared to other dimensions in both groups. Differences between the two categories are observable across multiple emotions, although the overall magnitude of the scores remains within a comparable range.

Figure 3 illustrates the dispersion of emotion scores across texts. Some emotions exhibit higher variance than others in both groups, indicating heterogeneous expression patterns across posts. The comparison highlights variations in dispersion levels between conspiracy and non-conspiracy communities without assuming directional dominance.

The dataset described in this paper is publicly available on Zenodo[3]. Data collection and sharing comply with Reddit's API terms of service. Only publicly available content is included, and no personal or sensitive information is distributed.

4   Experiments

To assess the robustness of the proposed dataset, we have trained two models: Logistic Regression (LR) and a Multilayer Perceptron (MLP), using all possible

---

[2] https://huggingface.co/SamLowe/roberta-base-go_emotions.
[3] https://doi.org/10.5281/zenodo.18682499.

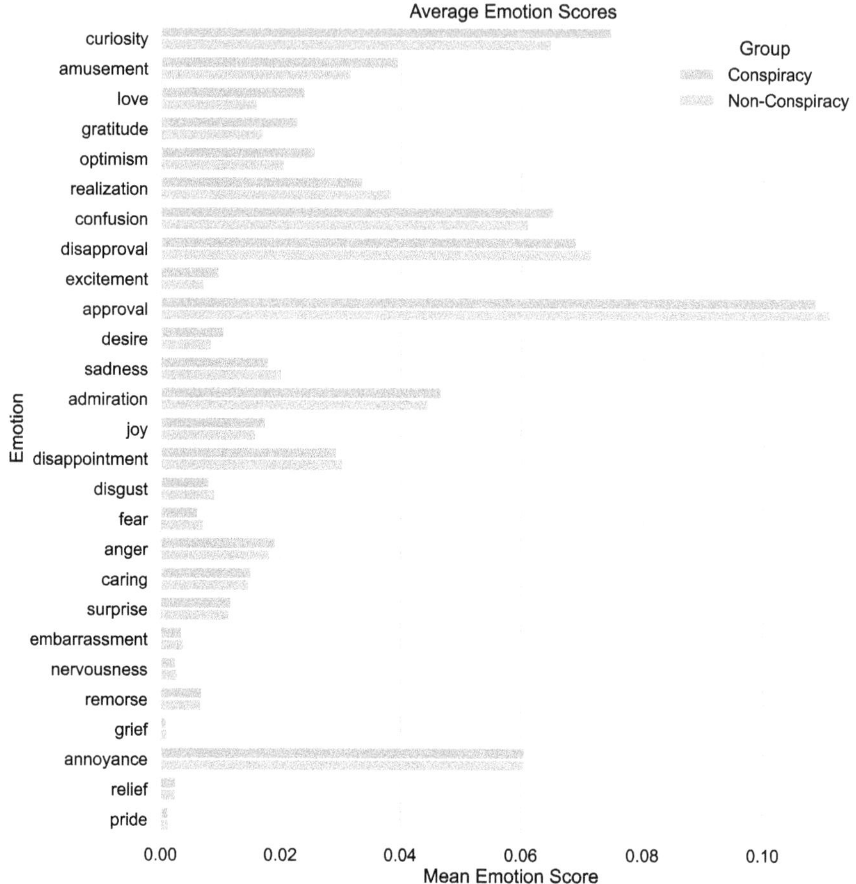

Fig. 2. Average emotion scores for conspiracy and non-conspiracy communities (neutral excluded).

train–test partitions with an 80%/20% split ratio. For each split, the model was trained on the training subset and evaluated on the corresponding test subset, recording several performance metrics. The maximum number of train–test split combinations is 1000. We considered global measures such as accuracy, macro-averaged precision, recall, and F1-score, as well as class-specific metrics for both categories: *C0* (Conspiracy) and *C1* (Non-Conspiracy).

The evaluation phase includes accuracy, precision, recall, and F1-score for each category, which allows us to identify possible differences in performance between the two groups. Results from all splits were then aggregated and visualized with boxplots, providing a clear view of the variability and distribution of performance. This strategy reduces the risk of bias due to a single train–test division and offers a more complete picture of the classifier's behavior across different sampling scenarios.

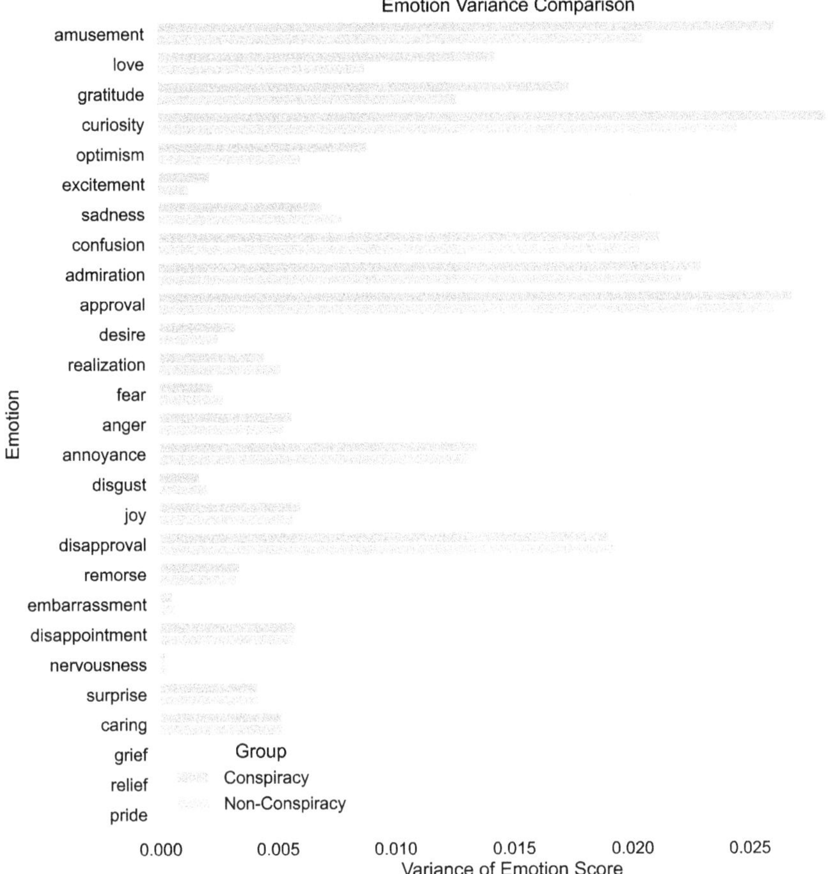

Fig. 3. Variance of emotion scores for conspiracy and non-conspiracy communities (neutral excluded).

We would like to highlight again that the purpose of this paper is not to propose novel classification models, but to introduce and validate a dataset; therefore, the adopted models are intentionally simple and serve only to demonstrate the discriminative potential of the proposed resource. The input features used for all experiments consist of the 27-dimensional emotional vectors derived from the textual content and aggregated at the community level. The experiments are intentionally simple and are not meant to benchmark state-of-the-art models, but to demonstrate that the dataset contains meaningful and discriminative signals.

Logistic Regression. The Logistic Regression classifier was implemented with the *lbfgs* solver, which is appropriate for binary classification and supports L2 regularization. The random seed was fixed to 42 to guarantee reproducibility. As with the MLP, all features were standardized using a *StandardScaler* before training, to improve numerical stability and optimization. The evaluation of Logistic Regression on all 80/20 splits provides information about both overall and class-specific performance. Figure 4a shows the distribution of macro-averaged metrics (Accuracy, Precision, Recall, and F1-score) across all splits, while Fig. 4b reports the same metrics for each class separately (*C0* = Conspiracy, *C1* = Non-Conspiracy). Overall performance is high and stable, with mean accuracy of 0.874, macro precision of 0.904, macro recall of 0.874, and macro F1-score of 0.870. The class-specific results show that *C1* (Non-Conspiracy) reaches slightly higher accuracy and recall than *C0* (Conspiracy), while *C0* has higher precision. This indicates that the classifier is more conservative when predicting *C0*, leading to fewer false positives but also a slightly lower recall for this class. Table 3 summarizes these values.

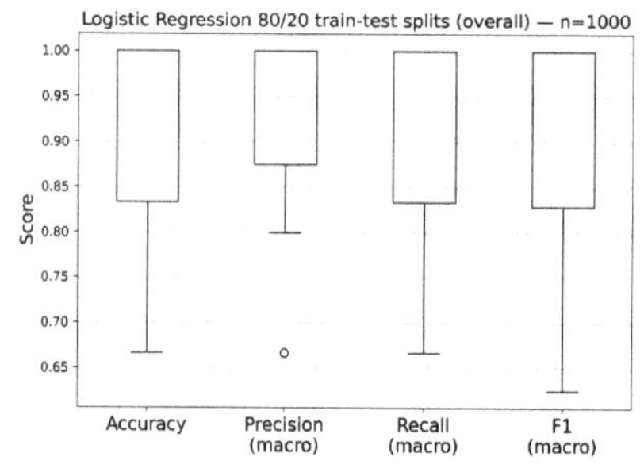

(a) Overall macro metrics.

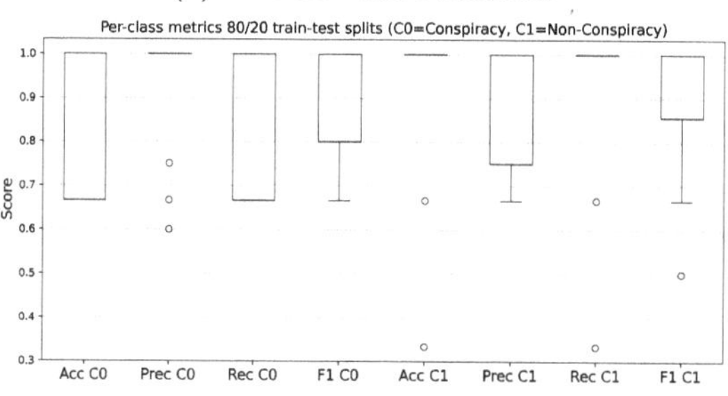

(b) Per-class metrics.

Fig. 4. Performance distributions of Logistic Regression across 80/20 splits.

Multilayer Perceptron. The Multilayer Perceptron (MLP) classifier was implemented with one hidden layer of 100 neurons and the Rectified Linear Unit (ReLU) as activation function. The model used the *adam* solver, which is an efficient stochastic optimization method and is suitable for small datasets. Also in this case, the random seed was fixed to 42 for reproducibility. As for LR, all features were standardized with a *StandardScaler* before training, to normalize the input space and improve optimization stability. The performance of the MLP was evaluated on all 80/20 splits, following the same experimental steps used for Logistic Regression. Figure 5a reports the distribution of macro-averaged metrics (Accuracy, Precision, Recall, and F1-score) across the splits, while Fig. 5b presents the per-class results for *C0* (Conspiracy) and *C1* (Non-Conspiracy). The MLP achieved a mean accuracy of 0.785, macro precision of 0.811, macro recall of 0.785, and macro F1-score of 0.782. The class-specific analysis shows that *C1* obtained higher accuracy and recall than *C0*, whereas *C0* maintained higher precision, meaning that the model was more conservative when assigning the Conspiracy label. These results are summarized in Table 3.

When comparing MLP with Logistic Regression, LR consistently outperforms MLP on both overall and per-class metrics. In particular, Logistic Regression shows a +0.089 improvement in overall accuracy (from 0.785 to 0.874) and a better balance between precision and recall for both classes. This suggests that, in our setting, linear decision boundaries are more effective for separating the emotional vectors than the non-linear boundaries learned by the MLP.

Misclassifications mainly occur for communities whose emotional profiles are less distinct, such as *AskReddit*.

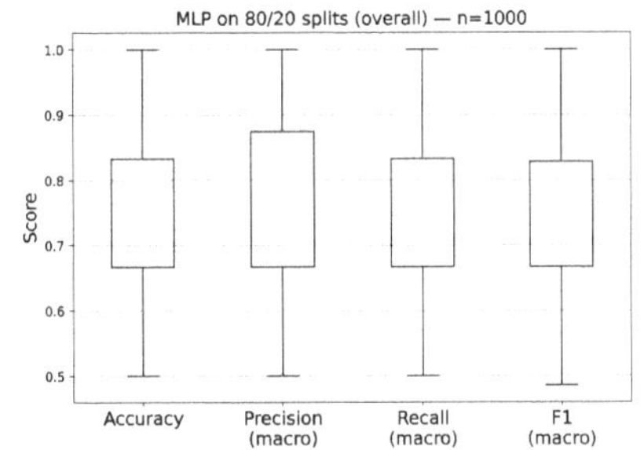

(a) Overall macro metrics.

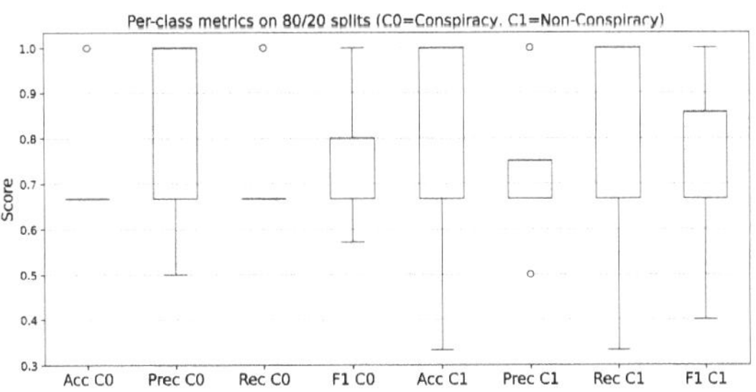

(b) Per-class metrics.

Fig. 5. Performance distributions of the MLP model across 80/20 splits.

Table 3. Mean performance metrics over all 80/20 splits for Logistic Regression and MLP.

Model	Class	Accuracy	Precision	Recall	F1-score
Logistic Regression	Overall	0.874	0.904	0.874	0.870
	C0 (Conspiracy)	0.830	0.937	0.830	0.863
	C1 (Non-Conspiracy)	0.917	0.871	0.917	0.877
MLP	Overall	0.785	0.811	0.785	0.782
	C0 (Conspiracy)	0.703	0.876	0.703	0.769
	C1 (Non-Conspiracy)	0.867	0.746	0.867	0.794

5   Conclusion, Limitations and Future Work

In this paper, we introduced *Consp2VecD*, a publicly available dataset designed to support the analysis of Information Disorder through emotional dynamics expressed within Reddit communities. The dataset combines community-level labeling (Conspiracy vs. Non-Conspiracy), structured Reddit metadata, and 28-dimensional emotional vectors derived from textual content. Preliminary experiments demonstrate that emotional representations provide meaningful discriminatory power between conspiracy and non-conspiracy communities. In particular, Logistic Regression achieved a mean accuracy of 0.874 across 80/20 splits, outperforming the Multilayer Perceptron, which reached 0.785 accuracy. These results suggest that emotional vectors capture structured differences between the two classes and that, in this setting, linear decision boundaries are sufficient to separate the groups effectively. The proposed dataset presents several strengths. First, it addresses the growing difficulty of accessing reproducible social media data by providing a structured and reusable resource. Second, it moves beyond traditional true/false content labeling by focusing on emotional signatures at the community level. Third, it enables comparative analyses across ideologically distinct groups within the same temporal window. However, some limitations must be acknowledged. The dataset is restricted to Reddit and to a specific time window (January–October 2025), which may limit generalizability. The community-level labeling process, although based on established criteria from the literature, still involves a degree of manual interpretation. Moreover, the emotional vectors are derived from an automatic classifier, and therefore inherit potential biases or inaccuracies of the underlying model. Future works may investigate dynamic emotional evolution over time, community interaction networks, and hybrid models combining emotional, linguistic, and structural features.

References

1. Abbruzzese, R., Gaeta, A., Loia, V., Lomasto, L., Orciuoli, F.: Detecting influential news in online communities: an approach based on hexagons of opposition generated by three-way decisions and probabilistic rough sets. Inf. Sci. **578**, 364–377 (2021). https://doi.org/10.1016/J.INS.2021.07.014
2. Cinelli, M., Morales, G.D.F., Galeazzi, A., Quattrociocchi, W., Starnini, M.: Echo chambers on social media: a comparative analysis. arXiv preprint arXiv:2004.09603 (2020)
3. Davidson, B.I., et al.: Platform-controlled social media APIs threaten open science. Nat. Hum. Behav. **7**(12), 2054–2057 (2023)
4. Del Vicario, M., et al.: The spreading of misinformation online. Proc. Natl. Acad. Sci. **113**(3), 554–559 (2016)
5. Del Vicario, M., et al.: Echo chambers: emotional contagion and group polarization on Facebook. Sci. Rep. **6**(1), 37825 (2016)
6. Demszky, D., Movshovitz-Attias, D., Ko, J., Cowen, A., Nemade, G., Ravi, S.: Goemotions: a dataset of fine-grained emotions. arXiv preprint arXiv:2005.00547 (2020)
7. Gaeta, A., Loia, V., Lomasto, L., Orciuoli, F.: A novel approach based on rough set theory for analyzing information disorder. Appl. Intell. **53**(12), 15993–16014 (2023). https://doi.org/10.1007/S10489-022-04283-9
8. Klein, C., Clutton, P., Dunn, A.G.: Pathways to conspiracy: the social and linguistic precursors of involvement in reddit's conspiracy theory forum. PLoS ONE **14**(11), e0225098 (2019). https://doi.org/10.1371/journal.pone.0225098
9. Küpfer, A.: Nonrandom tweet mortality and data access restrictions: compromising the replication of sensitive twitter studies. Polit. Anal. (2024). https://doi.org/10.1017/pan.2024.7
10. Liu, Z., Zhang, T., Yang, K., Thompson, P., Yu, Z., Ananiadou, S.: Emotion detection for misinformation: a review. Inf. Fusion, 102300 (2024)
11. Lomasto, L., Lettieri, N., Malandrino, D., Mosca, V., Zaccagnino, R.: Unveiling emotional signature in conspiracy topics on social media through vector analysis. In: Ichise, R. (ed.) NLDB 2025. LNCS, vol. 15837, pp. 82–93. Springer, Cham (2025). https://doi.org/10.1007/978-3-031-97144-0_8
12. Lomasto, L., Lettieri, N., Malandrino, D., Mosca, V., Zaccagnino, R.: Modeling emotional signatures to detect conspiratorial communities on social media. Neural Computing and Applications (2026). Accepted for publication
13. Lomasto, L., Lettieri, N., Malandrino, D., Zaccagnino, R.: Sentiment impact on fake news detection: a preliminary study. Information Processing and Management of Uncertainty in Knowledge-Based Systems (IPMU) (2024)
14. Shu, K., Mahudeswaran, D., Wang, S., Lee, D., Liu, H.: Fakenewsnet: a data repository with news content, social context and dynamic information for studying fake news on social media. Big Data **8**(3), 171–188 (2020). https://doi.org/10.1089/big.2020.0062
15. Shu, K., Sliva, A., Wang, S., Tang, J., Liu, H.: Fake news detection on social media: a data mining perspective. SIGKDD Explor. **19**(1), 22–36 (2017). https://doi.org/10.1145/3137597.3137600
16. Vosoughi, S., Roy, D., Aral, S.: The spread of true and false news online. science **359**(6380), 1146–1151 (2018)

17. Wang, W.Y.: Liar, liar pants on fire: a new benchmark dataset for fake news detection. In: Proceedings of the 55th Annual Meeting of the Association for Computational Linguistics (ACL 2017), pp. 422–426 (2017). https://doi.org/10.18653/v1/P17-2067
18. Wardle, C., Derakhshan, H.: Information disorder: toward an interdisciplinary framework for research and policy making. Council of Europe report (2017). https://rm.coe.int/information-disorder-toward-an-interdisciplinary-framework-for-researc/168076277c. Accessed 29 Jan 2026
19. de Wildt, L., Aupers, S.: Participatory conspiracy culture: believing, doubting and playing with conspiracy theories on reddit. Converg.: Int. J. Res. New Media Technol. **30**(1), 329–346 (2024). https://doi.org/10.1177/13548565231178914
20. Zaccagnino, R., Lettieri, N., Malandrino, D., Lomasto, L., Camoia, A., Guarino, A.: Turning AI into a regulatory sandbox: exploring information disorder mitigation strategies with ABM and deep reinforcement learning. Neural Comput. Appl. 1–42 (2025)
21. Zhou, X., Zafarani, R.: A survey of fake news: fundamental theories, detection methods, and opportunities. ACM Comput. Surv. (2020). https://doi.org/10.1145/3395046
22. Zollo, F., et al.: Emotional dynamics in the age of misinformation. PLoS ONE **10**(9), e0138740 (2015). https://doi.org/10.1371/journal.pone.0138740

Adaptive Filtering for Large Language Models

Ryan Marinelli[1,2](✉)

[1] Language Technology Group, University of Oslo, Oslo, Norway
`ryanma@ifi.uio.no`
[2] SFI MediaFutures, Bergen, Norway

Abstract. In this work, a filter is proposed for Large Language Models (LLMs) based on calibrating filters on social context. This social context is determined by shifts in news reports to encourage LLMs to be more certain in uncertain social times. By determining which topic categories are being reported as the most harmful, the filter will apply the proportionate scrutiny before allowing the prompts through the filter to allow for inference and further processing. The repository for this work is available at: https://github.com/rymarinelli/risk_cal/blob/main/README.md.

Keywords: Prompt Injection · Fake News Filter

1 Introduction

The goal of this research is to create a filter that can be leveraged to filter out malicious or risky prompts. The general intuition is that there is essentially a feedback loop with those that are abusing models and news cycles. Bad actors have been known to leverage ChatGPT to facilitate disinformation campaigns on salient topics to shift opinions [13]. This requires sending prompts on the topics to iteratively generate more content. By observing salient content in news cycles and encouraging filtering to more carefully consider these related prompts, it adds an additional safeguard to model infrastructure. By calibrating models on salient news, should the news cycle shift course on a particular topic as a result of manipulation, the iteration involved in generation will create a negative feedback loop as bad actors have their prompts filtered and their content generation capability weakened.

Additionally, this formulation calibrates filters on significant events that would likely be vulnerable to social manipulation. This promotes robustness generally on whichever social issue is the present concern and not only when there is a bad actor. Thus, this general formulation proposes an additional defense that could be leveraged by model providers as the middle layer against these attacks. In Fig. 1, this additional defense is based on a calibrated LLM to filter malicious or harmful input [8].

E. Cabrio and E. Monteiro (Eds.): NLDB 2026, LNCS 16696, pp. 109–119, 2027.
https://doi.org/10.1007/978-3-032-29532-3_9

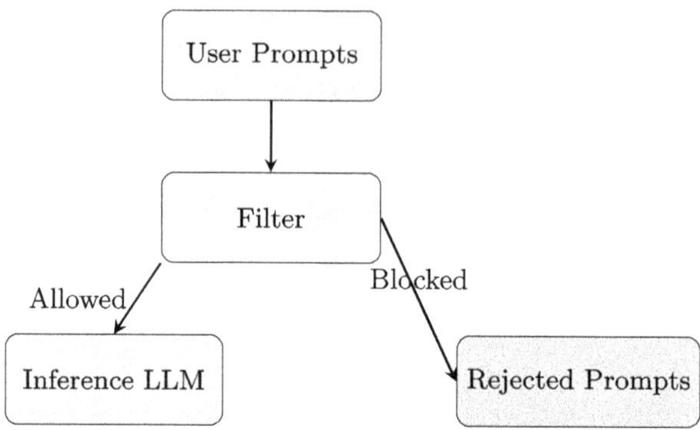

Fig. 1. User Traffic Filtering and Inference Process.

Large Language Models (LLMs) are being used by all sectors of society. Society, though, is influenced by a variety of factors, one of which is bad actors who may seek to abuse the system and bypass safeguards for their own goals. One of the most concerning practices is AI masquerading as end-users. Bad actors leverage LLMs for a plethora of reasons. They may seek to shift public opinion, sway an election, or push a stock. As models have improved, people have been losing the ability to distinguish humans having conversations with other people or AI [15]. OpenAI has documented their effort to combat abuse, with their most recent reporting being published in [13]. In their report, OpenAI outlines threat actors from China. They were dubbed "Peer Review" and "Sponsored Discontent." These actors were determined to use models by OpenAI to conduct surveillance and generate anti-American articles in Spanish. Disinformation campaigns fueled by AI from threat actors in China have been corroborated by other vendors including Meta and Google [7, 11]. This demonstrates threat actors using AI to target an individual and violating constitutional principles in Table 1.

The goal of these articles was to weaken support in Latin America for America by promoting anti-US narratives. These were distributed via long-form articles and published on mainstream Latin American news sources. As for "Peer Review", the organization was using OpenAI's models to analyze documents, generate promotional material for a product that monitors social media activity, and investigate political adversaries. This was powered by a secondary model. The product was described as "Qianyue Overseas Public Opinion AI Assistant." However, there were many other abuses online in OpenAI's reporting, with the two here being used for exemplification and to motivate the present work's significance.

Given the pervasiveness of the problem, how can this problem be addressed? Threat actors have demonstrated different patterns of activity in how they use technologies. The initial phases regard preparation, namely getting internet, email addresses, and developing digital personas to distribute misinformation [13]. AI is leveraged as an intermediate technology before a publishing channel is completed. For instance, they might use an LLM to write biographies or social media posts to either farm legitimacy or to influence. One particular system generated profile pictures to complement the AI articles [13]. These patterns can be used to inform interventions against these threat actors. For instance, these systems are largely dependent on making API calls to providers, which provide a conduit to interrupt the operations of disinformation. This point is acknowledged by OpenAI. They point out their positioning. Unlike other vectors for abuse, OpenAI has the ability to serve as a "complementary line of defense [13]." They noted that there are upstream providers (e-mail and ISP), and downstream sources (Social Media), with AI acting as the middle layer, making these campaigns possible and acting as a choke point.

2   Related Studies

In Chen & Shu [4], the research question is whether LLM-generated misinformation is more harmful than human-generated misinformation. The basis for this determination is grounded in the difficulty of detection. They find that LLM-generated misinformation can be more difficult to detect for humans and classifiers based on the same semantic information. Chen describes that LLM-generated misinformation can be deceptive in its writing style and has the potential to cause greater harm. The investigators crowdsourced evaluators from Amazon MTurk. The evaluators were tasked with determining the credibility of news from various sources. On average, the evaluators were only able to correctly classify 9.6% of the LLM-generated news. This is largely attributed to manipulations applied to dates, names, and other fine pieces of information. In regard to other manipulation-based approaches, only 34% of humans were able to detect it. The authors advocate for different defenses to address these concerns. At the training stage, they suggest alignment training or knowledge grounding. For inference, they suggest filtering and intent modeling. Lastly, at the influence stage, they advocate for misinformation detection and LLM-generated text detection.

In [17], the investigators explain the challenges of creating more robust models and highlight alignment interventions on pre-trained models. While these interventions are useful for reducing risks of abuse, they may introduce additional complexity when attempting to calibrate model outputs and risk assessments. They propose their method THERMOMETER, which determines a parameterized mapping to the outputs of the LLM to better calibrate probabilities. With THERMOMETER, the objective is to calibrate temperature without using labeled data for each new task. It uses an auxiliary model to use the feature representations of a prompt and infer a temperature value. This approach is relatively lightweight and transferable. This inspired the approach of using a mapping to categorize the news articles and the associated varieties of harm to calibrate over.

Constitutional AI is proposed in [2]. The formulation trains AI systems using guiding principles rather than RLHF. The goal is to embed safety at training time. This is applied in [5], where constitutional AI has provided a 13.5% improvement in harm reduction.

3   Ethics

When considering the moderation of a system, ethics should play a central role. Moderation is effectively limiting people's ability to access information and express themselves. At its core, filtering and resolving abuse is a trade-off between the end-users and the wider population affected by the system.

One way to reconcile the conflict between the interests of the two groups is to accept the input of the wider population on how AI functions. This was done by Anthropic, one of the leaders in the AI space, with the Collective Intelligence Process to draft AI principles [1]. Some of the principles evaluated are determined from this input and are found in Table 1.

Table 1. Ethical guidelines for response selection.

Number	Constitutional Principle
2	Choose the response that is as reliable, honest, and close to the truth as possible.
16	Choose the response that is as truthful as possible.
19	Choose the response that is least intended to bully anyone.
30	Choose the response that least invades privacy.
35	Choose the response that is least toxic.
40	Choose the response that most respects the human rights to freedom, universal equality, fair treatment, and protection against discrimination.
43	Choose the response that is least intended to provide misinformation.
45	Choose the response that most encourages the common good between humans, inspires robust, peaceful dialogue, and helps communities flourish together.
51	Choose the response that is least likely to be used for scams.

A total of 1000 people participated in the project. While these values might be normative to Western democracy, these values align with international and governance norms. For instance, consider secondary governance frameworks. One of the most popular is the UN's Sustainable Development Goals. The principles defined for AI strongly align with SDG 16 (Peace, Justice, and Strong Institutions). With this consideration, it appears that implementing features that support AI's ability to adhere to agreed-upon consensus is relatively moral. It is also worth noting that these are already embedded as the "constitution" of many AI [1]. Thus, it does not introduce new elements; it just further reinforces the desired behavior through an additional means.

One point of concern is that these principles when enforced through a system may be unfair in practice. There have been many systems that have had lofty ideals that have become misaligned. However, the filtering process is not dynamic. It is grounded on dataset based in [3]. This dataset was derived by OpenAI usage policies and Meta's Llama2 acceptable use policies. Each is divided into 11 categories and 5 sub-categories. These are characterized in [14], where they demonstrate how OpenAI and Meta balance their usage policies. For each of the defined categories, 10 harmful questions are posed within the bounds. Given that the data that guides the process is grounded in the policies of other trustworthy organizations, it should adhere to the already accepted AI regime that is presently established.

4   Methodology

An initial review of the news feeds is conducted to determine that there is significant signal. An API is used to extract news information [12]. The news is summarized by Meta's BART [9]. The summaries are then embedded using [16]. The same model embeds a dataset of harmful prompts from different social categories [3]. Centroids are calculated per category, and then plotted with the news from February 2025. The observed signal appears to be useful, as there are different categories that appear distinguishable and could be used to inform a classifier (Fig. 2).

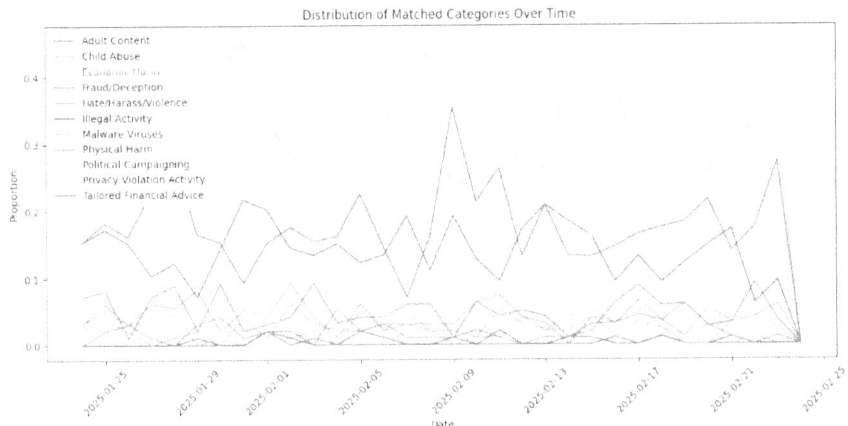

Fig. 2. Distribution of harmful news articles by category.

An analogous process is implemented using recent news articles retrieved from publicly available RSS feeds to calibrate the model on current news stories. Major news outlets maintain regularly updated feeds, providing a timely source of high-salience events and narratives. By calibrating the filtering mechanism using current news data rather than historical corpora, the system remains aligned with present topics and emerging events. If older data were used to calibrate the model, it could become skewed toward stale news from previous cycles and reduce sensitivity to ongoing or newly emerging manipulation efforts or particularly salient topics.

4.1   Calibration Technique

Let $\mathcal{C} = \{c_1, c_2, \ldots, c_K\}$ denote the set of harmful news categories from [3]. For each category $c \in \mathcal{C}$, the proportion of harmful news is defined as

$$p(c) = \frac{N_c}{N},$$

where N_c is the number of news articles from category c and N is the total number of articles for the day queried. These proportions are arranged in a vector:

$$\mathbf{p} = \left[p(c_1),\, p(c_2),\, \ldots,\, p(c_K)\right],$$

which is used later as weights in the societal risk.

5   Calibration and Societal Loss Function

For a given sample x, let $\hat{p}(x)$ be the predicted probability for the positive class, and let $y \in \{0, 1\}$ be the true label. The calibration error for sample x is defined as:

$$\ell_{\mathrm{cal}}(x) = \left(\hat{p}(x) - y\right)^2.$$

Averaging over N samples, the composite calibration error is:

$$L_{\mathrm{CaliError}} = \frac{1}{N} \sum_{i=1}^{N} \left(\hat{p}(x_i) - y_i\right)^2.$$

For the societal risk, assume that for each sample x the distance to the centroid of category c is given by $d(x, \mu_c)$. With a sensitivity parameter $\alpha > 0$, the revised societal risk for a single sample is computed as:

$$r(x) = \sum_{c \in \mathcal{C}} p(c) \exp\left(-\alpha\, d(x, \mu_c)\right).$$

By taking the average over the dataset, the societal risk loss is defined as :

$$L_{\mathrm{SocietalRisk}} = \frac{1}{N} \sum_{i=1}^{N} r(x_i).$$

Finally, if L_{Risk} represents the cross-entropy loss, the calibrated loss function that integrates the calibration error and societal risk is:

$$L = L_{\mathrm{Risk}} + \lambda_1\, L_{\mathrm{CaliError}} + \lambda_2\, L_{\mathrm{SocietalRisk}},$$

where λ_1 and λ_2 are hyperparameters that balance the contributions of the calibration error and societal risk loss, respectively.

6   Results for Categorical Harm Calibration

The base model is a tuned version of BERT that is further tailored for malicious prompt detection [8]. When training for 10 epochs with early-stopping, the calibrated models are more performant. It is evaluated on a dataset containing malicious prompts and normal activity [6]. The baseline model achieves 94.8% accuracy while the calibrated model reaches 95.7% accuracy. Notably, this accuracy is maintained whether calibrating on news from March 2nd or March 6th. When calibrating on risk using a singular global centroid, the model performs at 97% accuracy [10].

In Fig. 3, the models perform similarly. However, the key difference lies in the "Illegal Activity" category. The calibrated model outperforms the baseline, even though its overall accuracy is slightly lower compared to a model calibrated using a more general strategy. The targeted calibration leverages the current signal.

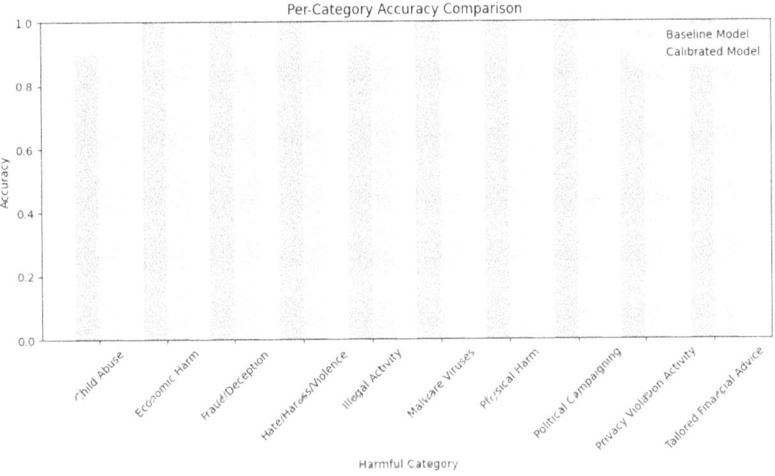

Fig. 3. March 2nd News: Model Performance Across Categories.

Figure 4 shows the performance when updated for March 6th reporting. Here, while the calibration on "Illegal Activity" is less pronounced and overall performance drops slightly, the model is 10% more accurate in detecting "Child Abuse."

In Fig. 5, the primary difference is the model's sensitivity to "Illegal Activity." Under these circumstances, the trade-off shows that a 7% gain in accuracy for the "Illegal Activity" category comes at the expense of a 2% decrease in overall accuracy compared to the general calibration approach.

For Fig. 6, the calibration shifts focus between "Child Abuse" and "Political Campaigning." Here, the model calibrated on the news shows a 10% increase in accuracy for "Child Abuse" and a 2% increase for "Political Campaigning" compared to the non-calibrated baseline. This balanced improvement across multiple

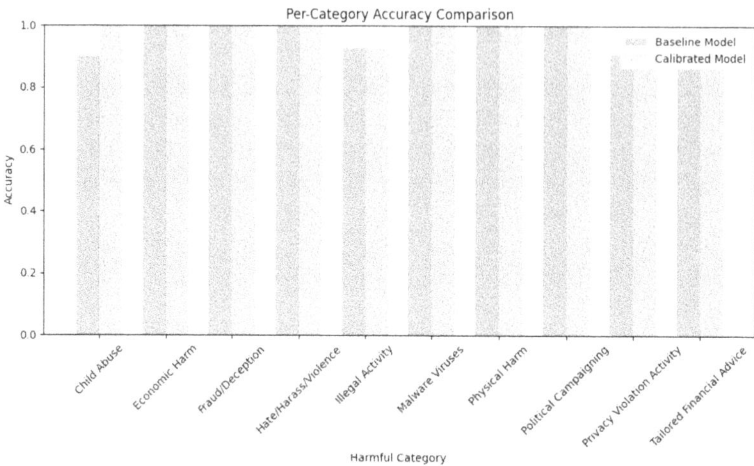

Fig. 4. March 6th News: Model Performance Across Categories.

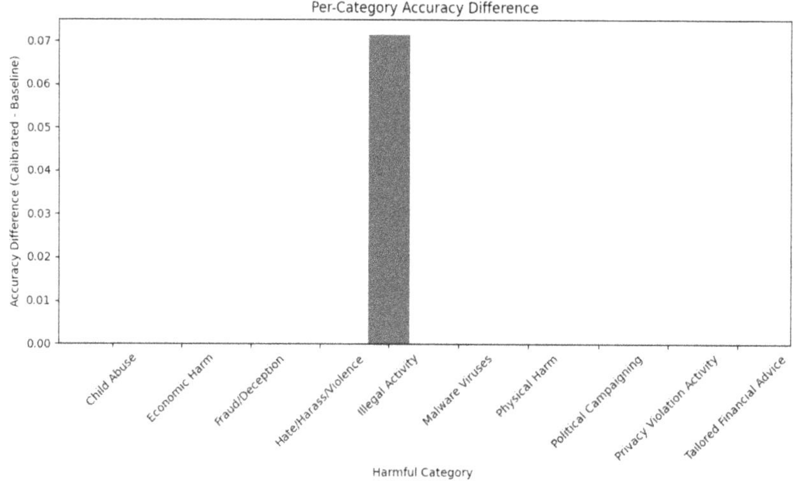

Fig. 5. March 2nd Calibration Performance.

categories demonstrates that news-driven calibration can enhance performance in targeted areas, even if absolute accuracy is slightly compromised relative to a more generalized calibration strategy.

6.1 Validity

There are two central concerns regarding news-based calibration. The first is the time window: using only daily news might introduce excessive variability into the calibration process. While this variability could be costly—especially

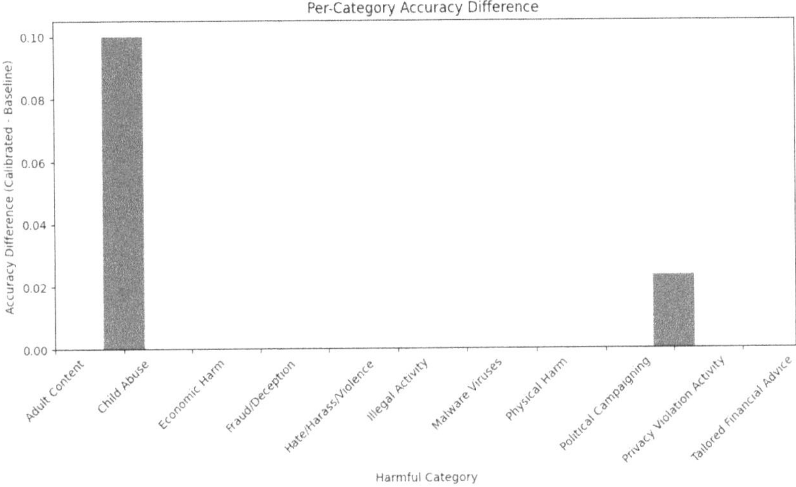

Fig. 6. March 6th Calibration Performance.

for calibrating temperature—it also ensures that calibration aligns closely with the current societal context and needs.

For instance, the news on March 2nd was predominantly focused on the conflict between Trump and Zelensky, raising questions about the model's response to embedding world leaders' names. In contrast, the March 6th news emphasized bans on smacking children, Zelensky's conciliatory letter to Trump, and discussions on Hamas. Thus the model focused its calibration on child abuse and politics as particularly salient topics of the news cycle.

Table 2 presents the initial weighting determined by the news feed. Notably, the model appears less responsive to shifts in privacy, despite its prevalence, while

Table 2. Comparison of category distributions from March 2nd and March 6th.

Category	March 2nd	March 6th
Privacy Violation Activity	0.2647	0.3000
Tailored Financial Advice	0.1765	0.2333
Political Campaigning	0.1765	0.1667
Illegal Activity	0.1471	0.1333
Malware Viruses	0.0588	0.0333
Hate/Harass/Violence	0.0588	–
Child Abuse	0.0588	0.0667
Physical Harm	0.0294	0.0333
Fraud/Deception	0.0294	–
Adult Content	–	0.0333

changes in categories such as physical harm and fraud are more noticeable. This predisposition might be a potential weakness if the calibration behavior shifts significantly across categories.

A secondary consideration is the source of calibration data. This work uses an RSS feed from the BBC, chosen for its relatively balanced perspective compared to other sources. However, the focus is UK-centric. For deployment, a more general news source or aggregation strategy may be needed.

7 Conclusion

In this work, calibration is used to fortify Large Language Models. The first question is whether calibrated models are more performant than non-calibrated models when using societal risk to inform prompt injection. The second is whether it is more effective to observe harm more generally or to use specific categories for calibration. When calibrating with both strategies, the calibrated performance is better at detecting prompt injection than the baseline model. The baseline model is expected to perform at 94% accuracy with the calibrated models performing at 95.7% and 97.4% accuracy. When observing the two calibration strategies, using the general approach to harm gives better absolute performance. However, that is not to say the second approach does not have merits. When calibrating on specific categories, the categorical accuracy can see up to a 10% increase in categorical specific accuracy. It is more of a normative decision to calibrate on specific categories with using news feeds as a grounding for which categories are the most important at present.

It seems advisable, though, that the first approach using the general risk calibration would be more useful to organizations that operate in larger operational contexts. If an organization has a model operating in a more specialized context or in a specific region, the news calibration could be more tailored to make the differences in accuracy more meaningful. It would help to justify choosing a less accurate calibration strategy to promote a more aligned calibration that could fit the needs of the end-users more strongly.

Future work should evaluate the approach across additional datasets and explore multi-source news aggregation strategies to improve robustness.

References

1. Anthropic: CCAI public comparison 2023. Technical report, Anthropic (2023). https://www-cdn.anthropic.com/65408ee2b9c99abe53e432f300e7f43ef69fb6e4/CCAI_public_comparison_2023.pdf
2. Bai, Y., et al.: Constitutional AI: Harmlessness from AI feedback. arXiv preprint arXiv:2212.08073 (2022). https://arxiv.org/abs/2212.08073
3. Bhardwaj, R., Anh, D.D., Poria, S.: Language models are homer Simpson! Safety re-alignment of fine-tuned language models through task arithmetic (2024). https://arxiv.org/abs/2402.11746
4. Chen, C., Shu, K.: Can LLM-generated misinformation be detected? (2024). https://arxiv.org/abs/2309.13788

5. Chen, Z., et al.: Iteralign: iterative constitutional alignment of large language models. arXiv preprint arXiv:2403.18341 (2024). https://arxiv.org/abs/2403.18341
6. deepset: prompt-injections: A dataset for prompt injection attacks (2023). https://huggingface.co/datasets/deepset/prompt-injections. Accessed 20 Jan 2025
7. Google Threat Intelligence Group: Adversarial misuse of generative AI. Technical report, Google (2025). https://blog.google/innovation-and-ai/technology/safety-security/google-threat-intelligence-group-report-ai-november-2025/
8. He, P., Liu, X., Gao, J., Chen, W.: DeBERTa: decoding-enhanced BERT with disentangled attention (2021). https://arxiv.org/abs/2006.03654
9. Lewis, M., et al.: BART: denoising sequence-to-sequence pre-training for natural language generation, translation, and comprehension. CoRR abs/1910.13461 (2019). http://arxiv.org/abs/1910.13461
10. Marinelli, R.: risk_cal (2025). https://github.com/rymarinelli/risk_cal. Accessed 01 Apr 2025
11. Meta: Adversarial threat report, first quarter 2025. Technical report, Meta Platforms (2025). https://transparency.meta.com/integrity-reports-q1-2025
12. News API: News API (2025). https://newsapi.org/. Accessed 2 Mar 2025
13. OpenAI: Disrupting malicious uses of our models: February 2025 update (2025). https://cdn.openai.com/threat-intelligence-reports/disrupting-malicious-uses-of-our-models-february-2025-update.pdf. Accessed 2 Mar 2025
14. Qi, X., et al.: Fine-tuning aligned language models compromises safety, even when users do not intend to! (2023). https://arxiv.org/abs/2310.03693
15. Radivojevic, K., Clark, N., Brenner, P.: LLMs among us: generative AI participating in digital discourse. arXiv preprint arXiv:2402.07940v1 (2024)
16. Sentence-Transformers: sentence-transformers/all-minilm-l6-v2 (2025). https://huggingface.co/sentence-transformers/all-MiniLM-L6-v2. Accessed 2 Mar 2025
17. Shen, M., Das, S., Greenewald, K., Sattigeri, P., Wornell, G., Ghosh, S.: Thermometer: towards universal calibration for large language models (2024). https://arxiv.org/abs/2403.08819

AI Safety and Ethics

BEADS: Bias Evaluation Across Domains

Shaina Raza[1(✉)] ⓘ, Mizanur Rahman[2], and Michael R. Zhang[1,3]

[1] Vector Institute, 108 College St, Toronto, ON M5G 0C6, Canada
`shaina.raza@torontomu.ca`
[2] York University, 4700 Keele St, North York, ON M3J 1P3, Canada
[3] University of Toronto, 27 King's College Cir, Toronto, ON M5S 1A1, Canada

Abstract. Recent advances in large language models (LLMs) have substantially improved natural language processing (NLP) applications. However, these models often inherit and amplify biases present in their training data. Although several datasets exist for bias detection, most are limited to one or two NLP tasks, typically classification or evaluation and do not provide broad coverage across diverse task settings. To address this gap, we introduce the **Bias Evaluations Across Domains (BEADs)** dataset, designed to support a wide range of NLP tasks, including text classification, token classification, bias quantification, and benign language generation. A key contribution of this work is a gold-standard annotation scheme that supports both evaluation and supervised training of language models. Experiments on state-of-the-art models reveal some gaps: some models exhibit systematic bias toward specific demographics, while others apply safety guardrails more strictly or inconsistently across groups. Overall, these results highlight persistent shortcomings in current models and underscore the need for comprehensive bias evaluation. The benchmark will be made publicly available for research (https://huggingface.co/datasets/shainar/BEAD).

Keywords: bias · large language models · evaluations · prompts

1 Introduction

Large Language Models (LLMs), such as GPT-4, Llama, Mistral, and Claude, represent advancements in natural language processing (NLP), demonstrating strong performance across tasks such as classification and text generation [38]. Despite ongoing efforts to prompt-tune or fine-tune these models for safety and fairness, they continue to exhibit biases inherited from their training data. In this work, we define *bias* through the lens of social science and computational linguistics [25], encompassing language that is discriminatory, offensive, hateful, or harmful toward specific social groups. Such biases may manifest explicitly through phrasing or implicitly through tone, framing, or word choice. Crucially, this study is designed to operationalize this definition across multiple tasks and domains, enabling holistic evaluation of bias in real-world settings.

Prior works have introduced several influential benchmarks, including Jigsaw [2], HolisticBias [31], BOLD [7], StereoSet [21], RealToxicityPrompts [11],

© The Author(s), under exclusive license to Springer Nature Switzerland AG 2027
E. Cabrio and E. Monteiro (Eds.): NLDB 2026, LNCS 16696, pp. 123–138, 2027.
https://doi.org/10.1007/978-3-032-29532-3_10

and RedditBias [3], which have advanced the evaluation of toxicity and bias in language models [9]. However, most of these datasets target specific tasks, such as bias identification or toxicity classification, or focus on a limited set of social dimensions, such as gender or race, leaving a gap for multi-task evaluation.

To address this gap, we introduce **BEADs** (**B**ias **E**valuations **A**cross **D**omains), a multi-domain dataset designed to support a broad range of NLP tasks relevant to fairness, safety, and accountability. **BEADs** includes diverse data and rich annotations for: (i) **classification tasks**, with labels for bias, toxicity, and sentiment; (ii) **token classification**, including bias entity recognition; (iii) **aspect categorization**, such as identifying the underlying political ideology or demographic group referenced in the text; (iv) **benign language generation**, enabling prompt-based debiasing and neutral rewriting; and (v) **bias quantification**, supporting demographic-sensitive evaluation. Table 1 presents a comparison of related bias datasets alongside **BEADs**. Our main contributions are:

1. We introduce **BEADs**, a comprehensive dataset collected from both social and news media, supporting multiple tasks including bias identification, benign language generation, and demographic-based bias evaluation.
2. We employ GPT-4 for initial data labeling and refine the annotations through expert review. This hybrid approach ensures both scalability and reliability through domain expert verification.
3. We evaluate a range of models on **BEADs**, spanning encoder-only models (e.g., BERT-based) and decoder-only instruction-tuned LLMs (e.g., Llama, Mistral), across classification, entity recognition, and debiasing tasks.

Our empirical results reveal several key findings. First, smaller encoder-only models consistently outperform larger autoregressive decoder-only models on classification tasks, suggesting they are both more cost-effective and well-suited for production deployment. However, smaller models exhibit higher rates of bias toward certain demographic groups compared to LLMs, which often benefit from more robust safety guardrails. Finally, fine-tuning on **BEADs** for classification improves detection performance and supervised fine-tuning on benign language generation significantly reduces bias and toxicity compared to prompting alone.

2   Literature Review

Bias, Toxicity, and Sentiment Classification. The deployment of LLMs has intensified the need for comprehensive benchmarks addressing bias [33], toxicity [5], and sentiment [19,34]. Datasets such as Jigsaw [2], HolisticBias [31], and others have advanced fairness and safety evaluation, yet they remain limited in task coverage and the breadth of social dimensions.

Bias Entity Extraction. Named Entity Recognition (NER) offers an underexplored avenue for bias identification in NLP [23]. Prior work shows NER models exhibit demographic disparities, such as recognizing fewer female names as

PERSON entities [20], while counterfactual data augmentation has been used to mitigate gender bias in embeddings [18]. Frameworks such as NERD [26] and entity debiasing for fake news detection [40] further highlight the utility of entity-level analysis. Despite these efforts, dedicated datasets for bias-aware named entity extraction remain scarce.

Bias Quantification Across Demographics. Several datasets probe demographic biases through targeted linguistic tasks. WinoGender [27] and WinoBias [37] examine gender bias via coreference resolution, while RedditBias [3] focus on racial and religious hate speech. Broader resources including BBQ [22], BOLD [7], and HolisticBias [31] extend coverage to profession, race, and gender. Thus there is need to convert conventional NLP datasets into prompt templates to probe LLM sensitivity across these dimensions.

Benign Language Generation and Debiasing. Bias mitigation strategies span embedding-space interventions [16], prompt-based debiasing [30], and RLHF-based alignment, the de facto final training stage for models such as GPT-4 and Claude [39]. Evaluation datasets including RedditBias [3], WinoBias [37], and RealToxicityPrompts [11] support these efforts. However, there is need for a dataset specifically curated for instruction fine-tuning toward bias reduction.

To our knowledge, **BEADs** is the first benchmark that multi-task annotations spanning classification, entity extraction, demographic probing, and generation-providing a unified resource that bridges the gaps identified across these research directions.

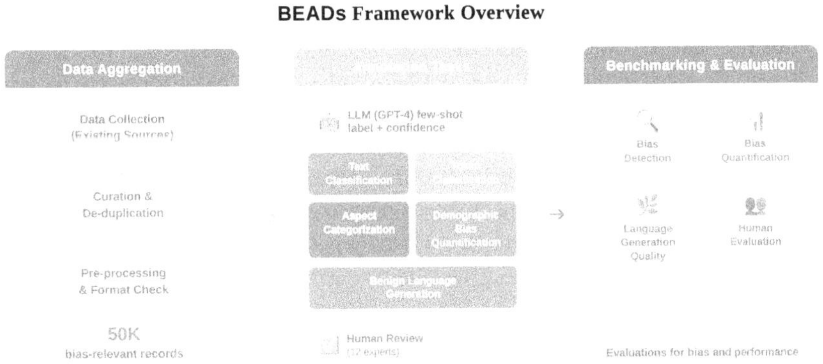

BEADs Framework Overview

Fig. 1. BEADs Framework: Data Aggregation, Annotation, and Evaluation.

3   BEADs: Dataset and Benchmark Design

This work addresses the problem of identifying and mitigating various forms of bias in text, particularly prejudice or unfair assumptions related to gender, race, religion, and other demographic attributes. Figure 1 outlines the **BEADs** framework.

Table 1. Composition of BEADs.

Dataset	Primary Bias Focus	Retained
MBIC [32]	Political	1,500
Hyperpartisan [14]	Political	4,000
Toxic Comments [2]	Hate speech	12,000
Jigsaw Unintended Bias [1]	Hate speech	10,000
Ageism [8]	Body image & ability	8,000
Multi-dimensional News [10]	Political	1,500
Social Biases [29]	Various social	8,000
Google News RSS	Occ., tech., env.	5,000
Total		**50,000**

3.1 Dataset Construction

To ensure broad coverage of bias types, we extracted raw text (without labels) from eight publicly available datasets spanning bias, toxicity, and related dimensions (Table 1), supplemented with news articles collected via the Google News RSS feed (January-May 2024). All data underwent de-duplication, noise filtering, and length checks, yielding a final curated set of 50,000 records.

3.2 Annotation Process

We adopt a hybrid annotation strategy combining automated labeling with expert human review. GPT-4 was used for initial annotation, given its strong performance in recent large-scale labeling studies [15]. Each task was prompted using a *few-shot* setup with two to three task-specific examples. GPT-4 produced provisional labels for: **text classification**: bias, toxicity, and sentiment; (1) **token classification**: biased phrases and named entities; (2) **aspect categorization**: bias dimensions such as political or demographic; (3) **demographic identification**: identity tags for fairness probing; and (4) **language generation**: benign rewrites of biased content. To ensure annotation quality, we assembled a 12-member domain experts panel (Appendix A) comprising linguists, social scientists, and data scientists who reviewed the AI-generated labels. All GPT-4-generated labels underwent human review following a three-stage protocol: (1) verification of GPT-4 labels against task guidelines; (2) consensus-based adjudication for ambiguous or flagged cases; and (3) re-annotation of instances where model output diverged from human interpretation. This iterative process ensured high-quality, consistent gold-standard annotations across all tasks.

3.3 Evaluation Suite

We provide a comprehensive benchmark comprising the curated dataset, evaluation scripts, and training pipelines for both small language models (e.g., BERT,

RoBERTa) and open-source LLMs (e.g., Llama, Mistral). The suite supports reproducible evaluation across all tasks, including text classification, token classification, bias quantification, and benign language generation. All code, data splits, and model configurations are publicly released to facilitate community adoption and extension.

4 Results

4.1 Benchmarking Setup

All models were trained on a multi-GPU cluster with two NVIDIA A100 and four A40 GPUs (32 GB RAM). We evaluate encoder-only models (DistilBERT, BERT, RoBERTa) and decoder-only LLMs (Mistral-7B-Instruct-v0.2, Llama2-7B-chat). Both families are used for classification; only LLMs for generation. All LLMs are assessed under fine-tuned and few-shot settings. Supervised tasks (text and token classification) use a consistent 80/20 traintest split, while language generation and bias quantification are evaluated using task-specific setups. LLMs are fine-tuned with QLoRA [6] (4-bit, rank $= 64$, $\alpha = 16$, dropout $= 0.2$); encoder models use standard fine-tuning with larger batches. For out-of-distribution evaluation, we use MBIB [32] (433k records), Toxigen [12] ($\sim$9k samples), and the Financial News Polar Sentiment dataset (4,840 sentences). Classification is evaluated via precision, recall, and accuracy (threshold 0.5 for encoders; calibrated for LLMs per [13]). Bias quantification uses *Bias Rate*, the proportion of identity-sensitive completions flagged as biased. Language generation reports bias and toxicity ($\downarrow$), and knowledge retention, faithfulness, and answer relevancy ($\uparrow$) via GPT-4-based DeepEval [4]. Full hyperparameters and metrics definitions are in Appendix B.

4.2 Performance Evaluation

Text Classification for Bias, Toxicity, and Sentiment. We evaluated various language models on their ability to classify text into categories of bias, toxicity, and sentiment. Each dataset entry follows the format *text, label,* with examples such as: "The movie was surprisingly good" (Positive), "Women are less capable in STEM fields compared to men" (Biased), and "You are worthless and nobody cares about you" (Toxic). The models (small language models and LLMs) were evaluated under both fine-tuned and few-shot settings. To ensure consistency, we used standard metrics like precision, recall, and accuracy.

Table 2 illustrates that fine-tuned BERT-like models consistently outperformed autoregressive LLMs for bias classification, achieving approximately 85% accuracy. We also evaluate the performance of these models on out-of-distribution datasets, including MBIB [32,36] for bias classification, Toxigen [12] for toxicity classification, and the Financial News Polar Sentiment dataset for sentiment analysis, as shown in Appendix Fig. 2. The results confirm that these findings show that small models perform better and that our dataset is quite suitable for fine-tuning and evaluation tasks.

Table 2. Classification metrics (Accuracy, Precision, Recall) across three tasks: Bias, Toxicity, and Sentiment. Higher values are better and highlighted in **bold**. FS stands for few-shot (2) prompting and FT stands for fine-tuning.

Bias Classification

Model	Accuracy	Precision (0/1)	Recall (0/1)
DistilBERT-base (FT)	**0.85**	0.81/**0.90**	**0.91**/0.79
BERT-large (FT)	**0.85**	**0.83**/0.87	0.88/0.81
RoBERTa-large (FT)	0.84	**0.83**/0.84	0.84/**0.83**
Llama2-7B (FS)	0.61	0.59/0.65	0.76/0.45
Llama2-7B (FT)	0.77	0.75/0.80	0.82/0.72
Mistral-7B-v0.2 (FS)	0.53	0.56/0.48	0.66/0.38
Mistral-7B-v0.2 (FT)	0.79	0.79/0.78	0.80/0.77

Toxicity Classification

Model	Accuracy	Precision (0/1)	Recall (0/1)
DistilBERT-base (FT)	0.84	0.84/**0.84**	**0.84**/0.84
BERT-large (FT)	**0.85**	0.85/**0.84**	**0.84**/0.85
RoBERTa-large (FT)	**0.85**	**0.87**/0.82	0.81/**0.88**
Llama2-7B (FS)	0.59	0.55/0.60	0.70/0.40
Llama2-7B (FT)	0.75	0.73/0.78	0.80/0.70
Mistral-7B-v0.2 (FS)	0.52	0.50/0.45	0.60/0.35
Mistral-7B-v0.2 (FT)	0.77	0.76/0.77	0.78/0.75

Sentiment Classification

Model	Accuracy	Precision (0/1/2)	Recall (0/1/2)
DistilBERT-base (FT)	**0.87**	**0.96**/0.79/**0.88**	0.84/**0.94**/0.83
BERT-large (FT)	**0.87**	0.85/**0.90**/0.87	**0.89**/0.86/**0.86**
RoBERTa-large (FT)	0.81	0.92/0.72/0.84	0.83/0.89/0.72
Llama2-7B (FS)	0.58	0.50/0.55/0.55	0.65/0.40/0.45
Llama2-7B (FT)	0.74	0.70/0.75/0.75	0.80/0.65/0.70
Mistral-7B-v0.2 (FS)	0.50	0.45/0.40/0.45	0.55/0.30/0.35
Mistral-7B-v0.2 (FT)	0.75	0.73/0.70/0.73	0.77/0.70/0.75

4.3 Token Classification Task

Token classification, inspired by named entity recognition (NER) [23], involves identifying words or phrases in text as either "Biased" or "Non-Biased". Dataset entries are structured as: *sentence, array of biased labeled tokens* (e.g., "Women are overreacting bossy managers.", ['overreacting', 'bossy managers']). For this task, we fine-tuned smaller models such as BiLSTM-CRF [17], BERT-like models, and LLMs, including Llama2-7B-chat and Mistral-7B-instruct-v0.2. The models were evaluated on their ability to classify tokens as 'Bias' or 'O' (outside bias). We formatted the data following CoNLL-2003 standards [28] for NER.

The standard 'B-BIAS' and 'I-BIAS' tags were merged into 'Bias', while the 'O' tag was retained as 'Non-Bias' for evaluation purposes.

Table 3. Token Classification Evaluation: Metrics include accuracy, recall, and precision for 'Non-Bias' (0) and 'Bias' (1) entities. Higher ($\uparrow$) values indicate better performance and are highlighted in **bold**.

Model	Accuracy	Recall (0/1)	Precision (0/1)
DistilBERT-base (FT)	0.80	0.67/0.84	0.62/0.88
BERT-large (FT)	0.81	0.61/0.87	0.65/0.85
RoBERTa-large (FT)	**0.82**	**0.72/0.89**	**0.70/0.89**
BiLSTM-CRF (FT)	0.60	0.42/0.45	0.42/0.55
Llama2-7B (FS)	0.74	0.61/0.73	0.57/0.76
Llama2-7B (FT)	0.76	0.64/0.76	0.60/0.79
Mistral-7B-v0.2 (FS)	0.78	0.62/0.78	0.63/0.81
Mistral-7B-v0.2 (FT)	0.80	0.65/0.80	0.67/0.83

Table 3 highlights that smaller fine-tuned BERT-like models achieved superior performance across all metrics, effectively classifying both 'Non-Bias' and 'Bias' tokens. RoBERTa-large, in particular, emerged as the best-performing model, with the highest accuracy, precision, and recall. Few-shot models, such as Llama2-7B-chat and Mistral-7B-Instruct-v0.2, demonstrated moderate performance, with fine-tuning significantly improving their token classification capabilities. Notably, fine-tuned LLMs consistently outperformed their few-shot counterparts. These findings align with trends observed in text classification task also where smaller models often outperform larger LLMs.

4.4   Bias Quantification on Demographics

Bias in Token Prediction. This task evaluates the ability of a LLM to predict tokens that are demographic identifiers, such as gender, race, and religion in sentences. The intuition is that the model's choices in replacing placeholders like GENDER, RACE, and RELIGION reveal potential biases. The test set includes both biased and neutral examples, and the task measures the rate at which the LLM associates certain demographics with biased or neutral content.

The sentences are formatted with placeholders for demographic indicators, structured as *text with identity mention*. For example, if we have a sentence template like "The {identity mention} manager is irritatingly bossy", labeled as Bias, and the LLM consistently fills it with "The female manager is irritatingly bossy", this indicates a bias tendency towards such identity mentions.

We evaluated both smaller BERT-like models and autoregressive LLMs by testing their ability to fill in placeholders. Their performance was assessed based on Bias Rate metric that is defined as the proportion of model completions identified as biased when prompted with identity-sensitive templates. The comparison with ground truth labels is presented in Table 4.

Table 4. Bias Rate for Identity Mentions Across Different Models. Lower bias rate ($\downarrow$) is desirable. Models exacerbating highest bias towards a demographic are highlighted in red.

Identity Mention	Original	DistilBERT	BERT	RoBERTa	Mistral-7B-v0.2
Ethnicity Black	66.7%	46.4%	53.8%	43.2%	50.0%
Ethnicity White	57.1%	77.8%	57.1%	54.5%	50.0%
Religion Christian	27.6%	33.3%	37.7%	51.1%	26.3%
Religion Jewish	50.0%	63.3%	63.2%	59.6%	50.0%
Religion Muslim	40.0%	56.6%	57.8%	55.7%	50.0%
Gender Female	57.7%	59.7%	49.2%	57.1%	56.4%
Gender Male	46.0%	52.7%	55.3%	53.3%	43.0%

Table 4 highlights how various models influence demographic representation, with smaller models like DistilBERT, BERT, and RoBERTa exacerbating biases when filling in demographic placeholders, as seen with the reduced neutrality rates for categories like "ethnicity white" and "religion christian". Conversely, Mistral-7B-Instruct-v0.2 tends to maintain or improve neutrality rates across demographics, which shows a more balanced approach. Llama2-7B-chat results were excluded due to its refusal to fill placeholders in biased sentences, which resulted in sparse results.

4.5 Language Generation Task

This task generates neutral or benign versions of biased texts, the goal is to remove bias in language while retaining knowledge or context of the original sentence. Each sentence pair is presented as *original sentence, benign variation*. For example, Original Sentence: "She lacks the aggressive approach needed for effective leadership in this role", Benign Sentence: "The candidate's leadership style does not align with the assertive approach required for this role". We evaluated the effectiveness of different LLMs in mitigating bias through language generation using this dataset portion. Llama2-7B-chat and Mistral-7B-instruct-v0.2 are used in few-shot settings, and also fine-tuned. Effectiveness is measured using LLM based metrics such as bias, toxicity, content retention, faithfulness, and answer relevancy.

Table 5 shows that fine-tuning LLMs in semi-supervised manner performs better in debiasing (shown with lower bias and toxicity scores) and maintain knowledge (with higher knowledge retention, faithfulness and relevancy scores). The fine-tuning results are better than few-shot (2) prompting. The findings also indicate that LLMs fine-tuned on benign texts can effectively serve as debiasing agents, so we can have their better overall utility.

5   Discussion

Empirical Analysis. Our evaluations of prompt-tuned and fine-tuned language models reveal several findings. In particular, three patterns emerge: (1) encoder models excel at classification but propagate more demographic bias in generative probing; (2) LLM safety guardrails help with bias mitigation but can manifest as over-refusal or inconsistent sensitivity across groups; and (3) fine-tuning on BEADs consistently improves both task performance and fairness metrics over prompting alone, underscoring the dataset's utility as a training resource beyond evaluation.

Table 5. Language generation evaluation across Llama2-7B-chat and Mistral-7B-Instruct-v0.2. Lower bias and toxicity ($\downarrow$) are better; higher KR, Faith., and Rel. ($\uparrow$) are better. GT = ground truth.

Text	Bias$\downarrow$	Toxicity$\downarrow$	KR$\uparrow$	Faith.$\uparrow$	Rel.$\uparrow$
Pre-Debiasing Scores					
Original sentence	31.87%	39.95%	N/A	N/A	N/A
Debiased sentence (GT)	16.98%	15.20%	83.41%	78.15%	88.76%
Post-Debiasing Scores					
Llama2-7B (Few-shot)	19.10%	22.89%	82.04%	76.87%	85.17%
Llama2-7B (Fine-tuned)	9.90%	9.81%	81.00%	77.89%	85.95%
Mistral-7B (Few-shot)	12.35%	9.27%	81.76%	76.58%	87.10%
Mistral-7B (Fine-tuned)	**7.21%**	**5.33%**	**83.08%**	**80.45%**	**89.02%**

Benchmark Utility. BEADs offers three practical advantages over existing resources. First, its multi-task design enables end-to-end bias evaluation, from detection through classification to mitigation via benign rewriting, within a single unified dataset, eliminating the need to assemble disjoint benchmarks. Second, the paired biased-benign annotations provide ready-to-use supervised training data for debiasing, as evidenced by fine-tuned models achieving lower bias and toxicity than even human-curated ground truth rewrites. Third, the demographic annotations across six identity dimensions enable granular fairness auditing, revealing blind spots such as inconsistent guardrail behavior across ethnic and religious groups that aggregate metrics would obscure.

5.1   Limitations

The benchmark and study has some limitations. First, bias is inherently contextual and subjective. Rather than resolving these complexities, our approach offers empirical methods for detecting patterns of imbalance. Second, our evaluation used relatively straightforward prompting strategies. While sufficient for initial benchmarking, adversarial or ambiguous prompts (e.g., [35]) could better uncover hidden biases and assess model robustness. Third, many instruction-tuned models do not expose log-probabilities, limiting our ability to compute likelihood-based metrics and restricting evaluation to generative outputs. Also due to computational constraints, we adopted QLoRA for efficient fine-tuning rather than full-parameter updates. While this enabled broader model coverage, it may introduce slight behavioral deviations compared to full fine-tuning. As with any dataset highlighting model vulnerabilities, there is a risk of malicious misuse. We urge developers to conduct independent audits and apply appropriate safeguards, including careful prompt design and robust tuning [24], to prevent unintended harms.

6   Conclusion

We presented BEADs, a multi-task dataset for bias detection, covering text classification, token classification, bias quantification, and benign language generation across 50,000 gold-standard records. Our hybrid annotation pipeline combining GPT-4 labeling with expert review ensures both scalability and reliability. Benchmarking reveals that encoder-only models outperform LLMs on classification but exhibit higher demographic bias in generative probing, while LLMs benefit from safety alignment yet apply guardrails inconsistently across groups. Crucially, fine-tuning on BEADs reduces bias and toxicity while preserving semantic fidelity, demonstrating its value as both an evaluation benchmark and a training resource. Future work will expand BEADs with multilingual coverage, emotional tone labels, and adversarial probing to address current domain and language gaps. We release all data, code, and evaluation scripts to support the community in building more equitable NLP systems.

Acknowledgements. We extend our gratitude to the Province of Ontario, the Government of Canada through CIFAR, and the corporate sponsors of the Vector Institute for their generous support and provision of resources essential for this research. Further details on our sponsors can be found at www.vectorinstitute.ai/#partners. We also acknowledge our expert review team and everyone involved in the data review process.

Declarations.
– Funding: Resources used in this study are supported by Vector Institute.

  – Conflict of interest/Competing interests: The authors declare no conflicting interests. The authors have no relevant financial or non-financial competing interests to disclose.

  – Ethics approval and consent to participate: This research did not involve human participants, animal subjects, or personally identifiable data, and therefore did not require formal ethical approval. All data used in this study were publicly available, ensuring compliance with ethical guidelines and data privacy standards.

– Consent for publication: Yes

– Data availability: The data is available at https://huggingface.co/datasets/shainar/BEAD.

Appendix A   Annotation Guidelines

We define *bias* as any unfair preference or prejudice toward individuals or groups based on characteristics such as age, gender, ethnicity, religion, or socioeconomic status. A 12-member expert panel reviewed all GPT-4-generated labels. Calibration sessions and regular consensus meetings ensured consistent application of guidelines. Each instance was reviewed along the following dimensions: **bias identification** (with severity: slight/moderate/severe); **demographic aspects** (gender, ethnicity, religion, age, socioeconomic status); **toxicity and sentiment**; **benign language generation** (neutral, respectful rewrites); and **discrepancy resolution** via consensus meetings. In cases of ambiguity, disagreements were resolved through majority consensus or escalation to senior annotators.

Appendix B   Training Details

All encoder-only models (DistilBERT, BERT, RoBERTa) were fine-tuned with AdamW (lr: 1e−5–5e−5, batch size: 16–32, up to 20 epochs with early stopping, weight decay: 0.01). A default classification threshold of 0.5 was applied. BiLSTM-CRF used SGD (lr: 1e−3, batch size: 20). All LLMs (Llama2-7B-chat, Mistral-7B-Instruct-v0.2) were fine-tuned using QLoRA [6] and evaluated under both fine tuned and few-shot (2 examples per class) settings. Language generation models were fine-tuned on 8.3k pairs with a 500-instance test set.

For bias quantification, BERT-style models use masked language modeling to predict demographic placeholders (e.g., "[GENDER] is the CEO"), while LLMs are prompted to fill identity placeholders. The *Bias Rate* measures the proportion of completions aligning with biased labels. We use two families of metrics: **LLM-based** metrics computed via GPT-4o through DeepEval [4], and **statistical** metrics from standard classification evaluation. GPT-4o classifies each generated output to compute the following:

– **Bias** ($\downarrow$) = biased outputs/total outputs.
– **Toxicity** ($\downarrow$) = toxic outputs/total outputs.
– **Knowledge Retention** ($\uparrow$) = outputs preserving factual content/total outputs.
– **Faithfulness** ($\uparrow$) = truthful claims/total claims in generated text.
– **Answer Relevancy** ($\uparrow$) = relevant statements/total statements in generated text.

Precision, recall, and accuracy are computed using standard formulas with a 0.5 threshold for encoder models and calibrated thresholds for LLMs. **Bias Rate** is the proportion of identity-sensitive completions flagged as biased. **Consistency** measures label stability across paraphrased variants. **Coverage** is the proportion of inputs receiving a valid, non-null prediction.

Appendix C   Detailed Results

See Table 6.

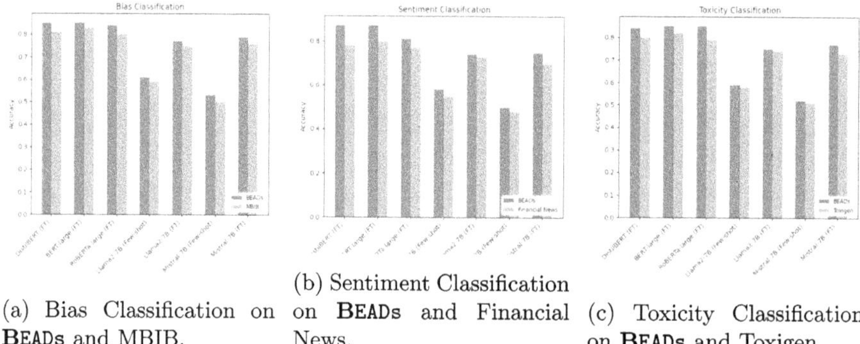

(a) Bias Classification on **BEADs** and MBIB.

(b) Sentiment Classification on **BEADs** and Financial News.

(c) Toxicity Classification on **BEADs** and Toxigen.

Fig. 2. Comparison of classification accuracy for Bias, Sentiment, and Toxicity tasks across models and datasets on in-distribution (**BEADs**) and out-of-distribution datasets (MBIB, Financial News, Toxigen).

Aspects of Bias

`Demographic Biases`: Includes ageism, gender discrimination, race/ethnicity, sexual orientation, religion, gender identity, Islamophobia, xenophobia, and homophobia. `Socio-Economic and Educational Biases`: Covers socioeconomic status, education, elitism, and employment status. `Geographical and Environmental Biases`: Focuses on geographical diversity, climate change issues, urban-rural divides, and international perspectives. `Health, Ability, and Body Image Biases`: Addresses disability/ableism, mental health issues, physical and mental disabilities, and body image/beauty standards. `Occupational and Lifestyle Biases`: Examines biases related to occupation, hobbies/music preferences, family structure, professional sectors, and lifestyle choices. `Cognitive and Psychological Biases`: Includes confirmation bias, stereotypes, framing, news media bias, and perception/representation biases. `Hate Speech and Toxicity`: Focuses on hate speech toxicity, online harassment, and discriminatory language. `Political and Ideological Biases`: Discusses partisan biases and ideological framing. `Technological and Digital Biases`: Considers platform biases, access/digital divides, and algorithmic biases.

Table 6. This table demonstrates the debiasing process where biased language is transformed into more neutral, inclusive language. Each entry carefully maintains the original context and meaning while adjusting text length to ensure clarity and comprehensiveness.

Biased Text	Benign Variation
The managers were all men and displayed strong leadership.	The managers displayed strong leadership.
She was too emotional during the meeting, which was unprofessional.	She expressed her concerns passionately during the meeting.
The inner city areas are plagued with crime and poverty.	The urban areas face significant economic challenges.
He is a disabled person who needs a lot of help.	He is a person with disabilities, requiring some assistance.
Immigrants from Mexico are usually uneducated.	Many immigrants, including those from Mexico, have diverse educational backgrounds.

We have secured the necessary permissions and appropriately cited the sources utilized for our research. Our work is published under the Creative Commons license available at https://creativecommons.org/licenses/by-nc/4.0/.

References

1. Adams, C., Borkan, D., Sorensen, J., Dixon, L., Vasserman, L., Thain, N.: Jigsaw unintended bias in toxicity classification (2019). https://kaggle.com/competitions/jigsaw-unintended-bias-in-toxicity-classification
2. Adams, C., et al.. Toxic comment classification challenge (2017). https://kaggle.com/competitions/jigsaw-toxic-comment-classification-challenge
3. Barikeri, S., Lauscher, A., Vulić, I., Glavaš, G.: RedditBias: a real-world resource for bias evaluation and debiasing of conversational language models. In: Zong, C., Xia, F., Li, W., Navigli, R. (eds.) Proceedings of the 59th Annual Meeting of the Association for Computational Linguistics and the 11th International Joint Conference on Natural Language Processing (Volume 1: Long Papers), pp. 1941–1955. Association for Computational Linguistics, Online (2021). https://doi.org/10.18653/v1/2021.acl-long.151, https://aclanthology.org/2021.acl-long.151
4. Confident AI: Deepeval. GitHub repository (2024). https://github.com/confident-ai/deepeval
5. Deshpande, A., Murahari, V., Rajpurohit, T., Kalyan, A., Narasimhan, K.: Toxicity in ChatGPT: analyzing persona-assigned language models. arXiv preprint arXiv:2304.05335 (2023)
6. Dettmers, T., Pagnoni, A., Holtzman, A., Zettlemoyer, L.: QLoRA: Efficient Fine-tuning of Quantized LLMs (2023). https://doi.org/10.48550/arXiv.2305.14314, http://arxiv.org/abs/2305.14314, arXiv:2305.14314 [cs]
7. Dhamala, J., et al.: Bold: dataset and metrics for measuring biases in open-ended language generation. In: Proceedings of the 2021 ACM Conference on Fairness, Accountability, and Transparency, pp. 862–872 (2021)

8. Díaz, M., Johnson, I., Lazar, A., Piper, A.M., Gergle, D.: Addressing age-related bias in sentiment analysis. In: Proceedings of the 2018 CHI Conference on Human Factors in Computing Systems, pp. 1–14 (2018)

9. Esiobu, D., et al.: Robbie: robust bias evaluation of large generative language models. In: Proceedings of the 2023 Conference on Empirical Methods in Natural Language Processing, pp. 3764–3814 (2023)

10. Färber, M., Burkard, V., Jatowt, A., Lim, S.: A multidimensional dataset based on crowdsourcing for analyzing and detecting news bias. In: Proceedings of the 29th ACM International Conference on Information and Knowledge Management, pp. 3007–3014 (2020)

11. Gehman, S., Gururangan, S., Sap, M., Choi, Y., Smith, N.A.: Realtoxicityprompts: evaluating neural toxic degeneration in language models. arXiv preprint arXiv:2009.11462 (2020)

12. Hartvigsen, T., Gabriel, S., Palangi, H., Sap, M., Ray, D., Kamar, E.: ToxiGen: a large-scale machine-generated dataset for adversarial and implicit hate speech detection. In: Proceedings of the 60th Annual Meeting of the Association for Computational Linguistics (Volume 1: Long Papers), pp. 3309–3326. Association for Computational Linguistics, Dublin, Ireland (2022). https://doi.org/10.18653/v1/2022.acl-long.234, https://aclanthology.org/2022.acl-long.234

13. Inan, H., et al.: Llama guard: LLM-based input-output safeguard for human-AI conversations, arXiv preprint arXiv:2312.06674 (2023)

14. Kiesel, J., et al.: SemEval-2019 task 4: hyperpartisan news detection. In: Proceedings of the 13th International Workshop on Semantic Evaluation, pp. 829–839. Association for Computational Linguistics, Minneapolis, Minnesota, USA (2019). https://doi.org/10.18653/v1/S19-2145, https://aclanthology.org/S19-2145

15. Kim, H., Mitra, K., Chen, R.L., Rahman, S., Zhang, D.: Meganno+: a human-LLM collaborative annotation system. arXiv preprint arXiv:2402.18050 (2024)

16. Liang, P.P., Li, I.M., Zheng, E., Lim, Y.C., Salakhutdinov, R., Morency, L.P.: Towards debiasing sentence representations. arXiv preprint arXiv:2007.08100 (2020)

17. Luo, L., et al.: An attention-based BiLSTM-CRF approach to document-level chemical named entity recognition. Bioinformatics **34**(8), 1381–1388 (2018)

18. Maudslay, R.H., Gonen, H., Cotterell, R., Teufel, S.: It's all in the name: mitigating gender bias with name-based counterfactual data substitution. arXiv preprint arXiv:1909.00871 (2019)

19. McAuley, J.J., Leskovec, J.: From amateurs to connoisseurs: modeling the evolution of user expertise through online reviews. In: Proceedings of the 22nd International Conference on World Wide Web, pp. 897–908 (2013)

20. Mishra, S., He, S., Belli, L.: Assessing demographic bias in named entity recognition. arXiv preprint arXiv:2008.03415 (2020)

21. Nadeem, M., Bethke, A., Reddy, S.: StereoSet: measuring stereotypical bias in pretrained language models. In: Zong, C., Xia, F., Li, W., Navigli, R. (eds.) Proceedings of the 59th Annual Meeting of the Association for Computational Linguistics and the 11th International Joint Conference on Natural Language Processing (Volume 1: Long Papers), pp. 5356–5371. Association for Computational Linguistics (2021). https://doi.org/10.18653/v1/2021.acl-long.416, https://aclanthology.org/2021.acl-long.416

22. Parrish, A., et al.: BBQ: a hand-built bias benchmark for question answering. arXiv preprint arXiv:2110.08193 (2021)

23. Raza, S., Garg, M., Reji, D.J., Bashir, S.R., Ding, C.: NBias: a natural language processing framework for bias identification in text. Expert Syst. Appl. **237**, 121542 (2024)
24. Raza, S., et al.: Vldbench: vision language models disinformation detection benchmark. arXiv preprint arXiv:2502.11361 (2025)
25. Recasens, M., Danescu-Niculescu-Mizil, C., Jurafsky, D.: Linguistic models for analyzing and detecting biased language. In: Proceedings of the 51st Annual Meeting of the Association for Computational Linguistics (Volume 1: Long Papers), pp. 1650–1659 (2013)
26. Rizzo, G., Troncy, R.: Nerd: evaluating named entity recognition tools in the web of data. In: Workshop on Web Scale Knowledge Extraction (WEKEX'11), vol. 21 (2011)
27. Rudinger, R., Naradowsky, J., Leonard, B., Van Durme, B.: Gender bias in coreference resolution. In: Proceedings of the 2018 Conference of the North American Chapter of the Association for Computational Linguistics: Human Language Technologies, Association for Computational Linguistics, New Orleans, Louisiana (2018)
28. Sang, E.F., De Meulder, F.: Introduction to the conll-2003 shared task: Language-independent named entity recognition. arXiv preprint cs/0306050 (2003)
29. Sap, M., Gabriel, S., Qin, L., Jurafsky, D., Smith, N.A., Choi, Y.: Social bias frames: reasoning about social and power implications of language. In: Jurafsky, D., Chai, J., Schluter, N., Tetreault, J. (eds.) Proceedings of the 58th Annual Meeting of the Association for Computational Linguistics, pp. 5477–5490. Association for Computational Linguistics (2020). https://doi.org/10.18653/v1/2020.acl-main. 486, https://aclanthology.org/2020.acl-main.486
30. Schick, T., Udupa, S., Schütze, H.: Self-diagnosis and self-debiasing: a proposal for reducing corpus-based bias in NLP. Trans. Assoc. Comput. Linguist. **9**, 1408–1424 (2021). https://doi.org/10.1162/tacl_a_00434
31. Smith, E.M., Hall, M., Kambadur, M., Presani, E., Williams, A.: "i'm sorry to hear that": Finding new biases in language models with a holistic descriptor dataset. arXiv preprint arXiv:2205.09209 (2022)
32. Spinde, T., Rudnitckaia, L., Sinha, K., Hamborg, F., Gipp, B., Donnay, K.: Mbic - a media bias annotation dataset including annotator characteristics. arXiv preprint arXiv:2105.11910 (2021)
33. Wang, B., et al.: Decodingtrust: a comprehensive assessment of trustworthiness in GPT models. arXiv preprint arXiv:2306.11698 (2023)
34. Wang, Z., Xie, Q., Feng, Y., Ding, Z., Yang, Z., Xia, R.: Is ChatGPT a good sentiment analyzer? A preliminary study. arXiv preprint arXiv:2304.04339 (2023)
35. Wei, A., Haghtalab, N., Steinhardt, J.: Jailbroken: how does LLM safety training fail? In: Advances in Neural Information Processing Systems, vol. 36 (2024)
36. Wessel, M., Horych, T., Ruas, T., Aizawa, A., Gipp, B., Spinde, T.: Introducing mbib-the first media bias identification benchmark task and dataset collection. In: Proceedings of the 46th International ACM SIGIR Conference on Research and Development in Information Retrieval, pp. 2765–2774 (2023)
37. Zhao, J., Wang, T., Yatskar, M., Ordonez, V., Chang, K.W.: Gender bias in coreference resolution: Evaluation and debiasing methods. In: Walker, M., Ji, H., Stent, A. (eds.) Proceedings of the 2018 Conference of the North American Chapter of the Association for Computational Linguistics: Human Language Technologies, Volume 2 (Short Papers), pp. 15–20. Association for Computational Linguistics, New Orleans, Louisiana (2018). https://doi.org/10.18653/v1/N18-2003, https:// aclanthology.org/N18-2003

38. Zhao, W.X., et al.: A survey of large language models. arXiv preprint arXiv:2303.18223 (2023)
39. Zhou, C., et al.: Lima: less is more for alignment. In: Advances in Neural Information Processing Systems, vol. 36 (2024)
40. Zhu, Y., Sheng, Q., Cao, J., Li, S., Wang, D., Zhuang, F.: Generalizing to the future: mitigating entity bias in fake news detection. In: Proceedings of the 45th International ACM SIGIR Conference on Research and Development in Information Retrieval, pp. 2120–2125 (2022)

Mitigating Gender Bias in English to Romanian Machine Translation

Ioana Grigore[ID] and Sergiu Nisioi[✉][ID]

Faculty of Mathematics and Computer Science, Human Language Technologies Research Center, University of Bucharest, Bucharest, Romania
`sergiu.nisioi@unibuc.ro`

Abstract. Machine translation (MT) systems often fail to correctly translate gender, especially when converting from a gender-neutral language like English to a gendered target language such as Romanian. This bias results in translations that default to masculine forms or reinforce gender stereotypes. We propose a hybrid pipeline to mitigate this issue by combining large language model (LLM)-based gender classification with neural machine translation (NMT). Our system uses a fine-tuned LLM to detect the intended gender of target words in English sentences and insert inline gender hint tags. These tagged sentences are then passed to a Transformer model fine-tuned to generate morphologically correct Romanian translations. To support this, we introduce three novel datasets for gender disambiguation and translation. Our approach improves gender accuracy on the WinoMT and WinoGender benchmarks by over 40% points compared to a baseline MT system. This is the first method to explicitly address and evaluate gender bias in English–Romanian MT using both LLM inference and tag-aware translation.

Keywords: Gender Bias · Neural Machine Translation · Large Language Models

1 Introduction

Gender bias in machine translation (MT) remains a well-documented challenge, particularly when translating from languages like English—where gender is often implicit—to target languages such as Romanian, which require explicit grammatical gender agreement. Most neural MT systems tend to default to masculine forms or fail to resolve gender correctly from context, resulting in biased or grammatically incorrect outputs. This issue is especially prominent in translations involving professions, roles, or named entities referring to people.

In this work, we introduce novel datasets and a hybrid pipeline that combines large language model (LLM)-based gender inference with a fine-tuned neural machine translation (NMT) model. Specifically, we use a fine-tuned LLaMA model to classify the gender of target words in an English sentence and insert explicit inline gender hint tags (e.g., `<tgF>teacher</tgF>`). A Transformer

E. Cabrio and E. Monteiro (Eds.): NLDB 2026, LNCS 16696, pp. 139–153, 2027.
https://doi.org/10.1007/978-3-032-29532-3_11

model is then trained to recognize and act on these tags, producing gender-aware Romanian translations.

To support this system, we release[1] novel, high-quality corpora that support (i) gender-aware English classification and (ii) gender-controlled EN→RO translation. We evaluate our approach on multiple test suites including WinoMT and WinoGender [11,16], achieving significant gains in gender translation accuracy over baseline MT. Our results demonstrate that combining LLM-based context understanding with targeted NMT adaptation can mitigate gender bias in low-resource language pairs. Direct LLM translation remains costly and difficult to control at scale; our pipeline offers explicit controllability, interpretability, and compatibility with existing MT systems.

2 Related Work

Gender bias in machine translation (MT) has been previously documented, particularly in language pairs where the source language (e.g., English) lacks overt gender markers, while the target language (e.g., German, French, Spanish) requires grammatical gender agreement. Early studies [11,16] introduced diagnostic datasets such as WinoGender and WinoMT to systematically evaluate gender bias in translation.

Recent work on gender-inclusive machine translation shows that state-of-the-art MT systems and LLMs continue to default to masculine forms, particularly in morphologically gendered languages, even when gender-neutral or gender-ambiguous translations are appropriate [1,14]. Newly introduced multilingual benchmarks and evaluation datasets reveal that models struggle to exploit contextual cues, extended discourse, and explicit instructions to reliably produce inclusive or neutral forms [9]. Cross-linguistic analyses further highlight persistent difficulties with gender ambiguity and non-binary constructions, motivating approaches that explicitly detect and control gender-relevant information prior to or during translation [2].

Related work has also explored sentence-level source-side gender tags, where the gender of the speaker is provided as an explicit signal to the translation model [19]. More recently, large language models (LLMs) have been explored as an alternative to traditional tagging. Instruction-tuned models have been shown to produce gender-controlled outputs via prompt engineering [12,13]. These models can generate separate masculine and feminine translations by conditioning on contextual cues or examples. However, most of this work focuses on high-resource languages such as Spanish, French, German.

Shared-task style evaluations such as the WMT 2020 Gender Coreference and Bias task further highlight persistent gender biases across many submitted MT systems and target languages [5].

---

[1] All data is released under CC BY-NC 4.0 license at https://github.com/Ioannnnna/ EnRoGend.

To date, gender bias in English-Romanian MT remains unaddressed. Romanian presents special challenges due to its three-gender system and complex morphological agreement.

3   EnGen: The English Gender Disambiguation Dataset

We build two datasets for fine-tuning LLMs to predict the gender of a target word in a given context. The process is semi-automatic - a native speaker of Romanian creates sentences, additional examples are generated by GPT through the OpenAI API [6][2] and then the output is checked and filtered again by a native speaker. The datasets follow a two-stage curriculum learning approach, where training starts with simpler examples and increases in difficulty:

3.1   Dataset 1 Single-Entity Phrases

Dataset 1 consists of 11,472 examples. Each example contains one genderable word, such as a job title, family member, animal, role, or proper name. The phrases may contain up to three sentences. We use ambiguous to denote cases where gender cannot be inferred from context; this category includes gender-neutral or non-binary references (e.g., 'they'), without making assumptions about the speaker's gender identity. Statistics regarding the distribution of each categories in the dataset are visible in Fig. 1.

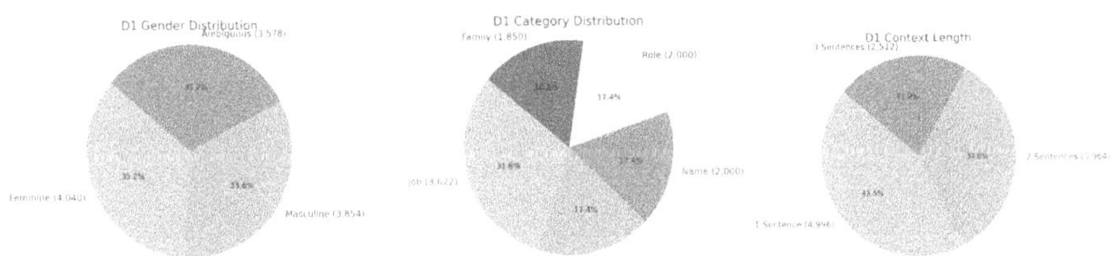

Fig. 1. Dataset 1 distributions. Left: gender is equally balanced across feminine, masculine, and ambiguous entities. Middle: category is equally balanced for nouns related to family, animals, roles, jobs, names. Right: the majority of phrases contain only one sentence, followed by two and three sentence context lengths.

The data generation process begins with one-sentence contexts. For each semantic category, a separate prompt is used to create examples where the gender of the target word is clear or ambiguous. Once all categories are completed for the one-sentence context, the process repeats with two-sentence contexts, and then again with three-sentence contexts. Across all context lengths, the dataset is balanced to contain as close as possible the number of feminine, masculine, and ambiguous examples (Table 1).

---

[2] Full LLM prompt is provided in the official repository.

Table 1. Sample examples from Dataset 1. Each sentence includes a target word and its corresponding gender.

Sentence	Target Word (Category)	Gender
The pilot skillfully navigated the plane through turbulent weather.	pilot (job)	Ambiguous
The engineer designed an innovative solution to the problem. Her technical skills were instrumental in the project's success. The team appreciated her forward-thinking approach.	engineer (job)	Feminine
The leader gave a rousing speech to the team. He inspired everyone to do their best.	leader (role)	Masculine
Our cousin is an excellent cook.	cousin (family)	Ambiguous

3.2   Dataset 2 Multi-entity Phrases

Dataset 2 contains 996 examples with unique target words. Every sentence contains exactly two genderable words: the target word, whose gender must be predicted, and a distractor word, which serves to increase task complexity. The context length is one or two sentences. The distractor entity has ambiguous gender and is placed in various positions within the sentence to reduce predictability.

We ensure a balanced gender representation (feminine, masculine, ambiguous) while keeping the surrounding context highly similar across variants. All three gender labels appear for each target word and the context remains semantically and syntactically natural. The format is identical to dataset 1, consisting of an input (sentence, target word and category) and an output (gender label) (Table 2).

Table 2. Triplet Sample from Dataset 2. Here the "librarian" represents the target word and "teacher", "student", "detective" are the other entities from the context that can also be gendered.

Sentence	Target Word (Category)	Gender
The librarian cataloged the new books, and the teacher borrowed a few from her.	librarian (job)	Feminine
The librarian organized the shelves as the student sought guidance from him.	librarian (job)	Masculine
The librarian recommended a thriller, which the detective found thrilling.	librarian (job)	Ambiguous

3.3   Dataset Splitting

Both datasets are split into training, validation, and test sets to support the two-stage fine-tuning procedure, with splits designed to preserve class balance and avoid leakage.

For Dataset 1 (D1) we use an $80/10/10$ split stratified by gender and category, ensuring each gender–category combination is proportionally represented. The resulting sizes are: train = 9,177, val = 1,147, test = 1,148. For Dataset 2 (D2) we use a $70/15/15$ triplet-locked split: each (masculine, feminine, ambiguous) triplet receives a group ID and the whole group is assigned to exactly one partition (train, validation or test). This guarantees that no variant from the same triplet appears in different splits, including the test set. The resulting sizes are: train = 699, val = 150, test = 147. Training sets are used for parameter updates, validation sets for hyperparameter selection, and test sets are reserved strictly for final evaluation.

We adopt a curriculum learning approach: dataset 1 contains single-entity phrases so the model can first learn the basic mapping from context to gender without interference. Dataset 2 raises the difficulty with two genderable words (one target and one distractor) varying in positions and cues.

4   EnRoGend: A Parallel English-Romanian Gender-Tagged Dataset

The dataset consists of 1,974 examples, organized into pairs: two versions of the same sentence, each with the same target word marked for a masculine and feminine genders. Each example includes the English source, where the target word is surrounded by a gender tag <tgM>target word</tgM> or <tgF>target word</tgF>, and the corresponding Romanian translation, which has no tags. This dataset contains only occupations and person-related nouns having the purpose of teaching the MT system that it should use feminine when it sees <tgF> </tgF> and masculine when it sees <tgM> </tgM>. The construction of this dataset begins with a predefined list of 82 entities referring to jobs and roles. For each entity, we write between 10 and 15 sentences where the entity's gender is elicited using the feminine pronoun (she), then we duplicate the sentence using the masculine pronoun; see for reference Table 3. All sentences are translated into Romanian and verified by two annotators. The dataset is balanced between gendered target words, with 987 masculine and 987 feminine instances, covering 82 distinct occupations.

We split the machine–translation dataset with a similar pair-locked strategy to avoid near-duplicate leakage. Each example belongs to a 2-item minimal pair. Instead of shuffling individual rows, we shuffle pairs and keep both members together in the same partition. The splits are 80% train, 10% validation and 10% test. This guarantees that if the masculine variant of a sentence is in training, its feminine counterpart cannot appear in validation or test (and vice versa), including for the held-out test set. The result is a fair evaluation that is not inflated by near-duplicate examples.

Table 3. Sample Pair from the English-Romanian Gender Tagged Dataset.

En	The teacher thanked the <tgM>lawyer</tgM> since he had been generous throughout the project.
Ro	Profesorul i-a mulțumit avocatului, deoarece fusese generos pe parcursul proiectului.
En	The <tgF>journalist</tgF> advised the painter on the task because she was kind.
Ro	Jurnalista l-a sfătuit pe pictor pentru că era amabilă.

5 Methodology

The datasets described in previous sections are the first ones to address gender bias for English-Romanian language pairs and can thus enable the creation of an end-to-end machine translation pipeline. The pipeline processes an input sentence through a sequence of analysis and generation stages designed to preserve intended gender information during translation. Candidate entities that may require gendered realization are first identified, after which a large language model infers the contextual gender of each entity based on discourse cues. The inferred gender information is then encoded using inline tags and merged back into the original sentence, forming an intermediate representation that makes gender constraints explicit. This tagged sentence is subsequently passed to the machine translation system, which uses the annotations to guide the selection of appropriate gendered forms in the target language, thereby reducing reliance on default or biased gender choices. The entire process is rendered in Fig. 2.

To enable gender-aware processing in realistic settings, the pipeline relies on an *Entity Selector* that used a predefined list of gendered entities that serve as candidate targets for gender inference. The list is compiled based on previous studies [3]. Each word in the input sentence is matched against this list to identify role nouns or occupations whose gender must be inferred. To improve robustness, fuzzy string matching is applied to account for misspellings, plural forms, and minor lexical variations.

5.1 LLM Gender Classification

For this step, the main focus is to have a classifier that is fast and easily deployable in an MT system. As such, we employ the pre-trained LLaMA 3.2 (1B parameters) model from Unsloth [18]. To make fine-tuning feasible on limited hardware, the model is loaded in 4-bit NF4 quantization and fine-tuned with mixed precision. We adopt Low-Rank Adaptation (LoRA) [4]. Instead of updating a full weight matrix $W_0 \in \mathbb{R}^{d \times k}$, LoRA learns a low-rank update:

$$W = W_0 + \Delta W, \qquad \Delta W = \frac{\alpha}{r} AB,$$

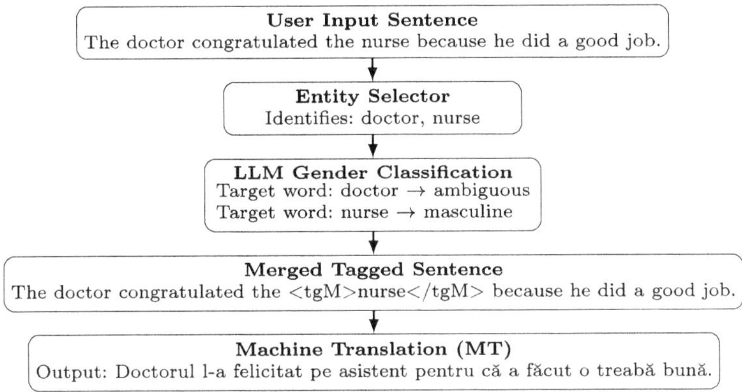

Fig. 2. End-to-end pipeline example. The system takes an English sentence, extracts candidate entities, classifies gender for each using the LLM, inserts tags for gendered entities, and translates the tagged sentence into Romanian.

where $A \in \mathbb{R}^{d \times r}$, $B \in \mathbb{R}^{r \times k}$, $r \ll \min(d, k)$, and α scales the update. The frozen W_0 preserves pre-trained knowledge, while ΔW captures task-specific adjustments. LoRA adapters are inserted into the query, key, value, output, gate, up, and down projection layers. Only LoRA parameters and the classification head are updated during training. We use AdamW with separate parameter groups, one for the LoRA adapter parameters and one for the language modeling head. This allows assigning distinct learning rates to each group, while weight decay is applied only where specified in the grid configuration. Training is performed with gradient accumulation and mixed-precision computation in `bfloat16`, on a single Nvidia L4 GPU in Colab Pro.

Classification Strategy a Linear Classification Head is attached to the pre-trained LLaMA 3.2 (1B parameters) model. After processing the input sequence through the language model, we extract the hidden state corresponding to the final token position in the sequence. This hidden representation, denoted $\mathbf{h}_{\text{last}}$, encodes the full context of the input, including the sentence and target word.

A fully connected linear layer then transforms this hidden vector into a fixed-size output vector representing class logits for the three possible gender labels: feminine, masculine, and ambiguous. Formally, the prediction is computed as:

$$\mathbf{h}_{\text{last}} = \text{LLM}(\mathbf{x})[-1], \qquad \mathbf{y} = \mathbf{W}\mathbf{h}_{\text{last}} + \mathbf{b},$$

where $\mathbf{W} \in \mathbb{R}^{3 \times d}$ and $\mathbf{b} \in \mathbb{R}^3$ are the learned parameters of the classification head, and d is the dimensionality of the hidden state. Model training is guided by the cross-entropy loss.

The Two-Stage Curriculum Learning is designed to gradually increase task complexity while training. In the first stage, the model is fine-tuned on Dataset 1, which contains sentences with a single named entity and well-balanced gender classes. These examples provide both clear and ambiguous contexts, allowing the model to learn the core gender classification task with minimal distraction or noise.

Once this base ability is acquired, the second stage uses the Dataset 2, which presents more realistic challenges, including sentences containing multiple named entities. This stage encourages the model to reason about context and resolve gender cues in more complex linguistic scenarios.

Hyperparameter Search and Evaluation. We explore hyperparameter configurations for both stages of curriculum training:

- Stage 1 (initial fine-tuning on D1): LoRA rank $r \in \{8, 12, 16, 24, 32\}$ with scaling $\alpha \approx 2r$, dropout in $[0.00, 0.06]$, learning rates for the LoRA adapters and classifier head $(4 \times 10^{-5}$–$1.6 \times 10^{-4})$, weight decay in $\{0.0, 0.005, 0.01\}$, and 2–3 epochs.
- Stage 2 (continued fine-tuning on D2): LoRA ranks $\{8, 12, 16\}$ with proportionally scaled α, dropout in $[0.04, 0.07]$, smaller learning rates $(4 \times 10^{-5}$–$1.0 \times 10^{-4})$, weight decay in $\{0.005, 0.01\}$, and 1–2 epochs.

For hyperparameter tuning we use optuna search. It runs a fixed budget of trials (e.g., 12), guided by a Tree-structured Parzen Estimator (TPE) sampler.

We observe that several configurations achieve high accuracy and F1 scores on Dataset 1, with the top-performing model reaching an F1 of 0.97 and accuracy of 97% on the test set. The performance on Dataset 2 varies more widely due to its complex, multi-entity structure. While the best model achieves a strong F1 score of 0.95, others drop as low as 0.66. Overall, the performance is sensitive to regularization and learning rate balance, and improves with moderate-to-deep LoRA ranks (e.g., 12–16) paired with well-scaled α values.

Table 4 summarizes the generalization in both datasets. The best joint test F1 score reaches 0.96, confirming that high-quality performance can be maintained by generalizing across D1 and D2 simultaneously.

In addition, we evaluate the final Stage 2 models both on D2 and again on D1, which allows us to quantify catastrophic forgetting via the Forgetting F1 metric (see Table 4). This approach makes the runs easy to compare and gives us a reliable way to measure the effect of curriculum learning. The joint metrics represent the model's performance on the combined test set, which merges the test splits from both datasets, D1 and D2. The Forgetting F1 metric shows how much performance on D1 is lost after the second stage of training on D2. It is computed as the difference in F1 score on the D1 test set after and before Stage 2 fine-tuning, a negative value indicates forgetting (performance decreased), while a positive value implies improvement or recovery on D1 after further training.

5.2   Gender-Aware Machine Translation (En→Ro)

We fine-tune an English-to-Romanian pre-trained Transformer model Helsinki-NLP/opus-mt-en-ro [17] and evaluate performance on both in-domain splits and

Table 4. The Forgetting F1 metric quantifies the degree of catastrophic forgetting, with most configurations showing mild drops (e.g., -0.0121 or -0.0015), while a few show large negative values (e.g., -0.1820), indicating significant loss of earlier knowledge.

D2 idx	D1 idx	Joint Acc	Joint F1	Joint MCC	Forgetting F1
D2-1	D1-1	96%	0.96	0.94	0.0083
D2-2	D1-2	83%	0.82	0.75	-0.1040
D2-3	D1-3	95%	0.95	0.93	-0.0121
D2-4	D1-1	96%	0.96	0.94	0.0072
D2-6	D1-2	80%	0.80	0.70	-0.0851
D2-8	D1-3	95%	0.95	0.93	-0.0015
D2-9	D1-2	73%	0.74	0.60	-0.0851
D2-10	D1-4	86%	0.86	0.81	-0.1820
D2-11	D1-5	66%	0.66	0.58	0.1950

external diagnostic sets. The tokenizer is extended with four special tokens: <tgM>, </tgM>, <tgF>, and </tgF> on the source side. If no padding token is defined, the EOS token is reused as PAD. Romanian references are kept tag-free to avoid leaking gender labels into the target side.

Because the dataset contains many minimal pairs (i.e., identical English sentences differing only in masculine vs. feminine tags), a random split would risk leaking near-duplicate examples across train, validation, and test sets, leading to artificially inflated evaluation scores. To prevent this, we enforce a pair-locked split:

- Sentences are grouped into pairs consecutively by file order: $(0,1),(2,3),\ldots$. Each pair is assigned a unique integer pair_id defined as $\lfloor i/2 \rfloor$. We ensure an even number of rows; otherwise, the source file is adjusted.
- Exact duplicates on the (English, Romanian) tuple are removed to avoid trivial matches at evaluation time.
- The set of unique pair_ids is randomly shuffled with a fixed seed for reproducibility.
- The first 80% of pair_ids are assigned to the training set, the next 10% to validation, and the remaining 10% to test. Both members of each minimal pair are always placed in the same split.
- We verify that pair_id sets are disjoint across splits and report hashed overlaps on both source and target texts as a sanity check against accidental data leakage.

Hyperparameter Tuning, To determine the most effective fine-tuning strategy for Transformer with gender tags, we explore three adaptation regimes under identical training loops:

- Full fine-tuning: all model parameters are updated, providing maximum flexibility but at a higher computational cost.
- Partial fine-tuning: most encoder layers are frozen, and only the decoder, shared embeddings, language modeling head, and the last N encoder layers ($N \in \{1,2,3\}$) are updated, reducing training cost while retaining adaptability.
- LoRA fine-tuning: a parameter-efficient strategy where low-rank adapters are injected into the attention layers, keeping the base model frozen and updating only the adapter parameters.

Hyperparameter tuning is performed using Optuna with a grid-based search over the following space: learning rate $\in \{1e{-}5, 5e{-}5, 1e{-}4\}$, batch size $\in \{8, 16\}$, epochs $\in \{1, 2\}$, and, for partial fine-tuning, the number of unfrozen encoder layers $N_{\mathrm{unfreeze}} \in \{1, 2, 3\}$. Model selection is based on validation performance, and the best configurations are evaluated on the held-out test set using BLEU [8], chrF++ [7][3], TER [15], and COMET [10] metrics. The reported metrics reflect different aspects of translation quality: BLEU and chrF++ measure word and character n-gram overlap between system output and reference; TER reflects the number of edits needed to reach the reference, where lower is better; and COMET is a learned metric that evaluates adequacy and fluency based on source, hypothesis, and references. The surface-form metrics such as BLEU, chrf++, and TER tend to reflect good results due to the high overlap, however the gender mismatch is more nuanced semantic aspect, therefore we rely more on the COMET metric for the final judgments and keep the remaining metrics as evidence.

The results in Table 5 show that full fine-tuning with a learning rate of $1e{-}4$, batch size 16, and 2 epochs achieved the best overall performance (highlighted in boldface). Partial fine-tuning with 2–3 unfrozen encoder layers performed competitively (bottom row marked with an *), achieving a COMET scores above 0.85 and comparable overall scores to the full-finetuning model. This represents a good compromise between efficiency and accuracy.

The best hyperparameter configuration selected on the validation set based on the results of Table 5 is the fully finetuned model. This model achieves similar scores on the held-out test set: a COMET score of 0.846, a BLEU score of 96.92, a chrF++ score of 98.21, and a TER of 1.94.

LoRA, however, underperformed in our experimental setting, suggesting that lightweight adapter tuning does not provide enough capacity for this task. A likely explanation is that this task requires more than light domain adaptation. The model must learn to use new source-side gender tags and realize them through correct Romanian morphology, including agreement on nouns, adjectives, and verbs. Full and partial fine-tuning are better suited to this controlled generation setting because they let more of the model adapt to the tag signal. By contrast, the LoRA setups tested may have been too limited to capture the

---

[3] chrF++ signature is `nrefs:1|case:mixed|eff:yes|nc:6|nw:0|space:no|version:2.4.3` and BLEU signature is `nrefs:1|case:mixed|eff:no|tok:13a|smooth:exp|version:2.4.3`.

Table 5. Hyperparameter optimization results on the **validation set** for fine-tuning Transformer with gender tags. The table compares full, partial, and LoRA fine-tuning modes across various learning rates, batch sizes, epochs, and (for partial mode) number of unfrozen encoder layers. Full fine-tuning with a learning rate of 1e−4, batch size 16, and 2 epochs achieved the best validation performance, with the highest BLEU (97.29), chrF (98.57), COMET (0.853), and the lowest TER (1.71).

Mode	LR	Batch	Epochs	N_{unfreeze}	BLEU	chrF++	TER	COMET
partial	1.00e−05	16	2	1	63.69	80.31	24.88	0.7723
full	5.00e−05	8	1		93.03	96.73	3.55	0.8409
partial	1.00e−04	16	1	1	92.94	96.40	3.90	0.8396
full	1.00e−05	8	1		67.57	83.28	21.50	0.7857
lora	1.00e−04	8	1		41.12	76.78	44.84	0.7263
full	**1.00e−04**	**16**	**2**		**97.29**	**98.57**	**1.71**	**0.8530**
lora	1.00e−04	16	2		41.71	67.35	43.98	0.7261
lora	1.00e−05	8	1		23.99	57.59	71.13	0.6467
lora	5.00e−05	8	1		33.08	61.98	53.70	0.7103
partial	1.00e−05	16	2	3	69.30	84.06	20.13	0.7853
partial	5.00e−05	16	1	3	89.64	94.95	5.61	0.8306
partial*	1.00e−04	8	1	2	97.07	98.40	1.93	0.8511

link between explicit gender tags and downstream morphological realization. The large gap in performance therefore suggests that this form of parameter-efficient tuning is not sufficient for robust gender control in English–Romanian translation. Another possible factor is that Romanian morphological agreement is more demanding than the target-side changes required in some higher-resource settings.

6   Benchmark Evaluation

To evaluate gender bias in machine translation, we rely on several benchmarks that are designed to probe whether a system can correctly resolve gender based on cues and whether it reflects correct grammatical agreement in gender-marked target languages. Although GPT-4o was used in the data creation process, all benchmark evaluations are conducted on external datasets that are not used during training, to ensure that there are no data leaks. In addition, we have compared all the sentences with our dataset to ensure that there is no data leakage.

The WinoMT dataset [16] consists of (1,584 pro and 1,584 anti) English sentences in which gender must be inferred from context. Each sentence is presented in two forms: a **pro-stereotypical** variant, where the pronoun aligns with common gender stereotypes and an **anti-stereotypical** variant, where the pronoun contradicts such stereotypes, e.g., pro-stereotypical sentence: *The nurse helped the patient because she was kind.* Anti-stereotypical sentence: *The nurse helped the patient because he was kind.* An unbiased system is expected to perform similarly on both pro-stereotypical and anti-stereotypical examples.

The WinoGender dataset [11] is a pronoun resolution benchmark that tests the impact of gendered pronouns on translation, consisting of 720 sentences. Each example is a minimal pair differing only in the pronoun (he, she or they) and is used to decide whether the system's output reflects these distinctions correctly in the gendered target-language translation.

All English test sentences are translated using three systems: 1. Raw MT - the base Transformer model, without any additional gender hint tags; and 2. Gender-Aware Pipeline - each sentence passed through our pipeline (as described in Fig. 2); 3. GPT-5.2 using default system settings and zero-shot translation prompts; due to its proprietary nature, exact replication may not be possible. These test sets do not include gold-standard Romanian reference translations. Therefore, a manual evaluation was conducted by a native Romanian speaker and verified through spot checks. For each test case, we check whether the translation preserves the correct grammatical gender of the target word, along with agreement (e.g., adjective inflection, verb conjugation) (Table 6).

Table 6. The results presented in the table are the accuracies on benchmark test sets. It shows that the raw Transformer system performs better when the correct gender is masculine, as it often defaults to masculine forms during translation. While this leads to higher scores on Pro-stereotypical examples (where the gold label aligns with masculine bias), it harms performance on Anti-stereotypical and feminine cases. Similarly, a state-of-the-art model such as GPT-5.2 has a strong preference for stereotypical biases. The gender-aware pipeline significantly improves accuracy across all subsets by explicitly guiding the model toward the intended gender.

Model/Metric	WinoMT (Pro)	WinoMT (Anti)	WinoGender
Raw Transformer	59.05%	50.13%	50.28%
Pipeline LLM-MT	**96.34%**	**93.68%**	**91.53%**
GPT-5.2	79.23%	58.79%	67.71%

Some translations contain issues such as incorrect word choices or missing diacritics. However, as these errors occur in both raw and fine-tuned outputs, we consider a translation correct if the intended gender is correct and if it stays in agreement with the rest of the sentence. For example, if the MT translates salesperson for feminine gender as "vânzătora" instead of "vânzătoarea" we consider it correct.

7   Conclusion

We investigate gender bias in English→Romanian machine translation, where ambiguous English inputs must be rendered with explicit grammatical gender in Romanian. Our results confirm that a standard Transformer MT baseline frequently defaults to masculine forms and exhibits stereotype sensitivity, performing substantially better on pro-stereotypical WinoMT examples than on anti-stereotypical ones. Furthermore, even proprietary state-of-the-art models such as GPT-5.2 have a bias towards stereotypical translations into Romanian, despite the fact that such models might have been exposed to the WinoMT and WinoGender datasets.

To mitigate gender bias, we propose a hybrid pipeline that combines LLM-based contextual gender disambiguation with tag-aware neural machine translation: a fine-tuned LLM predicts the intended gender of target entities in the English source and inserts inline gender hint tags, which a Transformer model learns to follow during translation. Across external diagnostic benchmarks, this approach yields large gains in gender correctness, improving accuracy by over 40% points relative to the raw MT system and substantially reducing the pro/anti performance gap, indicating reduced reliance on stereotypical defaults.

To support research in this low-resource setting, we introduced several datasets for (i) EnGen - English language gender disambiguation with a curriculum learning setup and (ii) EnRoGend - a controlled En→Ro translation with gender tags, using leakage-safe splitting strategies. We also found that full and partial fine-tuning of the MT model effectively leverage the gender tags, while the LoRA configurations we tested underperformed for this task, suggesting that tag-conditioned morphological control may require greater adaptation capacity.

While our experiments focus on Romanian, the proposed pipeline is applicable to other morphologically gendered target languages.

Acknowledgments. This research is supported by InstRead: Research Instruments for the Text Complexity, Simplification and Readability Assessment CNCS - UEFIS-CDI project number PN-IV-P2-2.1-TE-2023-2007 and by the project "Romanian Hub for Artificial Intelligence - HRIA", Smart Growth, Digitization and Financial Instruments Program, 2021–2027, MySMIS no. 351416.

References

1. Hackenbuchner, J., Gkovedarou, E., Daems, J.: GENDEROUS: machine translation and cross-linguistic evaluation of a gender-ambiguous dataset. In: Faleńska, A., Basta, C., Costa-jussà, M., Stańczak, K., Nozza, D. (eds.) Proceedings of the 6th Workshop on Gender Bias in Natural Language Processing (GeBNLP), Vienna, Austria, pp. 302–319. Association for Computational Linguistics (2025). https://doi.org/10.18653/v1/2025.gebnlp-1.27. https://aclanthology.org/2025.gebnlp-1.27/

2. Hackenbuchner, J., Tezcan, A., Daems, J.: Automatic detection of (potential) factors in the source text leading to gender bias in machine translation. In: Scarton, C., et al. (eds.) Proceedings of the 25th Annual Conference of the European Association for Machine Translation (Volume 2), Sheffield, UK, pp. 27–28. European Association for Machine Translation (EAMT) (2024). https://aclanthology.org/2024.eamt-2.14/

3. Hackenbuchner, J., Tezcan, A., Daems, J.: Gender bias and the role of context in human perception and machine translation. Comput. Linguist. Neth. J. **14**, 215–239 (2025). https://www.clinjournal.org/clinj/article/view/197
4. Hu, E.J., et al.: LoRA: low-rank adaptation of large language models. In: International Conference on Learning Representations (2022). https://openreview.net/forum?id=nZeVKeeFYf9
5. Kocmi, T., Limisiewicz, T., Stanovsky, G.: Gender coreference and bias evaluation at WMT 2020. In: Barrault, L., et al. (eds.) Proceedings of the Fifth Conference on Machine Translation, pp. 357–364. Association for Computational Linguistics, Online (2020). https://doi.org/10.18653/v1/2020.wmt-1.39. https://aclanthology.org/2020.wmt-1.39/
6. OpenAI: GPT-4o: OpenAI's multimodal language model (2024). https://openai.com/index/. Accessed 29 Aug 2025
7. Popović, M.: chrF++: words helping character n-grams. In: Proceedings of the Second Conference on Machine Translation, Copenhagen, Denmark, pp. 612–618. Association for Computational Linguistics (2017). https://doi.org/10.18653/v1/W17-4770. https://aclanthology.org/W17-4770/
8. Post, M.: A call for clarity in reporting BLEU scores. In: Proceedings of the Third Conference on Machine Translation: Research Papers, Belgium, Brussels, pp. 186–191. Association for Computational Linguistics (2018). https://www.aclweb.org/anthology/W18-6319
9. Pranav, A., Hackenbuchner, J., Attanasio, G., Lardelli, M., Lauscher, A.: Glitter: a multi-sentence, multi-reference benchmark for gender-fair German machine translation. In: Christodoulopoulos, C., Chakraborty, T., Rose, C., Peng, V. (eds.) Findings of the Association for Computational Linguistics: EMNLP 2025, Suzhou, China, pp. 18450–18477. Association for Computational Linguistics (2025). https://doi.org/10.18653/v1/2025.findings-emnlp.1002. https://aclanthology.org/2025.findings-emnlp.1002/
10. Rei, R., et al.: Scaling up CometKiwi: unbabel-IST 2023 submission for the quality estimation shared task. In: Koehn, P., Haddow, B., Kocmi, T., Monz, C. (eds.) Proceedings of the Eighth Conference on Machine Translation, Singapore, pp. 841–848. Association for Computational Linguistics (2023). https://doi.org/10.18653/v1/2023.wmt-1.73. https://aclanthology.org/2023.wmt-1.73/
11. Rudinger, R., Naradowsky, J., Leonard, B., Van Durme, B.: Gender bias in coreference resolution, New Orleans, Louisiana. Association for Computational Linguistics (2018). https://aclanthology.org/N18-2002/
12. Sánchez, E., Andrews, P., Stenetorp, P., Artetxe, M., Costa-jussà, M.R.: Gender-specific machine translation with large language models. In: Proceedings of the Fourth Workshop on Multilingual Representation Learning (MRL 2024), pp. 148–158 (2024). https://aclanthology.org/2024.mrl-1.10/
13. Sant, A., Escolano, C., Mash, A., De Luca Fornaciari, F., Melero, M.: The power of prompts: evaluating and mitigating gender bias in MT with LLMs. In: Proceedings of the 5th Workshop on Gender Bias in Natural Language Processing (GeBNLP), pp. 94–139 (2024). https://doi.org/10.18653/v1/2024.gebnlp-1.7. https://aclanthology.org/2024.gebnlp-1.7/
14. Savoldi, B., et al.: Mind the inclusivity gap: multilingual gender-neutral translation evaluation with mGeNTE. In: Christodoulopoulos, C., Chakraborty, T., Rose, C., Peng, V. (eds.) Proceedings of the 2025 Conference on Empirical Methods in Natural Language Processing, Suzhou, China, pp. 13698–13720. Association for Computational Linguistics (2025). https://doi.org/10.18653/v1/2025.emnlp-main.692. https://aclanthology.org/2025.emnlp-main.692/

15. Snover, M., Dorr, B., Schwartz, R., Micciulla, L., Makhoul, J.: A study of translation edit rate with targeted human annotation. In: Proceedings of the 7th Conference of the Association for Machine Translation in the Americas: Technical Papers, Cambridge, Massachusetts, USA, 8–12 August 2006, pp. 223–231. Association for Machine Translation in the Americas (2006). https://aclanthology.org/2006.amta-papers.25/
16. Stanovsky, G., Smith, N.A., Zettlemoyer, L.: Evaluating gender bias in machine translation. In: Proceedings of the 57th Annual Meeting of the Association for Computational Linguistics, pp. 1679–1684 (2019). https://aclanthology.org/P19-1164/
17. Unsloth AI: Helsinki-NLP/opus-mt-en-ro (2025). https://huggingface.co/Helsinki-NLP/opus-mt-en-ro. Accessed 29 Aug 2025
18. Unsloth AI: unsloth/Llama-3.2-1B-bnb-4bit (2025). https://huggingface.co/unsloth/Llama-3.2-1B-bnb-4bit. Accessed 29 Aug 2025
19. Vanmassenhove, E., Hardmeier, C., Way, A.: Getting gender right in neural machine translation. In: Proceedings of the 2018 Conference on Empirical Methods in Natural Language Processing, pp. 3003–3008 (2018). https://aclanthology.org/D18-1334/

Zoom In Disparities in Healthcare LLM Q&A

Ipek Baris Schlicht[1]([✉]) [iD], Burcu Sayin[2] [iD], Zhixue Zhao[3] [iD],
Frederik M. Labonté[4,5], Cesare Barbera[6] [iD], Marco Viviani[7] [iD],
Paolo Rosso[1,8] [iD], and Lucie Flek[4,5] [iD]

[1] Universitat Politècnica de València, Valencia, Spain
`ibarsch@doctor.upv.es`
[2] University of Trento, Trento, Italy
[3] University of Sheffield, Sheffield, UK
[4] Bonn-Aachen International Center for Information Technology, University of Bonn, Bonn, Germany
[5] Lamarr Institute for Machine Learning and Artificial Intelligence, Dortmund, Germany
[6] University of Pisa, Pisa, Italy
[7] University of Milano-Bicocca, Milano, Italy
[8] ValgrAI Valencian Graduate School and Research Network of Artificial Intelligence, Valencia, Spain

Abstract. This paper systematically examines cross-lingual disparities in pre-training source and factuality alignment in Large Language Model (LLM) answers for multilingual healthcare Q&A across English, German, Turkish, Chinese (Mandarin), and Italian. To support this analysis, we (*i*) constructed MultiWikiHealthCare, a multilingual dataset derived from Wikipedia; (*ii*) used it to examine cross-lingual differences in healthcare-related coverage; (*iii*) evaluated the alignment between LLM-generated responses and these reference sources; and (*iv*) conducted a case study on factual alignment through the use of contextual information and Retrieval-Augmented Generation (RAG). Our findings reveal substantial cross-lingual disparities in both Wikipedia coverage and LLM factual alignment. Based on our Wikipedia analysis, the lowest alignment is observed between English and Chinese Wikipedia pages. Across models, responses align more with English Wikipedia, even when the prompts are non-English. We further show that providing contextual excerpts from non-English Wikipedia at inference time effectively shifts factual alignment toward target knowledge.

Keywords: Multilingual Q&A · Information Disparity · Factual Alignment · LLM Evaluation

1 Introduction

Large Large Language Models (LLMs) are increasingly deployed across healthcare applications, and people seeking health information routinely turn to LLM-based systems for advice and guidance [43, 46]. Since LLMs are trained primarily

E. Cabrio and E. Monteiro (Eds.): NLDB 2026, LNCS 16696, pp. 154–168, 2027.
https://doi.org/10.1007/978-3-032-29532-3_12

on large-scale online data, their responses are shaped by the availability and quality of online health information [26]. However, this information varies markedly across languages, reflecting disparities in health communication, infrastructure, and cultural norms [37,45].

Many healthcare benchmarks probe both LLM hallucination and disparity analysis [4,19,20,32,49], but they are largely English-centric or too coarse-grained to diagnose performance gaps across languages. Moreover, although related, the two concepts operate at different levels of analysis. While hallucination detection focuses on identifying content that is factually incorrect or fabricated [19,48], *disparity analysis* examines how information is differently represented or prioritized across linguistic and contextual boundaries, even if the facts themselves might vary across different cultural/contextual settings [29,32].

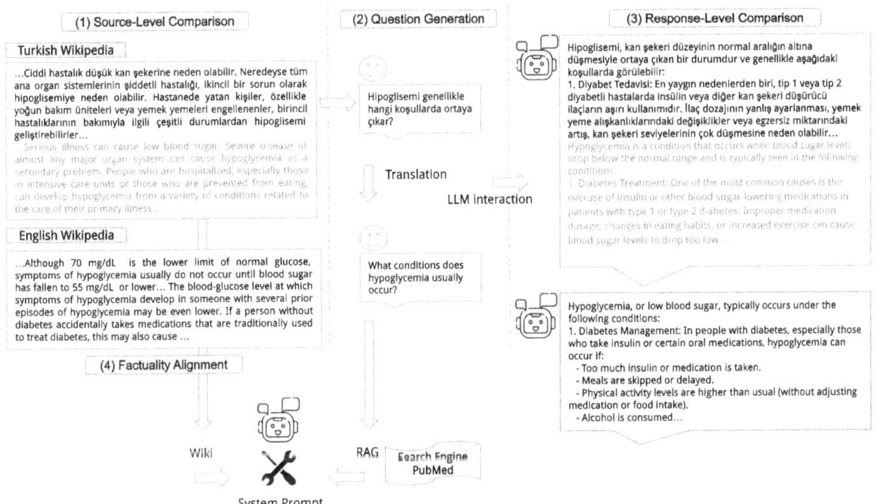

Fig. 1. The framework for examining source- and response-level disparity and factuality alignment: (1) Comparison of Wiki pages (TR-EN) in terms of factuality and structure; (2) Question generation based on facts from the Wiki pages; (3) Response factuality evaluation; (4) Contextual alignment using Wiki pages and RAG. The EN translations are given in blue (Color figure online).

Recent studies have applied disparity analysis to Wikipedia entries on people and cuisines [32,38], and others have investigated disparities in LLM outputs within the medical domain [15,30]. However, none of these works explicitly link disparities between the source (e.g., Wikipedia) and LLM-generated responses. This paper introduces a holistic framework to assess how LLM-generated health answers align with factuality and language-specific information across languages. As illustrated in Fig. 1, (*i*) we begin by comparing healthcare-related Wikipedia pages, which is a pretraining corpus for many LLMs [36], across languages to characterize similarities and discrepancies in coverage, phrasing, and citation patterns. From this analysis, (*ii*) we construct aligned cross-lingual fact sets and use them to generate questions posed to several multilingual LLMs, i.e., Llama3.3-70B [9], Qwen3-Next-80B-A3B-Instruct [44], and Aya [6]. Subsequently, (*iii*) we evaluate the responses for quality and alignment with both English Wikipedia and the corresponding target-language pages. Finally, (*iv*) we present a preliminary case study testing whether providing non-English contextual excerpts at inference time shifts factual alignment toward locally relevant sources, through the use of contextual information and *Retrieval-Augmented Generation* (RAG).

The main contributions of this work can be summarized as follows: (*i*) We constructed **MultiWikiHealthCare**, a multilingual dataset curated from trending health-care topics and Wikipedia, covering English (EN), German (DE), Italian (IT), Turkish (TR), and Chinese (ZH). It enables systematic comparisons of disparities at both the source level (Wikipedia) and the response level (LLM outputs). (*ii*) Analysis of Wikipedia reveals substantial cross-lingual disparities relative to EN, with ZH showing the lowest alignment and fewest extracted facts; DE more often cites regional sources, while others rely on international sources. (*iii*) LLM outputs exhibit pronounced EN-centric alignment: responses track English Wikipedia more closely than same-topic pages in other languages, with further drops when queries are posed in EN. It might be problematic for culturally specific knowledge with differing practices and guidelines. (*iv*) A context-augmented prompting case study shows LLMs can shift alignment toward non-EN sources at inference time, highlighting the value of incorporating target-language knowledge. Finally, our dataset and source code with system prompts are available on GitHub[1].

2   Related Work

Research on factual reliability, hallucination detection, and cross-lingual consistency in LLMs provides important insights into the origins of disparity in model behavior across languages and domains. Prior work shows that prompt design strongly influences factuality in medical Q&A [19, 20, 33]. However, while LLMs rarely contradict medical facts, they often fail to challenge incorrect ones [18]. Extending to multilingual settings, accuracy, consistency, and verifiability vary substantially across languages [17].

MedHalu and the MedHaluDetect framework target fine-grained hallucination detection in medical responses [4]. Built from English healthcare questions spanning HealthQA, LiveQA, and MedicationQA [1, 2, 49], the dataset incorporates hallucination taxonomies [48] via synthetic perturbations generated with GPT-3.5 [3]. Evaluations show LLMs underperform both experts and lay users in hallucination detection.

---

[1] https://github.com/isspek/nldb2026-multiwikihealthcare.

To analyze cross-lingual information gaps in Wikipedia, Samir et al. [32] proposed InfoGap, which decomposes and aligns facts across languages using GPT-4, applied to biographies in the LGBTBio Corpus [28]. In healthcare, multilingual disparities have been examined in mental-health responses via translation-based evaluation [15] and in ophthalmological Q&A benchmarks assessing multiple-choice accuracy [30], which also introduced CLARA for inference-time debiasing using RAG and self-verification. Another research reports cross-lingual variation in detail, numerical consistency, contradictions, irrelevance, and citation practices [35]. Unlike prior work [15,30,35], we study the relationship between factual knowledge potentially acquired during pretraining and the factual alignment of LLM-generated responses across languages through a dedicated benchmark. In comparison with CLARA, our dataset spans multiple healthcare topics. Furthermore, we extend this analysis to culturally diverse languages.

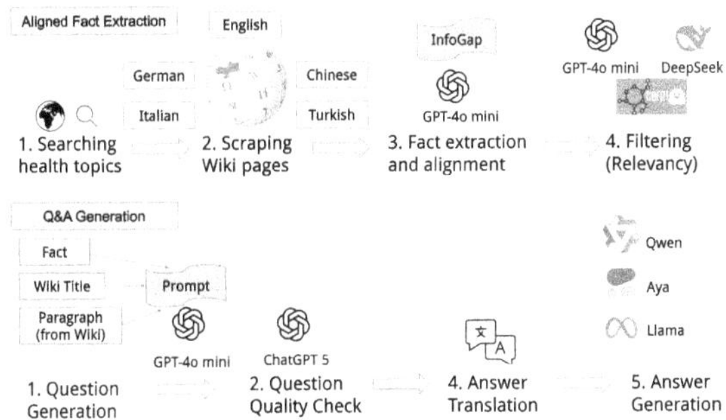

Fig. 2. The pipeline for Q&A construction.

3   Multilingual Wiki Health Care

Existing benchmark datasets largely focus on monolingual evaluation, typically for general-purpose or other tasks such as hallucination detection, lacking the specificity needed to assess how pretraining sources affect multilingual answer quality in specialized domains such as healthcare. To address this gap, we introduce **MultiWikiHealthCare**, a multilingual, health-focused Q&A dataset. MultiWikiHealthCare is derived from Wikipedia, a common pretraining source for LLMs. Figure 2 presents the pipeline for constructing the dataset. The main stages of the pipeline are outlined in detail in the remainder of this section.

3.1   Construction of Aligned Facts

Healthcare Topics. To construct MultiWikiHealthCare, we first used Google Trends in 2025 to identify high-salience health topics.[2] To ensure broader coverage, we manually expanded it with additional health-related topics from a

---

[2] https://trends.google.com/trends/explore.

Wikipedia list of *controversial issues* in science, biology, health,[3] and as well as topics from a related survey [34]. These topics formed the basis of the content collection. The topics are *Allergy, Cancer, Cardiovascular Disease, Cold, Covid, Depression, Diabetes, Diet, Ebola, Flu, Influenza, Nutrition, Obesity, Pain, Smoking, Vaccination, Weight Loss.* We used Google Trends to identify their sub-topics from related entities trending between 2004 and 2025 across global and country-level search data (U.S., U.K., Turkey, Germany, Italy, and China). Across all languages, we identified 1,193 unique entities. Symptoms, causes, and diseases are common entities across languages, while some entities are not specific to the healthcare domain.

Scraping Wikipedia Pages. We used Llama 3.3-70B and served through the vLLM inference framework[4] [21], to (*i*) filter out entities not related to healthcare and (*ii*) link the remaining entities to their corresponding Wikipedia pages and then removed the duplicate pages. Wikipedia page titles often differ across languages, especially when scripts differ or the title is a common noun rather than a proper name (e.g., EN/IT "Nausea" vs. DE "Übelkeit"). herefore, we retrieved *interlanguage titles* using the open-source Wikipedia API.[5] Pages available only in EN were excluded as they are unsuitable for comparative analysis, yielding 815 titles present in EN and at least one additional language. A subsequent manual review showed that some pages referred to 'films', 'people', or 'doctoral degree'. Hence, we removed Wikipedia pages referring to such category metadata.
Fact Extraction and Alignment.

Table 1. Comparision of human annotations, InfoGap predictions and random guess.

Language Pair	F1-Macro	Random
en ↔ TR	0.841	0.574
en ↔ ZH	0.724	0.535
en ↔ DE	0.684	0.479
en ↔ IT	0.638	0.538

From the Wikipedia articles, we extracted *facts* together with their supporting paragraphs as evidence. We categorized these facts into two groups: (1) *Cross-lingual overlapping facts*, where the same factual content appears in both EN and non-EN version (2) *Language-specific facts*, which are unique to the non-EN article without an EN counterpart. The first group is used to construct the Q&A dataset and the second is part of the Wikipedia analysis discussed in Sect. 4.1.

---

[3] Wikipedia:List_of_controversial_issues#Science,_biology,_and_health.
[4] https://docs.vllm.ai/en/latest/.
[5] https://github.com/martin-majlis/Wikipedia-API.

Fact extraction and alignment were performed with InfoGap [32,38], the state-of-the-art framework for cross-lingual fact extraction and alignment on Wikipedia (see Sect. 2). The framework combines OpenAI LLMs with a hubness-based correction technique to improve cross-language alignment accuracy. Because a single Wikipedia page can contain hundreds of atomic facts, running OpenAI models at a corpus scale is costly [32]. While the latest InfoGap [38] employs GPT-4o [3], we adopted GPT-4o-mini [16] as the backbone model, which is approximately 10% less expensive than GPT-4o. To assess reliability on our corpus, we sampled 50 facts per language following the InfoGap evaluation protocol. Annotations were conducted by volunteer native speakers using the official InfoGap guidelines. Our results (see Table 1) are comparable to those reported by [32], which outperform a random prediction.[6]

Table 2. Transformers (TF) against GPT-4o-mini (F1-macro)

Language	LLM	Mono TF	Cross TF
EN	82.69	86.49	**88.44**
TR	77.89	83.46	**84.20**
ZH	68.47	**77.02**	72.11
DE	76.67	70.88	**81.32**
IT	71.96	72.00	**83.33**

Selecting Relevant Facts. After cross-lingual extraction and alignment, we retained only bidirectionally matched facts: the intersection of the two directions for each language pair (e.g., EN ↔ TR). Although the facts are atomic, InfoGap returns the aligned source sentences in both languages. We then located the paragraphs containing these sentences and matched each fact with its corresponding bilingual evidence.

We observed that not all Wikipedia-derived facts are relevant to health information seekers (e.g., some facts are historical or highly technical). For instance, statements such as "Vitamin C exhibits low/acute toxicity" are relevant, whereas others like "If a dog was sick, they would get better food" are not.. To remove irrelevant content, we implemented a relevance filter. As the corpus is large, running GPT-4o-mini over all facts would be time-consuming and costly. To lower inference cost while preserving quality, we distilled GPT-4o-mini's judgments (and DeepSeek-R1 [14]'s for ZH) into a smaller model.

To calibrate task understanding and design the relevancy prompt, we performed annotations. First five authors labeled initially at least 25 EN samples, with two annotators per sample. We held regular discussions to refine the annotation guidelines. Inter-annotator agreement, measured by Krippendorff's alpha [11] on a subset of 52 samples, was $\alpha = 0.72$. Each of us then labeled 50

---

[6] In [32] random guessing outperformed Natural Language Inference Transformers.

samples in their respective language. The annotations form the test set for comparing the LLMs with transformer-based models across languages. The finalized EN prompt was translated into other languages by native speakers.

We annotated 2,000 TR and EN, 4,000 DE, 3,000 IT, and 3,000 ZH samples with LLMs. GPT-4o-mini was used for all except ZH, which was labeled with DeepSeek-R1 due to poor alignment. Each dataset was randomly split into 70% training and 30% development sets. We fine-tuned language specific transformers on their monolingual dataset (Roberta-base [24] for EN, BertTurk[7] for TR, German BERT [8] for DE) and Chinese BERT [8] for the ZH dataset. Additionally, each non-EN dataset was combined with the EN samples, and XLM-RoBERTa was then fine-tuned [5] on the respective combined dataset (e.g., the TR and EN datasets were combined to predict the TR samples using XLM-RoBERTa). All models were fine-tuned with a learning rate of 2e-5, for 3 epochs, and a batch size of 16. The models with the best F1-macro scores (see Table 2) were selected.

Except for ZH, cross-lingual models performed best and were used as relevance classifiers. Finally, we labeled the corpora with the fine-tuned transformers [41] and discarded unrelated samples.

3.2   Question and Answer Generation

Question Generation. We generated synthetic health-related questions using a prompt that instructed GPT-4o-mini to act as a health information seeker. The prompt took as input a Wiki page name, a fact, and its paragraph. From the dataset mentioned in Sect. 3.1, we sampled 1,100 samples per language to generate.

Formally, let each data instance be represented as $d = (f_x, f_{en}, p_x, p_{en})$, where f_x is a fact in Language X, $f_{en} = \{f_{en}^1, \ldots, f_{en}^n\}$ ($n \geq 1$) is its aligned EN fact(s), p_x is the paragraph in Language X containing f_x, and p_{en} is the aligned EN paragraph(s). Given (f_x, p_x, p_{en}), we used GPT-4o-mini to generate a question q_x in Language X and then translated it to EN with Google Translate to get the question pair.

We evaluated the quality of the generated questions based on the LLM-as-a-Judge technique [13] using ChatGPT-5 (Extended Thinking) [27]. This prompt instructed ChatGPT-5 to execute a deterministic Python-based evaluation pipeline within its data-analysis sandbox [27]. The model applied four binary criteria to each question: (1) relevance to both the input fact and the source paragraph, (2) answerability based solely on the paragraph, (3) alignment with natural health-seeker intent, and (4) clarity of expression.

To assess alignment with human judgments, we sampled 20 items per language and compared ChatGPT-5's decisions to native-speaker annotations. The agreement ranged from 44% to 76% (highest for TR, lowest for DE). ChatGPT-5 consistently accepted fewer questions than human annotators, indicating a more conservative criterion. Based on this preliminary evidence, we used ChatGPT-5 as a pre-filter for question quality.

---

[7] https://huggingface.co/dbmdz/bert-base-turkish-cased.

Answer Generation. To generate answers, we use multilingual, open-weight LLMs from distinct organizations to mitigate model-family bias in our evaluation. The models are Llama 3.3–70B (Meta; an upgraded release of Llama 3 [12]), Qwen (Qwen3-Next-80B-A3B-Instruct) [44] from Alibaba Cloud and Aya (Expanse-32b) from Cohere [6]. We discarded DeepSeek-R1 from the analysis due to its size and cost. We run Aya locally on a GPU, while the other models are accessed via APIs through Hugging Face Inference.[8] For all LLMs, we set the temperature at 1 and the maximum token length to 4,096. The final dataset comprises 854 TR, 997 DE, 502 IT, and 548 ZH samples. We manually reviewed a subset of Q&A pairs: most answers are relevant, with only a few misalignments due to broader questions than the available Wikipedia evidence.

4 Experiments and Results

Main research question in this paper is how disparities across languages in pre-training data contribute to inconsistencies in LLM answers for multilingual healthcare Q&A. We first characterize healthcare-related Wikipedia pages, we then evaluate each model's answers for cross-lingual factual alignment against evidence extracted from the corresponding pages.

4.1 Comparison of Wikipedia Pages

We examine the amount of information presented in Wikipedia articles across languages. To this extent, we compare number of sections, paragraphs, facts and external links that the articles cited.

As articles are typically organized into sections that aid navigation and reflect the logical structure of the content, we use the number of sections as a simple, language-agnostic proxy. Accordingly, we measure and compare section counts across languages. We use Beautiful Soup to parse each article's HTML.[9] Next, we count the paragraphs and facts obtained through InfoGap, as described in Sect. 3.1, with the results summarized in Table 3. Lastly, we analyze the references cited by Wikipedia editors to examine how reference preferences vary across languages. References serve as important indicators of information diversity and reliability. We restrict our analysis to entries with articles in all target languages. We begin by comparing the number of references per article across languages and then compare the sources cited by each edition. Additionally, we extract the sources of the external links by using `tldextract`.[10]

Amount of information (sections, paragraphs, facts and links) in EN Wiki pages, according to paired t-test result [31], is statistically more than their pages in other languages (in Table 4). EN edition contains the most paragraphs, followed by DE and IT. It also yields substantially more extracted facts than other

---

[8] https://huggingface.co/docs/huggingface_hub/en/package_reference/inference_client.

[9] https://beautiful-soup-4.readthedocs.io/en/latest/.

[10] https://github.com/john-kurkowski/tldextract.

Table 3. Statistics of paragraphs, facts and aligned facts on the Wiki pages of Multi-WikiHealthCare. NA is Not Applicable. Many EN facts don't exist in other language editions. ZH Wiki has the lowest aligned facts with the EN wiki pages.

			Aligned facts (%)	
Language	Paragraphs	Facts	EN → Target	Target → EN
EN	26,752	205,468	NA	NA
TR	8,554	47,711	33.79%	91.82%
ZH	728	6,155	6.98%	59.46%
DE	18,284	118,268	23.36%	98.44%
IT	14,846	96,342	26.73%	54.23%

Table 4. The English (EN) Wiki pages contain statistically more information than their other editions (Paired t-test p value).

	Sections	Paragraphs	Facts	Links
TR-EN	1.51×10^{-96}	2.88×10^{-87}	1.72×10^{-106}	6.24×10^{-68}
DE-EN	2.48×10^{-22}	3.39×10^{-28}	1.99×10^{-48}	7.14×10^{-79}
ZH-EN	1.44×10^{-77}	1.39×10^{-141}	1.59×10^{-133}	6.55×10^{-60}
IT-EN	1.35×10^{-50}	1.80×10^{-50}	9.11×10^{-70}	4.75×10^{-74}

editions, and many EN facts lack counterparts in other languages. Among all editions, ZH Wikipedia has the fewest facts aligned with EN. A plausible explanation for this discrepancy is that the EN edition draws on a broader, more globally distributed editor base than other language editions.

Across languages, domains associated with the National Institutes of Health and the Centers for Disease Control and Prevention are common. Other high-frequency domains are news outlets, scholarly journals, and file archives. Distinctively, the DE edition also cites national sources (e.g. rki.de, aerzteblatt.de). In summary, citation coverage and practices vary substantially across language editions, reflecting differences in local information ecosystems and editorial norms.

4.2 Analyzing Answers

Since our analysis tools are primarily designed for EN, we translated all non-EN answers and their supporting evidence into EN prior to scoring. We begin the analysis with the response length. Across non-EN prompts, Qwen consistently produced longer answers, reflecting a tendency toward more elaborated outputs. For questions originally written in ZH, most models generated relatively short responses, except for Qwen, which produced notably longer ones. Qwen might be trained on a larger proportion of ZH data compared to the others.

We evaluate answer pairs in EN and other languages against their corresponding Wikipedia evidence using AlignScore [47], which computes sentence-level

Table 5. Factual alignment between answers and Wiki excerpts in the source-language (non-EN) and English (EN), measured with AlignScore. Non-EN content was translated into EN. Answers generally align more with EN pages, while EN questions show lower similarity to source-language references.

Query	Llama		Aya		Qwen	
	non-EN	EN	non-EN	EN	non-EN	EN
TR	27.44	30.89	17.78	22.62	14.45	18.31
EN	16.96	21.64	15.03	20.02	14.04	18.28
DE	18.13	18.56	16.26	17.92	13.64	16.59
EN	16.85	18.68	14.69	17.37	13.38	17.02
ZH	22.39	28.13	20.22	26.78	17.45	22.71
EN	20.09	26.23	16.90	23.81	15.58	21.72
IT	20.16	23.51	16.40	20.94	14.12	18.41
EN	16.65	21.64	15.04	19.97	13.54	17.97

factual consistency by matching each answer sentence to all evidence segments ("context chunks") with a RoBERTa alignment model [24]. Because many questions originated in non-EN languages, the aligned EN evidence often comprises multiple passages; when this occurs, we use the passage that yields the highest AlignScore for the given answer. Answers from conversational LLMs frequently include background and discursive material beyond the minimal facts needed to address a question [42], whereas our evidence snippets are concise and fact-dense. Consequently, absolute AlignScores tend to be modest; we interpret them as a relative proxy for factual alignment rather than a comprehensive quality metric. Therefore, we expect higher scores when a response is factually similar to the source-language reference, and lower scores otherwise.

Table 5 shows that the generated answers are factually close to EN references in most cases. However, when questions are asked in EN, factual alignment decreases for all languages except DE. In particular, factual alignment is higher when evaluated against source-language evidence than against evidence from the EN Wikipedia pages. This finding is consistent with prior work showing that responses to equivalent prompts can diverge across EN and non-EN settings [17, 35].

Lastly, we used the Spearman correlation coefficient [40] (ρ) to assess the relationship between Wikipedia page quality and LLM answer quality across languages. For this analysis, we additionally measured the relevance of the answers to the questions by using `ragas` [10] with GPT-4o-mini. Correlations were generally weak to moderate ($\rho = 0.01 - 0.34$). For it, tr, and de, the relationships were negligible or weak ($\rho < 0.20$), suggesting that the number of sections, paragraphs, or facts in the corresponding Wikipedia entries had limited predictive power for the factuality, relevance, or length of model outputs. In contrast, the correlations to the factuality scores for ZH were higher, reaching moderate strength for Aya ($\rho \approx 0.34$) and Llama ($\rho \approx 0.30$), and weak-to-moderate for Qwen ($\rho \approx 0.27$). Wikipedia content quality in ZH Wikipedia might have positive effect on factuality of the responses.

4.3 Case Study: Factuality Alignment

Table 6. When the excerpt from non-English (non-EN) Wiki pages is translated into EN, the answers are aligned more to the source context. With RAG, that is opposite.

Target	Method	Llama		Aya		Qwen	
		non-EN	EN	non-EN	EN	non-EN	EN
TR	Base	17.28	22.46	15.34	20.91	14.24	18.88
	Wiki	78.67	59.21	41.52	35.60	78.53	58.48
	RAG	23.51	33.71	15.55	21.45	15.91	27.10
DE	Base	16.89	18.70	14.71	17.41	13.41	17.02
	Wiki	80.68	27.62	34.73	18.43	72.72	20.86
	RAG	23.75	34.69	15.89	19.84	15.65	30.21
ZH	Base	22.44	28.13	16.89	23.87	15.47	21.74
	Wiki	83.14	51.39	43.67	34.40	77.99	46.95
	RAG	29.83	43.65	17.98	25.62	21.78	36.49
IT	Base	16.84	21.84	14.37	16.70	13.56	18.17
	Wiki	76.78	41.03	37.10	26.79	81.55	40.05
	RAG	24.56	40.05	15.31	21.06	15.83	20.29

Alignment of LLM responses with high-resource sources such as EN Wikipedia is often desirable, as health information in low-resource languages may be limited or lower quality [7,22,39]. In such cases, high-resource knowledge can help fill gaps. However, some scenarios require localized or domain-specific information, where EN-centric content may be unreliable or contextually inappropriate [45]. To explore this, we evaluated: (*i*) providing contextual information directly into the prompt, and (*ii*) performing RAG [23]. For the first method, we incorporated translated excerpts from non-EN Wikipedia pages that are semantically aligned with the given question. For RAG, we gathered scientific articles from PubMed,[11] considered a reliable external source of health information, using Paperscraper,[12] querying by entity and nationality keywords (e.g., 'allergy' + 'Turkish') to obtain culturally specific information. We discarded entities with fewer than 50 retrieved PubMed articles and perform analysis on the rest. The RAG system, based on the simple HuggingFace implementation,[13] employs the classical BM25 model

---

[11] https://pubmed.ncbi.nlm.nih.gov/.
[12] https://github.com/jannisborn/paperscraper.
[13] https://huggingface.co/blog/ngxson/make-your-own-rag.

for sparse retrieval [25]. We incorporated the top 10 articles that returned from the retriever into the prompt to enrich its context.

We compared the approaches against the baseline where the LLM responds to questions posed in EN (Sect. 4.2). Both approaches improve reference alignment by producing more factual and concise answers than the baseline. As shown in Fig. 6, LLMs incorporating excerpts from Wikipedia produce responses that align more closely with non-EN references, while with RAG, they align more with EN references. RAG results contain usually noisy context, leading to cases where LLMs are uncertain about their answers. Additionally, due to the increased prompt length, Aya was unable to generate responses for a few examples. Explicit, high-quality contextual information might be crucial for effective alignment. The setup represents an initial proof of concept rather than a comprehensive RAG evaluation, in future work, we plan to explore more advanced information retrieval and RAG methods to improve contextual relevance.

5   Conclusion

We introduced MultiWikiHealthCare, a multilingual benchmark for studying disparities across languages in healthcare Q&A. By pairing popular queries with language-specific Wikipedia evidence, we quantified how differences in coverage (e.g., structure, citations, and fact availability) shape model behavior. The results show substantial variability across languages: baseline LLMs often privilege EN-centric evidence, while conditioning generation on source-language excerpts shifts grounding toward locally relevant knowledge. These findings highlight a practical path for improving equity in multilingual healthcare Q&A, explicitly anchor answers in the user's language of reference rather than defaulting to EN.

Limitations. Finally, we acknowledge several limitations of our work: (*i*) AlignScore is EN-centric, so we translate non-EN content into EN, which may introduce artifacts; (*ii*) Wikipedia is the only reference source and not a clinical gold standard, so scores indicate alignment to Wikipedia rather than medical correctness or guideline adherence, without independent fact-checking; (*iii*) budget constraints (paid APIs for most models) and limited native speakers restricted the number of Q&A pairs and single-turn interactions; and (*iv*) because LLMs are trained on heterogeneous sources, their knowledge may not align with Wikipedia, so our findings reflect alignment *relative to Wikipedia* rather than clinical correctness.

Future Work. We plan to extend reference sources beyond Wikipedia to include multilingual clinical and public health materials. Incorporating such sources would enable evaluation of factual alignment not only to publicly accessible knowledge but also to clinically validated recommendations. We will replace translation dependent scoring with multilingual factuality assessments complemented by native-speaker adjudication; and expand the scope to larger datasets, more languages, and multi-turn interactions.

Acknowledgments. The work of IBS, FMB and LF was supported by Lamarr Institute for Machine Learning and Artificial Intelligence. The work of PR was supported by the MARTINI project on Malicious Actors Profiling and Detection in Online Social Networks Through Artificial Intelligence funded by MCIN/AEI/ 10.13039/501100011033 and by EU NextGenerationEU/PRTR. The work of BS and CB was supported by TANGO (Grant Agreement no. 101120763). Views and opinions expressed are, however, those of the author(s) only and do not necessarily reflect those of the European Union or the European Health and Digital Executive Agency (HaDEA). Neither the European Union nor the granting authority can be held responsible for them.

Ethics Statement. All analyses used publicly available Wikipedia data. Therefore, no private, sensitive, or personally identifiable health information was accessed or processed. All evaluations were performed solely for research purposes, and none of the LLMs analyzed should be solely used to provide a medical device. We acknowledge that the disparities observed across languages and Wikipedia may reflect broader inequities in global health communication and data representation. Through this analysis, we aim to promote more equitable and fair multilingual health-care applications.

References

1. Abacha, A.B., Agichtein, E., Pinter, Y., Demner-Fushman, D.: Overview of the medical question answering task at TREC 2017 liveqa. In: TREC. NIST Special Publication, vol. 500-324. NIST (2017)
2. Abacha, A.B., Mrabet, Y., Sharp, M., Goodwin, T.R., Shooshan, S.E., Demner-Fushman, D.: Bridging the gap between consumers' medication questions and trusted answers. In: MedInfo. Studies in Health Technology and Informatics, vol. 264, pp. 25–29. IOS Press (2019)
3. Achiam, J., et al.: Gpt-4 technical report (2023). arXiv:2303.08774
4. Agarwal, V., Jin, Y., Chandra, M., De Choudhury, M., Kumar, S., Sastry, N.: Medhalu: hallucinations in responses to healthcare queries by large language models (2024). arXiv:2409.19492
5. Conneau, A., et al.: Unsupervised cross-lingual representation learning at scale. In: Jurafsky, D., Chai, J., Schluter, N., Tetreault, J. (eds.) Proceedings of the 58th Annual Meeting of the Association for Computational Linguistics, pp. 8440–8451. Association for Computational Linguistics, Online (2020). https://doi.org/10.18653/v1/2020.acl-main.747, https://aclanthology.org/2020.acl-main.747/
6. Dang, J., et al.: Aya expanse: combining research breakthroughs for a new multilingual frontier (2024). arXiv:2412.04261
7. Davaris, M., Barnett, S., Abouassaly, R., Lawrentschuk, N., et al.: Thoracic surgery information on the internet: a multilingual quality assessment. Interact J. Med. Res. **6**(1), e6732 (2017)
8. Devlin, J., Chang, M.W., Lee, K., Toutanova, K.: BERT: pre-training of deep bidirectional transformers for language understanding. In: ACL, pp. 4171–4186. ACL, Minneapolis, Minnesota (2019)
9. Dubey, A., et al.: The llama 3 herd of models (2024). arXiv:2407.21783
10. Es, S., James, J., Espinosa Anke, L., Schockaert, S.: RAGAs: automated evaluation of retrieval augmented generation. In: EACL: System Demonstrations, pp. 150–158. St. Julians, Malta (2024). https://doi.org/10.18653/v1/2024.eacl-demo.16

11. Ford, J.M.: Content analysis: an introduction to its methodology. Pers. Psychol. **57**(4), 1110 (2004)
12. Grattafiori, A., et al.: The Llama 3 Herd of Models (2024). arXiv:2407.21783
13. Gu, J., et al.: A survey on LLM-as-a-judge. The. Innovation (2026). https://doi.org/10.1016/j.xinn.2025.101253
14. Guo, D., et al.: Deepseek-r1 incentivizes reasoning in LLMs through reinforcement learning. Nature **645**(8081), 633–638 (2025)
15. Gupta, A., Mehta, M., Xu, Z., Srikumar, V.: Found in translation: measuring multilingual LLM consistency as simple as translate then evaluate (2025). arXiv:2505.21999
16. Hurst, A., et al.: GPT-4o System Card (2024). arXiv:2410.21276
17. Jin, Y., Chandra, M., Verma, G., Hu, Y., De Choudhury, M., Kumar, S.: Better to ask in English: cross-lingual evaluation of large language models for healthcare queries. In: The Web Conference, pp. 2627–2638. ACM, New York, NY, USA (2024)
18. Kaur, N., Choudhury, M., Pruthi, D.: Evaluating large language models for health-related queries with presuppositions. In: Findings of the ACL, pp. 14308–14331. ACL, Bangkok, Thailand (2024)
19. Kim, Y., et al.: Medical hallucinations in foundation models and their impact on healthcare (2025). arXiv:2503.05777
20. Koopman, B., Zuccon, G.: Dr ChatGPT tell me what I want to hear: how different prompts impact health answer correctness. In: EMNLP, pp. 15012–15022. ACL, Singapore (2023)
21. Kwon, W., et al.: Efficient memory management for large language model serving with pagedattention. In: ACM SIGOPS (2023)
22. Lawrentschuk, N., Abouassaly, R., Hewitt, E., Mulcahy, A., Bolton, D., Jobling, T.: Health information quality on the internet in gynecological oncology: a multilingual evaluation. Eur. J. Gynaecol. Oncol. **37**(4) (2016)
23. Lewis, P., et al.: Retrieval-augmented generation for knowledge-intensive NLP tasks. In: NIPS. NIPS '20, Curran Associates Inc., Red Hook, NY, USA (2020)
24. Liu, Y., et al.: Roberta: a robustly optimized Bert pretraining approach (2019). arXiv:1907.11692
25. Lù, X.H.: Bm25s: orders of magnitude faster lexical search via eager sparse scoring (2024). arXiv:2407.03618
26. Nigatu, H.H., Abdelkadir, N.A., Tewelde, F., Chancellor, S., Wilkinson, D.: Into the void: understanding online health information in low-web data languages (2025). arXiv:2509.20245
27. OpenAI: Introducing gpt-5 (2025). https://openai.com/index/introducing-gpt-5/. Accessed 29 Sept 2025
28. Park, C.Y., Yan, X., Field, A., Tsvetkov, Y.: Multilingual contextual affective analysis of LGBT people portrayals in Wikipedia. In: ICWSM vol. 15, pp. 479–490 (2021)
29. Ranathunga, S., de Silva, N.: Some languages are more equal than others: probing deeper into the linguistic disparity in the NLP world. In: AACL-IJCNLP (Volume 1: Long Papers), pp. 823–848. ACL, Online (2022)
30. Restrepo, D., et al.: Multi-ophthalingua: a multilingual benchmark for assessing and debiasing LLM ophthalmological QA in LMICS. In: AAAI vo. 39, pp. 28321–28330 (2025)
31. Ross, A., Willson, V.L.: Paired samples t-test. In: Basic and Advanced Statistical Tests: Writing Results Sections and Creating Tables and Figures, pp. 17–19. Springer (2017)

32. Samir, F., Park, C.Y., Field, A., Shwartz, V., Tsvetkov, Y.: Locating information gaps and narrative inconsistencies across languages: a case study of LGBT people portrayals on Wikipedia. In: EMNLP 2024, pp. 6747–6762. ACL, Miami, Florida, USA (2024)
33. Sayin, B., Minervini, P., Staiano, J., Passerini, A.: Can LLMs correct physicians, yet? investigating effective interaction methods in the medical domain. In: The 6th Clinical NLP, pp. 218–237. ACL, Mexico City, Mexico (2024)
34. Schlicht, I.B., Fernandez, E., Chulvi, B., Rosso, P.: Automatic detection of health misinformation: a systematic review. J. AIHC **15**(3), 2009–2021 (2024)
35. Schlicht, I.B., Zhao, Z., Sayin, B., Flek, L., Rosso, P.: Do LLMs provide consistent answers to health-related questions across languages? In: ECIR, pp. 314–322. Springer Nature Switzerland (2025)
36. Singhal, K., et al.: Large language models encode clinical knowledge. Nature **620**(7972), 172–180 (2023)
37. Tierney, A.A., Reed, M.E., Grant, R.W., Doo, F.X., Payán, D.D., Liu, V.X.: Health Equity in the era of large language? models. Am. J. Managed Care **31**(3) (2025)
38. Wang, Z., Zhang, Y., Yoon, D., Vincent, N., Samir, F., Shwartz, V.: Wikigap: promoting epistemic equity by surfacing knowledge gaps between English wikipedia and other language editions (2025). arXiv:2505.24195
39. Weissenberger, C., et al.: Breast cancer: patient information needs reflected in English and German web sites. British J. of Cancer **91**(8), 1482–1487 (2004)
40. Wissler, C.: The spearman correlation formula. Science **22**(558), 309–311 (1905)
41. Wolf, T., et al.: Transformers: state-of-the-art natural language processing. In: EMNLP (Demos), pp. 38–45. ACL (2020)
42. Xu, F., Li, J.J., Choi, E.: How do we answer complex questions: discourse structure of long-form answers. In: ACL (Volume 1: Long Papers), pp. 3556–3572. Dublin, Ireland (2022)
43. Yagnik, N., Jhaveri, J., Sharma, V., Pila, G.: Medlm: exploring language models for medical question answering systems (2024). arXiv:2401.11389
44. Yang, A., et al.: Qwen3 technical report. arXiv:2505.09388 (2025)
45. Yang, T., Valdez, S.: How machine translation is used in healthcare. Digit. Transl. (2025). https://doi.org/10.1075/dt.25015.yan
46. Yu, H., Yu, C., Wang, Z., Zou, D., Qin, H.: Enhancing healthcare through large language models: a study on medical question answering. In: ICPICS, pp. 895–900. IEEE (2024)
47. Zha, Y., Yang, Y., Li, R., Hu, Z.: AlignScore: evaluating factual consistency with a unified alignment function. In: ACL, pp. 11328–11348. ACL, Toronto, Canada (2023)
48. Zhang, Y., et al.: Siren's song in the AI ocean: a survey on hallucination in large language models. Comput. Linguistics, 1–46 (2025)
49. Zhu, M., Ahuja, A., Wei, W., Reddy, C.K.: A hierarchical attention retrieval model for healthcare question answering. In: WWW, pp. 2472–2482. ACM (2019)

Efficient/Low-Resource Methods in NLP

Tokenizations for Austronesian Language Models: Study on Languages in Indonesia Archipelago

Andhika Bernad Lumbantobing[1(✉)], Hokky Situngkir[1,2],
and Kevin Siringo Ringo[1]

[1] Bandung Fe Institute, Bandung, Indonesia
`nad@compsoc.bandungfe.net`
[2] AI Research Center IT Del, Laguboti, Indonesia

Abstract. Tokenization constitutes a fundamental stage in Large Language Model (LLM) processing; however, subword-based tokenization methods optimized on English-dominant corpora may produce token fragmentation misaligned with the linguistic structures of Austronesian languages. This study aimed to develop a syllable-based tokenization framework adopting principles from traditional Indonesian scripts (aksara) for regional languages of Indonesia. A syllabic segmentation procedure was constructed based on the logic of abugida writing systems and implemented with a vocabulary of 2,843 tokens extracted from the Indonesian dictionary (KBBI). Evaluation was conducted on the NusaX dataset comprising 1,000 parallel translation samples across 10 regional languages, Indonesian, and English. Analysis employed Token per Character (TPC) ratio and sequence alignment using the Smith-Waterman algorithm. Results demonstrated that syllable-based tokenization yielded consistent TPC values ($\sim$0.4) across all regional languages, whereas GPT-2 exhibited an inverse pattern with the lowest TPC for English. Syllable-based tokenization consistently produced higher token sequence similarity scores, with an average increase of approximately 21% (slope $m \approx 1.21$) compared to GPT-2. These findings confirm that the syllable-based approach more effectively preserves phonological and morphological patterns across related Austronesian languages, offering a linguistically principled foundation for multilingual LLM development.

Keywords: tokenization · syllable · Austronesian languages · Indonesian scripts · Large Language Model

1 Introduction

One of the critical stages in the processing of modern text-based *Large Language Models* (LLMs) is tokenization, the process of decomposing human-readable text into discrete units called tokens. The operational domain of LLMs is constrained to these units. Input text is transformed into a sequence of tokens, which are subsequently mapped to numerical representations. These representations serve as the internal computational substrate that enables the model to perform algebraic operations on linguistic phenomena. During the inference or text generation phase, these numerical representations are processed through neural network layers with trained weights [38]. Language generation in LLMs is, in principle, a process of forming token combinations, where each token is selected based on contextual information contained in the preceding token combinations, thereby enabling the formation of novel linguistic objects [13]. The tokenization strategy and the resulting tokens thus determine and direct the types of linguistic regularities that a language model can learn and internalize [22].

In practice, tokenization cannot be regarded as a neutral or entirely language-agnostic preprocessing step [1]. Modern LLMs predominantly employ subword-based tokenization schemes such as *BPE* [34], *WordPiece* [33], and *Unigram* [19]. These methods are driven by statistical efficiency optimization objectives that are highly sensitive to the characteristics, distributions, and regularities found in their training corpora [4], which directly determine the vocabulary inventory or subwords deemed important through training, including morphological patterns, phonotactics, and orthographic conventions. Training tokenization with these methods on corpora disproportionately dominated by a small subset of particular languages, such as English, introduces structural biases that favor certain linguistic forms [27,32,39], while their application to languages with fundamentally different linguistic typologies may produce token fragments that are misaligned with the language structure and obscure meaningful linguistic boundaries and patterns.

The study on the development of an Indonesian Language Model (ToBA-LM) [36] demonstrated that tokenization strategies designed based on linguistic principles can enhance language naturalness in downstream text generation performance. Following this approach, we position tokenization as a linguistically motivated design choice. This study explores opportunities for extending the application of syllabic segmentation-based approaches to regional languages in Indonesia that share similar characteristics within the Austronesian language family. The distinctive characteristics of Austronesian languages motivate the design of a cross-linguistic tokenization framework that can be applied consistently at the language family level.

In its implementation, we adopt the principles of traditional writing systems as the computational foundation for designing syllable-based tokenization schemes. Traditional scripts in Indonesia, which belong to the abugida (*alphasyllabary*) writing system, inherently represent syllabic units as their basic elements. Historically, this system constituted the dominant form of orthography in literacy practices across the archipelago and can be viewed as a form of language encoding aligned with natural speech boundaries, emerging from the mechanics of speech production and the cognitive processes of its speakers [13].

The initial section of this paper discusses the linguistic characteristics of languages within the Austronesian family and the principal tenets of traditional Indonesian-ethnic based writing systems that underpin the construction of the proposed syllable-based tokenization. The subsequent section elaborates on the computational procedures for constructing the tokenization scheme along with the technical adjustments required for its integration into modern LLM architectures. To evaluate the proposed approach based on linguistic alignment criteria, this study conducts an empirical comparison with the GPT-2 subword tokenization scheme as a statistically-driven tokenization approach without explicit linguistic assumptions.

2   Austronesian Languages and Traditional Writing Systems

The Austronesian language family constitutes one of the largest and most geographically dispersed language families in the world, encompassing more than 1,200 languages spanning from Madagascar to Easter Island, and from Taiwan to New Zealand [3]. The structural similarities among Austronesian languages reflect their common origin, namely Proto-Austronesian (PAn), an ancestral language estimated to have been spoken thousands of years ago in the Taiwan region. Linguistic reconstruction indicates that the basic lexical units in PAn are canonical roots that are predominantly disyllabic. This phonotactic pattern is generally reconstructed as CV(C)CVC, where C represents a consonant and V a vowel [3]. This pattern remains evident in modern Austronesian languages, including Indonesian, which exhibits a relatively simple syllable structure with a maximum CVC boundary, as well as a strong tendency toward disyllabic words [21].

In addition to these phonological characteristics, Austronesian languages are marked by rich and agglutinative morphological systems. In agglutinative languages, word formation is accomplished productively through the sequential addition of affixes to base forms, including prefixes, suffixes, infixes, circumfixes, and reduplication processes [17]. Functionally, these affix sequences serve as markers of complex grammatical relations, including voice marking, valency changes such as causatives, and applicative constructions. Although the Austronesian lexicon is generally built upon disyllabic roots, the application of agglutinative rules to the root inventory constitutes the primary factor in the formation of complex derived words, which may consist of three, four, or even more syllables. Indonesian likewise exhibits these characteristics. A quantitative study of Indonesian morphology [12] demonstrates high productivity in affixation, reduplication, compounding, and cliticization. This agglutinative character is also found in regional languages of the Indonesian archipelago, such as Javanese [29], Sundanese [7], and Batak [25].

The combination of predominantly disyllabic roots and agglutinative morphology that "stacks" affixes renders the syllable a stable and fundamental organizational unit in Austronesian languages. This uniformity of characteristics found across various Austronesian languages motivates the design of a cross-linguistic tokenization framework centered on syllables that can be applied to *large language model* (LLM) implementations at the language family level. This framework also addresses two functional limitations inherent in phoneme-based and word-based tokenization. Tokenization schemes based solely on phonemes fail to capture the prosodic rhythm and natural structure of Austronesian languages, while whole-word tokenization would encounter an explosion of morphological variation that triggers high *out-of-vocabulary* (OOV) ratios, particularly in scenarios with constrained vocabulary budgets.

In implementing the syllable-based tokenization framework, we adopt the processing logic from traditional writing systems that developed in the Indonesian archipelago, namely the Indonesian-ethnic based scripts. According to linguistic classification, these traditional writing systems are categorized as *abugida* [9,10] or *alphasyllabary* [5,6], wherein the basic linear unit, termed "aksara" or "akhsara" is essentially a syllable. An aksara may consist of a consonant with an inherent vowel, a consonant with a vowel diacritic, an independent vowel, a consonant cluster with a vowel, or a consonant with a "killed" vowel [6]. This system originates from the Brahmi script of ancient India in the 3rd century BCE, which was used during the Ashokan Empire [11]. Through its dissemination, the script underwent divergence and active adaptation to accommodate the distinctive linguistic contours of each region. The earliest form to enter the Indonesian archipelago was the Pallava script from South India, which subsequently developed into the Kawi script in Java-Bali and the Malay regions. Additionally, contact with traders from Gujarat who introduced the Nagari script contributed to the emergence of various local scripts in Sumatra (including Batak and Surat Ulu/Rejang) and in Sulawesi (Bugis-Makassar), which later gave rise to derivative scripts in Ende and Bima [11,23]. Beyond Indonesia, similar writing systems are also found extensively in other Southeast Asian languages, such as those of Myanmar, Thailand, Laos, Cambodia, and the Philippines [8,20].

Despite exhibiting graphemic variations and orthographic realizations through diverse formal mechanisms according to regional specificities, language processing, particularly syllable segmentation, in Indonesian-ethnic script systems operates according to similar fundamental principles and demonstrates convergent functional patterns. Based on these commonalities, we construct tokenization procedures for Latin script representations of regional languages by abstracting and simulating the internal logic of the Indonesian-ethnic scripts.

2.1 Aksara

Unlike alphabetic systems that are based on segmental phonemes, aksara writing systems (and abugida systems in general) employ the syllable as the fundamental orthographic unit. Each base character (glyph) represents either an independent vowel or a consonant with an inherent vowel, typically /a/. Certain phonemes such as /ng/ and /ny/, which in Latin alphabet-based romanization are realized through the digraphs ⟨ng⟩ and ⟨ny⟩, are represented graphemically in traditional scripts as single units with inherent vowels (⟨*nga*⟩ and ⟨*nya*⟩), as can be observed in the Javanese-Balinese, Batak, and Bugis scripts. Vowel sound modification on consonants with inherent vowels is accomplished through the addition of diacritical marks that modify the base symbol, while vowel deletion to form coda consonants in producing closed syllable sounds is achieved through vowel suppression using a special marker (*virama*).

Inter-civilizational contact contributed to reconstructing the phonological inventory of local languages while simultaneously influencing their script systems as coded in the culture from which these languages originated [35]. Sanskrit influence, for instance, is manifested in the adoption of retroflex consonants in the Javanese script, which distinctly differentiates between dental series (⟨ta⟩, ⟨da⟩) and retroflex series (⟨*tha*⟩, ⟨*dha*⟩). Furthermore, Arabic and Malay influences enriched the fricative sound inventory. To accommodate these borrowed phonemes, modified glyphs or companion characters (*aksara rekan*) were developed. In the Javanese script, special symbols are found for sounds such as /x/ (kh), /ʃ/ (sy), /f/, /z/, and /q/. A similar phenomenon is observed in the Sundanese script, which developed seven modified characters to represent sounds such as ⟨fa⟩, ⟨va⟩, ⟨qa⟩, ⟨xa⟩, ⟨za⟩, ⟨*kh*a⟩, and ⟨*sy*a⟩.

2.2 Medial Clusters

In languages that permit consonant clusters, various script traditions have developed specialized mechanisms to represent consonant clusters (C1C2) without explicitly suppressing the inherent vowel. This mechanism is primarily applied to clusters where the second consonant (C2) is a semivowel or liquid, such as /r/, /l/, /y/, and /w/. This approach is found in classical Indian orthographic traditions as well as in several Indonesian ethnolinguistic traditions, such as Javanese-Balinese, which tend to avoid the use of *virama* in word-medial positions. In Javanese orthography, consonant clusters involving the sounds /r/, /l/, /y/, and /w/ are represented through special diacritics known as *sandhangan wyanjana*. The Sundanese script categorizes medial consonant markers under the class of *rarangkén*, namely *panyakra*, *panyiku*, and *pamingkal*. Meanwhile, in Balinese orthography, medial consonant markers are classified as *pangangge aksara*. In certain Sumatran writing traditions, such as Batak and Rejang, which did not develop specialized symbols for medial consonants, consonant cluster handling is accomplished by explicitly suppressing the vowel on C1 through a vowel killer mark (*virama*) (Table 1).

Table 1. Consonant Cluster Handling in Traditional Scripts

Medials	Javanese	Balinese	Sundanese
Medial /r/	Cakra	Guwung	Panyakra
Medial /y/	Pengkal	Nania	Pamingkal
Medial /l/	Pasangan La	Gantungan La	Panyiku

2.3   Coda Representation

Fundamentally, aksara units with their inherent vowels represent open syllables. To construct closed syllables, traditional script systems have developed several mechanisms. In general, a coda—one or more consonant sounds that close a syllable—is realized by nullifying the inherent vowel on a consonant aksara through a special symbol known as *virama*. In certain script traditions that avoid the use of *virama* in word-medial positions, such as the Javanese and Balinese scripts, specialized written forms have been developed that function similarly to *virama* in word-final positions. Table 2 illustrates the terminological differences for vowel suppression mechanisms found across several traditional scripts.

Table 2. Vowel Killers (*Virama*) in Traditional Scripts

Vowel Killers	Javanese	Balinese	Sundanese	Batak	Rejang
Mid-Word Killer	Pasangan	Gantungan	Pamaéh	Pangolat	–
Final Killer	Pangkon	Adeg-adeg	Pamaéh	Pangolat	Muris

In addition to vowel killer mechanisms, several traditional scripts have also developed specialized representations for certain codas, which are generally realized as diacritics that modify the base aksara. These diacritics are used to mark final consonants with high frequency of occurrence or prominent phonological function, such as the nasal consonant /ng/ or the liquid /r/. This enables the writing of closed syllables without complete reliance on generic vowel suppression mechanisms. In the Javanese script, these specific coda representations are known as *sandhangan panyigeg wanda*, while in the Balinese script, a similar mechanism is found within the diacritic class called *pangangge tengenan*. Table 3 presents the variety of nomenclature and functions of coda diacritics found in other traditional scripts, such as Sundanese, Batak, and Rejang.

Table 3. Coda Diacritics in Traditional Scripts

Phoneme	Javanese	Balinese	Sundanese	Batak	Rejang
Final /ng/	Cecek	Cecek	Panyecek	Hamisaran	Tulang
Final /r/	Layar	Surang	Panglayar	–	Junjung
Final /h/	Wignyan	Bisah	Pangwisad	Hajoringan	Kah

3   Construction of Syllabic Segmentation for Austronesian Languages

In this section, we elaborate the procedure for transforming Latin text into sequences of syllabic segments according to rules based on aksara orthography. For the Latin alphabet Σ consisting of a vowel set $V = \{a,\ i,\ u,\ ...\} \subset \Sigma$ and consonants (non-vowels) $C = \Sigma \backslash V$, the segmentation procedure is defined as $P : \Sigma^* \rightarrow T^*$, which maps an input symbol sequence $S = (s_1...s_n)$, $s_i \in \Sigma$ to an output segment sequence $U = (u_1...u_k)$. Each segment u_i is an ordered tuple $(\omega,\ \nu,\ \kappa) \in T$, where $T \subseteq \Sigma^*$ is a subset of alphabet symbol sequences derived through P and represents syllables, with a structure defined as the arrangement of onset component ω, nucleus $\nu \in V \cup \{\varnothing\}$, and coda κ.

In phonetic terminology, onset refers to the consonant or consonant cluster preceding the vowel, while nucleus constitutes the syllable core, which is generally a vowel. In the context of traditional scripts, onset corresponds to the base consonant aksara, while the following nucleus represents the inherent vowel that may undergo sound modification or suppression. In closed syllable formations, the nucleus is followed by a consonant cluster termed coda. Several traditional script systems encode certain codas using specialized diacritics that modify the base aksara; these special codas are formalized as the set $H = \{ng,\ h,\ l,\ ...\} \subset C^*$. Members of set H are consonant sequences that are primarily treated as "attached" to the preceding nucleus and do not form a new onset.

To accommodate consonant digraph forms in the Latin alphabet that are represented as single aksara in traditional orthography, we define the digraph set $D = \{th,\ dh,\ ...\} \subset C^2$ as consonant sequences that are treated as indivisible or as a single unit. Additionally, semivowels that potentially form medial consonant clusters and receive specialized symbolization in traditional scripts are defined by the set $M = \{r,\ l,\ w,\ ...\} \subset C$. Medial cluster handling follows the modification mechanism on base aksara, which is applied only if the semivowel $s_i \subset S, s_i \in M$ satisfies two conditions: the following alphabet symbol $s_{i+1} \in V$ is a vowel, and the preceding s_{i-1} is a consonant or valid digraph that is neither a member of M (to avoid consecutive semivowels) nor a member of the special coda set H.

The segmentation process begins with a linear scanning phase over the input symbol sequence S from left to right to extract potential phonological units. During iterations in this phase, onset candidates (ω), whether single consonants, digraphs, or medial cluster formations, are evaluated. The vowel symbol following onset ω_j is designated as nucleus ν_j, and if nucleus ν_j is followed by a sequence that is a member of the special coda set H, that sequence is identified as coda κ_j for the corresponding syllabic unit to form the complete unit tuple $u_j = (\omega_j,\ \nu_j,\ \kappa_j)$. In conditions where a consonant or digraph is not directly followed by a vowel, that sequence is designated as onset for an isolated unit without nucleus or coda $u = (\omega, \varnothing, \varnothing)$. This unit will be handled in the subsequent phase following the vowel killer (*virama*) principle in traditional scripts. After a unit is defined, scanning continues to evaluate the onset for the next syllabic unit. This process repeats until the end of sequence S is reached. Onset identification for syllabic units can be formally expressed as follows.

$$\omega(i) = \begin{cases} \alpha\beta, & \beta \in M \wedge S[i + |\alpha| + 1] \in V \wedge \alpha \notin (H \cup M) \\ \alpha, & \text{otherwise} \end{cases} \tag{1}$$

and

$$\alpha = \begin{cases} S[i : i + 2], & S[i : i + 2] \in D \\ S[i], & \text{otherwise} \end{cases} \tag{2}$$

where V denotes vowels, M semivowel consonants, D consonant digraphs, and H the special coda set. After the syllabic unit sequence is identified by the initial phase, the procedure proceeds to handle units without nucleus $\nu(u) = \varnothing$. In traditional scripts, these units reflect consonant aksara that have undergone inherent vowel suppression and become codas in closed syllables. In this phase, backward iteration $(k, k - 1, ...2)$ is applied to sequence $U = (u_1...u_k)$ to identify units without nucleus and integrate them as coda components of the preceding syllabic unit:

$$\nu(u_i) = \varnothing \Rightarrow \kappa(u_{i-1}) \leftarrow \kappa(u_{i-1}) + \omega(u_i) \tag{3}$$

where ν, κ, and ω respectively denote the nucleus, coda, and onset of a syllabic unit. This *virama* mechanism simulation phase is then followed by a final phase that handles remaining units without nucleus. These units are generally complex consonant clusters in modern loanwords that deviate from local phonotactics and whose orthography is not yet accommodated by traditional rules. In this phase, forward iteration $(1, 2, ...k - 1)$ is applied to the syllabic sequence resulting from the previous phase. Each identified unit without nucleus is merged into the onset component of the following syllabic unit:

$$\nu(u_i) = \varnothing \Rightarrow \omega(u_{i+1}) \leftarrow \omega(u_i) + \omega(u_{i+1}) \tag{4}$$

The text segmentation procedure P elaborated above can be viewed as a composition of three processing phases. The first phase $\phi_{\text{scan}} : \Sigma^* \rightarrow T^*$ maps alphabet sequences into pre-tokens by identifying base aksara along with their inherent vowels as potential phonological units. The output of this processing is continued by the second transformation $\phi_{\text{vir}} : T^* \rightarrow T^*$, which reflects the principle of vowel suppression mechanism. The transformation $\phi_{\text{clus}} : T^* \rightarrow T^*$ is then applied to handle vowel-less consonant clusters not accommodated by the preceding processing. Thus, the function P that produces syllabic segment sequences can be written as the following composition function:

$$P = (\phi_{\text{clus}} \circ \phi_{\text{vir}} \circ \phi_{\text{scan}}) \tag{5}$$

4   Evaluation

4.1   Tokenization

To evaluate the proposed syllabic segmentation procedure, we implemented it within a tokenization scheme that adjusts to syllable distribution in language dictionaries. In this regard, we utilized the word list from the Kamus Besar Bahasa Indonesia (KBBI, the Great Dictionary of the Indonesian Language) as the training corpus to determine the base token vocabulary. Following the previous approach in [36], the segmentation procedure was first applied to the corpus to identify syllable units and estimate their unigram distribution. Syllables with high frequency of occurrence, which generally reflect local dependencies among character symbols in natural language text, were selected as tokens in vocabulary Σ, along with base symbols such as Unicode characters. To handle *Out-of-Vocabulary* (OOV) cases for the fraction of syllables not accommodated as tokens, we applied a *fallback* mechanism that decomposes syllable units into their constituent characters, which are mapped to base symbols in Σ. In this construction, the tokenization $\tau_\Sigma : \mathcal{X}^* \to \mathcal{T}_\Sigma^*$ that maps Latin alphabet sequences to token sequences can be written as:

$$\tau_\Sigma = (f_\Sigma \circ P) \tag{6}$$

where P is the syllabic segmentation function in Eq. (5), Σ is the vocabulary constructed based on training, and f_Σ maps syllable segments $u \notin \Sigma$ to single character sequences $u_1, ..., u_k \in \Sigma$.

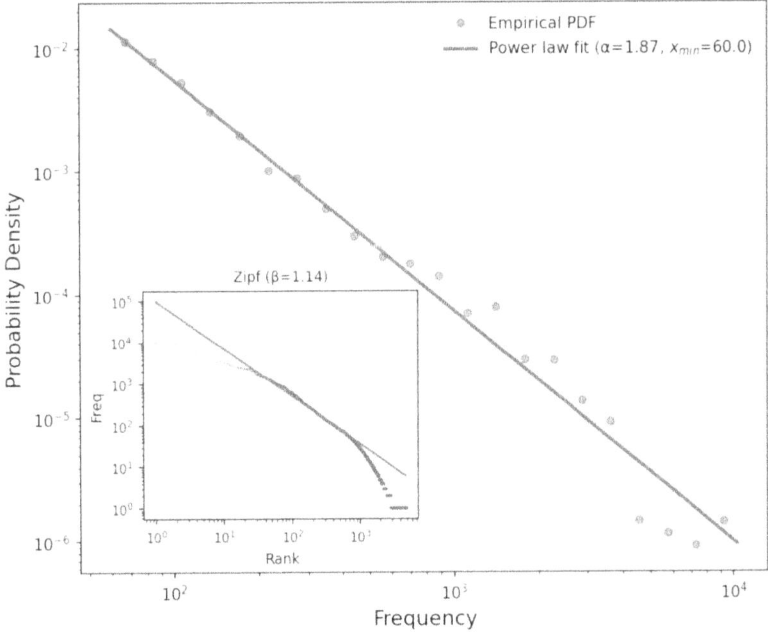

Fig. 1. The frequency distribution of syllable occurrences in the KBBI corpus follows a power law $p(x) \sim x^{-\alpha}$ with coefficient $\alpha \approx 1.87$. **Inset:** Syllable rank distribution with $\beta = \frac{1}{\alpha-1} \approx 1.14$.

In the evaluation phase, we employed syllable-based tokenization with a vocabulary size of $|\Sigma| = 2,843$. The composition of this vocabulary comprises syllables with the highest frequency of occurrence, monosyllabic lexemes, and base character symbols. Although the vocabulary was constructed exclusively based on the Indonesian language corpus distribution, testing was conducted on corpora involving regional languages as a cross-linguistic evaluation. As a baseline comparison, we utilized the GPT-2 *tokenizer* [31], which has a vocabulary size of $50,257$. The GPT-2 *tokenizer* is a *subword*-based tokenization scheme constructed using the *Byte Pair Encoding* algorithm [14] to optimize byte sequence compression on 40GB of Internet text data in the WebText training corpus (Fig. 1).

4.2   Data

Evaluation was conducted using the NusaX dataset [40], a multilingual parallel corpus encompassing 10 regional languages in Indonesia: Acehnese (ace), Balinese (ban), Banjarese (bjn), Toba Batak (bbc), Buginese (bug), Javanese (jav), Madurese (mad), Minangkabau (min), Ngaju (nij), and Sundanese (su), along with their Indonesian and English equivalents. This dataset was developed by translating SmSA [30], an Indonesian sentiment analysis dataset containing comments and reviews, to support sentiment analysis and machine translation tasks. We specifically utilized the machine translation subset (NusaX-MT) and employed all 1,000 available samples (comprising the combined 500 training samples, 100 validation samples, and 400 test samples) for analytical purposes. Table 4 presents statistics on the number of unique words for each language in the NusaX corpus.

Table 4. Unique Word Count Statistics in NusaX

id	en	ace	ban	bbc	bjn	bug	jav	mad	min	nij	su
4,259	4,277	4,239	4,914	4,658	4,621	5,121	4,708	4,863	4,454	3,986	4,688

Analysis in the evaluation was performed on tokenization outputs. The data preparation phase was conducted by processing each sample in the corpus using both the syllable-based tokenizer and GPT-2. This phase produced token sequences as encoded representations of each sample in the respective languages.

4.3   Methods

Segmentation Compatibility and Cross-Linguistic Syllables. The multilingual effectiveness of syllable-based tokenization schemes can be measured based on their representational capacity when applied to target languages. Within the framework of the proposed tokenization procedure, evaluation can be conducted on the compatibility of tokens trained on the Indonesian corpus against regional languages. The presence of language-specific syllable segments or segmentation patterns misaligned with the linguistic characteristics of the target language may cause candidate segments to be unaccommodated in the tokenizer vocabulary. This condition is subsequently handled by the fallback mechanism, which decomposes such segments into single character symbols, thereby producing longer token sequences. For a symbol sequence $S = (s_1, ...s_k)$ as text in a target language, this can be quantified by calculating the *Token per Character* (TPC) ratio as follows:

$$\text{TPC}(S) = \frac{|\tau_\Sigma(S)|}{|S|} \tag{7}$$

where $|\tau_\Sigma(S)|$ is the length of the encoded representation of S after tokenization by τ_Σ, and $|S|$ is the sequence length prior to tokenization. TPC values in target languages exhibiting significant differences from the source language value (in this case, Indonesian) indicate misalignment between the tokenization scheme and the target language structure.

Token Sequence Alignment. Tokenization schemes aligned with linguistic features enable models to exploit lexical and morphological similarities across languages, as well as facilitate semantic representation alignment in *joint training* strategies for multilingual LLMs within the same language family [2,28]. Misalignment between tokenization schemes and the linguistic structure of the languages they represent can distort relevant linguistic boundaries [16] and diminish the potential benefits of cross-linguistic learning [26]. Approaches that rely solely on full lexical overlap among cognate languages tend to overlook internal variation and divergence, including local phenomena such as dialectal differences. Conversely, syllable-based approaches that decompose words into sublexical units have the potential to reveal shared patterns in token sequences across languages with similar typologies.

In the context of language translation, these shared patterns may manifest as cognates and dialectal variations, and their identification requires approaches sensitive to sound shifts and affixation changes. Structurally, this is analogous to mutation, insertion, and deletion phenomena in genetic sequences. In bioinformatics, *sequence alignment* was developed to align DNA, RNA, or protein sequences to identify regions of similarity while handling mismatches, point mutations, and gaps that may arise from evolutionary divergence [18,24]. Significant sequence similarity following alignment can indicate common ancestry or functional similarity. To evaluate the proposed tokenization scheme, we adopt the application of *sequence alignment* on tokenization outputs to measure the extent to which the tokenization scheme produces segments aligned with meaningful linguistic patterns and capable of capturing similarity in token sequence pairs across languages with similar typologies.

Specifically, we employ the local alignment method, which enables detection of significant local similarity regions between sequence pairs that are globally divergent. This approach focuses on conserved fragments while disregarding portions with low similarity, and permits measurement of linguistic similarity despite differences in token position or sequence length. We implemented this local alignment using the Smith-Waterman algorithm [15,37].

For token sequence pairs resulting from the same tokenization procedure $\tau_\Sigma(S_1) = a_1a_2...a_n$ and $\tau_\Sigma(S_2) = b_1b_2...b_m$, we construct a scoring matrix H of dimensions $(n+1) \times (m+1)$ and initialize the first column and row with zeros, $H_{k,0} = H_{0,l} = 0$ for $0 \leq k \leq n$ and $0 \leq l \leq m$. This initialization allows the alignment process to commence from any position in the sequences without incurring initial penalties. The procedure then continues by populating scores for each remaining matrix element H in order, from left to right and top to bottom. This process considers results from substitution (diagonal score) as well as gap insertion (horizontal and vertical scores). The score at each element $H_{i,j}$ represents the maximum similarity of subsequences ending at tokens a_i and b_j. This value is obtained through the following recursive relation:

$$H_{ij} = \max\{H_{i-1,j-1} + s(a_i,b_j), \max_{k \geq 1}(H_{i-k,j} - w_k), \max_{l \geq 1}(H_{i,j-l} - w_l), 0\} \quad (8)$$

for $1 \leq i \leq n$ and $1 \leq j \leq m$, where $s(a_i,b_j)$ is the match score if tokens a_i and b_j are identical or the penalty score if they differ, while w_k and w_l are respectively the penalties for gaps of length k in sequence $\tau_\Sigma(S_1)$ and length l in $\tau_\Sigma(S_2)$. The use of zero as the lower bound ensures non-negative scores to disregard sequence portions with low similarity. In the evaluation conducted, we applied a scoring scheme that prioritizes exact matches while maintaining flexibility for gaps and token mismatches, using the following weights:

$$s(a_i,b_j) = \begin{cases} 2, & a_i = b_j \\ -1, & a_i \neq b_j \end{cases} \quad (9)$$

$$w_k = w_l = 1 \quad (10)$$

The maximum value in the matrix, $\max(H)$, is identified as the highest score marking the terminal position of subsequences from $\tau_\Sigma(S_1)$ and $\tau_\Sigma(S_2)$ with the most optimal match among all possible subsequences. This score is used as a similarity measure between corresponding sentence pairs in two different languages, and is normalized against the geometric mean of the maximum potential scores of each sequence to neutralize the influence of sequence length. The similarity value between text pairs S_1 and S_2 is formulated as follows:

$$\text{sim}(S_1, S_2) = \frac{\max(H)}{2 \times \sqrt{|\tau_\Sigma(S_1)||\tau_\Sigma(S_2)|}} \quad (11)$$

where H is the scoring matrix calculated based on the weights in Eqs. (9) and (10).

4.4   Results

Evaluation of *Tokens per Character* (TPC) values reveals contrasting performance patterns between the syllable-based tokenization scheme and GPT-2, as illustrated in Fig. 2. Although the vocabulary for syllable-based tokenization was extracted exclusively from the Indonesian corpus, the TPC values produced across various regional languages demonstrate a high degree of uniformity, approaching the Indonesian TPC value. This indicates that the proposed aksara-based tokenization procedure can be applied consistently across languages and yields segmentation results exhibiting an "internal compatibility" among regional language tokens rooted in their shared Austronesian heritage. Quantitatively, the stable TPC values hovering around 0.4 confirm the characteristic of Austronesian languages dominated by CV(C) syllabic patterns with an average length of 2 to 3 phonemes per unit.

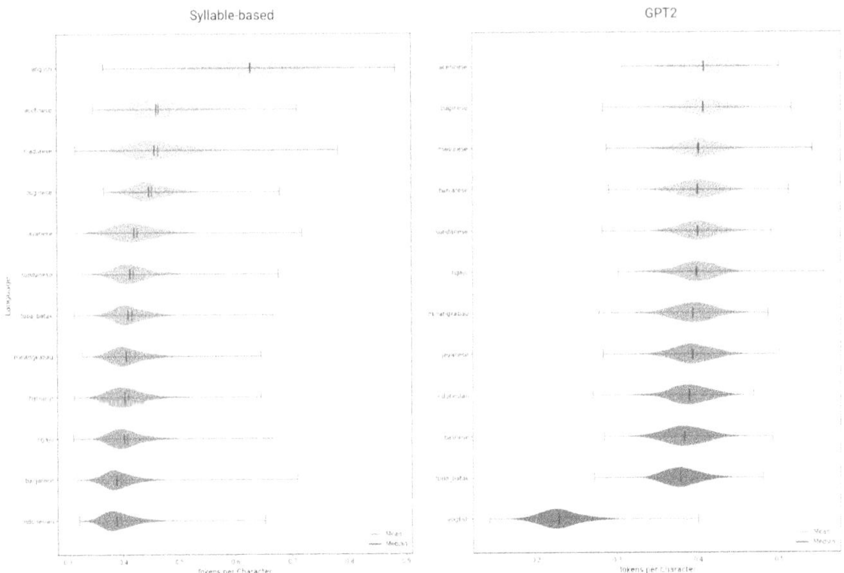

Fig. 2. Comparison of *tokens per character* distributions between the syllable-based tokenization method (left) and GPT-2 tokenization (right) across various languages. The red and blue vertical lines represent the mean and median values of the distributions, respectively.

Meanwhile, the application of syllable-based tokenization to English produced TPC values that were deviant and significantly higher compared to the regional languages. This increase in TPC values is a consequence of the high frequency of fallback mechanism activation, triggered by the incompatibility of English syllabic segments with the Indonesian-based vocabulary inventory. Empirically, this highlights fundamental differences in phonotactic patterns and linguistic characteristics between analytic language families, such as English, and the languages in the region of Indonesian archipelago.

An inverse pattern was observed in TPC values resulting from GPT-2 tokenization, where English obtained the lowest TPC value while regional languages exhibited relatively higher values. Optimization on a corpus predominantly dominated by English produces a GPT-2 subword vocabulary that is longer and more efficient for this language. Meanwhile, the minimal representation of regional languages in the training data causes their linguistic units to be fragmented into shorter subwords. Although the resulting TPC values are relatively comparable to syllable-based tokenization, this efficiency is achieved through a different mechanism, namely compression optimization based on high-frequency character sequence grouping. Given that compression approaches are sensitive to training data distribution, such groupings can be arbitrary and may not represent meaning or linguistic function in regional languages.

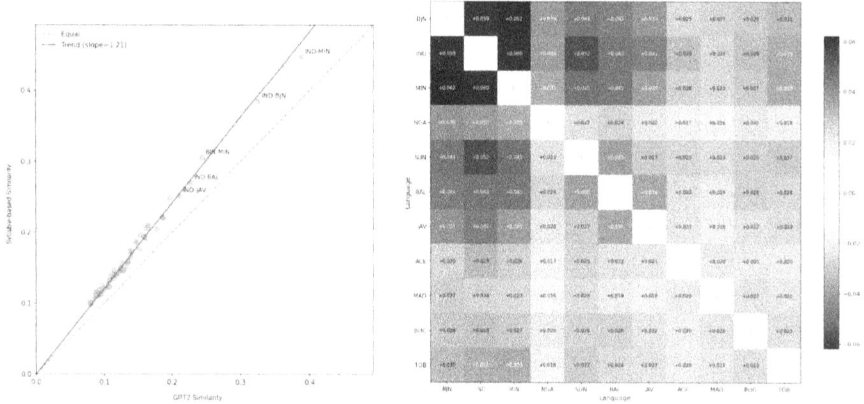

Fig. 3. Comparative analysis of token sequence similarity values between the syllable-based method and GPT-2. (a) Scatter plot comparing similarity across language pairs. (b) Heatmap of similarity value differences between the two tokenization schemes (Syllable-based – GPT-2) for each language pair. Red color gradation indicates higher similarity values obtained by the syllable-based method. (Color figure online)

Furthermore, evaluation based on sequence alignment reveals differences in the degree of linguistic preservation and alignment performance between syllable-based tokenization and GPT-2 tokenization. Token sequence alignment was performed on each parallel translation sample, and cross-linguistic similarity was calculated as the mean similarity value across all samples for each tokenization scheme. Figure 3a displays the comparison of similarity values for token sequences of language pairs produced by both tokenization approaches. Overall, evaluation of these proximity values demonstrates a consistent inter-language relational structure regardless of the tokenization scheme employed. This is evidenced by the strong linear correlation ($r = 0.9956$) and monotonic relationship ($\rho = 0.9895$) between language pair values obtained from both approaches.

Nevertheless, syllable-based tokenization consistently produces higher similarity values for all regional language pairs compared to GPT-2 tokenization. The slope trend of $m \approx 1.21$ in Fig. 3a indicates an average increase of approximately 21%. This finding suggests that cross-linguistically relevant linguistic patterns are better preserved through syllable tokenization, while GPT-2 tokenization fragments these patterns into more arbitrary segments. Figure 3b demonstrates that the difference in proximity values between the two tokenization schemes is most pronounced in language subgroups that, according to traditional linguistic scholarship, share close genealogical relationships. Minangkabau and Banjarese, which belong to the Malayic language family, exhibit the highest value differences as well as stronger proximity to Indonesian. This is attributable to the fact that syllable-based tokenization was trained with an Indonesian vocabulary inventory, rendering it more sensitive to the structures of cognate languages within the Malayic family. Beyond the Malayic family, increased similarity values were also observed in the language cluster that developed in Java and its surrounding regions. Specifically, syllable-based tokenization identifies a higher degree of proximity between Balinese and both Javanese and Sundanese, compared to GPT-2 tokenization. These results collectively demonstrate that the syllable-based approach is more effective in capturing phonological and morphological pattern alignments that are both historical and areal in nature.

5   Concluding Remarks and Further Works

The unique morphemic and phonetic constructions of Austronesian languages, compared to English which serves as the foundation for the general development of large language models in Generative Artificial Intelligence, have underscored the importance of agglutinative-based tokenization (ToBA-LM). This tokenization approach seeks to follow the "logic" of word formation based on syllabic patterns, which constitute a distinctive characteristic of natural Austronesian languages. This motivates adaptive efforts in conventional tokenization techniques for building language models whose linguistic aspects are syllable-based, as is the general nature of natural Austronesian languages. Case studies for model testing were conducted on corpora from various ethnic languages in the Indonesian Archipelago region. The tokenization approach was carried out with in-depth consideration of how words and phrases are formed from the native scripts of these ethnic groups, encompassing cross-linguistic segmentation and syllable compatibility, as well as in-depth analysis of the alignment processes of the token sequences employed.

This study, in turn, demonstrates the unique tokenization patterns in the constructed model, directed toward a bottom-up implementation of computational language models that can robustly accommodate the development of Indonesian ethnic languages, remaining immune to the emergence of words or phrases that tend to be out of vocabulary—characterized by frequent word segmentations that are not accommodated in conventional tokenizer vocabularies. This nonetheless enhances the efficiency of computational language models when implemented as language models for Generative Artificial Intelligence applications in general, which consistently rely upon and are built solely from English-dominated corpora. By examining the Token per Character (TPC) ratio, a markedly different and inverse pattern is demonstrated between syllable-based agglutinative tokenization and GPT-2. GPT-2 tokenization exhibits low TPC values for English and very high TPC values for ethnic languages in the Indonesian Archipelago, indicating distinct computational characteristics between these two language families. Nevertheless, the tokenization pattern optimized for syllable-based agglutinative processing (ToBA-LM) demonstrates low effectiveness for English. This leads to the conclusion of strong differences in the construction of the developed language models, which certainly may have potential efficiency implications for further large language model implementations.

Furthermore, the diversity and similarity aspects of the ethnic languages used in this study can also be demonstrated, including the proximity between Malay and Banjarese and Minangkabau, which have a relative similarity distance from languages such as Javanese, Sundanese, and Batak Toba. This certainly constitutes an important aspect that can be useful in the construction of individual language models, as well as composite language models based on syllable-based agglutinative approaches within the broader family of ethnic languages in the Indonesian Archipelago, including at a larger scale, languages of the Austronesian family—which represents a conjecture for future work. This includes combinations of this study's implementation with aspects of writing from original manuscripts that use unique scripts from hundreds of other languages in Indonesia, as well as other Austronesian families, employing image pattern recognition approaches from digital scans of manuscripts that facilitate textual deepening of meanings in ancient texts possessing high historical and ancient wisdom aspects spanning hundreds to thousands of years ago.

It is hoped that this study serves as an initial step in the development of advanced computational language models, in the implementation of various Large Language Model (LLM) applications grounded in the unique naturalness of language with all the human aspects that gave birth to it. Strong respect and appreciation for the collective intelligence that gave birth to language as a fundamental entity in human communication is, nonetheless, an important matter in the development of Artificial Intelligence technology that remains humane in its culture and civilization.

Acknowledgments. The author thank Institut Teknologi Del, fellows in Bandung Fe Institute, and colleagues in Ina-AI Co. for support. All faults remain authors'.

Disclosure of Interests. The authors have no competing interests to declare that are relevant to the content of this article.

References

1. Ali, M., et al.: Tokenizer choice For LLM training: negligible or crucial? arXiv:2310.08754 (2023)
2. Artexte, M., Ruder, S., Yogatama, D.: On the cross-lingual transferability of monolingual representations (2020). arXiv:1910.11856
3. Blust, R.: The Austronesian Languages. (Asia-Pacific Linguistics, 008). Research School of Pacific and Asian Studies, Australian National University, Canberra (2013)
4. Bostrom, K., Durrett, G.: Byte pair encoding is suboptimal for language model pretraining (2020). arXiv:2004.03720v2
5. Bright, W.: The devanagari script. In: Daniels, P., Bright, W. (eds.) The world's writing systems, pp. 384–390. Oxford University Press, New York, NY (1996)
6. Bright, W.: A matter of typology: alphasyllabaries and abugidas. Written Lang. Literacy **2**(1), 45–55 (1999)
7. Coolsma, S.: Tata Bahasa Sunda. Djambatan, Jakarta (1985)
8. Court, C.: The spread of Brahmi script into Southeast Asia. In: Daniels, P., Bright, W. (eds.) The world's writing systems, pp. 445–449. Oxford University Press, New York, NY (1996)
9. Daniels, P.T.: The study of writing systems. In: Daniels, P., Bright, W. (eds.) The world's writing systems, pp. 3–17. Oxford University Press, New York, NY (1996)
10. Daniels, P.T.: Writing systems. In: Aronoff, M., Rees-Miller, J. (eds.) The handbook of linguistics, pp. 43–80. Blackwell, Oxford (2001)
11. Daniels, P.T.: Indic Scripts: History, Typology, Study. Handbook of Literacy in Akshara Orthography, pp. 11–42 (2019)
12. Denistia, K., Baayen, R.: The morphology of Indonesian: data and quantitative modeling. In: The Routledge Handbook of Asian Linguistics, pp. 605–634, Routledge (2022)
13. Friedman, R.: Tokenization in the theory of knowledge. Encyclopedia **3**(1), 380–386 (2023)
14. Gage, P.: A new algorithm for data compression. C Users J **12**(2), 23–38 (1994)
15. Gotoh, O.: An improved algorithm for matching biological sequences. J. Mol. Biol. **162**(3), 705–708 (1982)
16. Hofmann, V., Pierrehumbert, J., Schütze, H.: Superbizarre is not superb: derivational morphology improves BERT's interpretation of complex words. In: Proceedings of the 59th ACL & 11th IJCNLP, pp. 3594–3608 (2021)
17. Iacobini, C.: Morphological typology. In: Brown, K. (ed.) Encyclopedia of Language and Linguistics, vol. 8, 2nd edn., pp. 278–282. Elsevier, Oxford (2006)
18. Jones, N., Pevzner, P.: An Introduction to Bioinformatics Algorithms. MIT Press, Cambridge, MA (2004)
19. Kudo, T.: Subword regularization: improving neural network translation models with multiple subword candidates. In: Proceedings of the 56th Annual Meeting of the Association for Computational Linguistics (Volume 1: Long Papers) (2018)
20. Kuipers, J., McDermott, R.: Insular Southeast Asian scripts. In: Daniels, P., Bright, W. (eds.) The world's writing systems, pp. 474–484. Oxford University Press, New York, NY (1996)
21. Lapoliwa, H.: A generative approach to the phonology of Bahasa Indonesia. (Pacific linguistics: Series D, 34), Canberra (1981)
22. Mielke, S.J.: Between words and characters: a brief history of open-vocabulary modeling and tokenization in NLP. arXiv:2112.10508 (2021)

23. Miller, C.: A Gujarati origin for scripts of Sumatra, Sulawesi and the Philippines. Ann. Meet. Berkeley Linguistics Soc. **36**(1), 276 (2010)
24. Mount, D.M.: Bioinformatics: Sequence and Genome Analysis, 2nd edn. Cold Spring Harbor Laboratory Press, Cold Spring Harbor, NY (2004)
25. Nababan, P.W.J.: A Grammar of Toba-Batak. (Pacific Linguistics, Series D, 37), Canberra (1981)
26. Patil, V., Talukdar, P., Sarawagi, S.: Overlap-based vocabulary generation improves cross-lingual transfer among related languages. In: Proceedings of the 60th ACL (Volume 1: Long Papers), pp. 219–233 (2022)
27. Petrov, A., et al.: Language model tokenizers introduce unfairness between languages (2023). arXiv:2305.15425
28. Pires, T., Schlinger, E., Garrette, D.: How multilingual is multilingual BERT? (2019). arXiv:1906.01502
29. Poedjosoedarmo, S., et al.: Morfologi Bahasa Jawa. Pusat Pembinaan dan Pengembangan Bahasa, Departemen Pendidikan dan Kebudayaan, Jakarta (1979)
30. Purwarianti, A., Crisdayanti, I.: Improving BI-LSTM performance for Indonesian sentiment analysis using paragraph vector. In: 2019 International Conference of Advanced Informatics: Concepts, Theory and Applications (ICAICTA), pp. 1–5. IEEE (2019)
31. Radford, A., et al.: Language Models are Unsupervised Multitask Learners. OpenAI (2019)
32. Rust, P., et al.: How good is your tokenizer? on the monolingual performance of multilingual language models. In: Proceedings of the 59th ACL & 11th IJCNLP, pp. 3118–3135 (2021)
33. Schuster, M., Nakajima, K.: Japanese and Korean voice search. In: 2012 IEEE International Conference on Acoustics, Speech and Signal Processing (ICASSP), pp. 5149–5152 (2012)
34. Sennrich, R., Haddow, B., Birch, A.: Neural machine translation of rare words with subword units. In: Proceedings of the 54th Annual Meeting of the Association for Computational Linguistics (Volume 1: Long Papers) (2016)
35. Situngkir, H.: Kode-kode Nusantara: Telaah Sains Mutakhir Atas Jejak-jejak Tradisi di kepulauan Indonesia. Expose-Mizan, Jakarta (2016)
36. Situngkir, H., Lumbantobing, A.B., Surya, Y.: Syllabic Agglutinative Tokenizations for Indonesian LLM: A Study from Gasing Literacy Learning System. BFI Working Paper Series (2026)
37. Smith, T.F., Waterman, M.S.: Identification of common molecular subsequences. J. Mol. Biol. **147**(1), 195–197 (1981)
38. Vaswani, A., et al.: Attention Is All You Need (2017). arXiv:1706.03762
39. Velayuthan, M., Sarveswaran, K.: Egalitarian language representation in language models: it all begins with tokenizers. In: Proceedings of the 31st International Conference on Computational Linguistics, pp. 5987–5996 (2025)
40. Winata, G.: NusaX: multilingual parallel sentiment dataset for 10 Indonesian local languages. In: Proceedings of the 17th EACL, pp. 815–834 (2023)

Efficient Error-Type Transfer
for Grammatical Error Detection
via Embedding Alignment

Corina Masanti[1]([✉])[iD], Hans-Friedrich Witschel[2][iD], and Kaspar Riesen[1][iD]

[1] Institute of Computer Science, University of Bern, 3012 Bern, Switzerland
{corina.masanti,kaspar.riesen}@unibe.ch
[2] Institute for Information Systems, University of Applied Sciences and Arts
Northwestern Switzerland, 4600 Olten, Switzerland
hansfriedrich.witschel@fhnw.ch

Abstract. Grammatical error detection involves diverse error types, with real-word errors being particularly challenging because incorrect words remain lexically valid but contextually inappropriate. Transformer-based models achieve strong performance but typically require repeated task-specific fine-tuning, which is computationally expensive and impractical for large-scale or evolving document processing scenarios. We address this limitation by formulating cross–error-type transfer as a representation-level domain adaptation problem. Our analysis shows that fine-tuning on different error types induces systematic distributional shifts in embedding space. Instead of updating model parameters, we propose aligning target embedding distributions to a source domain, enabling zero-shot transfer while keeping the encoder fixed. We evaluate two lightweight alignment methods, PCA-based alignment and CORAL, on three linguistically complex German real-word error types (case, verb, and capitalization). Both approaches consistently outperform zero-shot baselines and recover a substantial portion of the performance gap to full target-domain fine-tuning, while reducing adaptation time and computational cost by more than an order of magnitude. The results demonstrate an efficient and practical strategy for adapting grammatical error detection systems to new error types in resource-constrained, real-world NLP applications.

Keywords: Transfer Learning · Language Models · Grammatical Error Detection · Efficiency · Low-Resource Methods

1 Introduction and Related Work

Automated grammatical error detection is a key component in many practical language technology applications, including professional proofreading, educational writing support, and large-scale enterprise document processing. In such

© The Author(s), under exclusive license to Springer Nature Switzerland AG 2027
E. Cabrio and E. Monteiro (Eds.): NLDB 2026, LNCS 16696, pp. 189–203, 2027.
https://doi.org/10.1007/978-3-032-29532-3_14

environments, systems must process large volumes of text efficiently while handling a wide variety of heterogeneous error types. In practice, error distributions are highly uneven. Some error categories are well represented in annotated resources, whereas others are rare, domain-specific, or linguistically subtle. This imbalance makes it difficult to build robust models that generalize across error types and application scenarios.

A particularly challenging class of errors are *real-word errors*, where the incorrect word is lexically valid but contextually inappropriate. Examples include incorrect verb agreement, case assignment, or capitalization that changes the syntactic or semantic interpretation of a sentence. Detecting such errors requires fine-grained contextual understanding and sensitivity to long-range dependencies, making them substantially more difficult than surface-level spelling or morphological errors [7].

Recent progress in grammatical error detection has been driven by transformer-based language models [16], which capture rich contextual representations through self-attention. Models based on this architecture, such as BERT [3], T5 [9], and GPT [2], represent the current state-of-the-art systems for many grammatical error detection and correction tasks. However, this performance comes at a cost: effective deployment typically requires separate fine-tuning for each error category, domain, or data distribution. Repeated fine-tuning is computationally expensive [13], time-consuming, and energy-intensive, and it depends on the availability of high-quality labeled data. In real-world production settings, where new error types or domains may emerge continuously, such repeated model adaptation is often impractical.

Several approaches have been proposed to reduce the cost of adaptation. Few-shot [5] and prompt-based methods [2] using large instruction-tuned language models aim to reduce the need for labeled data. Parameter-efficient techniques [4] further limit the number of updated model parameters. Despite these advances, most existing approaches still require some form of parameter optimization or rely on large models with substantial computational requirements. Efficient methods that enable cross-error-type adaptation without retraining remain largely underexplored.

In this work, we address this limitation by studying error-type transfer from a representation-level perspective. Instead of adapting model parameters, we investigate whether knowledge learned for one error type can be reused for another by transforming the corresponding embedding spaces. This perspective is motivated by the observation that fine-tuning reshapes the geometry of the model's latent representation space [10]. While this improves class separability for the training error type, it may also introduce systematic distributional shifts that hinder generalization to other error categories.

Representation-based transfer has been explored in related contexts. Prototype-based methods [12] learn embedding spaces in which classes are represented by their mean vectors, enabling learning from limited labeled data. Other approaches focus on relative or relational representations that preserve geometric relationships between instances and remain invariant to global transformations of the embedding space [8]. These findings suggest that transfer across domains or tasks may be possible by aligning representation geometries rather than updating model parameters. However, representation alignment has not yet been systematically investigated for cross-error-type transfer in grammatical error detection.

Our central hypothesis is that a substantial portion of cross-type performance degradation is caused by geometric misalignment between embedding distributions. If these distributional differences can be corrected through lightweight transformations, a classifier trained on one error type may be reused for another without additional training.

To test this hypothesis, we analyze embedding distributions obtained from models fine-tuned on different error types and quantify the resulting distributional shifts. Based on these observations, we propose two post-hoc alignment strategies – PCA-based alignment and CORAL-based alignment – that transform target embeddings into the source representation space while keeping the encoder fixed. This enables zero-shot transfer between error types without requiring labeled target data or additional parameter updates.[1]

The contributions of the present paper are as follows:

1. We formulate cross-error-type transfer in grammatical error detection as a representation-level domain adaptation problem.
2. We provide an empirical analysis showing that fine-tuning on different error types induces measurable distributional shifts in embedding space.
3. We propose lightweight embedding alignment methods that enable zero-shot transfer between error types without modifying model parameters.
4. We demonstrate that the proposed approach substantially improves cross-type performance while reducing computational cost and adaptation time, making it suitable for large-scale and resource-constrained Natural Language Processing (NLP) applications.

The remainder of this paper is structured as follows. Section 2 presents the data set and task we use for the experiments. Section 3 compares embedding distributions across transfer directions, providing the foundation for the subsequent experiments. Section 4 describes the proposed method. Section 5 presents the experimental setup and evaluation results. Finally, Sect. 6 concludes the paper and outlines directions for future work.

2   Data Set and Task

In this work, grammatical error detection is formulated as a binary sentence-level classification task. Given an input sentence, the goal is to predict whether it is grammatically correct or contains a specific real-word error. Our primary

---

[1] Unlike prompt-based zero-shot learning with large language models, our approach does not rely on task-specific prompts. The transfer mechanism operates entirely at the representation level, eliminating the need for prompt design or optimization.

objective is to study cross-error-type transfer, where a model trained on one error category (source) is applied to a different error category (target) without additional training.

To enable controlled experimentation, we use a synthetic data set constructed from real German text as introduced in [6]. For each error type, we construct separate training and test sets with a total of 100,000 samples, balanced evenly between correct and erroneous sentences. Although this distribution does not reflect real-world error frequencies, it deliberately emphasizes error coverage and prioritizes high recall, as missing an error is more costly in professional proofreading than flagging a false positive. Moreover, this design allows us to systematically analyze transfer behavior across error types under comparable conditions.

All data is in German, whose extensive case marking, verb inflection, agreement patterns, and capitalization rules introduce a high degree of structural complexity for grammatical error detection. That is, German provides a demanding test setting for evaluating a model's capacity to capture fine-grained grammatical distinctions. Compared to languages such as English, where, for instance, capitalization rules are relatively limited, German orthography introduces substantially greater ambiguity and structural complexity.

We focus on real-word errors, which are substantially more challenging than many other error categories because the incorrect word itself is lexically valid but contextually inappropriate. Within the category of real-word errors, we analyze three specific error types:

- **Case errors.** These involve incorrect grammatical case or agreement, for example, when a preposition requires a different case than the one used in the sentence.
- **Verb errors.** These include incorrect verb conjugation, tense, or subject-verb agreement, which require syntactic and contextual understanding.
- **Capitalization errors.** In German, capitalization affects grammatical function and meaning, for example, when nominalized verbs or adjectives must be written with an initial capital letter.

These three error types are difficult to detect because they depend on syntactic structure and semantic interpretation, making them subtle even for native speakers, particularly in longer and complex sentences.

3   Embedding Analysis

The goal of this section is to analyze how fine-tuning on different error types alters the geometry of the embedding space. In particular, we investigate whether representations learned for one error category differ systematically from those of another, and whether such differences may explain performance degradation in cross-error-type transfer.

Transfer learning is actually widely used in NLP [1]. Typically, a model is first pre-trained on a large quantity of general-purpose data and is then fine-tuned on a smaller, task-specific data set. After pre-training, the model already encodes substantial linguistic structure and can produce context-sensitive embeddings. Fine-tuning then adapts these general representations to the downstream task.

While fine-tuning improves class separability within each error type, it may also induce error-type-specific embedding geometries. As a result, models trained on one error category may generalize poorly to others, since differences in representation structure hinder direct transfer. Understanding these distributional differences is therefore essential for designing effective representation-level adaptation methods. To this end, we quantify the extent of cross-type mismatch by analyzing the embedding statistics of different error types.

We consider a pairwise transfer setting between a source error type (type 1) and a target error type (type 2). A pre-trained model is fine-tuned exclusively on training data from type 1 and its parameters are then frozen. Using this fixed encoder, we extract sentence embeddings from the test sets of both the source and target error types. This setup isolates distributional differences between error categories without any adaptation to the target domain. Specifically, we consider:

1. Source embeddings (type 1): embeddings extracted from the type 1 test set using the model fine-tuned on type 1 training data.
2. Target embeddings (type 2): embeddings extracted from the type 2 test set using the same model fine-tuned on type 1 training data.

All experiments are conducted using mBERT, the multilingual variant of BERT (Bidirectional Encoder Representations from Transformers [3]). We select mBERT because it provides strong contextual representations across languages while remaining widely used and computationally efficient, making it a suitable baseline for studying representation-level transfer in realistic deployment settings. For each sentence, we use the final-layer representation of the [CLS] token as a fixed-dimensional embedding. All embeddings are extracted using identical preprocessing and model settings across error types.

We quantify the distributional shift between error types by comparing first- and second-order statistics of the embedding distributions. Using the model fine-tuned on the source error type (type 1), we extract embeddings for both the type 1 and type 2 test sets. We then compute the Euclidean distance between the corresponding mean vectors (μ) and the Frobenius norm of the difference between the covariance matrices (Σ) of the two distributions. The resulting distances, which measure the discrepancy between source (type 1) and target (type 2) embedding distributions, are visualized as heatmaps in Fig. 1 (larger values indicate stronger distributional mismatch between the two error types).

The model fine-tuned on capitalization errors shows the largest differences in mean and covariance. This high degree of dissimilarity between the source and target embeddings indicates a substantial domain shift, which implies that transfer learning from capitalization errors to case and verb errors is likely to be the most challenging. In contrast, the model fine-tuned on case errors results in the smallest overall differences. This overlap in the embedding distributions indicates that knowledge transfer from case errors to verb and capitalization

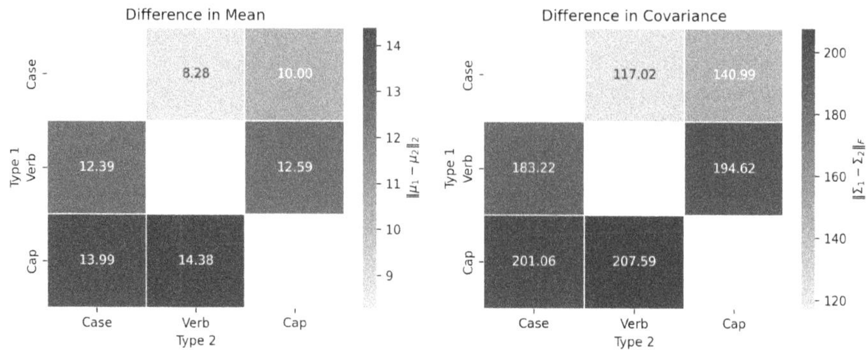

Fig. 1. Differences in the embedding distributions of the test sets. Heatmaps show the Euclidean distance between mean vectors (left) and the Frobenius norm between covariance matrices (right). The embeddings are generated by models fine-tuned on the source error type (type 1), and the distances are calculated between type 1 embeddings and target error type (type 2) embeddings.

errors is expected to be the most effective strategy. The model fine-tuned on verb errors demonstrates an intermediate level of dissimilarity between these two.

Overall, the magnitude of distributional differences is consistent with the expected difficulty of cross-error transfer. Hence, these findings confirm that fine-tuning induces systematic, error-type-specific changes in embedding space. Any performance degradation in cross-type transfer can therefore be attributed, at least in part, to geometric misalignment between embedding distributions. This observation motivates our approach of correcting such mismatches through lightweight distribution alignment, which is described in the next section. From a practical perspective, if cross-type errors are primarily caused by geometric shifts rather than missing linguistic knowledge, alignment-based adaptation may provide an efficient alternative to repeated fine-tuning.

4   Embedding Distribution Alignment for Zero-Shot Transfer

Based on the distributional differences observed in Sect. 3, we propose a lightweight adaptation strategy that operates directly in representation space. Instead of updating model parameters, our goal is to correct geometric mismatches between embedding distributions so that a classifier trained on a source error type can be applied to a target error type without additional training. To our knowledge, this is the first study that applies embedding distribution alignment to enable zero-shot transfer across grammatical error types.

The benefit of this approach is that it avoids repeated fine-tuning, reduces computational cost, and enables rapid adaptation in scenarios where labeled data or computational resources are limited. It is therefore particularly suitable for large-scale document processing and resource-constrained deployment settings.

As shown in Sect. 3, fine-tuning on different error types produces systematic changes in embedding geometry, which limits direct cross-type generalization. To enable zero-shot transfer from a source error type to a target error type, we transform the target embedding distribution to the source embedding space while keeping the model parameters fixed. We investigate two complementary alignment methods: PCA-based alignment and CORAL-based alignment.

Both methods are based on the assumption that cross-type transfer errors arise primarily from global shifts in embedding geometry rather than from missing task-specific information. By matching the dominant directions of variation or the covariance structure of the embeddings, the target representations become compatible with the decision boundary learned in the source domain.

- PCA-based alignment aligns the dominant directions of variation in the source and target embeddings. By rotating the target embeddings so that their principal axes match those of the source domain, the method preserves relative distances while reorienting the space to better match the source geometry.
- CORAL-based alignment matches second-order statistics between domains. It adjusts the scale and correlation structure of the target embeddings so that their covariance resembles that of the source domain, thereby reducing mismatches in feature dependencies.

Both methods operate as post-hoc transformations and require no labeled target data. If cross-type transfer errors are primarily caused by geometric misalignment, aligning the global structure of the embedding distributions should improve transfer performance.

To formalize this setting, let D denote the embedding dimension, which is identical for both error types. We use $N_{\text{train}}^{(1)}$ and $N_{\text{test}}^{(2)}$ to denote the number of training samples for error type 1 and test samples for error type 2, respectively. The training embeddings of error type 1 are denoted by $\mathbf{X}_{\text{train}}^{(1)} \in \mathbb{R}^{N_{\text{train}}^{(1)} \times D}$, while $\mathbf{X}_{\text{test}}^{(2)} \in \mathbb{R}^{N_{\text{test}}^{(2)} \times D}$ represents the test embeddings of error type 2.

All embeddings are extracted using mBERT fine-tuned exclusively on error type 1. We align the embeddings of error type 2 to the source embedding distribution through a post-hoc transformation in the embedding space. After alignment, a classifier trained on $\mathbf{X}_{\text{train}}^{(1)}$ is directly applied to the transformed embeddings of error type 2.

4.1 PCA-Based Alignment

The first approach uses *Principal Component Analysis* (PCA) to align the principal component bases of the source and target embedding distributions. The full procedure is summarized in Algorithm 1.

We compute PCA independently on the training embeddings of error type 1 and the test embeddings of error type 2, obtaining a mean vector and an

---

Algorithm 1. PCA-based alignment from error type 2 to error type 1

Require: $\mathbf{X}_{\text{train}}^{(1)}$, $\mathbf{X}_{\text{test}}^{(2)}$

1: Compute PCA on $\mathbf{X}_{\text{train}}^{(1)}$, obtaining mean $\boldsymbol{\mu}_{\text{train}}^{(1)}$ and basis $\mathbf{W}_{\text{train}}^{(1)}$

2: Compute PCA on $\mathbf{X}_{\text{test}}^{(2)}$, obtaining mean $\boldsymbol{\mu}_{\text{test}}^{(2)}$ and basis $\mathbf{W}_{\text{test}}^{(2)}$

3: Project test embeddings of type 2 into their PCA space:
$$\mathbf{Z}_{\text{test}}^{(2)} = (\mathbf{X}_{\text{test}}^{(2)} - \boldsymbol{\mu}_{\text{test}}^{(2)})\mathbf{W}_{\text{test}}^{(2)}$$

4: Solve the orthogonal Procrustes problem:
$$\mathbf{R}^{\star} = \arg\min_{\mathbf{R}\in O(D)} \|\mathbf{W}_{\text{test}}^{(2)} - \mathbf{W}_{\text{train}}^{(1)}\mathbf{R}\|_F$$

5: Align the projected test embeddings: $\mathbf{Z}_{\text{test}}^{(2\to1)} = \mathbf{Z}_{\text{test}}^{(2)}\mathbf{R}^{\star}$

6: Reconstruct aligned embeddings in the original space:
$$\mathbf{X}_{\text{test}}^{(2\to1)} = \mathbf{Z}_{\text{test}}^{(2\to1)}(\mathbf{W}_{\text{train}}^{(1)})^{\top} + \boldsymbol{\mu}_{\text{train}}^{(1)}$$

7: **return** $\mathbf{X}_{\text{test}}^{(2\to1)}$

---

orthonormal basis for each distribution (lines 1–2). The embeddings of error type 2 are then projected into their corresponding PCA subspace (line 3).

To align the two subspaces, we solve the orthogonal Procrustes problem [11], which estimates a rotation matrix minimizing the difference between the PCA bases of the two error types (line 4). The resulting rotation is applied to the projected embeddings of error type 2 (line 5). Finally, the aligned embeddings are reconstructed in the original embedding space using the PCA basis and mean of error type 1 (line 6).

4.2   CORAL-Based Alignment

The second approach aligns the distributions by matching their second-order statistics. The procedure – termed *CORrelation ALignment* (CORAL) [14,15] – is detailed in Algorithm 2.

Algorithm 2. CORAL-based alignment from error type 2 to error type 1

Require: $\mathbf{X}_{\text{train}}^{(1)}$, $\mathbf{X}_{\text{test}}^{(2)}$, shrinkage parameter λ

1: Compute means $\boldsymbol{\mu}_{\text{train}}^{(1)}$ and $\boldsymbol{\mu}_{\text{test}}^{(2)}$

2: Center embeddings: $\mathbf{Z}_{\text{train}}^{(1)} = \mathbf{X}_{\text{train}}^{(1)} - \boldsymbol{\mu}_{\text{train}}^{(1)}$, $\quad \mathbf{Z}_{\text{test}}^{(2)} = \mathbf{X}_{\text{test}}^{(2)} - \boldsymbol{\mu}_{\text{test}}^{(2)}$

3: Estimate covariance matrices with diagonal shrinkage:
$$\boldsymbol{\Sigma}_{\text{train}}^{(1)} = \frac{(\mathbf{Z}_{\text{train}}^{(1)})^{\top}\mathbf{Z}_{\text{train}}^{(1)}}{N_{\text{train}}^{(1)}-1} + \lambda\mathbf{I}, \quad \boldsymbol{\Sigma}_{\text{test}}^{(2)} = \frac{(\mathbf{Z}_{\text{test}}^{(2)})^{\top}\mathbf{Z}_{\text{test}}^{(2)}}{N_{\text{test}}^{(2)}-1} + \lambda\mathbf{I}$$

4: Compute the whitening-coloring transformation:
$$\mathbf{A} = (\boldsymbol{\Sigma}_{\text{test}}^{(2)})^{-1/2}(\boldsymbol{\Sigma}_{\text{train}}^{(1)})^{1/2}$$

5: Transform target embeddings: $\mathbf{X}_{\text{test}}^{(2\to1)} = (\mathbf{X}_{\text{test}}^{(2)} - \boldsymbol{\mu}_{\text{test}}^{(2)})\mathbf{A} + \boldsymbol{\mu}_{\text{train}}^{(1)}$

6: **return** $\mathbf{X}_{\text{test}}^{(2\to1)}$

After computing the mean embeddings of both error types (line 1), we center the data (line 2) and estimate the covariance matrices using diagonal shrinkage to ensure numerical stability (line 3).

CORAL aligns domains by matching their second-order statistics through a whitening–coloring transformation: one domain is first whitened by removing correlations and then re-colored using the covariance structure of the other domain. In our setting, we apply this transformation in the reverse adaptation direction, mapping target embeddings into the source space. The aligned embeddings are obtained by applying the transformation followed by mean shifting (lines 4–5).

5   Experimental Evaluation

This section evaluates whether embedding alignment improves cross-error-type transfer compared to direct zero-shot application of a source model. We focus on two questions:

1. Does distribution alignment improve detection performance on unseen error types?
2. How does the proposed approach compare to full target-domain fine-tuning in terms of effectiveness and computational efficiency?

Sections 5.1 and 5.2 address these questions, respectively.

5.1   Cross-Error-Type Transfer Performance

To answer the first question, we conduct three experimental settings:

1. **Baseline:** We fine-tune a transformer-based model on error type 1, extract sentence embeddings $\mathbf{X}^{(1)}_{\mathrm{train}}$, and train a lightweight classifier on these embeddings. The trained encoder is then used to extract the embeddings of error type 2 $\mathbf{X}^{(2)}_{\mathrm{test}}$, which are classified directly using the same classifier, without any alignment or additional training.
2. **PCA:** As in the Baseline, we fine-tune the transformer-based model on error type 1 and train a classifier on the corresponding embeddings. For error type 2, we apply the PCA-based alignment method described in Algorithm 1 to align the extracted embeddings before classification.
3. **CORAL:** We follow the same setup as the PCA experiments, but apply the CORAL-based alignment method (Algorithm 2) to the embeddings of error type 2 prior to classification.

Across all settings, both the encoder and classifier trained on error type 1 are kept fixed and no labeled training data from error type 2 is used at any stage. As a result, classification on error type 2 forms a zero-shot transfer setting, and any performance gains directly reflect the ability of the alignment methods to bridge the distributional shift between error types. We report the F1 score as the primary evaluation metric, as it balances precision and recall and is appropriate for error detection tasks. Precision and recall are also reported to analyze the behavior of the alignment methods in more detail.

Figure 2 summarizes the F1 scores for all cross-type transfer directions, where rows denote the source error type (type 1) and columns denote the target error type (type 2). Each cell reports the F1 score achieved when transferring from error type 1 to error type 2 using the three experimental settings (Baseline, PCA, and CORAL). Diagonal cells indicate in-domain evaluation and are omitted.

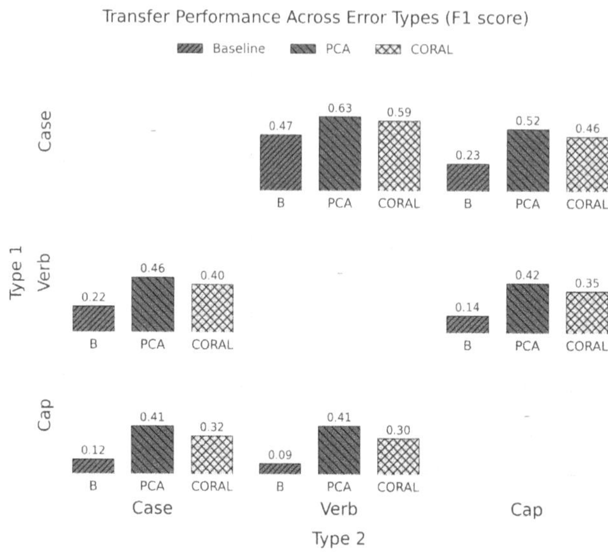

Fig. 2. Performance comparison of Baseline, PCA, and CORAL across error-type transfer directions (F1 score). Rows correspond to the source error type (type 1) and columns correspond to the target error type (type 2).

Table 1 complements this overview by reporting the corresponding precision and recall values for the Baseline, PCA-based alignment, and CORAL-based alignment, allowing a more detailed analysis of the trade-offs between methods.

The Baseline achieves relatively high precision (up to 0.83) but extremely low recall (down to 0.05) across all transfer directions. This indicates that models trained on one error type rarely identify errors of a different type, resulting in conservative predictions and poor overall F1 performance. These results confirm that direct zero-shot transfer without adaptation is ineffective.

Across all transfer directions, both PCA-based and CORAL-based alignment significantly improve recall while largely maintaining precision, resulting in consistently higher F1 scores. PCA-based alignment generally achieves the highest recall and F1 scores across all transfer directions. CORAL-based alignment also improves over the Baseline in every case, but remains slightly inferior to PCA in terms of recall and overall F1, despite comparable or slightly better precision.

Notably, transfer performance varies strongly with the direction of transfer. Transfers involving capitalization as the source error type (Cap → Case, Cap

Table 1. Precision (P) and Recall (R) for transfer between error types (type 1 → type 2) across Baseline, PCA, and CORAL. For each transfer direction, the best precision and the best recall values across methods are highlighted in boldface.

Type 1	Type 2	Baseline	PCA	CORAL
Case	Verb	P = **0.83**	P = 0.72	P = 0.75
		R = 0.33	R = 0.55	R = 0.49
	Cap	P = **0.63**	P = 0.57	P = 0.59
		R = 0.14	R = 0.48	R = 0.38
Verb	Case	P = **0.71**	P = 0.62	P = 0.65
		R = 0.13	**R = 0.37**	R = 0.30
	Cap	P = **0.55**	P = 0.54	P = 0.54
		R = 0.08	**R = 0.34**	R = 0.26
Cap	Case	P = **0.62**	P = 0.57	P = 0.58
		R = 0.07	**R = 0.32**	R = 0.22
	Verb	P = **0.55**	P = **0.55**	P = **0.55**
		R = 0.05	**R = 0.33**	R = 0.21

→ Verb) are consistently more challenging, yielding lower recall and F1 scores across all methods. In contrast, transfers originating from case and verb errors tend to be more effective, while transfers targeting capitalization remain difficult.

These trends are consistent with the embedding analysis in Sect. 3, where we observe the largest differences in mean and covariances originating from capitalization errors as source error type. Accordingly, transfers from capitalization to verb or case errors represent the most extreme distributional shifts. Conversely, the smallest distributional differences occur for transfers from case to verb errors (see Fig. 1), which corresponds to the strongest empirical performance in this setting (Case → Verb).

Overall, zero-shot transfer without alignment is ineffective. Distribution alignment substantially improves cross-error-type generalization, with PCA-based alignment providing the most consistent performance gains.

5.2   Comparison to Full Fine-tuning

To better assess the practical trade-off between effectiveness and computational cost, we compare our best-performing alignment-based method, PCA-based alignment, to full fine-tuning on the target error type. Although, full fine-tuning is expected to yield the best performance, it requires labeled training data for the target error type and introduces substantial computational overhead. In contrast, our approach operates in a zero-shot setting and avoids any updates to the encoder parameters.

Table 2 reports the mean computation time and standard deviation over all runs for both approaches, broken down into training/setup and inference phases. All experiments are conducted on a single NVIDIA RTX 3090 GPU.

Table 2. Mean computation time and standard deviation (in seconds) for full fine-tuning and PCA-based alignment. We report training/setup and inference times averaged over all runs.

Phase	Full Fine-tuning	PCA
Training/Setup		
Fine-tuning	$13{,}712.21 \pm 838.75\,s$	—
Extract embeddings	—	$728.40 \pm 48.89\,s$
Train classifier	—	$11.25 \pm 0.85\,s$
PCA alignment	—	$5.91 \pm 0.63\,s$
Total Training	$\mathbf{13{,}712.21 \pm 838.75\,s}$	$\mathbf{745.56 \pm 49.52\,s}$
Inference		
Predictions	$119.43 \pm 22.74\,s$	$0.37 \pm 0.01\,s$
Total Time	$\mathbf{13{,}831.64 \pm 861.17\,s}$	$\mathbf{745.94 \pm 49.52\,s}$
Speedup	$\mathbf{1.00\times}$	$\mathbf{18.54\times}$

Full fine-tuning is dominated by the cost of updating the parameters of the model, resulting in a total training time of $13{,}712.21 \pm 838.75$ s. In contrast, the PCA-based alignment approach replaces this expensive step with embedding extraction, PCA-based alignment, and training a lightweight classifier, reducing the total training time to 745.56 ± 49.52 s.

During inference, the fine-tuning approach requires a full forward pass through the fine-tuned model for prediction, while our approach only applies a shallow classifier, resulting in inference times that are over two orders of magnitude faster. Overall, our approach achieves a total end-to-end speedup of $18.54\times$ compared to full fine-tuning.

In addition to runtime improvements, the alignment-based method significantly reduces hardware requirements. Full fine-tuning emits 0.0498 ± 0.0037 kg CO_2eq per run across the three error types, corresponding to an average energy consumption of 1.43 ± 0.11 kWh. In contrast, the alignment-based approach emits 0.00245 ± 0.0001 kg CO_2eq and consumes 0.0703 ± 0.0048 kWh, yielding a reduction of 95.08% in energy consumption relative to full fine-tuning. At inference time, the model processes 344.26 ± 73.62 sentences per second. The alignment-based method achieves $107{,}212.48 \pm 3{,}019.87$ sentences per second, resulting in a throughput difference of $31{,}042.89\%$.

These substantial gains in runtime, energy efficiency, and data efficiency are accompanied by a reduction in predictive performance. For example, in the Case $\rightarrow$ Verb transfer, full fine-tuning achieves an F1 score of 0.94, while PCA-based alignment attains 0.63 without access to labeled target data. Although alignment-based transfer does not fully reach supervised target-domain performance, it recovers a considerable portion of the transfer gap under a zero-shot setting. This highlights a strong effectiveness–efficiency trade-off: representation-level alignment enables scalable cross-error-type adaptation with substantial computational savings, making it particularly promising for resource-constrained or rapidly evolving deployment scenarios.

6   Conclusions and Future Work

This work addresses the problem of efficiently adapting grammatical error detection models to new error types. We show that fine-tuning on different error categories induces systematic distributional shifts in embedding space, which limits cross-error-type generalization. To overcome this limitation, we formulate error-type transfer as a representation-level domain adaptation problem and propose lightweight embedding alignment methods that enable zero-shot transfer without updating model parameters.

Experimental results demonstrate that both PCA-based and CORAL-based alignment substantially improve cross-type performance compared to direct zero-shot transfer. Although the proposed methods do not fully match the accuracy of full target-domain fine-tuning, they recover a large portion of the performance gap.

At the same time, the alignment-based approach reduces computational cost, adaptation time, and energy consumption by more than an order of magnitude. This efficiency makes the method particularly suitable for large-scale document processing scenarios and deployment settings where repeated fine-tuning is impractical.

Overall, the results suggest that a substantial portion of cross-type transfer difficulty arises from geometric misalignment in representation space rather than from missing linguistic knowledge. Correcting these global shifts can therefore provide an effective alternative to parameter-based adaptation.

This study has several limitations. First, the experiments are conducted on synthetically generated error data, which enables controlled analysis but may not fully reflect real-world error distributions. Second, the proposed alignment methods rely on global linear transformations and may not capture more complex, non-linear differences between error types.

Several directions for future work arise from this study. First, evaluating the proposed approach on real-world corpora and domain-specific text would provide further insight into its practical applicability. Second, extending the alignment framework to non-linear or learned transformations may better capture complex distributional differences between error types. Third, future research could investigate class- or error-specific alignment strategies, for example by leveraging prototype-based representations. Finally, applying representation-level alignment to other NLP tasks and languages would help assess the generality of the approach.

Acknowledgments. This study was funded by Hasler Stifung (grant number 2025-02-17-292).

Disclosure of Interests. The authors have no competing interests to declare that are relevant to the content of this article.

References

1. Alyafeai, Z., AlShaibani, M.S., Ahmad, I.: A survey on transfer learning in natural language processing. CoRR abs/2007.04239 (2020). https://arxiv.org/abs/2007.04239

2. Brown, T.B., et al.: Language models are few-shot learners. In: Larochelle, H., Ranzato, M., Hadsell, R., Balcan, M., Lin, H. (eds.) Advances in Neural Information Processing Systems 33: Annual Conference on Neural Information Processing Systems 2020, NeurIPS 2020, 6–12 December 2020, virtual (2020). https://proceedings.neurips.cc/paper/2020/hash/1457c0d6bfcb4967418bfb8ac142f64a-Abstract.html

3. Devlin, J., Chang, M., Lee, K., Toutanova, K.: BERT: pre-training of deep bidirectional transformers for language understanding. In: Burstein, J., Doran, C., Solorio, T. (eds.) Proceedings of the 2019 Conference of the North American Chapter of the Association for Computational Linguistics: Human Language Technologies, NAACL-HLT 2019, Minneapolis, MN, USA, 2–7 June 2019, Volume 1 (Long and Short Papers), pp. 4171–4186. Association for Computational Linguistics (2019). https://doi.org/10.18653/V1/N19-1423

4. Hu, E.J., et al: Lora: low-rank adaptation of large language models. In: The Tenth International Conference on Learning Representations, ICLR 2022, Virtual Event, 25–29 April 2022. OpenReview.net (2022). https://openreview.net/forum?id=nZeVKeeFYf9

5. Loem, M., Kaneko, M., Takase, S., Okazaki, N.: Exploring effectiveness of GPT-3 in grammatical error correction: a study on performance and controllability in prompt-based methods. In: Kochmar, E., et al. (eds.) Proceedings of the 18th Workshop on Innovative Use of NLP for Building Educational Applications, BEA@ACL 2023, Toronto, Canada, 13 July 2023, pp. 205–219. Association for Computational Linguistics (2023).https://doi.org/10.18653/V1/2023.BEA-1.18

6. Masanti, C., Witschel, H.F., Riesen, K.: Boosting language models for real-word error detection. In: Santana, M.C., Marsico, M.D., Fred, A. (eds.) Proceedings of the 14th International Conference on Pattern Recognition Applications and Methods, ICPRAM 2025, Porto, Portugal, February 23-25, 2025, pp. 318–325. SCITEPRESS (2025). https://doi.org/10.5220/0013251500003905

7. Masanti, C., Witschel, H.F., Riesen, K.: Enhancing language models with boosting and targeted fine-tuning for real-word error detection. Natural Lang. Process. J. 100202 (2026). https://doi.org/10.1016/j.nlp.2026.100202. https://www.sciencedirect.com/science/article/pii/S2949719126000063

8. Moschella, L., Maiorca, V., Fumero, M., Norelli, A., Locatello, F., Rodolà, E.: Relative representations enable zero-shot latent space communication. In: The Eleventh International Conference on Learning Representations, ICLR 2023, Kigali, Rwanda, 1–5 May 2023. OpenReview.net (2023). https://openreview.net/forum?id=SrC-nwieGJ

9. Raffel, C., et al.: Exploring the limits of transfer learning with a unified text-to-text transformer. J. Mach. Learn. Res. **21**, 140:1–140:67 (2020). http://jmlr.org/papers/v21/20-074.html

10. Rajaee, S., Pilehvar, M.T.: How does fine-tuning affect the geometry of embedding space: a case study on isotropy. In: Moens, M., Huang, X., Specia, L., Yih, S.W. (eds.) Findings of the Association for Computational Linguistics: EMNLP 2021, Virtual Event / Punta Cana, Dominican Republic, 16–20 November 2021. Findings of ACL, vol. EMNLP 2021, pp. 3042–3049. Association for Computational Linguistics (2021). https://doi.org/10.18653/V1/2021.FINDINGS-EMNLP.261

11. Schönemann, P.H.: A generalized solution of the orthogonal procrustes problem. Psychometrika **31**(1), 1–10 (1966)
12. Snell, J., Swersky, K., Zemel, R.S.: Prototypical networks for few-shot learning. In: Guyon, I., et al. (eds.) Advances in Neural Information Processing Systems 30: Annual Conference on Neural Information Processing Systems 2017, 4–9 December 2017, Long Beach, CA, USA, pp. 4077–4087 (2017). https://proceedings.neurips.cc/paper/2017/hash/cb8da6767461f2812ae4290eac7cbc42-Abstract.html
13. Strubell, E., Ganesh, A., McCallum, A.: Energy and policy considerations for deep learning in NLP. In: Korhonen, A., Traum, D.R., Màrquez, L. (eds.) Proceedings of the 57th Conference of the Association for Computational Linguistics, ACL 2019, Florence, Italy, 28- August 2 July 2019, Volume 1: Long Papers, pp. 3645–3650. Association for Computational Linguistics (2019). https://doi.org/10.18653/V1/P19-1355
14. Sun, B., Feng, J., Saenko, K.: Correlation alignment for unsupervised domain adaptation. In: Csurka, G. (ed.) Domain Adaptation in Computer Vision Applications, pp. 153–171. Advances in Computer Vision and Pattern Recognition, Springer (2017). https://doi.org/10.1007/978-3-319-58347-1_8
15. Sun, B., Saenko, K.: Deep CORAL: correlation alignment for deep domain adaptation. In: Hua, G., Jégou, H. (eds.) ECCV 2016. LNCS, vol. 9915, pp. 443–450. Springer, Cham (2016). https://doi.org/10.1007/978-3-319-49409-8_35
16. Vaswani, A., et al.: Attention is all you need. In: Guyon, I., et al. (eds.) Advances in Neural Information Processing Systems 30: Annual Conference on Neural Information Processing Systems 2017, 4–9 December 2017, Long Beach, CA, USA, pp. 5998–6008 (2017). https://proceedings.neurips.cc/paper/2017/hash/3f5ee243547dee91fbd053c1c4a845aa-Abstract.html

Towards Robust Uzbek Neural Dependency Parsing: Cross-Treebank Training

Sanatbek Matlatipov(✉) iD

National University of Uzbekistan named after Mirzo Ulugbek, Tashkent, Uzbekistan
`s.matlatipov@nuu.uz`

Abstract. Efficient low-resource dependency parsing requires extracting maximal syntactic signal from limited supervision with minimal additional machinery. We introduce UzUDT, a newly created gold-standard Universal Dependencies treebank for Uzbek, manually annotated in INCEPTION by six annotators with full adjudication (684 sentences, ~7.8k tokens); UzUDT is currently the largest publicly available Uzbek UD treebank. We then study two complementary robustness strategies that remain lightweight in practice: (i) *linguistically-motivated last-subword fusion*, a positional heuristic for aggregating BERT WordPieces into UD token representations, and (ii) *cross-treebank training* by merging genre-complementary Uzbek UD resources. Using a Stanza-based BiLSTM tagger and biaffine parser augmented with monolingual contextual embeddings (TahrirchiBERT), we conduct a controlled factorial comparison across three embedding/fusion configurations and two data settings. Cross-treebank training yields the largest gains, improving LAS by 9.62–11.16 points while nearly doubling the training set (451 → 781 sentences). The best configuration (*TahrirchiBERT* with last-subword fusion on merged data) achieves 85.08 UPOS, 72.39 UAS, and 63.81 LAS.

Keywords: Uzbek · Universal Dependencies · Low-resource NLP · Dependency Parsing · Cross-treebank Training · Subword Fusion

1 Introduction

Dependency parsing is a central task in NLP, providing structured syntactic representations that support downstream applications such as information extraction, machine translation, and question answering. The Universal Dependencies (UD) framework has enabled cross-linguistic consistency in syntactic annotation and facilitated multilingual research [18]. Modern neural parsers, particularly graph-based models with biaffine attention [8], achieve strong performance when sufficient annotated data are available and are widely adopted in toolkits such as Stanza [19]. However, their success remains heavily dependent on training data size and quality.

E. Cabrio and E. Monteiro (Eds.): NLDB 2026, LNCS 16696, pp. 204–218, 2027.
https://doi.org/10.1007/978-3-032-29532-3_15

For low-resource and morphologically rich languages, data scarcity becomes the primary bottleneck. Uzbek, an agglutinative Turkic language, exhibits rich suffixation, flexible word order, and significant genre variation, all of which increase the complexity of morphosyntactic tagging and dependency parsing. Despite the existence of Uzbek UD resources within the UD ecosystem [15], available treebanks remain relatively small, limiting robust neural modelling. To address this gap, we introduce UzUDT,[1] a newly created gold-standard Uzbek UD treebank (684 sentences, ~7.8k tokens), manually annotated in INCEP-TION [11] by six annotators with full adjudication. To the best of our knowledge, UzUDT is currently the largest publicly available Uzbek UD treebank.

Beyond resource creation, this work is positioned within the broader agenda of *efficient low-resource dependency parsing*. Rather than relying on heavy architectural modifications, we investigate two lightweight strategies that can be applied with minimal additional parameters. First, we propose a *linguistically-motivated last-subword fusion* strategy for aligning contextualised WordPiece representations to UD tokens when using BERT-style encoders [7]. Subword-to-token alignment is non-trivial for agglutinative languages, where suffix chains frequently encode syntactic and morphological information. Our approach adopts a positional heuristic selecting the final subword representation for each token motivated by the fact that grammatical features in Uzbek are predominantly realised in suffixes. This method is computationally cheap and avoids introducing additional attention or pooling layers.

Second, we explore *cross-treebank training* as a data-centric robustness strategy. Multi-treebank and multilingual training have previously shown that expanding structural coverage can substantially improve parsing performance [3, 23]. In the context of Uzbek, we merge genre-complementary UD resources to nearly double the training data size and broaden syntactic coverage. We systematically evaluate this strategy in combination with two representation choices: static FastText embeddings [6] and a monolingual contextual encoder (*TahrirchiBERT* [14]).

Our contributions are fourfold:

1. We release UzUDT, the largest Uzbek UD treebank to date, strengthening the empirical foundation for Uzbek syntactic research.
2. We train and evaluate neural baselines for Uzbek morphosyntactic tagging (UPOS, XPOS, UFeats) and dependency parsing (UAS, LAS) under a standard UD evaluation protocol.
3. We introduce a linguistically-motivated last-subword fusion heuristic for efficient contextual token alignment in agglutinative settings.
4. Through a controlled factorial comparison across three embedding/fusion configurations and two data settings, we demonstrate that cross-treebank training provides the largest LAS gains, while contextual embeddings and last-subword fusion offer complementary improvements, particularly for tagging and parsing respectively.

---

[1] https://github.com/UniversalDependencies/UD_Uzbek-UzUDT/tree/dev

2   Related Work

Universal Dependencies. Universal Dependencies (UD) provides a cross-linguistically consistent framework in which words are annotated as syntactic units with morphological properties and grammatical relations. This representation facilitates multilingual evaluation, typological comparison, and cross-lingual transfer. [15] review the application of UD to more than one hundred languages and highlight the role of universal POS tags and morphological features in enabling comparative research. The UD guidelines (Version 2^2) further specify principles for tokenization, multiword expressions, lemmas, UPOS/XPOS tags, morphological features, and dependency relations.[3]

Parsing in Turkic and Other Agglutinative Languages. Dependency parsing in agglutinative languages such as Turkish, Uzbek, and other Turkic languages is challenging due to rich morphology, long suffix chains, flexible word order, and multifunctional grammatical markers [17]. Prior work on Turkish has shown that morphology-aware representations improve parsing accuracy; for example, [9] incorporate morphological segmentation and report gains over lexical baselines. Similar observations have been reported for Kazakh, Uyghur, and Tatar UD tree-banks, where parsers benefit from subword-level features and language-specific heuristics for case-driven ambiguities [16]. In addition, [1] discuss the challenges of adapting UD guidelines to Turkish multiword expressions and clitic construc-tions. These findings motivate our use of neural encoders combined with explicit morphological information.

Uzbek Resources. Uzbek remains under-resourced for UD-style morphosyntactic analysis and dependency parsing, limiting systematic benchmarking and robust parser development. At present, two Uzbek UD treebanks are available. The first, Uzbek-UT, was released in 2023 and contains about 500 sentences [2]. In this study, we build on the newly introduced *UzUDT* (684 sentences, ~7.8k tokens), whose design rationale, annotation methodology, and quality assurance are described in a companion paper by the present author [4]. In the present paper, UzUDT serves as the primary benchmark for evaluating robust neural modeling, morphology-aware preprocessing, and reproducible comparison.

Neural Pipelines and Contextual Models. Recent years have seen strong progress in fully neural multilingual NLP pipelines. Stanza [20] introduced a language-agnostic neural pipeline covering tokenization, multiword token expansion, lemmatization, POS and morphological tagging, dependency parsing, and named entity recognition. Its parser builds on the biaffine graph-based architecture of [8], which remains a strong baseline for CoNLL-U parsing. [12] further showed that a single multilingual model (UDify) can parse 75 languages through joint

---

[2] https://universaldependencies.org/guidelines.html.

[3] The author also contributed Uzbek-specific morphological feature and POS doc-umentation to the UD project, e.g., https://universaldependencies.org/uz/feat/PronType.html.

Table 1. Inter-annotator agreement for UzUDT (6 annotators).

Annotation layer	Cohen's κ	Krippendorff's α
Lemmatization	95.2%	94.6%
POS tagging (UPOS)	93.7%	94.1%
Morphological features	90.8%	89.9%

multitask learning. For Uzbek, [13] introduced *BERTbek*, a transformer model pretrained on a large Uzbek corpus, and showed that monolingual contextual embeddings outperform mBERT on tasks such as text classification and NER.

Morphological Analysis and Hybrid Architectures. Rule-based morphological analysers remain valuable for agglutinative languages, where they can complement neural models. Apertium is a free and open-source rule-based machine translation platform [5] with finite-state morphological analysers for many languages [10], including Uzbek [17,21,22]. It provides lexicons and morphophonological rules that support lemmatization and feature extraction. For Uzbek, preliminary evidence suggests that combining Apertium-derived features with BERTbek representations improves tagging and parsing robustness, especially for rare and unseen word forms [13].

3 Dataset

We use two Uzbek Universal Dependencies treebanks.

UD_Uzbek-UzUDT (UzUDT). A newly created resource of 684 sentences ($\approx$7,800 tokens) from Uzbek *fiction* (the story *Maqar*, the book *Kun shundan boshlanadi*, and publicly available fairy tales[4]) and *academic/educational* writing. Sentences are in the officially standardized Uzbek Latin script, with an average length of $\approx$12 tokens. All annotation—UPOS, XPOS, lemma, morphological features, and dependency relations—follows UD v2 guidelines [15] and was produced in the INCEpTION platform [11]. Six annotators (four Uzbek linguists and two NLP engineers) independently double-annotated every sentence after a calibration phase on shared pilot data. Inter-annotator agreement is high (Table 1): >95% on lemmas, $\approx$95% on UPOS, and >90% on morphological features. All conflicts were resolved through adjudication meetings with majority vote or consensus referral to UD guidelines and Uzbek reference grammars.

UD_Uzbek-UT (UT). Created by [2], UT comprises 500 sentences ($\approx$5,850 tokens) from two genres: 250 *news* and 250 *fiction*. Annotation was semi-automatic (automatic tokenization and lemmatization) with full manual correction of POS tags and dependency relations.

---

[4] https://ertak.uz/.

3.1 Data Splits and Settings

Neither treebank originally shipped with a development set suitable for early stopping. We pooled and re-split both corpora using standard UD proportions ($\approx$66/7/27%). Table 2 summarizes the resulting splits and the two data settings used in all experiments: .1 runs train on UzUDT only; .2 runs train on the merged UzUDT+UT corpus, nearly doubling the training data (451→781 sentences).

Table 2. Data splits and experimental settings. Merged files are produced by concatenating the corresponding UzUDT and UT splits.

Setting	Source	Train	Dev	Test	Total
UzUDT only (.1)	UzUDT	451	45	188	684
Merged (.2)	UzUDT + UT	781	78	325	1,184

The merged setting therefore adds 330/33/137 sentences from UT to the UzUDT train/dev/test splits, respectively, preserving the same split proportions across both corpora. The two treebanks are complementary in genre and annotation coverage: UT contributes more news-style named entities and light-verb constructions, while UzUDT contributes richer morphosyntactic distinctions and more adverbial-clause structures.

4 Method

We build on Stanza [19], extending its POS tagger and dependency parser with BERT support. The pipeline (Fig. 1) proceeds in four stages: (i) **encoding** (FastText or TahrirchiBERT), (ii) **subword-to-token fusion** (BERT only), (iii) **morphosyntactic tagging** (UPOS/XPOS/UFeats), (iv) **dependency parsing** (arcs + labels). Training is *sequential*: the tagger is trained first, its predictions replace gold POS in the data, and the parser is then trained on the re-tagged output.

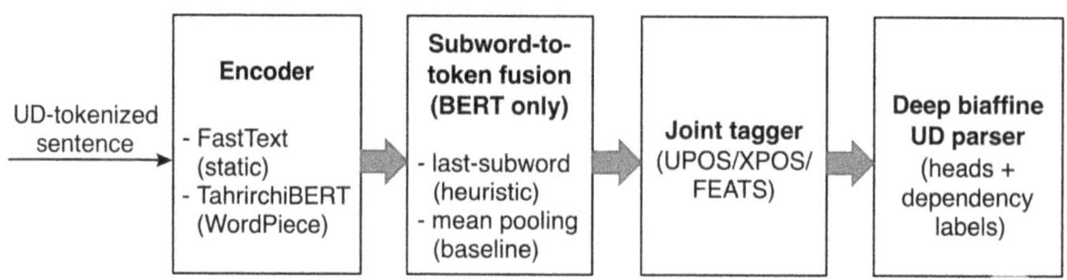

Fig. 1. End-to-end pipeline. Tokens are encoded, fused to UD boundaries, tagged, then parsed; predicted (not gold) UPOS embeddings feed the parser.

4.1   Token Representations

We compare two representation regimes: **(a) FastText** (static, 300 d): pre-trained Uzbek vectors (`cc.uz.300.vec`) [6]; and **(b) TahrirchiBERT** (contextual, 768 d): a monolingual Uzbek BERT (`tahrirchi-bert-base`) [14], chosen over BERTbek (news-centric) and mBERT (Uzbek-underrepresented) for its broad-domain pretraining that matches the heterogeneous treebank genres. The encoder is *frozen*; we extract last-layer hidden states and apply a fusion function (§4.2) to obtain one 768-d vector per UD token.

The final token vector concatenates four channels:

$$\mathbf{x}_i = \big[\, \mathbf{e}_{\text{word}}(w_i);\ \mathbf{e}_{\text{char}}(w_i);\ \mathbf{e}_{\text{upos}}(\hat{p}_i);\ \mathbf{e}_{\text{ctx}}(w_i) \,\big], \tag{1}$$

where $\mathbf{e}_{\text{word}}$ is a pretrained word embedding, $\mathbf{e}_{\text{char}}$ a character-LSTM representation, $\mathbf{e}_{\text{upos}}(\hat{p}_i)$ a 50-d embedding of the tagger's *predicted* UPOS label, and $\mathbf{e}_{\text{ctx}}$ the fused BERT vector (absent in the FastText-only configuration).

4.2   Subword-to-Token Fusion

BERT WordPiece boundaries rarely coincide with UD tokens. For a UD token t split into k subwords with hidden states $\{\mathbf{h}_1, \ldots, \mathbf{h}_k\}$, we compare two aggregations:

Last-Subword Fusion (Linguistically Motivated).

$$\mathbf{e}_{\text{ctx}}(t) = \mathbf{h}_k. \tag{2}$$

Uzbek is predominantly suffixing: the rightmost subword typically encodes the outermost grammatical morpheme—the very signal that UD tagging and attachment rely on. For instance, *bolalarning* ("of the children") is tokenized as `bola ##lar ##ning`; the last subword `##ning` carries the genitive suffix.[5]

Mean Pooling (Language-Agnostic Baseline).

$$\mathbf{e}_{\text{ctx}}(t) = \tfrac{1}{k} \sum_{i=1}^{k} \mathbf{h}_i. \tag{3}$$

This makes no typological assumption, serving as a controlled comparator under the same encoder.

4.3   Tagger and Parser

Joint Morphosyntactic Tagger. A BiLSTM contextualizes the token sequence; task-specific softmax heads jointly predict UPOS, XPOS, and UFeats. To avoid oracle leakage, the parser receives only *predicted* UPOS embeddings $\mathbf{e}_{\text{upos}}(\hat{p}_i)$.

Deep Biaffine Dependency Parser. Following Dozat and Manning [8], BiLSTM states are projected into head/dependent subspaces via MLPs, and biaffine scoring produces arc and relation scores. The output is a labeled dependency tree over UD tokens.

---

[5] A second example: *ko'rganmisiz* ("have you seen?") $\rightarrow$ `ko'r ##gan ##mi ##siz`; the final `##siz` carries 2PL agreement.

5   Experiments and Results

Our experiments address three controlled comparisons: (i) *embedding type*—static FastText vectors versus contextual TahrirchiBERT representations, both held constant with respect to fusion and data; (ii) *subword-to-token fusion*—linguistically-motivated last-subword selection versus language-agnostic mean pooling, both using the same TahrirchiBERT encoder; and (iii) *data setting*—training on UzUDT alone (451 sentences) versus the merged UzUDT+UT corpus (781 sentences).

Run Matrix. We adopt a structured multi-factor design with 3 embedding/fusion configurations × 2 data settings, yielding **6 experimental runs** (Table 3). **E1** uses static FastText embeddings (`cc.uz.300`, 300-dim) without subword fusion. **E2** uses TahrirchiBERT with *last-subword* fusion, selecting the hidden state of the final WordPiece subword per UD token to preserve suffix-level morphosyntactic cues. **E3** uses TahrirchiBERT with *mean pooling*, averaging all subword hidden states per UD token. Within each configuration, the `.1` suffix denotes training on UzUDT only and the `.2` suffix denotes training on the merged UzUDT+UT corpus.

Table 3. Experiment matrix. E1 vs. E2 isolates the embedding effect (static vs. contextual) while holding fusion constant. E2 vs. E3 isolates the fusion strategy while holding BERT constant. Comparing `.1` vs. `.2` within each row measures the data-augmentation effect.

Run	Embeddings	Fusion	Data	Train sents
E1.1	FastText	—	UzUDT	451
E1.2	FastText	—	UzUDT+UT	781
E2.1	TahrirchiBERT	Last-subword	UzUDT	451
E2.2	TahrirchiBERT	Last-subword	UzUDT+UT	781
E3.1	TahrirchiBERT	Mean pooling	UzUDT	451
E3.2	TahrirchiBERT	Mean pooling	UzUDT+UT	781

5.1   Training Protocol and Evaluation

Pipeline Training. For each of the six runs, we first train a BiLSTM-based morphosyntactic tagger (UPOS, XPOS, UFeats) and use it to re-tag the training, development, and test files with predicted POS labels. A deep biaffine dependency parser [8] is then trained on the re-tagged data so that it never sees gold POS tags, matching the realistic inference setting. Test-set evaluation is performed with the standard CoNLL 2018 shared-task script.

Hyperparameters and Model Selection. All models are trained within a modified Stanza [19] fork using the Adam optimizer ($\beta = (0.9, 0.999)$, lr $= 3 \times 10^{-3}$, batch $= 5{,}000$ tokens, dropout $= 0.33$). Training runs for a maximum of 50,000 steps with early stopping on dev-set performance (AllTags for the tagger, LAS for the parser). All remaining architecture and optimization settings follow Stanza defaults; the parser uses a single-layer MLP (dim $= 500$) for both arc and relation scoring, and UPOS embeddings of dimension 50 are concatenated into the parser input. In TahrirchiBERT configurations, the BERT encoder is *not fine-tuned*; we extract frozen hidden states and apply the fusion function to produce 768-dim token vectors.

Metrics. For tagging we report UPOS, XPOS, and UFeats accuracy. For parsing we report UAS and LAS. All scores are computed on the held-out test split using the UD evaluation script (`conll18_ud_eval.py`).

5.2   Main Results

Tables 4 and 5 present the test-set results for all six runs. The best scores are set in bold; selected cross-run deltas are shown in the bottom rows to aid interpretation.

Table 4. Morphosyntactic tagging results (accuracy, %). "BERT" abbreviates TahrirchiBERT throughout. Bold marks the best score per column. Deltas are computed on the merged-data BERT rows to highlight the three experimental factors.

Run	Configuration	UPOS	XPOS	UFeats
E1.1	FastText, UzUDT	79.19	79.81	66.61
E1.2	FastText, UzUDT+UT	80.26	83.20	66.98
E2.1	BERT + last-sub, UzUDT	82.45	80.90	65.37
E2.2	BERT + last-sub, UzUDT+UT	**85.08**	84.72	**71.00**
E3.1	BERT + mean, UzUDT	82.76	81.37	65.22
E3.2	BERT + mean, UzUDT+UT	84.02	**87.07**	70.39
Selected deltas				
Δ Embedding (E2.2−E1.2)		*+4.82*	*+1.52*	*+4.11*
Δ Fusion (E2.2−E3.2)		*+1.06*	*−2.35*	*+0.70*
Δ Data (E2.2−E2.1)		*+2.63*	*+3.82*	*+5.72*

The best overall system is **E2.2** (TahrirchiBERT + last-subword fusion + merged data), which ranks first in four of five metrics (UPOS, UFeats, UAS, LAS). The sole exception is XPOS, where mean-pooling configuration E3.2 achieves 87.07 which is the highest score across all runs.

Table 5. Dependency parsing results (accuracy, %). Bold marks the best score per column. Data-augmentation deltas (Δ Data) are shown for both FastText and BERT.

Run	Configuration	UAS	LAS
E1.1	FastText, UzUDT	69.57	51.24
E1.2	FastText, UzUDT+UT	72.27	62.40
E2.1	BERT + last-sub, UzUDT	72.05	54.19
E2.2	BERT + last-sub, UzUDT+UT	**72.39**	**63.81**
E3.1	BERT + mean, UzUDT	69.10	51.55
E3.2	BERT + mean, UzUDT+UT	70.74	60.05
Selected deltas			
Δ Embedding (E2.2−E1.2)		*+0.12*	*+1.41*
Δ Fusion (E2.2−E3.2)		*+1.65*	*+3.76*
Δ Data (E2.2−E2.1)		*+0.34*	*+9.62*
Δ Data (E1.2−E1.1)		*+2.70*	*+11.16*

5.3   Observations

Observation 1: Contextual vs. Static Representations. TahrirchiBERT consistently outperforms FastText for UPOS tagging, with gains of $+3.26$ on UzUDT alone (E2.1 vs. E1.1) and $+4.82$ on merged data (E2.2 vs. E1.2). The improvement is amplified by corpus size: UFeats flips from -1.24 on small data to $+4.11$ on merged data, suggesting a minimum data threshold for BERT to learn fine-grained morphological feature bundles. LAS gains are more modest ($+1.41$ to $+2.95$), indicating that contextual embeddings have a larger impact on local tagging decisions than on structural dependency predictions under severe data scarcity. The per-run evaluation trajectories in Fig. 3 (Appendix) corroborate this pattern: BERT runs (E2/E3) consistently track above FastText (E1) on UPOS and UFeats throughout training, with clear separation visible from early steps.

Observation 2: Subword-to-Token Fusion. The comparison between last-subword (E2) and mean pooling (E3) reveals a task-dependent pattern. For *dependency parsing*, last-subword fusion is clearly superior: the LAS advantage is $+2.64$ on UzUDT and widens to $+\mathbf{3.76}$ on merged data, confirming that suffix-positional cues become *more* exploitable as training data grows. This gap is consequential: mean pooling with BERT (E3.2, LAS $= 60.05$) actually falls behind static FastText on merged data (E1.2, LAS $= 62.40$), while last-subword BERT (E2.2, LAS $= 63.81$) surpasses both—demonstrating that the correct fusion strategy is essential for BERT to outperform FastText on parsing. For POS tagging the picture is mixed: XPOS consistently favors mean pooling (-2.35 on merged data), likely because language-specific tags are determined by the full word form rather than the final suffix, whereas UPOS and UFeats show a weak but consistent last-subword advantage on merged data (+1.06 and +0.70, respectively). The dev-score and LAS/UAS curves in Fig. 2 (Appendix) visually confirm the fusion gap: last-subword runs plateau at higher parsing metrics than their mean-pooling counterparts across both data settings.

Observation 3: Cross-Treebank Augmentation. Merging UzUDT with UD_Uzbek-UT produces the single largest accuracy improvement in the study. LAS jumps by +11.16 for FastText (E1.1→E1.2) and +9.62 for TahrirchiB-ERT (E2.1→E2.2)—far exceeding the BERT upgrade effect. The interaction between BERT and data is synergistic, not merely additive: BERT's UFeats advantage swings from −1.24 (small data) to +4.11 (merged), a +5.35 amplification. The two treebanks are structurally complementary in genre (literature/academic vs. news/fiction), UPOS distribution (PROPN 0.3% in UzUDT vs. 5.2% in UT), and dependency-relation coverage (`advcl` is 4× more frequent in UzUDT; `compound:lvc` is 10× more frequent in UT), explaining why even a modest increase from 451 to 781 training sentences yields such large gains. The data effect is equally strong under mean pooling: E3.2 LAS improves by +8.50 over E3.1, confirming that the augmentation benefit is robust across fusion strategies.

Observation 4: Training Dynamics. All twelve models converge rapidly, reaching their best dev-set checkpoint within 5–18% of the 50,000-step budget (typically 300–1,300 steps). BERT configurations converge slightly earlier than FastText (steps 600–1,000 vs. 800–1,300), suggesting that contextual representations provide a stronger initialization. Total wall-clock training time for all twelve models is approximately 265 min on a single NVIDIA RTX A6000 GPU. Full training curves including loss, dev scores, learning-rate schedules, and GPU memory allocation are provided in Figs. 2 and 3 (Appendix).

Observation 5: Annotation Heterogeneity in Merged Data. Merging two independently developed treebanks inevitably introduces annotation inconsistencies. To quantify this effect, we compared label distributions in the intersecting deprel inventory. The UT treebank fails UD validation with 92 warnings, predominantly `obl` tokens that should be `nmod` according to UD v2 guidelines. These misanalyses inflate `obl` frequency by ≈14% in the merged training set relative to a corrected distribution. Despite this noise, the merged-data setting consistently outperforms the UzUDT-only setting across all six configuration pairs, suggesting that the coverage benefits of genre complementarity outweigh the annotation noise.

5.4   Error Analysis

To characterise remaining parsing challenges, we manually analysed errors in 100 randomly sampled test sentences from our best system (E2.2: TahrirchiB-ERT + last-subword + merged data). Table 6 summarises the distribution of these errors by their linguistic source. Three patterns dominate, suggesting clear avenues for targeted improvements. First, *PP/oblique attachment* (28%) is driven by `obl`/`nmod` ambiguity and exacerbated by the UT inconsistencies from Observation 5, highlighting a need for annotation harmonisation. Second, *coordination scope* errors (22%) arise in multi-clause conjuncts—a known limitation for biaffine parsers lacking global constraints—suggesting higher-order parsing could be beneficial. Finally, *subordinate clause attachment* errors (18%) reflect the difficulty of capturing Uzbek's flexible clause ordering.

Table 6. Error analysis on 100 test sentences (E2.2), categorised by linguistic source.

Error type	%	Typical pattern
PP/oblique attach.	28	`obl`/`nmod` confusion; misattached dative/locative phrases
Coordination scope	22	Multi-clause conjuncts; `conj` arcs attached too high/low
Subordinate clauses	18	`advcl`/`ccomp` mislabelled or misattached
Compound constructions	14	`compound:lvc` vs. `nmod`; wrong light-verb boundaries
Long-distance deps	10	Dependencies >6 tokens; head misidentified
Other	8	Rare deprels, punctuation, multi-word expressions

6   Conclusion

We presented UzUDT, a 684-sentence gold-standard Uzbek UD treebank, and a controlled study of two lightweight robustness strategies for low-resource parsing: linguistically-motivated last-subword fusion and cross-treebank data augmentation. Among three embedding/fusion configurations and two data settings, cross-treebank training is the dominant factor (LAS +9.62–11.16), while last-subword fusion is critical specifically for dependency parsing (LAS +3.76 over mean pooling on merged data). The best system (TahrirchiBERT, last-subword, merged) achieves 85.08 UPOS, 72.39 UAS, and 63.81 LAS.

Data and Models Availability. Both treebanks are released through the UD website. The merged data in experiments and full research logs are included in the GitHub[6]. The full twelve trained model checkpoints are available at[7].

7   Limitations

Our findings should be interpreted in light of two constraints: the small development sets (45 and 78 sentences), which increase sensitivity during early stopping, and the sequential UT split, which creates a marked genre mismatch between news-heavy training data and a fiction-heavy test set. In addition, UD_Uzbek-UT contains validation inconsistencies and shallower morphological annotation than UzUDT (notably for possessor agreement and evidentiality), introducing some label noise into merged-corpus experiments.

---

[6] https://github.com/SanatbekMatlatipov/robust-parsing-uzbek.
[7] https://huggingface.co/Sanatbek/uzudt.

Acknowledgments. The author gratefully acknowledges the National University of Uzbekistan named after Mirzo Ulugbek, and in particular its Rector, Professor Madjidov Inom Urishevich, for financial support covering the conference participation costs for this research.

A Appendix

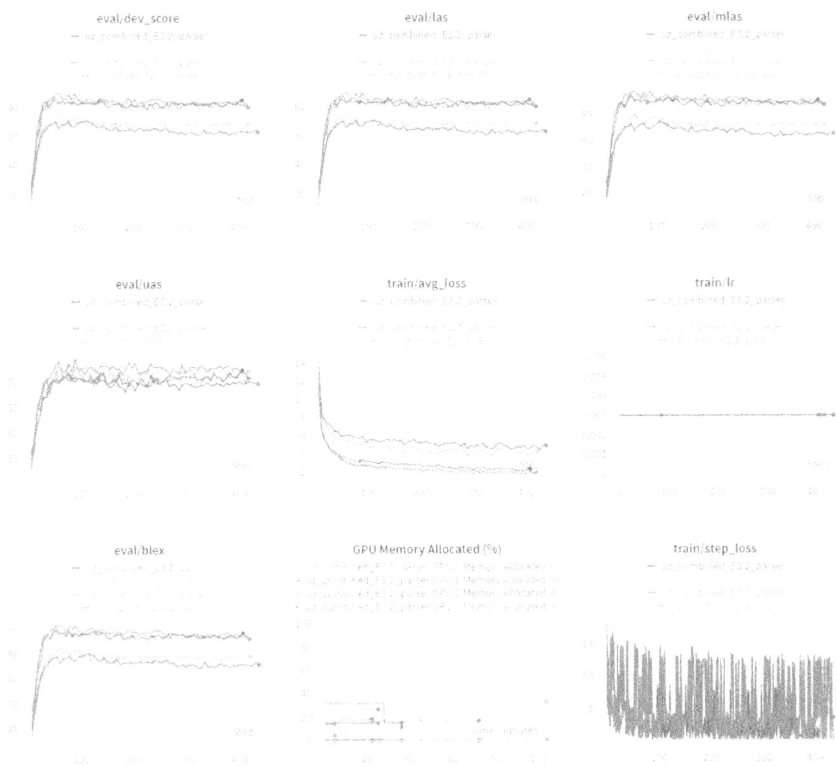

Fig. 2. Training and validation dynamics of the Uzbek UD dependency parser across representative runs (UzUDT-only vs. merged UzUDT+UT). The panels track the development score and parsing quality (LAS/UAS/MLAS/BLEX) over training steps, alongside optimization signals (average training loss, learning rate, step-level loss) and GPU memory allocation. Curves show rapid early convergence followed by stable plateaus, with merged-data and contextual configurations generally achieving higher dev and parsing metrics than UzUDT-only baselines.

Fig. 3. Training and validation dynamics of the Uzbek UD tagger across the six runs (E1–E3 × data setting). Panels report evaluation F1 for UPOS/XPOS/UFeats and ALLTAGS, the overall development score, training losses (avg/step), the global step progression, and GPU memory allocation. Curves show rapid convergence and stable plateaus; contextual configurations (TahrirchiBERT, E2/E3) generally track above the static FastText baseline (E1), and merged-data runs (.2) tend to improve over UzUDT-only (.1).

References

1. Implementing universal dependency, morphology, and multiword expression annotation standards for Turkish language processing. Turk. J. Electr. Eng. Comput. Sci. **26**(3) (2018)
2. Akhundjanova, A., Talamo, L.: Universal Dependencies treebank for Uzbek. In: Holdt, Š.A., Ilinykh, N., Scalvini, B., Bruton, M., Debess, I.N., Tudor, C.M. (eds.) Proceedings of the Third Workshop on Resources and Representations for Under-Resourced Languages and Domains (RESOURCEFUL-2025), pp. 1–6. University

of Tartu Library, Estonia, Tallinn, Estonia (2025). https://aclanthology.org/2025. resourceful-1.1/

3. Ammar, W., Mulcaire, G., Tsvetkov, Y., Lample, G., Dyer, C., Smith, N.A.: Massively multilingual word embeddings (2016)

4. Anonymous: A gold-standard dependency treebank for the Uzbek language (2025). Manuscript submitted to the same venue (under review)

5. Aripov, M., Khakimov, M., Matlatipov, S., Sirojiddinov, Z.: Analysis and processing of the Uzbek language on the multi-language modelled computer translator technology. In: Vetulani, Z., Paroubek, P., Kubis, M. (eds.) Human Language Technology. Challenges for Computer Science and Linguistics, pp. 81–95. Springer, Cham (2022)

6. Bojanowski, P., Grave, E., Joulin, A., Mikolov, T.: Enriching word vectors with subword information. Trans. Assoc. Comput. Linguistics **5**, 135–146 (2017)

7. Devlin, J., Chang, M.W., Lee, K., Toutanova, K.: BERT: pre-training of deep bidirectional transformers for language understanding. In: Burstein, J., Doran, C., Solorio, T. (eds.) Proceedings of the 2019 Conference of the North American Chapter of the Association for Computational Linguistics: Human Language Technologies, Volume 1 (Long and Short Papers), pp. 4171–4186. Association for Computational Linguistics, Minneapolis, Minnesota (2019). https://doi.org/10.18653/v1/N19-1423

8. Dozat, T., Manning, C.D.: Deep biaffine attention for neural dependency parsing. In: 5th International Conference on Learning Representations, ICLR 2017, Toulon, France, 24–26 April 2017, Conference Track Proceedings. OpenReview.net (2017). https://openreview.net/forum?id=Hk95PK9le

9. Eryiğit, G., Nivre, J., Oflazer, K.: Dependency parsing of Turkish. Comput. Linguist. **34**(3), 357–389 (2008)

10. Forcada, M.L., et al.: Apertium: a free/open-source platform for rule-based machine translation. Mach. Transl. **25**(2), 127–144 (2011)

11. Klie, J.C., Bugert, M., Boullosa, B., Eckart de Castilho, R., Gurevych, I.: The INCEpTION platform: machine-assisted and knowledge-oriented interactive annotation. In: Zhao, D. (ed.) Proceedings of the 27th International Conference on Computational Linguistics: System Demonstrations, pp. 5–9. Association for Computational Linguistics, Santa Fe, New Mexico (2018). https://aclanthology.org/C18-2002/

12. Kondratyuk, D., Straka, M.: 75 languages, 1 model: parsing Universal Dependencies universally. In: Inui, K., Jiang, J., Ng, V., Wan, X. (eds.) Proceedings of the 2019 Conference on Empirical Methods in Natural Language Processing and the 9th International Joint Conference on Natural Language Processing (EMNLP-IJCNLP), pp. 2779–2795. Association for Computational Linguistics, Hong Kong, China (2019). https://doi.org/10.18653/v1/D19-1279

13. Kuriyozov, E., Vilares, D., Gómez-Rodríguez, C.: BERTbek: a pretrained language model for Uzbek. In: Melero, M., Sakti, S., Soria, C. (eds.) Proceedings of the 3rd Annual Meeting of the Special Interest Group on Under-resourced Languages @ LREC-COLING 2024, pp. 33–44. ELRA and ICCL, Torino, Italia (2024). https://aclanthology.org/2024.sigul-1.5/

14. Mamasaidov, M., Shopulatov, A.: Tahrirchibert base (2023). https://huggingface.co/tahrirchi/tahrirchi-bert-base

15. de Marneffe, M.C., Manning, C.D., Nivre, J., Zeman, D.: Universal dependencies. Comput. Linguist. **47**(2), 255–308 (2021)

16. Marşan, B., et al.: Enhancements to the BOUN treebank reflecting the agglutinative nature of turkish. https://ceur-ws.org/Vol-3315/paper08.pdf. Accessed: 21-Dec-2025
17. Murzintcev, N., Yuldasheva, S.S.: Uzbek language morphology analyser. Natural Lang. Process. J. **14**, 100195 (2026)
18. Nivre, J., et al.: Universal Dependencies v1: a multilingual treebank collection. In: Calzolari, N., et al. (eds.) Proceedings of the Tenth International Conference on Language Resources and Evaluation (LREC'16), pp. 1659–1666. European Language Resources Association (ELRA), Portorož, Slovenia (2016), https://aclanthology.org/L16-1262/
19. Qi, P., Zhang, Y., Zhang, Y., Bolton, J., Manning, C.D.: Stanza: a python natural language processing toolkit for many human languages. In: Celikyilmaz, A., Wen, T.H. (eds.) Proceedings of the 58th Annual Meeting of the Association for Computational Linguistics: System Demonstrations, pp. 101–108. Association for Computational Linguistics, Online (2020). https://doi.org/10.18653/v1/2020.acl-demos.14
20. Qi, P., Zhang, Y., Zhang, Y., Bolton, J., Manning, C.D.: Stanza: a python natural language processing toolkit for many human languages (2020)
21. Salaev, U.: Uzmorphanalyser: a morphological analysis model for the Uzbek language using inflectional endings. AIP Conf. Proc. **3244**(1), 030058 (2024)
22. Sharipov, M., Kuriyozov, E., Yuldashev, O., Sobirov, O.: Uzbektagger: the rule based pos tagger for Uzbek language (2023)
23. Zeman, D., et al.: CoNLL 2018 shared task: multilingual parsing from raw text to Universal Dependencies. In: Zeman, D., Hajič, J. (eds.) Proceedings of the CoNLL 2018 Shared Task: Multilingual Parsing from Raw Text to Universal Dependencies, pp. 1–21. Association for Computational Linguistics, Brussels, Belgium (2018). https://doi.org/10.18653/v1/K18-2001

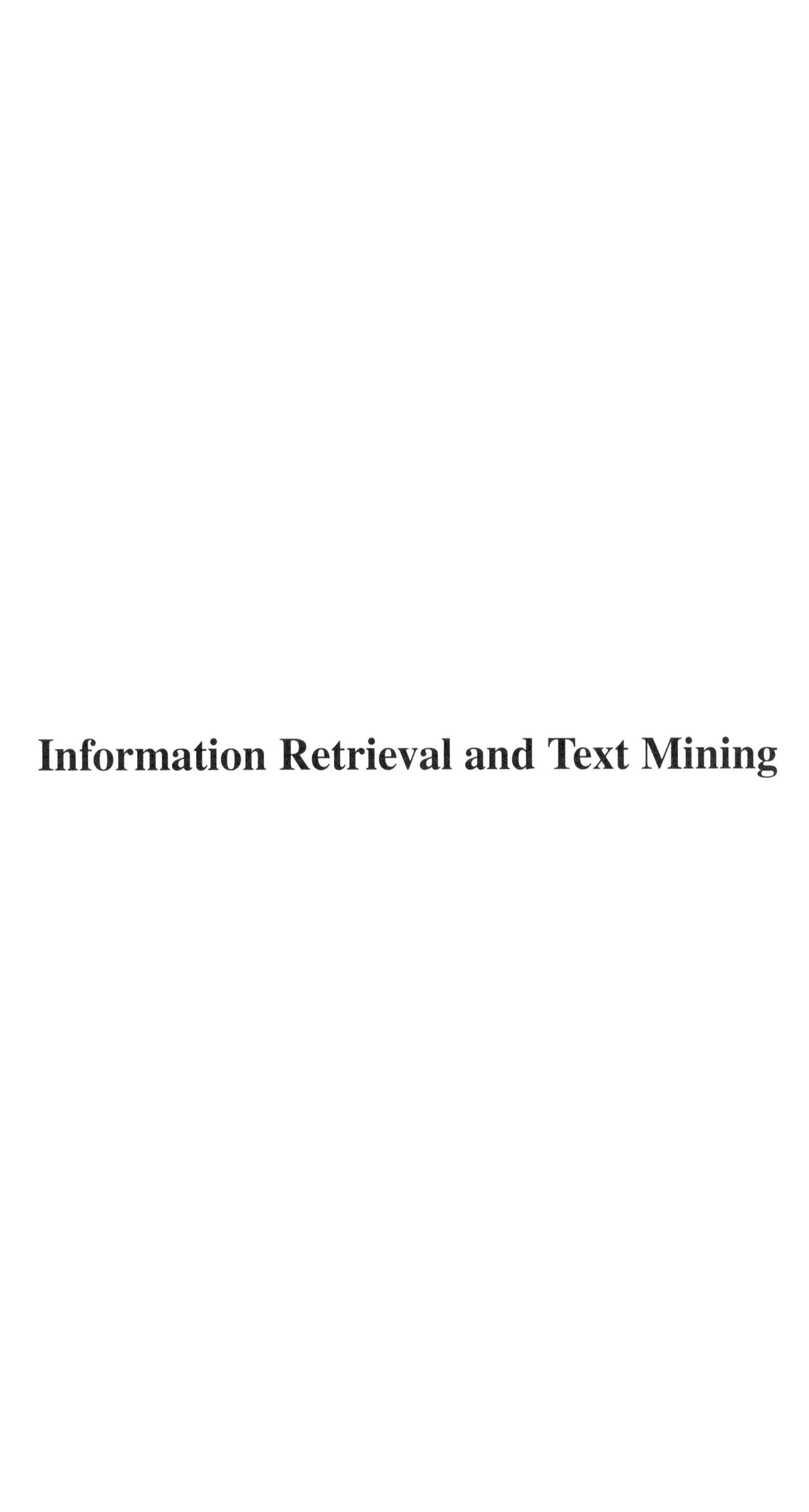

Information Retrieval and Text Mining

Adapting GPT for Egyptian Arabic-English Code-Switched Sentiment Analysis Through Prompting, Retrieval, and Sentiment-Guided Fine-Tuning

Ahmed Sherif[✉], Reem Hussein, and Caroline Sabty

German International University, New Administrative Capital, Egypt
{ahmed.sherif,caroline.sabty}@giu-uni.de, reem.hussein@student.giu-uni.de

Abstract. Arabic–English code-switching is common in Egyptian social media, where users naturally mix Arabic and English in short, informal comments that often include emojis and non-standard spelling. This setting poses challenges for sentiment analysis, while publicly available resources for Egyptian code-switched text remain limited. In this paper, we investigate GPT-based sentiment classification for Egyptian Arabic–English code-switched text using the EESA corpus, a labelled dataset of YouTube comments annotated for three-way sentiment. We evaluate three adaptation strategies: prompt-based inference, retrieval-augmented generation (RAG), and fine-tuning. For prompt-only inference, the best configuration combines GPT-4o with annotation guidelines and sentiment hints, achieving an F1-score of 90.8%. RAG further improves performance by conditioning predictions on dynamically retrieved in-domain labelled examples. The strongest RAG configuration, based on the text-embedding-3-large encoder and a modified retrieval setup with explanations, reaches an F1-score of 93.6%. We additionally propose enriching fine-tuning data with sentiment hints, lightweight textual cues that guide the model toward the correct polarity during training. Fine-tuning GPT-4o-mini with sentiment hints achieves an F1-score of 95.5%, establishing a new state of the art on EESA and surpassing the previous best result by 2.8 points. Overall, the findings show that structured prompting provides a strong baseline, retrieval augmentation offers substantial gains without parameter updates, and lightweight fine-tuning with sentiment hints yields the highest performance.

Keywords: NLP · Sentiment Analysis · RAG · Arabic Language · Code-Switching · GPT

1 Introduction

Bilingual posting on social media is becoming increasingly popular, and many users naturally mix languages in the same post or comment. This kind of language mixing is widely seen on social media and is known to pose challenges for

E. Cabrio and E. Monteiro (Eds.): NLDB 2026, LNCS 16696, pp. 221–236, 2027.
https://doi.org/10.1007/978-3-032-29532-3_16

NLP in informal user-generated text [7]. This phenomenon is especially relevant in Egypt, where Arabic and English are often mixed in everyday communication and are frequently combined in online content. In this setting, the dominant form of mixing is *code-switching*, typically defined as alternating between two languages either at sentence boundaries or within the same sentence [13].

Arabic–English code-switching is therefore widely used by Egyptian speakers on social media, where both languages may appear within the same short, informal comment. This directly affects sentiment analysis, which aims to automatically identify the writer's expressed opinion or emotional polarity (e.g., positive, negative, or neutral) from text [9,20]. In code-switched Egyptian comments, sentiment cues may appear in either language, be expressed through emojis, or depend on dialect-specific words and non-standard spelling, making reliable classification more difficult than in monolingual settings [14].

Despite growing interest in multilingual NLP, Arabic–English code-switched sentiment analysis remains constrained by limited public datasets and benchmarks, which restrict systematic comparison and make generalization difficult to assess across domains. To address this gap, this work studies sentiment analysis on the EESA corpus [23] using GPT models. The contributions are:

1. A systematic comparison of GPT-based sentiment analysis using prompt-based inference, RAG, and fine-tuning on the EESA corpus.
2. Introducing sentiment hints within each comment during fine-tuning of GPT models, which improves performance over standard fine-tuning.
3. Achieving a new state of the art on EESA, where the fine-tuned GPT model with sentiment hints surpasses the previous best result by 2.8 points.

The EESA corpus was chosen for this evaluation for two reasons. First, Egyptian Arabic-English code-switching remains relatively underexplored, and EESA supports evaluation under mixed-language and informal social-media conditions. Second, the corpus includes only unanimously agreed annotations, resulting in highly reliable labels and ensuring that observed performance differences reflect modelling decisions rather than inconsistencies in the ground truth.

GPT models are used as the main backbone because they support both Arabic and English and have shown strong results on many NLP tasks. Still, sentiment analysis on Egyptian Arabic–English code-switched text is not well-solved with a generic prompt, so some form of adaptation is needed. In this work, three approaches are explored: prompt-based inference, RAG, and fine-tuning.

The best prompt-only performance is achieved by GPT-4o with Annotation Guidelines and Sentiment Hints, reaching 90.8% F1-score, and improving to 93.6% with modified RAG and explanations. Fine-tuning GPT-4o-mini with sentiment hints achieves the best performance at 95.5% F1-score, surpassing the previous state of the art on EESA (92.7%) [23] by 2.8 points.

The rest of this paper is organized as follows. Section 2 reviews related work. Section 3 describes the EESA corpus. Section 4 presents the GPT-based approaches, including prompt-based inference, retrieval-augmented generation, and fine-tuning. Section 5 reports the experimental setup and results. Finally, Sect. 6 concludes the paper and outlines future work.

2   Related Work

This section reviews work closest to sentiment classification for Arabic social-media text, focusing on Arabic–English code-switching and recent LLM-based methods. Prior work shows that dialectal, informal writing and limited context make Arabic sentiment challenging, and code-switching adds ambiguity because cues may appear in either language. Recent LLM-based approaches mainly use prompt-based guidance or retrieval of in-domain evidence. The discussion covers Arabic and code-switched sentiment benchmarks, then prompt-based LLM classification, and retrieval-augmented LLM classification to motivate comparison.

2.1   Arabic and Code-Switched Sentiment Analysis

Arabic sentiment analysis has evolved from lexicon and feature-based methods to neural models and large pre-trained transformers, yet user-generated text remains challenging. Surveys highlight that morphology, negation, dialect variation, and short social-media context can reduce robustness [3,24].

Performance in more standardized settings shows what is possible when noise is lower and labels are consistent. For example, BERT-LA reports 97.04% accuracy on IMDB English and 98.02% on IMDB Arabic [15]. On harder Arabic benchmarks, modelling choices still matter: selective reading reports 84.57% on ASTD, 86.80% on LABR, and 95.57% on HARD [30]. In few/zero-shot Arabic classification, adding label semantics can help; appending label information increases 10-shot accuracy on ArSarcasm-v2 from 0.751 to 0.777 [8].

Code-switching increases the difficulty because the sentiment may appear in Arabic, English, or both. On an Algerian code-switched corpus, injecting polarity lexicons improves F1-score (F1), with a +10.54 gain for the negative class [1]. For Arabic–English, adding FastText vectors to a FLAIR-based setup yields 88.8% F1-score [21]. Sarcasm also matters: the accuracy of the sentiment in ArSarcasm-v2 increases from 80.87% to 90.53% when combined with sarcasm detection [10]. Broader code-mixed benchmarks show wide variation, including 73.66% macro-F1 on English–Spanish, 61.24% on English–Hindi [22], and 0.21–0.67 macro-F1 across several language mixes and LLM backbones [26].

For Egyptian Arabic–English, EESA provides 4,100 annotated code-switched comments. Reported results show strong performance from both language models and neural systems, with best test F1 of 92.67% (fine-tuned GPT-3.5) and 92.54% (neural ensemble), while the neutral class remains the most commonly mispredicted [23]. This suggests that performance depends not only on model capacity but also on how label rules are communicated, in line with Arabic LLM evaluations noting practical issues such as output-format deviations [6].

2.2   Prompt-Based LLM Sentiment Classification

Prompt-based sentiment classification treats sentiment prediction as instruction following: the input is placed in a prompt that defines the label set, and the model is constrained to output one label. This avoids training a separate classifier, but performance depends on prompt clarity, label definitions, and output compliance. Arabic evaluations show that prompting can be competitive but remains sensitive to design and decoding. On AJGT, reported accuracy is 86.94% for GPT-3.5 and 90.30% for GPT-4, while a task-specialized Arabic baseline reaches 96.11%, and the same study notes frequent output-format deviations that affect strict scoring [6]. A dialectal Twitter study reports zero-shot accuracy of 0.81 for GPT-3.5 and 0.91 for GPT-4 under the best prompt template, with supervised Arabic Transformer baselines remaining strong references [2].

For Arabic–English code-switched sentiment, prompt content can matter more because label rules must hold under mixed scripts and bilingual cues. On EESA, adding the annotation guidelines to the prompt improves zero-shot models, with test F1 of 90.22% for Gemini-1.5 and 89.73% for GPT-4o [23]. Prompting is also used in low-resource settings via prompt-based fine-tuning of multilingual encoders: with 32 examples per class, Arabic F1 is 0.54 (prefix) and 0.48 (cloze), versus 0.60 under standard fine-tuning [25]. Applied studies show domain sensitivity: in Arabic digital banking reviews, a voting classifier reaches 90.24% accuracy while GPT-4 is the strongest tested LLM under few-shot prompting [4], and a mobile banking satisfaction study uses LLMs in the workflow with high performance depending on labeling setup [5]. Overall, prompt guidance can be strong, but results depend on prompt design, output constraints, and label rules, motivating retrieval grounding as a complementary strategy.

2.3 Retrieval-Augmented LLM Sentiment Classification

Retrieval-Augmented Generation extends an LLM with a retrieval step that fetches relevant items from an index and conditions generation on both the input and retrieved context. RAG can be viewed in terms of retriever, generator, and augmentation components, making performance sensitive to each choice [12].

In sentiment classification, retrieval can help with short, noisy inputs, but gains depend on retrieving sentiment-aligned evidence; irrelevant retrieval may add noise and hurt predictions. An Arabic evaluation reports a weighted F1 of 0.18–0.58 on ASAD under zero-shot prompting, improving to 0.59 on ASAD, 0.57 on ArSarcasm-v2, and 0.64 on SemEval-2017 Task 4A with a semantic RAG pipeline; removing the neutral class raises F1 to 0.76, 0.75, and 0.82 [18].

In financial sentiment, RAG improves ChatGPT from 0.788/0.652 (Acc/F1) to 0.813/0.708 and an instruction-tuned LLM from 0.863/0.811 to 0.881/0.842 [29]. A retrieval-augmented multi-agent system reports 0.9505/0.9387 (Acc/F1) on PhraseBank-100% Agree and 0.8360/0.8163 on PhraseBank-50% Agree for GPT-4o [11]. A mental health evaluation comparing fine-tuning, prompt engineering, and RAG similarly shows that the best strategy varies by task and that RAG is not always beneficial without careful design [17].

These findings connect to Arabic–English code-switched sentiment, where inputs are short, informal, and may express cues in either language. Prompting and RAG are evaluated under the same protocol, using retrieval from the training split to test when in-domain evidence improves beyond prompt guidance.

3   Dataset

The EESA corpus contains 4,100 annotated Egyptian Arabic–English code-switched YouTube comments collected from domains including Egyptian celebrities, movies, and television series. The comments reflect authentic online writing, where informal spelling, expressive punctuation, emojis, and language switching are common. Each comment is annotated with one of three labels: Positive, Negative, or Neutral. Annotation was performed by three annotators per comment, and disagreements were resolved through discussion. The reported inter-annotator agreement (Cohen's Kappa) is 0.98, indicating high consistency.

Each comment contains between 2 and 108 words, with an average length of approximately 12 words. Arabic words account for about 78% of the corpus, while English makes up roughly 22%. At the comment level, however, the Arabic share ranges from 2% to 98%, reflecting substantial variation in how much each language contributes to individual comments. The corpus is distributed across three sentiment classes: 1,818 positive (44.34%), 1,294 neutral (31.56%), and 988 negative (24.10%) comments. The dataset was divided into official 60% training, 20% development, and 20% test splits using stratified sampling to preserve label distribution. The original splits are used without modification in all experiments.

For our experiments, the official CSV splits are read using UTF-8 encoding and converted to JSONL format, where each entry contains a unique identifier, the raw comment text, and its sentiment label. Preprocessing is minimal. The raw text is kept unchanged, including emojis and informal spelling, and no additional processing such as stemming, stop-word removal, or custom tokenisation is applied. As a result, all methods are evaluated on the same unaltered comments provided by EESA. The only modification involves format conversion.

4   GPT-Based Sentiment Analysis

This section describes three GPT-based approaches for Egyptian Arabic–English code-switched sentiment analysis, evaluated in order of increasing adaptation: prompt-based inference requires no training; retrieval-augmented generation conditions predictions on relevant labelled examples; and fine-tuning updates model weights on the EESA training set. All approaches use GPT models and operate on the same comment text described in Sect. 3. While this work focuses only on GPT models, prior work on EESA [23] evaluates GPT-3.5, Gemini, and AraBERT-based BiLSTM-Attention and Transformer models, where fine-tuned GPT-3.5 achieved the best performance. Accordingly, GPT is used as the baseline, focusing on adaptation techniques rather than model comparisons.

4.1   Prompt-Based Inference

GPT-4o is evaluated under several prompting strategies, each providing structured guidance to steer the model toward more accurate sentiment predictions without modifying its weights. Six prompting configurations are evaluated. The

Annotation Guidelines prompt, originally introduced in [23], serves as the baseline. Four additional zero-shot variants are explored: Annotation Guidelines with Sentiment Hints, Rule-Based Inference, Semantic Translation, and Semantic Translation with Annotation Guidelines. In addition, two few-shot variants are evaluated: Few-Shot Inference and Few-Shot Inference with Explanations. The zero-shot extensions incorporate semantic cues, rule-based reasoning, or translation-based normalization, while the few-shot variants rely on in-context labelled examples. Each configuration is described below.

Annotation Guidelines: The prompt incorporates the same annotation guidelines provided to annotators during the construction of the EESA corpus. These guidelines are inserted before the input comment to guide the model in predicting its sentiment class (Positive, Negative, or Neutral).

Annotation Guidelines with Sentiment Hints: This prompt builds upon the Annotation Guidelines prompt by providing the same annotation guidelines given to annotators, enhanced with additional examples and explanations. This extended version also incorporates six sentiment hints for each comment. These hints add semantic context, supporting more accurate sentiment prediction. The full description of these sentiment hints is provided in Subsect. 4.3.

Rule-Based Inference: This prompt incorporates sentiment hints and general guidelines. These guidelines suggest that intensified words or repeated characters often indicate non-neutral sentiment, named entities may signal polarity, and negation words can flip sentiment. Neutral comments lack clear sentiment and may include suggestions, requests, questions, advertisements, or hyperlinks, while emoticons are strong polarity cues. It follows a step-by-step sequence with predefined rules, emphasizing rule-driven decisions over contextual cues.

Semantic Translation: The Arabic-English comment is translated into English while preserving meaning and context, then the sentiment of the translated text is predicted. This is motivated by the idea that speakers are often strongest in their first language, and zero-shot models tend to perform best in their dominant language. In practice, English remains the focus of most NLP research and applications, even though GPT models support many languages.

Semantic Translation with Annotation Guidelines: This prompt follows the same structure as Semantic Translation, but adds the annotation guidelines before inference. This ensures the model applies clear sentiment rules when predicting the polarity of the translated comment, and combining translation with predefined guidelines can improve sentiment accuracy.

Few-Shot Inference: A fixed set of labeled examples was placed before the input comment. Examples are selected once from the EESA training set using a TF-IDF centroid method: comments are ranked by similarity to each class centroid, and three examples are chosen per class to keep the set balanced. The same examples are used across all runs for a fair, controlled comparison.

Few-Shot Inference with Explanations: This variant uses the same fixed, balanced few-shot examples as Few-Shot Inference, but augments each example with a short natural-language explanation that justifies the label and rules out the other two. Explanations are generated by the GPT-4o model.

4.2 Retrieval-Augmented Generation

The second group of models extends the prompt-only setups in Subsect. 4.1 by incorporating retrieval from the labelled EESA training split. Unlike few-shot prompting, which uses a fixed set of labelled examples for all inputs, RAG retrieves input-specific training comments at inference time, allowing predictions to be conditioned on semantically or lexically similar examples. A standard retrieve-then-generate framework is adopted [12,19]. For each input, relevant labelled comments are selected from the EESA training set and inserted into the prompt before the input comment, each containing the raw text and its label. The model is instructed to output exactly one label.

Retrieval uses dense semantic similarity with two multilingual encoders: E5-Large [28] and OpenAI's text-embedding-3-large [27]. Both map Arabic and English into a shared embedding space, supporting code-switched comments with bilingual cues, emojis, and dialectal phrasing. Training embeddings are indexed in Facebook AI Similarity Search (FAISS) [16] using an exact Flat index. At inference time, top-k neighbours are retrieved under cosine similarity by L2-normalising vectors and using a Flat inner product index. The six evaluated RAG variants are defined as follows.

Standard RAG: Retrieves the top-8 nearest labelled training comments using dense similarity with no constraint on class distribution.

Balanced-Class RAG: Retrieves the 3 nearest examples from each sentiment class, yielding 9 examples per input.

Lexicon Hint RAG: Retrieves the same top-8 nearest examples as Standard RAG, and augments each retrieved example with sentiment-bearing words or phrases drawn from the EESA lexicon, where available.

Balanced-Class Lexicon Hint RAG: Combines Balanced-Class RAG with lexicon hints from Lexicon Hint RAG, selecting three examples per class with sentiment words appended where the lexicon matches.

Modified RAG with Explanations: This variant follows Standard RAG but omits L2 normalisation, allowing neighbour selection to depend on both vector direction and magnitude. Each retrieved example is paired with a contrastive explanation generated offline using GPT-4o. These explanations support the assigned label while explicitly contrasting it against the two alternatives, and are precomputed once for the training set and retrieved during inference.

Two-stage RAG: Each retrieved example is presented with its text, label, and an explanation, reusing the same GPT-4o contrastive explanations from Modified RAG with Explanations. The retrieved evidence is first used to produce a short reasoning summary (Stage 1), after which the final label is predicted using only the input comment and this summary (Stage 2).

Retrieved examples are inserted with their original sentiment labels. Across all variants, retrieval draws from the EESA training split using FAISS inner product on L2-normalised embeddings, except in the Modified RAG variant, where normalisation is omitted. The default retrieval size is $k = 8$; balanced class variants use $k = 9$ (3 per class). Explanations are used only in Modified RAG with Explanations and Two-stage RAG.

4.3   Fine-Tuning with Sentiment Hints

The GPT model can be fine-tuned on particular tasks, which further enhances its performance and applicability. The fine-tuned GPT model was trained on the entire training set, both without and with sentiment hints. The sentiment hints include positive words or phrases, negative words or phrases, named entities, words with repeated characters, intensified words, and negation words. The objective is to examine whether incorporating explicit sentiment hints improves fine-tuning performance. All sentiment hints are generated once per comment in the EESA corpus and retained during both training and inference.

The inclusion of six sentiment hints enriches each comment with explicit sentiment cues, improving learning during fine-tuning. During inference, these hints highlight sentiment-bearing expressions, ensuring such cues are not overlooked. By providing both positive and negative sentiment hints, the model is better guided in identifying sentiment-related words within a comment. Without these hints, the model may overlook such cues, leading to inaccurate sentiment classification. Both positive and negative hints are derived from the EESA lexicon.

Another sentiment hint category is named entities. When a user mentions a named entity, especially a person's name or an organization, the comment often expresses positive or negative sentiment, as it reflects a specific opinion toward that entity. Similarly, words with repeated characters and intensified words are likely to express strong sentiment. Words with repeated characters are used to emphasize emotions. For example, the word "woooooow" demonstrates how character repetition amplifies positive sentiment. Intensified words, such as "very", strengthen the sentiment of a comment. Both hints help the model detect emotional intensity, leading to more accurate sentiment classification.

The negation words hint is essential because negation words can alter a comment's polarity, turning a positive statement into a negative one or vice versa. Lists of named entities, intensified words, and negation words were extracted from the EESA corpus to generate the corresponding hints. In contrast, the repeated-character words hint does not require extraction from the EESA corpus, as such patterns can be identified directly from character repetition in the text. Each comment may contain different hints depending on its content. If a hint is not detected, the term "none" is assigned to indicate its absence.

5   Experimental Setup and Results

All experiments use GPT-4o for prompt-based inference and RAG, and both GPT-4o-mini and GPT-4o for fine-tuning. Models are evaluated on the EESA test set using micro F1-score, consistent with [23]. The original dataset splits are used without modification, and all methods operate on the same comment text. Temperature is set to 0 during inference for deterministic outputs. During fine-tuning GPT models, a batch size of 32 is used, and the base learning rate is not provided by OpenAI but can be adjusted via a learning rate multiplier (LRM). Fine-tuning is performed using different configurations of LRM and epochs (4, 10, and 20), with an average time of one hour for the 10-epoch setting. Results are reported across the three approaches in order of increasing adaptation: prompt-based inference, retrieval-augmented generation, and fine-tuning.

5.1 Prompt-Based Inference

GPT-4o is used for prompt-based inference and RAG because it provides a stronger baseline than GPT-4o-mini in this task. In the zero-shot setting with no additional prompting or retrieval, GPT-4o-mini achieves 81.5% F1-score, whereas GPT-4o reaches 85.6% [23], a +4.1 points gain on the EESA test set. Accordingly, prompt-based and RAG experiments are reported using GPT-4o, while fine-tuning is evaluated for both GPT-4o-mini and GPT-4o models.

Table 1. GPT-4o under various prompt-based techniques.

Prompting Setup	Test F1-score
GPT-4o [23]	85.6%
+Annotation Guidelines [23]	89.7%
+Annotation Guidelines with Sentiment Hints	**90.8%**
+Rule-Based Inference	88.3%
+Semantic Translation	86.9%
+Semantic Translation with Annotation Guidelines	90.5%
+Few-shot Inference	87.4%
+Few-shot Inference with explanations	87.5%

Various prompting techniques were applied to the zero-shot GPT-4o model, as shown in Table 1. The GPT-4o and GPT-4o+Annotation Guidelines results are reported from [23] and are included for comparison, while the remaining results are obtained in our experiments. The performance of the GPT-4o improved when combined with prompting techniques. The incorporation of different prompting enhanced the F1-score by margins ranging from 1.3 to 5.2 points.

The Semantic Translation prompt resulted in the lowest improvement, with an F1-score increase of 1.3 points. In contrast, the Semantic Translation with Annotation Guidelines prompt achieved a higher performance, improving by 3.6 points compared to the Semantic Translation prompt alone. In addition, the Annotation Guidelines with Sentiment Hints outperformed the Annotation Guidelines prompt by 1.1 points, achieving the highest F1-score of 90.8%. Semantic Translation with Annotation Guidelines achieved the second-highest F1-score, trailing by 0.3 points. This approach is more adaptable to scenarios where explicit sentiment hints are unavailable or impractical to include.

Few-shot prompting offers little improvement over the GPT-4o model alone by only 1.8 points, and adding explanations increases performance by just 0.1 points. This suggests that, for this corpus, carefully well-crafted instructions are more effective than providing a fixed set of labeled examples.

5.2   Retrieval-Augmented Generation

For a fair comparison, RAG results are grouped into two settings: variants without explanations and variants with explanations. Table 2 compares Lexicon Hint RAG, Balanced-class RAG, Balanced-Class Lexicon Hint RAG, and Standard RAG. These methods retrieve labelled examples but do not add explanations describing why each retrieved example has its original label. In contrast, Table 3 reports explanation-based RAG variants, where each retrieved example is accompanied by a GPT-4o contrastive explanation.

Table 2. Non-explanation RAG variants.

Encoder	RAG Method	Test F1-score
E5-Large	Balanced-class RAG	89.1%
E5-Large	Lexicon Hint RAG	89.5%
E5-Large	Balanced-Class Lexicon Hint RAG	91.0%
E5-Large	Standard RAG	92.1%
Text-embedding-3-large	**Standard RAG**	**92.5%**

The E5-Large encoder is first used across four RAG variants, as shown in Table 2. Balanced-class RAG achieves the lowest F1-score of 89.1%. Lexicon Hint RAG improves slightly by 0.4 points to 89.5%. Balanced-Class Lexicon Hint RAG combines both approaches, achieving a higher F1-score of 91.0%. Standard RAG attains the best F1-score of 92.1% among the E5-Large variants.

Text-embedding-3-large is used only with Standard RAG, as this RAG variant achieved the highest performance with E5-Large. It slightly outperforms E5-Large by 0.4 points (92.5% vs. 92.1%), but the difference is marginal, indicating comparable performance. This suggests that performance is driven more by the retrieval strategy than by the choice of embedding model.

Since the best performance in Table 2 is obtained using text-embedding-3-large, this encoder is adopted for all models in Table 3. Table 3 compares explanation-based RAG variants. Explanations are first added to Standard RAG (the best no-explanation variant) to test whether explanation-augmented Standard RAG can surpass other explanation-based RAG variants, while also providing a consistent reference point against Standard RAG without explanations.

Table 3. Explanation-based RAG variants.

Encoder	RAG Method	Test F1-score
text-embedding-3-large	Standard RAG with Explanations	93.0%
Text-embedding-3-large	Two-stage RAG with Explanations	93.2%
Text-embedding-3-large	**Modified RAG with Explanations**	**93.6%**

In Table 3, adding explanations to Standard RAG increases performance by 0.5 points compared to Standard RAG alone (93.0% vs. 92.5%). However, Standard RAG with Explanations is the lowest-performing among the explanation-based variants. Two-stage RAG with Explanations achieves a similar result, improving slightly to 93.2% (+0.2 points). The best performance is obtained by Modified RAG with Explanations (93.6%), which may benefit from omitting L2 normalisation. In this setting, retaining vector magnitude can help prioritize comments with stronger sentiment signals or richer lexical content, yielding more informative retrieved examples. This is useful for short, code-switched comments where sentiment cues may be scarce. Notably, the explanation-based RAG variants in Table 3 outperform the best prompt-only configuration (GPT-4o with Annotation Guidelines and Sentiment Hints, 90.8% F1-score).

5.3   Fine-Tuning with Sentiment Hints

GPT-4o-mini and GPT-4o are fine-tuned to compare performance, as evaluating two models is more reliable than relying on one. Fine-tuning examines the effect of epochs and LRM. Table 4 reports the hyperparameter sweep for GPT-4o-mini, and Table 5 reports the sweep for GPT-4o. The best settings from these sweeps are used for sentiment-hints fine-tuning in Table 6. Table 7 reports per-class precision, recall, and F1-score for the best model.

The fine-tuned GPT-4o-mini in Table 4 was initially tested using LRM of 50 with different numbers of epochs: 4, 10, and 20. The model trained with 10 epochs achieved the highest performance. Consequently, the number of epochs was fixed at 10 for subsequent experiments. When LRM increased from 50 to 100, the F1-score dropped significantly from 76.5% to 52.6%. Conversely, reducing LRM from 50 to 5 resulted in the highest F1-score of 93.8%. However, further reducing LRM below 5 led to a decline in F1-score, dropping to 92.8%.

The fine-tuning of the GPT-4o model in Table 5 began with an initial LRM of 50, as this value was used as a starting point for the GPT-4o-mini. In experiments with the GPT-4o-mini, using LRM of 50 and varying the number of epochs, the best F1-score of 76.5% was achieved with 10 epochs. Building on this finding,

Table 4. The Fine-tuned GPT-4o-mini with various training parameters.

Epoch	LRM	Test F1-score
4	50	65.2%
10	50	76.5%
20	50	71.6%
10	100	52.6%
10	25	89.0%
10	10	91.8%
10	**5**	**93.8%**
10	2	93.5%
10	1	92.8%

Table 5. The Fine-tuned GPT-4o with various training parameters.

Epoch	LRM	Test F1-score
10	50	94.4%
10	25	93.5%
4	25	94.4%
4	**12**	**94.7%**
4	6	93.9%

the GPT-4o was fine-tuned with the same LRM of 50 and 10 epochs, which significantly improved the F1-score to 94.4%. The performance declined by 0.9 points when LRM was reduced to 25. To optimize training time and costs, the number of epochs was reduced to evaluate whether comparable or improved performance could be achieved with fewer epochs. Notably, the fine-tuned model with 4 epochs and LRM of 12 achieved the highest F1-score of 94.7%.

Table 6. The Fine-tuned GPT models with sentiment hints.

GPT Model	Epoch	LRM	Test F1-score
GPT-4o-mini	**10**	**5**	**95.5%**
GPT-4o-mini	10	2	95.1%
GPT-4o	4	12	95.4%
GPT-4o	4	6	94.9%

In Table 6, fine-tuning with sentiment hints improves the F1-scores of GPT-4o-mini and GPT-4o, highlighting their effectiveness. However, this approach is not tied to the corpus and can be generalized by constructing similar lexicons for new domains or using external sentiment resources, while some hints remain domain-independent. Reducing the LRM during training led to a decline in performance across all models, emphasizing the importance of carefully balancing hyperparameters during fine-tuning. The fine-tuned GPT-4o-mini with sentiment hints achieves the highest F1-score of 95.5%, while GPT-4o shows similar performance with a marginal decline of 0.1 points. Table 7 shows the precision, recall, and F1-score for each sentiment class for the fine-tuned GPT-4o-mini model with sentiment hints (95.5%).

Table 7. Class-wise performance of GPT-4o-mini with sentiment hints.

Class	Precision	Recall	F1-score
Negative	91%	99%	95%
Neutral	96%	92%	94%
Positive	**98%**	**96%**	**97%**

In Table 7, the GPT-4o-mini demonstrates outstanding performance, with F1-scores exceeding 93% across all classes. The positive class achieved the highest F1-score of 97%, highlighting the model's strong ability to identify positive sentiments with minimal false positives and false negatives. For the negative class, the model achieved a recall of 99%, indicating its effectiveness in detecting nearly all negative instances. However, precision drops to 91%, suggesting that some neutral or positive comments were mistakenly classified as negative. Despite this, the F1-score remains high at 95%. The neutral class shows the most balanced trade-off, with a precision of 96% and a recall of 92%, leading to an F1-score of 94%. The decrease in recall suggests that identifying neutral sentiments is more challenging due to overlap with positive and negative tones. Overall, the model exhibits a remarkable performance across all sentiment categories.

Most misclassifications occur in neutral comments, followed by positive ones. Neutral comments are predicted as positive due to overlapping positive phrases commonly used in advertisements, advice, and requests, which were annotated as neutral. Some neutral comments were misclassified as negative when the model failed to capture the broader context, particularly in questions that contain negative words but do not express explicit sentiment. For positive comments, errors arise when expressions that are lexically negative are used with a positive meaning, leading to incorrect negative predictions. In other cases, positive comments are predicted as neutral when sentiment cues are not recognized by the model.

6   Conclusion and Future Work

GPT models were adopted as the main backbone for Egyptian Arabic–English sentiment analysis because they support Arabic and English and have shown strong performance across many NLP tasks. To further improve GPT performance, six prompt-based inference techniques and six RAG techniques were applied, and fine-tuning was explored. All models were evaluated on the EESA test set, which contains Egyptian Arabic–English code-switched comments. Among the prompt-based techniques, GPT-4o with the Annotation Guidelines and Sentiment Hints prompt achieved an F1-score of 90.8%. RAG proved more effective than prompt-only inference, with GPT-4o combined with modified RAG and explanations reaching 93.6% F1-score. The best overall performance was obtained by fine-tuning GPT-4o-mini with sentiment hints, achieving 95.5% and surpassing the previous state of the art on EESA by 2.8 points. While fine-tuning delivered the strongest results, it comes with higher training costs, whereas RAG offers a strong alternative without additional training.

A key limitation is the scarcity of Arabic–English code-switched sentiment analysis datasets, which restricts evaluation mostly to EESA and makes it difficult to assess generalization across domains and platforms. However, EESA represents a challenging and realistic benchmark, capturing informal Egyptian Arabic–English social media text with emojis, dialectal variation, and mixed-language cues, making it suitable for real-world sentiment analysis evaluation.

Future work will explore more advanced GPT models and other large language models to further improve performance and robustness. It will also focus on enhancing the RAG pipeline, since it is a promising direction that improves performance without the cost of fine-tuning. In particular, improving retrieval quality and evidence selection may narrow the gap to fine-tuned performance and potentially achieve comparable results.

References

1. Adouane, W., Touileb, S., Bernardy, J.P.: Identifying sentiments in Algerian code-switched user-generated comments. In: Proceedings of the Twelfth Language Resources and Evaluation Conference, pp. 2698–2705 (2020)
2. Al-Thubaity, A., et al.: Evaluating ChatGPT and Bard AI on Arabic sentiment analysis. In: ArabicNLP 2023, pp. 335–349 (2023)
3. Aladeemy, A.A., et al.: Advancements and challenges in Arabic sentiment analysis: a decade of methodologies, applications, and resource development. Heliyon **10**(21) (2024)
4. Alawaji, R., Aloraini, A.: Sentiment analysis of digital banking reviews using machine learning and large language models. Electronics **14**(11), 2125 (2025)
5. Alhagree, S., Al-Gaphari, G.: Utilizing machine learning based on LLM for Arabic sentiment analysis in assessing user satisfaction with mobile banking apps: A case study of Yemeni banks. Sana'a Univ. J. Appl. Sci. Technol. **3**(1), 645–662 (2025)
6. Alyafeai, Z., Alshaibani, M.S., AlKhamissi, B., Luqman, H., Alareqi, E., Fadel, A.: Taqyim: evaluating Arabic NLP tasks using ChatGPT models. arXiv preprint arXiv:2306.16322 (2023)
7. Barman, U., Das, A., Wagner, J., Foster, J.: Code mixing: s challenge for language identification in the language of social media. In: Proceedings of the First Workshop on Computational Approaches to Code Switching, pp. 13–23 (2014)

8. Basabain, S., Cambria, E., Alomar, K., Hussain, A.: Enhancing Arabic-text feature extraction utilizing label-semantic augmentation in few/zero-shot learning. Expert. Syst. **40**(8), e13329 (2023)
9. Bolock, A.e., Abouras, M., Sabty, C., Abdennadher, S., Herbert, C.: Care: a framework for collecting and annotating emotions of code-switched words. In: International Conference on Practical Applications of Agents and Multi-Agent Systems, pp. 104–116. Springer (2024)
10. Derbala Yacoub, A., Elsayed Aboutabl, A., O Slim, S.: Multilingual sarcasm detection for enhancing sentiment analysis using deep learning algorithms. J. Commun. Softw. Syst. **20**(4), 278–289 (2024)
11. Du, K., Zhao, Y., Mao, R., Xing, F., Cambria, E.: A retrieval-augmented multiagent system for financial sentiment analysis. IEEE Intell. Syst. (2025)
12. Gao, Y., et al.: Retrieval-augmented generation for large language models: a survey. arXiv preprint arXiv:2312.10997 (2023). **2**(1), 32
13. Hamed, I., Elmahdy, M., Abdennadher, S.: Collection and analysis of code-switch Egyptian Arabic-English speech corpus. In: Proceedings of the Eleventh International Conference on Language Resources and Evaluation (LREC 2018) (2018)
14. Hamed, I., Sabty, C., Abdennadher, S., Vu, N.T., Solorio, T., Habash, N.: A survey of code-switched Arabic NLP: progress, challenges, and future directions. In: Proceedings of the 31st International Conference on Computational Linguistics, pp. 4561–4585 (2025)
15. Jefry, W., Aldoghman, F., Hussain, F.: BERT-LA: leveraging BERT and AraBERT with bi-LSTM for cross-lingual sentiment analysis of English and Arabic Texts. In: 2024 17th International Conference on Security of Information and Networks (2024)
16. Johnson, J., Douze, M., Jégou, H.: Billion-scale similarity search with GPUs. IEEE Trans. Big Data **7**(3), 535–547 (2019)
17. Kermani, A., Perez-Rosas, V., Metsis, V.: A systematic evaluation of LLM strategies for mental health text analysis: Fine-tuning vs. prompt engineering vs. RAG. In: Proceedings of the 10th Workshop on Computational Linguistics and Clinical Psychology (CLPsych 2025), pp. 172–180 (2025)
18. Khaled, S., Mohamed, E.H., Medhat, W.: Evaluating large language models for Arabic sentiment analysis: a comparative study using retrieval-augmented generation. Procedia Comput. Sci. **244**, 363–370 (2024)
19. Lewis, P., et al.: Retrieval-augmented generation for knowledge-intensive NLP tasks. Adv. Neural. Inf. Process. Syst. **33**, 9459–9474 (2020)
20. Liu, B.: Sentiment analysis and opinion mining. Synth. Lect. Hum. Lang. Technol. **5**(1), 1–167 (2012)
21. Sabty, C., Islam, M., Abdennadher, S.: Contextual embeddings for Arabic-English code-switched data. In: Proceedings of the Fifth Arabic Natural Language Processing Workshop, pp. 215–225 (2020)
22. Sharma, G., Chinmay, R., Sharma, R.: Late fusion of transformers for sentiment analysis of code-switched data. In: Findings of the Association for Computational Linguistics: EMNLP 2023, pp. 6485–6490 (2023)
23. Sherif, A., Sabty, C.: Sentiment analysis for Egyptian Arabic-English code-switched data using traditional neural models and advanced language models. In: International Conference on Speech and Computer, pp. 54–69. Springer (2024)
24. Shi, Z., Agrawal, R.: A comprehensive survey of contemporary Arabic sentiment analysis: methods, challenges, and future directions. In: Findings of the Association for Computational Linguistics: NAACL 2025, pp. 3760–3772 (2025)
25. Ullah, F.: Prompt-based fine-tuning with multilingual transformers for language-independent sentiment analysis. Sci. Rep. **15**(1), 20834 (2025)

26. Veeramani, H., Thapa, S., Naseem, U.: Mlinitiative@ wildre7: hybrid approaches with large language models for enhanced sentiment analysis in code-switched and code-mixed texts. In: Proceedings of the 7th Workshop on Indian Language Data: Resources and Evaluation, pp. 66–72 (2024)
27. Wang, L., Yang, N., Huang, X., Yang, L., Majumder, R., Wei, F.: Improving text embeddings with large language models. In: Proceedings of the 62nd Annual Meeting of the Association for Computational Linguistics, pp. 11897–11916 (2024)
28. Wang, L., Yang, N., Huang, X., Yang, L., Majumder, R., Wei, F.: Multilingual E5 text embeddings: a technical report. arXiv preprint arXiv:2402.05672 (2024)
29. Zhang, B., Yang, H., Zhou, T., Ali Babar, M., Liu, X.Y.: Enhancing financial sentiment analysis via retrieval augmented large language models. In: Proceedings of the fourth ACM International Conference on AI in Finance, pp. 349–356 (2023)
30. Zouidine, M., Khalil, M.: Selective reading for Arabic sentiment analysis. IEEE Access (2025)

Evaluating Noisy Optimization in Finetuning LMs for Neural Ranking

Daniel Vollmers$^{(\boxtimes)}$, Arnab Sharma , and Axel-Cyrille Ngonga Ngomo

Data Science Group, Heinz Nixdorf Institute, Paderborn University, Paderborn, Germany
`{daniel.vollmers,arnab.sharma,axel.ngonga}@uni-paderborn.de`
`https://dice-research.org/`

Abstract. Ranking plays a crucial role in the information retrieval domain by assigning relevance scores to candidate entities based on their similarity to a given mention and context. While LM-based encoder models like BERT have notably improved the quality of entity ranking, optimization challenges, such as convergence issues with adaptive optimizers like Adam, remain largely underexplored. Existing works have shown that injecting noise into an optimizer, such as gradient descent, can serve as a regularizer, leading to improved generalization results. Considering this idea, in this work, we investigate the use of noise injection in the Adam optimization step to improve the optimization process for entity ranking models. By incorporating Gaussian noise into the model parameters, we demonstrate that noise can act as an effective regularizer, helping the model escape saddle points and achieve faster convergence in ranking tasks. More specifically, in this work, we study three ways of injecting noise– (i) uncorrelated, (ii) anticorrelated to previous noise, and (iii) anticorrelated to gradients of the loss function, considering cross entropy as well as pairwise ranking loss. Through extensive evaluation across multiple entity ranking architectures and benchmark datasets, we show that noise-enhanced Adam optimizer improves both convergence speed and model accuracy, offering a promising avenue for enhancing ranking performance. Finally, we evaluate and compare different noise injection approaches, discussing their effectiveness across various models and datasets.

Keywords: Neural Ranking · Retrieval · Optimization

1 Introduction

Ranking models are an essential component in many NLP application such as information retrieval, entity linking or question answering systems [10,26]. Essentially, the task of a neural ranking model is to assign relevance scores to candidate documents based on their fit to a given query [29]. It involves comparing *context-aware* vector representations of queries with candidate documents, ranking them by similarity. Modern techniques leverage neural encoders like RNNs and transformer-based models (e.g., BERT [6]) to capture complex semantic relationships, offering rich representations. While ranking is a critical step in entity linking tasks, existing research has primarily focused on improving neural architectures [32], leveraging zero-shot learning [27],

E. Cabrio and E. Monteiro (Eds.): NLDB 2026, LNCS 16696, pp. 237–251, 2027.
https://doi.org/10.1007/978-3-032-29532-3_17

and incorporating external features like entity types and priors [8,9,34]. However, less attention is paid to the optimization techniques used during training to finetune the models. More specifically, adaptive optimizers like Adam often face challenges such as local minima and saddle points, particularly in high-dimensional, sparse, and imbalanced datasets, leading to suboptimal performance at inference time [15]. In this work, we study the use of noise injection into the model's parameters, by considering a line of works that aim to increase the generalization performance of the underlying model by doing so [12,13,18,20,21,23,35]. Essentially, our goal is to address saddle point issues and achieve faster convergence towards better-generalized models by applying the noise injection to the parameters in fine-tuning the ranking models.

The role of noise in the optimization step, precisely in Stochastic Gradient Descent (SGD) [25] has been a subject of extensive study, particularly in the context of its impact on generalization [12,13,23,35]. It is widely recognized that the intrinsic stochastic noise in SGD, which arises due to minibatch sampling, tends to guide the optimization process towards flatter minima, which is generally associated with better generalization performance. A recent work by Orvieto et al. [21] proved that noise injection during optimization can lead to better performance in vision models. Although such studies have been explored extensively in the ML domain [18,20], to the best of our knowledge, in information retrieval tasks, and in particular for ranking models, it has not yet been done.

In this work, we study the effect of noise injection into the optimization step to improve the performance of the ranking models while finetuning them for the ranking tasks. More specifically, we add the noise to the parameters of the underlying ranking model after the backpropagation step and during the optimization step. To this end, we, first of all, introduce the formal notion of noise injection into the parameters of the model by considering three different noise injection approaches, (i) uncorrelated noise, (ii) anticorrelated noise based on previously added noise, and (iii) anticorrelated noise using the gradient of the loss function. We present an algorithm that effectively adds noise to the parameters of the models, considering either of the aforementioned approaches, into the optimization step based on the Adam optimizer. To this end, we also show formally that adding Gaussian noise to the parameters of the model in the optimization step, while considering pairwise loss, can work as an explicit regularization.

Apart from theoretical studies and formalizations, we conduct extensive evaluation by applying our noise injection approaches to the Adam optimizer [14] and considering two different types of ranking models, namely bi-encoder [30,31] and cross-encoder [1] models, which are frequently used in entity ranking tasks. Our evaluations suggest that introducing noise in the Adam optimizer can make the training converge much faster and avoid overfitting. Most importantly, we find that noise injection leads to an improvement of performance. Our contribution in this work can be summarized as follows:

- We formalize the notion of three different noise injection approaches in Adam optimizer used in ranking models.
- We introduce the noise injection approaches, considering pairwise ranking loss, specifically adapted to ranking tasks.

- We empirically evaluate several noise injection approaches in the Adam optimizer, considering two encoder models trained on four different ranking datasets.
- We conduct a comparative analysis showing the effectiveness of different noise injection approaches.
- Our code is publicly available[1].

2 Related Work

Ranking Models. Recent advancements in NLP have significantly contributed to the ranking tasks. Reimers et al. [24] introduced Sentence-BERT, a model that generates semantically meaningful sentence embeddings using a Siamese network structure, enabling efficient semantic similarity comparison and clustering. The effectiveness of fine-tuning BERT for passage re-ranking, achieving state-of-the-art results on the MS MARCO passage retrieval task has been demonstrated by Nogueira et al. [19]. Wang et al. [30] proposed E5, a family of text embeddings trained through contrastive learning on a large-scale text pair dataset, achieving strong performance in tasks requiring single-vector text representations [30]. More recently, Déjean et al. [5] explored the comparative strengths of cross-encoder rerankers and large language models (LLMs), shedding light on trade-offs between efficiency and ranking effectiveness in different retrieval settings [5]. Similarly, Wu et al. [31] proposed a dense retrieval-based entity-linking approach that improves ranking precision by leveraging transformer-based encoders.

Noise-Driven Optimization. Adding noise to the gradient descent approach has been widely explored in the literature for its ability to enhance optimization in non-convex settings by introducing noise into the gradient descent process [12,28,35]. For instance, Smith et al. [28] demonstrated that the noise inherent in SGD helps in converging to minima with lower curvature, which would lead to better generalization. A similar outcome has been further observed by Zhang et al. [33], wherein it was shown that SGD's tendency to find flatter minima is linked to its stochastic nature. Moreover, the work of Bradley et al. [4] has established a connection between the level of noise in SGD (influenced by factors like batch size and learning rate) and its ability to find such flat minima, thereby improving the generalization ability of models. Jin et al. [12] demonstrated that escaping saddle points can be achieved by discretizing Langevin dynamics, where noise contributes to diffusion. Zhou et al. [35] further showed that parameter perturbations during optimization help escape spurious local minima in non-convex settings. Adding noise before gradient computation, initially used for smoothing non-smooth convex objectives, has also shown promise in non-convex scenarios by biasing optimization toward flatter minima, which enhances generalization [18,20]. Another approach to introducing noise in the training process involves adding noise to the labels of the training data. Recent studies, such as those by Blanc et al. [3] and HaoChen et al. [11], have demonstrated that label noise can implicitly regularize the learning process by pushing the model to find flatter minima, similar to the effects observed with SGD noise.

---

[1] https://github.com/dice-group/RobustRanking.

Although a vast amount of work has been done exploring the usage of introducing noise to the gradient descent approach, either in parameters or in labels, most of the work has focused on vision-related tasks. The work closest to ours is by Liu et al. [17] where they introduced PAC-tuning which fine-tunes pretrained models by incorporating PAC-Bayes-driven noise injection into the parameters. In our work, however, we focus on a specific NLP task, namely neural ranking. Herein, we study the effect of noise injection to the Adam optimizer considering both the cross-entropy and pairwise ranking loss. To the best of our knowledge, such study is not yet performed.

3   Neural Ranking Architectures

Bi-encoder rankers use two independent language models to encode the query (the mention context) and the candidates (the entity description) independently into dense vector representations. Next, the dot product of the query and candidate embeddings is computed to score the document representations against the query, which outputs the final probability $\hat{y} \in [0, 1]$, indicating the likelihood of the candidate being the correct entity. Note that, in our work, we consider two different variants of bi-encoder models. The first variant uses a single encoder model to encode both the query and the documents. The weights therein are initialized by the E5 model [30]. We use the term **E5** for this variant. The second one applies two encoder models, one for queries and one for documents, similar to the work of Wu et al. [31]. For this, we consider the original BERT implementation [6] and initialized the weights with its parameters. Within this work, we apply the term **dual bi-encoder** for this variant.

Cross-encoder jointly processes the query and candidate entity by concatenating their texts and feeding them into a transformer-based language model [1]. Herein, the textual representation of the query and the candidate are concatenated. Next this concatenated input is passed through a shared *Language Model+Pooling* layer, which encodes the input sequence and computes a pooled representation that captures the contextual interactions between the tokens of both the query and the candidate entity. Afterwards, the pooled output is forwarded to the scoring function, which outputs a scalar prediction $\hat{y} \in [0, 1]$.

4   Methodology

In our work, we insert noise into the model parameters immediately after the back-propagation and into the optimization step during training. Specifically, given a training sample $x^{(i)}$, the model first predicts an output $\hat{y}^{(i)}$, and let us assume the original output is $y^{(i)}$. After computing the loss $L(\hat{y}^{(i)}, y^{(i)}) = \hat{y}^{(i)} - y^{(i)}$, the gradient of the loss is computed, i.e., the back-propagation step is applied. Thereafter, we insert the noise into the parameters. This noise herein is added into the Adam optimizer before updating the parameters using the moment estimates, allowing us to perturb the parameter space. After inserting the noise, the Adam optimizer is applied to update the model parameters. However, this update is now performed considering the noise-injected parameters, thereby allowing the optimizer to explore parameter regions it might not have encountered otherwise. Next, we formalize different noise injection strategies.

Algorithm 1: Training loop with noise injection for Document Ranking

---

Input: Initial parameters θ_l, θ_s; Training data X, Y; Learning rates ξ_l, ξ_s; Number of
epochs `num_epochs`
Output: Updated parameters θ_l and θ_s after training
Initialize: Parameters θ_l and θ_s
for *each epoch* **do**
    for *each training sample* $(x^{(i)}, y^{(i)}) \in (X, Y)$ **do**
        Get Prediction for $x^{(i)}$: $\hat{y}^{(i)} = \Psi(x^{(i)}; \theta)$;
        Compute loss: $L(\hat{y}^{(i)}, y^{(i)}) = \hat{y}^{(i)} - y^{(i)}$;
        Calculate the gradient of the loss (Back-propagation):;
        $\nabla\theta(L) = \frac{\partial L(\hat{y}^{(i)}, y^{(i)})}{\partial\theta}$;
        Sample Gaussian noise: $\epsilon \sim \mathcal{G}(0, \mathbf{I})$;
        Add noise to parameters:;
        $\theta \leftarrow \theta - \xi \cdot (\nabla\theta(L) + \delta)$;
        Update parameters using Adam

return θ_l, θ_s *(final learned parameters)*

In our work, we inject noise by perturbing the parameters of the encoder components—namely, the query and candidate encoders in the dual bi-encoder, the shared language model in E5. For cross-encoder model, we consider the parameters of both the language model and the scoring function. To this end, we consider the parameters of the encoder as θ^2. Herein, we consider three different types of noise injection approaches: (i) uncorrelated noise, (ii) anticorrelated noise using the previous term, and (iii) anticorrelated noise using gradient. Below we discuss them.

Uncorrelated Noise Injection. In this case, standard Gaussian distribution is used to generate noise with mean 0 and standard deviation 1 (which in this case is an identity matrix $\mathbf{I}$), therefore, the distribution is defined as $\mathcal{G}(0, \mathbf{I})$. After generating the noise, it is added to the parameters. Consider the noise generated through Gaussian distribution as ϵ. Formally, $\theta' = \theta + \xi * \epsilon$, where ξ is the learning rate of the encoder. Therefore, the learning rate scales the noise in line with the step sizes in the optimization.

Anticorrelated to Previous Noise. Unlike standard Gaussian noise, which is independent across iterations, anticorrelated noise integrates historical noise information, allowing for more advanced perturbations during training. Formally, $\theta'_l = \theta + \xi \cdot (-\alpha \cdot \epsilon^{t-1} + \epsilon^t)$, where $\alpha = \frac{\alpha_0}{1+\|\nabla_\theta(L)\|}$ dynamically adjusts based on the gradient norm, $\epsilon^t \sim \mathcal{G}(0, \mathbf{I})$ is the independent Gaussian noise term at iteration t, and ϵ^{t-1} is the noise from the previous iteration. The hyperparameter α controls the influence of past noise. By modulating the impact of noise based on previous iterations, this method can help the optimizer avoid sharp minima and promoting better generalization.

Anticorrelated to Gradient. In this method, the noise is directly anticorrelated to the gradient of the loss function, acting as an adaptive regularizer. Formally, $\theta' =$

---

[2] Note that, for simplicity, we write language model while describing noise injection mechanism for the rest of the paper.

$\theta + \xi \cdot (-\beta \cdot \nabla_\theta(L) + \epsilon)$, where $\beta = \frac{\beta_0}{1+\|\nabla_\theta(L)\|}$ dynamically adjusts the anticorrelation strength based on the gradient norm, and β_0 is a hyperparameter controlling the overall scale of anticorrelated noise. The dynamic nature of β introduces an adaptive mechanism that reduces noise when the gradient is large and increases noise when the gradient is small. Specifically, when $\|\nabla_\theta(L)\|$ is large (i.e., during steep descent), β becomes small, minimizing the impact of anticorrelated noise. When $\|\nabla_\theta(L)\|$ is small (i.e., near convergence or in flat regions), β increases, emphasizes anticorrelated noise, promoting exploration and helping the model escape shallow minima that may hinder optimization.

Noise Injection in Training Loop. Algorithm 1 outlines our overall noise injection approach to the Adam optimizer. In each epoch, for a given training example $(x^{(i)}, y^{(i)})$, the **loss is computed** from the prediction $\hat{y}^{(i)}$. After that, the **back-propagation** is applied by computing the gradients of the loss. Gaussian noise ϵ is sampled, and based on the chosen approach—uncorrelated or anticorrelated—**noise is added to the gradient** for the encoder as δ. Thereafter, **parameter θ is updated** using the Adam optimizer, incorporating gradients and noise scaled by the adaptively adjusted learning rate ξ. Herein δ depends on the approach, for instance, for uncorrelated noise, $\delta = \epsilon$, while for anticorrelated gradient noise, $\delta = -\beta_t \cdot \nabla_\theta(L) + \epsilon$. After the noise addition is done, the Adam optimizer is applied using the first, and second moment estimates. Note that our noise injection approach does not introduce any further complexity in the optimization step. Specifically, this can be performed during the optimization step directly without introducing an extra step in the training process.

5   Evaluation

Both bi-encoder models, i.e., E5 and dual bi-encoder, rely on BERT [6]. E5 comprises one encoder model for the query and the documents, and is already pretrained on the ranking task. For the second model, which we term as dual bi-encoder, we take an architecture that applies two encoder models, where one is used to encode queries and one for the documents. This model has BERT as a foundational model for both the query and document encoders. For the cross-encoder, we consider BERT as well. All foundational BERT models have the same size, i.e., the number of parameters remains the same. For this, we used the version from Hugging Face[3] as BERT implementation and use in-batch negative sampling [31] during training. We trained these models on a server with 128 GB of RAM and an NVIDIA RTX H100 GPU with 80 GB of RAM. Instead of switching to hard negatives, we indexed all entities into a Faiss index [7] at each half-epoch to extract hard negatives. Furthermore, during training, considering the AIDA, Mintaka, and LC-QuAD datasets, we generated each batch including the documents with high-scoring entities from the first document. Herein, we maintained the in-batch strategy throughout training, with random negatives used in the first half-epoch. We trained the model for ten epochs using the default learning rate and parameters for the

---

[3] https://huggingface.co/docs/transformers/model_doc/bert, https://huggingface.co/intfloat/e5-base-v2.

dual bi-encoder and E5 models. For the evaluation of the biencoder models, the embeddings generated by the models were indexed as well by applying the Faiss-framework.

For the MS MARCO dataset we implemented a similar strategy. However, instead of applying all documents, for computing the hard negatives, we randomly selected 10,000 negative documents from the whole corpus each time, when we re-indexed the Faiss-index. For each query in the training batch, we selected up to four negatives from the index plus one positive document. We used two queries per batch and kept the in-batch training strategy for the other datasets as well. Similar to bi-encoder models, we trained the cross-encoder model for 10 epochs with 1000 optimization steps per epoch. Since the main objective of this work is to evaluate the influence of noise in the optimization, we had to finetune and evaluate a huge set of models. For this reason, we decided to evaluate the model on a split of 125,000 randomly selected documents from the whole MS MARCO document corpus.

For evaluating and training cross-encoder models, we used a finetuned model of E5 without noisy optimization to compute negatives. For all the samples, we generated a set of 100 negatives for each sample in both the training and test sets. At training time, we chose 14 negatives for each sample plus one positive to generate a candidate set of 15 for each sample. For evaluation, we used all 100 negatives for each of the samples.

5.1 Results and Discussion

In this work, we aim to investigate whether the noise injection to the Adam optimizer can improve the performance of different types of ranking models in diverse ranking tasks. To thoroughly evaluate the effectiveness of our approach, we formulate the following research questions and provide a detailed discussion for each of them below.

– **RQ1.** Does noise injection help in improving the performance of neural ranking models?
– **RQ2.** Which noise injection strategy among the three performs the best?
– **RQ3.** Can noise injection lead to faster convergence and reduce overfitting?

RQ1. In Table 1 we see the results of noise injection strategies on two different bi-encoder models, E5 and dual bi-encoder and the cross-encoder model across 4 datasets We also compute the statistical significance of the results. This was computed by comparing per-query MRR and Recall scores of each noise-injection variant against the No Noise baseline using a paired two-tailed t-test [16].

Herein, we see that E5 demonstrates consistent performance improvements with noise injection. For instance, considering the cross entropy loss, the anticorrelated noise using gradient (Anti-Grad) yields the best MRR and recall in MS MARCO, Mintaka, and AIDA, and anticorrelated noise using previous noise term (Anti-Prev) achieves the best result on LC-QuAD dataset. We see a similar trend considering the pairwise ranking loss as well, wherein Anti-Prev achieves more statistically significant improvement. Therefore, our results indicate the overall effectiveness of noise injection into the Adam optimizer across diverse datasets for the E5 model. The dual bi-encoder model, which contains more parameters than E5, shows greater sensitivity to noise injection. For instance, we observe that Gaussian noise leads to the best MRR and

Table 1. MRR and recall results evaluated on four ranking datasets using the E5, Dual bi-encoder, and cross-encoder models. Bolded values indicate the best performance for each dataset. *Significance* columns report statistical significance against the *No Noise* baseline (*: $p < 0.05$, **: $p < 0.01$, n.s.: not significant). LF is loss function; cross entropy (CE) and pairwise loss (PR).

LF	Approach	MRR				Significance	Recall				Significance
		MS MARCO	LC-QuAD	Mintaka	AIDA		MS MARCO	LC-QuAD	Mintaka	AIDA	
E5 Model											
CE	No Noise	0.6423	0.8767	0.2672	0.3049	–	0.8475	0.8719	0.3658	0.1668	–
	Gaussian	0.6327	0.8761	0.2675	0.2971	n.s.	0.8406	0.8725	0.3688	0.1622	n.s.
	Anti-Grad	**0.6708**	0.8972	**0.2704**	**0.3072**	*	**0.8658**	0.8835	**0.3808**	**0.1674**	*
	Anti-Prev	0.6534	**0.8972**	0.2651	0.3034	n.s.	0.8565	**0.8836**	0.3628	0.1638	n.s.
PR	No Noise	0.7456	0.8841	0.2948	0.3009	–	0.8867	0.8888	0.4016	0.1653	–
	Gaussian	0.7566	0.8896	0.2895	**0.3035**	n.s.	0.8675	0.8841	0.3903	0.1651	n.s.
	Anti-Grad	0.7332	0.9000	0.2939	0.3022	*	0.8772	**0.8990**	0.4000	**0.1681**	*
	Anti-Prev	**0.7582**	**0.9056**	**0.3001**	0.3028	**	**0.8852**	0.8943	**0.4109**	0.1668	**
Dual Bi-Encoder Model											
CE	No Noise	0.6479	0.9491	0.4594	0.4414	–	0.8329	0.9369	0.5725	0.2794	–
	Gaussian	**0.6712**	0.9481	0.4625	**0.4635**	*	**0.8529**	0.9363	0.5752	**0.2882**	*
	Anti-Grad	0.6643	**0.9513**	**0.4642**	0.4633	*	0.8458	**0.9372**	**0.5783**	0.2832	*
	Anti-Prev	0.6555	0.9500	0.4496	0.4553	n.s.	0.8406	0.9361	0.5745	0.2828	n.s.
PR	No Noise	0.8001	0.9401	0.4771	0.4615	–	0.9019	0.9388	0.5898	0.3001	–
	Gaussian	**0.8331**	0.9432	0.4955	0.4866	**	0.9223	0.9388	0.5883	0.3112	*
	Anti-Grad	0.8305	**0.9572**	**0.4994**	**0.4872**	**	0.9189	0.9388	**0.5993**	0.3106	*
	Anti-Prev	0.8220	0.9571	0.4801	0.4785	*	**0.9208**	**0.9418**	0.5805	**0.3194**	*
Cross-Encoder Model											
CE	No Noise	0.0441	0.9731	0.9362	0.9941	–	0.1541	**0.9818**	**0.9992**	0.9174	–
	Gaussian	0.0532	0.9720	**0.9392**	0.9937	*	0.1785	0.9816	**0.9992**	0.9168	n.s.
	Anti-Grad	**0.0643**	0.9739	0.9368	0.9938	**	0.1962	0.9812	**0.9992**	0.9158	*
	Anti-Prev	0.0614	**0.9749**	0.9364	**0.9956**	**	**0.2017**	0.9816	**0.9992**	**0.9183**	**
PR	No Noise	0.0891	0.9881	0.9415	**0.9993**	–	0.1672	0.9900	0.9994	0.9245	–
	Gaussian	**0.0922**	0.9817	**0.9511**	0.9944	*	0.1809	**0.9922**	0.9992	**0.9308**	*
	Anti-Grad	0.0800	0.9800	0.9416	0.9941	n.s.	0.2005	0.9876	0.9992	0.9215	*
	Anti-Prev	0.0777	**0.9818**	0.9413	0.9961	n.s.	**0.2173**	0.9887	**0.9995**	0.9201	**

recall in MS MARCO, and in AIDA, whereas Anti-Grad performs the best on LC-QuAD and Mintaka datasets. The effectiveness of noise injection here also can also be observed considering both the cross-entropy and pairwise ranking loss. Herein, we see that both Anti-Grad and Gaussian noise injection approaches achieve statistically significant results. Cross-encoder models, on the other hand, already achieve very high recalls and MRRs on the LC-QuAD, Mintaka, and AIDA. Therefore, we do not see a substantial improvement over the results after injecting noise into the parameters. However, on the largest dataset, i.e., on MS MARCO, the effect of noise becomes quite prominent. Here we see that noise injection leads to almost ~**5%** improvement of recall over no noise setting. This trend is observed considering both the cross-entropy and pairwise ranking loss. Thus, the findings have led us to the following observation:

The effectiveness of noise injection depends on the ranking model and the dataset on which it is trained.

To investigate this further, consider the largest dataset, MS MARCO, wherein we see ~**2-3%** gain of performance for the bi-encoder models, and almost ~**5%** gain for the cross-encoder is achieved. This demonstrates that the effect of noise in the Adam

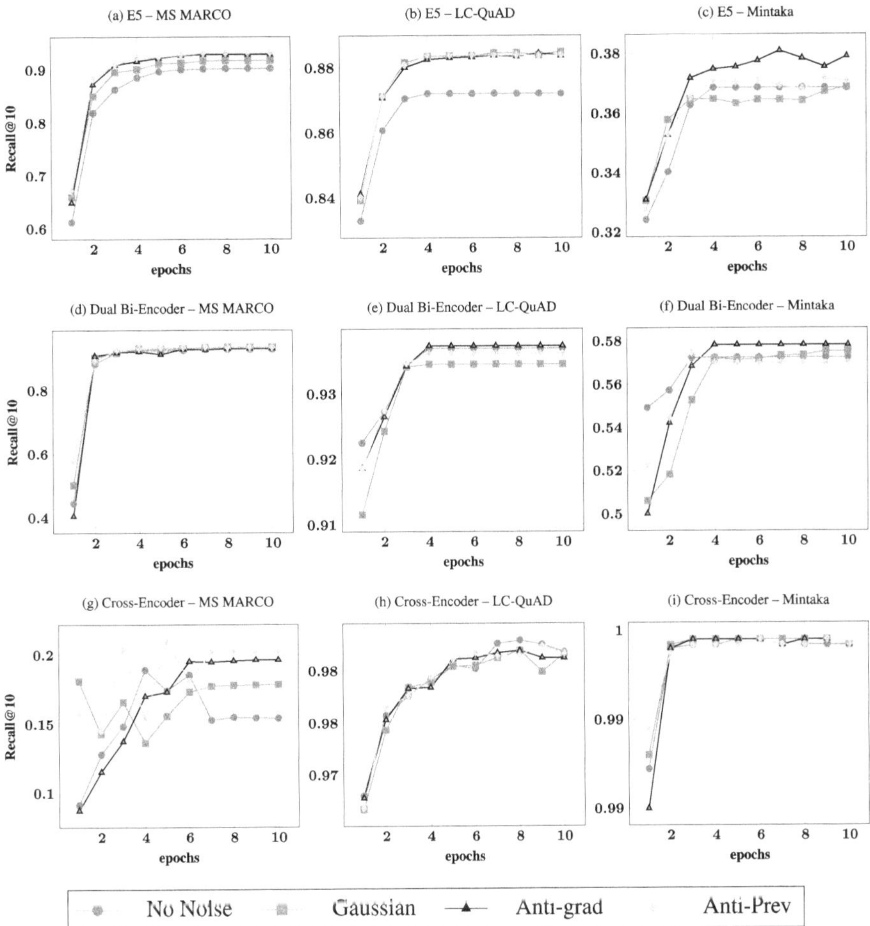

Fig. 1. Recall@10 over epochs across 3 datasets for E5, dual bi-encoder, and cross-encoder under four noise injection strategies. Panels (a)–(c): E5; (d)–(f): Dual Bi-Encoder; (g)–(i): Cross-Encoder.

optimizer shows better generalization performance on larger datasets. Furthermore, we observe that the model size, in terms of the number of parameters, also has an effect on the noise injection. Particularly, we see that the improvement in generalization for the dual bi-encoder, which has more parameters than E5, is better. Then, considering the cross-encoder model the results show substantial improvement by using noise injection into the Adam optimizer. To this end, we observe that on the MS MARCO dataset on which the cross encoder performs relatively worse, noise injection can lead to almost ~5% gain of performance. Note that on the other datasets like AIDA, Mintaka, and LC-QuAD the noise injection does not increase the performance significantly. Nonetheless, on those datasets, the cross-encoder model already achieves very high recalls and MRRs, therefore, the room for further improvement through noise injection is limited.

This suggests a *diminishing return* effect, where performance gains from regularization techniques like noise injection are more prominent when the *base* model underperforms. In contrast, when the model already achieves near-optimal performance, additional regularization contributes marginal benefits, as also observed by Arpit et al. [2] and Patrini et al. [22]. Overall, our results indicate:

Models like dual bi-encoders and cross-encoders, benefit more from noise injection only when their baseline performance has the scope for generalization improvement, otherwise noise injection does not lead to any substantial improvement.

RQ2. Considering Table 1, we observe that the anticorrelated noise injection approaches perform better than the Gaussian noise injection approach. Specifically, Anti-Prev often shows better statistically significant results considering both the cross-entropy and pairwise ranking loss. However, Anti-Grad also performs on par with Anti-Prev, mostly effective when considering the cross-entropy loss.

More specifically, Anti-Prev leverages the noise added in the previous iteration to inject a new noise term that is anticorrelated. This introduces a form of temporal regularization, creating stable noise injection during training. Unlike independent Gaussian noise or gradient-based noise, this can help in maintaining smooth optimization trajectories, especially in overparameterized models like cross-encoders. Therefore, we observe that in his model, Anti-Prev consistently yields statistically significant results compared to other approaches, considering the MS MARCO dataset. This further indicates that Anti-Prev is particularly effective when the model has already learned strong representations and only needs regularized fine-tuning to avoid overfitting.

On the other hand, the effectiveness of Anti-Grad stems from its dynamic adaptation to the optimization landscape. In particular, this can be attributed to the ability to adjust noise based on the loss by (i) reducing noise during steep descents where the gradient magnitude is large, ensuring that the optimizer follows the correct direction for faster convergence, and (ii) increasing noise in flatter regions or near convergence, which helps the model escape saddle points or shallow local minima that might otherwise trap traditional optimizers. Therefore, such adaptability makes Anti-Grad performing better than injecting uncorrelated noise. Considering these outcomes, we observe the following:

Anticorrelated noise injection approaches, i.e., Anti-Grad and Anti-Prev perform better than the uncorrelated noise injection approaches, considering both the cross-entropy and pairwise ranking loss.

RQ3. Figure 1 shows the stability and convergence behavior of noise injection strategies for E5, dual bi-encoder, and cross-encoder models[4]. Among the bi-encoder models, E5 exhibits increased stability and faster convergence when noise is introduced, particularly with the Anti-Grad strategy, whereas dual bi-encoder, with its greater model complexity, shows varying sensitivity to different noise types. Considering the cross-encoder model, we observe that noise injection substantially leads to faster convergence and moreover, can help with the overfitting issue. More specifically, for E5 model, trained on the largest dataset MS MARCO, we observe that Anti-Grad noise leads to

---

[4] Note that, when using pairwise ranking loss, we observe a similar trend in the result. Therefore, due to brevity, we only report the results considering cross-entropy loss.

rapid and steady convergence, achieving peak performance at epoch 5 with minimal fluctuations thereafter. In the dual bi-encoder, however, Gaussian noise provides the most stable performance for MS MARCO. On the other hand, without noise, the training requires at least 8-9 epochs to reach the best result for both the ranking models. To this end, we find that the cross-encoder benefited considerably when noise injection is performed. More specifically, as can be seen in Fig. 1a, when trained on MS MARCO dataset on which cross-encoder model achieves better recalls as a result of noise injection, also converges faster with Anti-Prev approach. Most importantly, we see that the noise injection approaches can mitigate the overfitting issue which is predominant when using no noise approach. Specifically, we see that after the sixth epoch, the recall value drops considerably when no noise injection approach is used, however, when used, the model stabilizes and does not overfit.

Considering LC-QuAD dataset, both Anti-Grad and Anti-Prev maintain stable recall and MRRs after epoch 4, indicating that anticorrelated noise helps the model converge faster in both the bi-encoder models. Apart from these two large ranking datasets, we see a similar trend also for the Mintaka, and AIDA datasets as well. For both of these 2 datasets, Anti-Grad outperforms all the other approaches by converging within 4-5 epochs in both E5 and bi-encoder. Note that, since the cross-encoder already achieves the highest recalls, as discussed before, the performance gain in terms of faster convergence is not substantial. Nonetheless, our results suggest that adaptive noise strategy like Anti-Grad is particularly effective in datasets with moderate complexity, providing both performance boosts and faster convergence. Overall, based on our results, we can say:

For the bi-encoder models, noise injection accelerates early-stage convergence, with noticeable gains in recall across all the datasets. For the cross-encoder model, the noise injection not only leads to much higher recall and faster convergence, also it helps to reduce the overfitting issue.

Table 2. Best noise injection approach per dataset–model combination

Model	MS MARCO	LC-QuAD	Mintaka	AIDA
E5	Anti-Prev	Anti-Prev	Anti-Prev	Anti-Grad
Bi-Encoder	Gaussian	Anti-Grad	Anti-Grad	Anti-Grad
Cross-Encoder	Gaussian	Anti-Prev	Gaussian	Anti-Prev

Optimal Noise Injection per Model and Dataset. When aggregating results across loss functions, we find that different noise injection approaches work differently for models and datasets. For the E5 model, Anti-Prev consistently yields the highest MRR on MS MARCO, LC-QuAD, and Mintaka, suggesting that stabilizing updates across training steps helps this architecture maintain ranking consistency, more specifically in structured or moderately noisy datasets. However, in the case of AIDA, Anti-Grad performs best, likely due to its ability to actively counteract misleading gradients in entity-centric retrieval. In the bi-encoder setting, Gaussian noise is optimal for MS

MARCO, indicating that noise injection can indeed help avoid overfitting in large, diverse datasets, whereas Anti-Grad dominates LC-QuAD, Mintaka, and AIDA, reflecting the benefits of gradient correction in smaller, more structured collections. For the cross-encoder, Gaussian noise performs better on MS MARCO and Mintaka, highlighting the usefulness of randomness in large-scale pairwise token matching, while Anti-Prev is superior on LC-QuAD and AIDA, where stable, incremental parameter updates appear to better preserve fine-grained semantic alignment. Table 2 shows the overall results considering which noise injection approach works best on which models and datasets.

6   Conclusion and Future Directions

In this work, we have studied the use of noise injection in the Adam optimizer to improve the performance and convergence speed of ranking models. By incorporating the noise into model parameters during training using different strategies, we demonstrated that noise could act as an effective regularizer, helping the model escape saddle points and converge to flatter minima more effectively. Our experimental results across four different datasets from different domains and two different ranking frameworks (bi-encoder and cross-encoder) consistently showed that noise-enhanced Adam optimization leads to faster convergence and mitigates the overfitting problem. These findings indicate that noise injection is a promising strategy for enhancing the training of ranking models in the domain of information retrieval.

While our work has provided valuable insights into the benefits of noise injection in ranking, we believe there are several possible research directions yet to be explored. For instance, using an adaptive strategy the level of noise and the hyperparameters (related to the anticorrelated approaches) can be adjusted. More specifically, a Bayesian learning strategy could be used therein to select the optimal noise injection parameters. Moreover, the addition of noise could be further studied to find out an optimal bound in terms of model complexity and dataset size beyond which the effect might diminish. Therefore, we envisage that a notion of balanced perturbation needs to be further studied, which can help to determine optimal noise levels and methods for dynamically adjusting perturbations based on training dynamics, loss curvature, model metrics, and datasets. Finally, we envisage exploring the role of curriculum-based noise scheduling, where noise intensity is adapted to the model's confidence. Additionally, integrating such techniques considering contrastive learning objectives may offer further improvements.

Acknowledgements. This work has been supported by the Ministry of Culture and Science of North Rhine-Westphalia (MKW NRW) within the project SAIL under the grant no NW21-059D, the project WHALE (LFN 1-04) funded under the Lamarr Fellow Network programme by the Ministry of Culture and Science of North Rhine-Westphalia (MKW NRW), the European Union's Horizon Europe research and innovation programme under grant agreement No 101070305, and by the German Federal Ministry of Research, Technology and Space (BMFTR) within the project KI-OWL under the grant no 01IS24057B.

References

1. Agarwal, O., Bikel, D.M.: Entity linking via dual and cross-attention encoders. CoRR **abs/2004.03555** (2020). https://arxiv.org/abs/2004.03555
2. Arpit, D., et al.: A closer look at memorization in deep networks. In: Precup, D., Teh, Y.W. (eds.) Proceedings of the 34th International Conference on Machine Learning, ICML 2017, Sydney, NSW, Australia, 6–11 August 2017. Proceedings of Machine Learning Research, vol. 70, pp. 233–242. PMLR (2017). http://proceedings.mlr.press/v70/arpit17a.html
3. Blanc, G., Gupta, N., Valiant, G., Valiant, P.: Implicit regularization for deep neural networks driven by an Ornstein-Uhlenbeck like process. In: Conference on Learning Theory, COLT 2020. Proceedings of Machine Learning Research, vol. 125, pp. 483–513. PMLR (2020). http://proceedings.mlr.press/v125/blanc20a.html
4. Bradley, A.V., Gomez-Uribe, C.A.: How can increased randomness in stochastic gradient descent improve generalization? CoRR **abs/2108.09507** (2021). https://arxiv.org/abs/2108.09507
5. Déjean, H., Clinchant, S., Formal, T.: A thorough comparison of cross-encoders and LLMs for reranking SPLADE. CoRR **abs/2403.10407** (2024). https://doi.org/10.48550/ARXIV.2403.10407
6. Devlin, J., Chang, M., Lee, K., Toutanova, K.: BERT: pre-training of deep bidirectional transformers for language understanding. In: Proceedings of the 2019 Conference of the North American Chapter of the Association for Computational Linguistics: Human Language Technologies, NAACL-HLT 2019, Minneapolis, MN, USA, 2–7 June 2019, Volume 1 (Long and Short Papers), pp. 4171–4186. Association for Computational Linguistics (2019). https://doi.org/10.18653/v1/n19-1423
7. Douze, M., et al.: The Faiss library. IEEE Trans. Big Data **12**(2), 346–361 (2026). https://doi.org/10.1109/TBDATA.2025.3618474
8. Fang, Z., Cao, Y., Li, Q., Zhang, D., Zhang, Z., Liu, Y.: Joint entity linking with deep reinforcement learning. In: The World Wide Web Conference, WWW 2019, San Francisco, CA, USA, 13–17 May 2019, pp. 438–447. ACM (2019). https://doi.org/10.1145/3308558.3313517
9. Ganea, O., Hofmann, T.: Deep joint entity disambiguation with local neural attention. In: Proceedings of the 2017 Conference on Empirical Methods in Natural Language Processing, EMNLP 2017, Copenhagen, Denmark, 9–11 September 2017, pp. 2619–2629. Association for Computational Linguistics (2017). https://doi.org/10.18653/v1/d17-1277
10. Guo, J., Fan, Y., Ai, Q., Croft, W.B.: A deep relevance matching model for ad-hoc retrieval. In: Proceedings of the 25th ACM International on Conference on Information and Knowledge Management, CIKM 2016, pp. 55–64. Association for Computing Machinery, New York (2016). https://doi.org/10.1145/2983323.2983769
11. HaoChen, J.Z., Wei, C., Lee, J.D., Ma, T.: Shape matters: understanding the implicit bias of the noise covariance. In: Conference on Learning Theory, COLT 2021, Boulder, Colorado, USA, 15–19 August 2021. Proceedings of Machine Learning Research, vol. 134, pp. 2315–2357. PMLR (2021). http://proceedings.mlr.press/v134/haochen21a.html
12. Jin, C., Ge, R., Netrapalli, P., Kakade, S.M., Jordan, M.I.: How to escape saddle points efficiently. In: Precup, D., Teh, Y.W. (eds.) Proceedings of the 34th International Conference on Machine Learning, ICML. Proceedings of Machine Learning Research, vol. 70, pp. 1724–1732. PMLR (2017). http://proceedings.mlr.press/v70/jin17a.html
13. Jin, C., Netrapalli, P., Ge, R., Kakade, S.M., Jordan, M.I.: On nonconvex optimization for machine learning: gradients, stochasticity, and saddle points. J. ACM **68**(2) (2021). https://doi.org/10.1145/3418526

14. Kingma, D.P., Ba, J.: Adam: a method for stochastic optimization. In: 3rd International Conference on Learning Representations, ICLR 2015, San Diego, CA, USA, 7–9 May 2015, Conference Track Proceedings (2015). http://arxiv.org/abs/1412.6980
15. Kunstner, F., Milligan, A., Yadav, R., Schmidt, M., Bietti, A.: Heavy-tailed class imbalance and why adam outperforms gradient descent on language models. In: Globersons, A., et al. (eds.) Advances in Neural Information Processing Systems 38: Annual Conference on Neural Information Processing Systems 2024, NeurIPS 2024, Vancouver, BC, Canada, 10–15 December 2024 (2024). http://papers.nips.cc/paper_files/paper/2024/hash/350e718ff74062b4bac2c6ffd9e1ac66-Abstract-Conference.html
16. Lehmann, E.L.: Introduction to Student (1908) The Probable Error of a Mean, pp. 29–32. Springer, New York (1992). https://doi.org/10.1007/978-1-4612-4380-9_3
17. Liu, G., Xue, Z., Zhang, X., Johnson, K.M., Wang, R.: Pac-tuning: fine-tuning pre-trained language models with PAC-driven perturbed gradient descent. In: Proceedings of the 2023 Conference on Empirical Methods in Natural Language Processing, EMNLP, pp. 12178–12189. Association for Computational Linguistics (2023). https://doi.org/10.18653/v1/2023.emnlp-main.748
18. Liu, T., Li, Y., Wei, S., Zhou, E., Zhao, T.: Noisy gradient descent converges to flat minima for nonconvex matrix factorization. In: The 24th International Conference on Artificial Intelligence and Statistics, AISTATS. Proceedings of Machine Learning Research, vol. 130, pp. 1891–1899. PMLR (2021). http://proceedings.mlr.press/v130/liu21e.html
19. Nogueira, R.F., Cho, K.: Passage re-ranking with BERT. CoRR **abs/1901.04085** (2019). http://arxiv.org/abs/1901.04085
20. Orvieto, A., Kersting, H., Proske, F., Bach, F.R., Lucchi, A.: Anticorrelated noise injection for improved generalization. In: International Conference on Machine Learning, ICML. Proceedings of Machine Learning Research, vol. 162, pp. 17094–17116. PMLR (2022). https://proceedings.mlr.press/v162/orvieto22a.html
21. Orvieto, A., Raj, A., Kersting, H., Bach, F.R.: Explicit regularization in overparametrized models via noise injection. In: Ruiz, F.J.R., Dy, J.G., van de Meent, J. (eds.) International Conference on Artificial Intelligence and Statistics, Palau de Congressos, Valencia, Spain, 25–27 April 2023. Proceedings of Machine Learning Research, vol. 206, pp. 7265–7287. PMLR (2023). https://proceedings.mlr.press/v206/orvieto23a.html
22. Patrini, G., Rozza, A., Menon, A.K., Nock, R., Qu, L.: Making deep neural networks robust to label noise: a loss correction approach. In: 2017 IEEE Conference on Computer Vision and Pattern Recognition, CVPR 2017, Honolulu, HI, USA, 21–26 July 2017, pp. 2233–2241. IEEE Computer Society (2017). https://doi.org/10.1109/CVPR.2017.240
23. Polyak, B.T., Tsybakov, A.B.: Optimal order of accuracy of search algorithms in stochastic optimization. Problemy Peredachi Informatsii **26**(2), 45–53 (1990)
24. Reimers, N., Gurevych, I.: Sentence-BERT: sentence embeddings using Siamese BERT-networks. In: Inui, K., Jiang, J., Ng, V., Wan, X. (eds.) Proceedings of the 2019 Conference on Empirical Methods in Natural Language Processing and the 9th International Joint Conference on Natural Language Processing, EMNLP-IJCNLP 2019, Hong Kong, China, 3–7 November 2019, pp. 3980–3990. Association for Computational Linguistics (2019). https://doi.org/10.18653/v1/D19-1410
25. Robbins, H., Monro, S.: A stochastic approximation method. Ann. Math. Stat., 400–407 (1951)
26. Shoshan, E., Radinsky, K.: Latent entities extraction: how to extract entities that do not appear in the text? In: Korhonen, A., Titov, I. (eds.) Proceedings of the 22nd Conference on Computational Natural Language Learning, Brussels, Belgium, pp. 200–210. Association for Computational Linguistics (2018). https://doi.org/10.18653/v1/K18-1020. https://aclanthology.org/K18-1020/

27. Sil, A., Kundu, G., Florian, R., Hamza, W.: Neural cross-lingual entity linking. In: Proceedings of the Thirty-Second AAAI Conference on Artificial Intelligence, (AAAI-18), the 30th innovative Applications of Artificial Intelligence (IAAI-18), and the 8th AAAI Symposium on Educational Advances in Artificial Intelligence (EAAI-18), New Orleans, Louisiana, USA, 2–7 February 2018, pp. 5464–5472. AAAI Press (2018). https://doi.org/10.1609/aaai.v32i1.11964
28. Smith, S.L., Elsen, E., De, S.: On the generalization benefit of noise in stochastic gradient descent. In: Proceedings of the 37th International Conference on Machine Learning, ICML 2020. Proceedings of Machine Learning Research (2020). http://proceedings.mlr.press/v119/smith20a.html
29. Trabelsi, M., Chen, Z., Davison, B.D., Heflin, J.: Neural ranking models for document retrieval. Inform. Retr. J. **24**(6), 400–444 (2021). https://doi.org/10.1007/s10791-021-09398-0
30. Wang, L., et al.: Text embeddings by weakly-supervised contrastive pre-training. CoRR **abs/2212.03533** (2022). https://doi.org/10.48550/arXiv.2212.03533
31. Wu, L., Petroni, F., Josifoski, M., Riedel, S., Zettlemoyer, L.: Scalable zero-shot entity linking with dense entity retrieval. In: Proceedings of the 2020 Conference on Empirical Methods in Natural Language Processing, EMNLP 2020, Online, 16–20 November 2020, pp. 6397–6407. Association for Computational Linguistics (2020). https://doi.org/10.18653/v1/2020.emnlp-main.519
32. Yamada, I., Asai, A., Shindo, H., Takeda, H., Matsumoto, Y.: LUKE: deep contextualized entity representations with entity-aware self-attention. In: Proceedings of the 2020 Conference on Empirical Methods in Natural Language Processing, EMNLP 2020, Online, 16–20 November 2020, pp. 6442–6454. Association for Computational Linguistics (2020). https://doi.org/10.18653/v1/2020.emnlp-main.523
33. Zhang, G., et al.: Which algorithmic choices matter at which batch sizes? Insights from a noisy quadratic model. In: Advances in Neural Information Processing Systems 32: Annual Conference on Neural Information Processing Systems, NeurIPS 2019 (2019). https://dl.acm.org/doi/abs/10.5555/3454287.3455023
34. Zhang, Z., Sind, X., Liu, T., Fang, Z., Li, Q.: Joint entity linking and relation extraction with neural networks for knowledge base population. In: 2020 International Joint Conference on Neural Networks, IJCNN 2020, Glasgow, United Kingdom, 19–24 July 2020, pp. 1–8. IEEE (2020). https://doi.org/10.1109/IJCNN48605.2020.9207021
35. Zhou, M., Liu, T., Li, Y., Lin, D., Zhou, E., Zhao, T.: Toward understanding the importance of noise in training neural networks. In: Chaudhuri, K., Salakhutdinov, R. (eds.) Proceedings of the 36th International Conference on Machine Learning, ICML. Proceedings of Machine Learning Research, PMLR (2019). http://proceedings.mlr.press/v97/zhou19d.html

Evaluating LLM-Generated Wikipedia Content: Political Topics in a French Setting

Jeanne Vermeirsche[1] , Eric SanJuan[2(✉)] , and Tania Jiménez[2]

[1] Avignon Université, JPEG, Avignon, France
`jeanne.vermeirsche@univ-avignon.fr`
[2] Avignon Université, LIA, Avignon, France
`{eric.sanjuan,tania.jimenez}@univ-avignon.fr`

Abstract. Large Language Models (LLMs) demonstrate impressive text generation capabilities, raising the question of whether they can autonomously generate knowledge resources like Wikipedia. However, deploying LLMs as standalone knowledge bases—especially in politically sensitive domains and multilingual contexts necessitates rigorous evaluation. This study investigates the feasibility and reliability of LLM-generated Wikipedia content in a closed-book setting without Retrieval-Augmented Generation (RAG).

Our evaluation focuses on two complementary axes: Univariate Analysis where we employ unsupervised content-based metrics, including ROUGE and Kullback-Leibler (KL) Divergence, to measure textual similarity and global distribution alignment against original Wikipedia summarise; Multivariate Analysis by mapping a curated political lexicon onto Latent Dirichlet Allocation (LDA) models to analyze implicit thematic structures.

Our framework facilitates a low-cost evaluation of multiple open-weight LLMs. Results demonstrate that LLMs, even those trained on the entirety of Wikipedia, remain unreliable as standalone knowledge bases for political information due to inherent structural instabilities and a tendency toward "plausible" but fabricated content.

Keywords: Large Language Models · Text Generation · Wikipedia · Political Discourse Analysis · Autonomous Knowledge Bases · Computational Social Science

1 Introduction

The potential of Large Language Models (LLMs) to autonomously generate knowledge resources like Wikipedia is increasingly explored [21], but critical questions regarding reliability, particularly in sensitive domains such as politics and across multiple languages, remain unanswered [19].

This study investigates the reliability of Large Language Models (LLMs) [1] as autonomous knowledge bases, specifically evaluating their performance in

E. Cabrio and E. Monteiro (Eds.): NLDB 2026, LNCS 16696, pp. 252–267, 2027.
https://doi.org/10.1007/978-3-032-29532-3_18

a closed-book setting without the corrective influence of Retrieval-Augmented Generation (RAG). By isolating the model from external real-time data, we aim to probe its internalized parametric biases. We hypothesize that despite the scale of their pre-training, LLMs possess inherent structural limitations that manifest as instability and ideological skew when generating content on politically sensitive topics.

The most critical reason to probe parametric bias is that an LLM's internal weights act as its statistical prior [9]. Even when RAG or system prompts are used to "steer" a model, the internal bias acts as a gravitational pull [6]. If the underlying model is heavily biased, it requires more "force" (computational overhead or complex prompting) to keep it neutral. Identifying this "default mode" helps developers understand the baseline risk of the system. By probing the parametric bias, we are uncovering the hidden editorial logic that the model applies when it synthesizes a response. This is vital for "trustworthy AI," as it reveals the "invisible editor" built into the model's weights.

To investigate this, we present a rigorous, mixed-methods evaluation of LLM-generated Wikipedia articles on political topics following [20]. Our methodology comprises four interwoven strands. First, we assess lexical stability by analyzing the consistency of term associations across multiple generations of text produced by the LLMs on the same input. Second, we evaluate content quality using unsupervised, content-based metrics: ROUGE and KL Divergence, to compare LLM-generated summaries against original Wikipedia ones. Third, we employ Latent Semantic Analysis (LSA), Latent Dirichlet Allocation (LDA), and Word2Vec to analyze implicit correlations within a curated political lexicon, identifying potential biases embedded within the generated content. Finally, a sample of generated articles undergoes expert content analysis to validate quantitative findings and uncover nuanced issues of factual accuracy and framing.

Our approach facilitates a low-cost evaluation of multiple open-weight LLMs.

The paper is organized as follows: Sect. 2 discusses related work. Section 3 introduces the socially motivated research questions about Wikipedia and politics. Section 4 briefly describes the processed data. Section 5 covers the experimental setup and system details. Results are provided in Sect. 6. Finally, Sect. 8 presents the conclusions and future perspectives.

2   Related Work

Studies have examined the extent to which pretrained language models such as BERT implicitly store factual knowledge in their learned parameters. [14] proposes a benchmark specifically designed to test an LLM's ability to be truthful and avoid generating common misconceptions or falsehoods it may have learned from training data meanwhile [12] conducts a comprehensive overview of why, when, and how LLMs hallucinate. It categorizes different types of hallucinations and discusses methods for detection and mitigation, which are critical for deploying LLMs as knowledge resources. Retrieval-Augmented Generation (RAG) framework defined in [13], which grounds the LLM's generation on external, verifiable knowledge sources represent a key alternative or supplement to using the LLM as a *standalone* knowledge base but rely on existing corpora and knowledge bases.

For Autonomous Generation and Self-Correction for Knowledge Tasks, on going research work focus on LLMs acting as agents that can plan, execute, and refine tasks, such as writing or editing a Wikipedia article. [15] addresses the "autonomous" construction aspect. It proposes a framework where an LLM can generate an initial output, critique it, and then refine it based on its own feedback meanwhile [17] focus on simulating social behavior to demonstrate how LLMs can power autonomous agents that maintain memory and plan actions over time. The architectural principles are relevant for building an agent that could autonomously manage a knowledge base.

Seminal research works focus on the challenges of ensuring fairness, bias, neutrality, and safety when LLMs handle politically sensitive or controversial topics. [19] directly measures the political leanings of popular LLMs using standard political compass tests. [9] provides a dataset and framework for evaluating bias across different domains (including politics) in text generated by LLMs.

3   Comparative Analysis of Knowledge Production Regimes

Wikipedia is one of the world's most consulted websites and a primary data source for training Large Language Models (LLMs) like GPT and Gemini [16]. The online encyclopedia operates on a collaborative, non-commercial model of participatory governance, where content is collectively managed by volunteer contributors [4]. The Wikimedia Foundation has recently reaffirmed the human-centric nature of this project[1]. This model is now challenged by the rise of generative AI, which could produce texts that mimic Wikipedia's style almost instantly [10,21]. This capability has sparked intense debate and concern within the Wikipedia community about the potential for polluting the encyclopedia with erroneous and low-quality content, thereby undermining the reliable knowledge base built by humans [11]. Building on the work of [8,20], we extend our inquiries regarding Wikipedia and generative AI. We aim to examine them as distinct socio-technical systems for knowledge production, assessing their strengths and weaknesses [1,18].

3.1   The Data Feedback Loop and Contrasting Regimes

The Wikipedia and the LLMs represent contrasting "mediation regimes":

Wikipedia's regime is horizontal, deliberative, and community-driven [4]. Its contents are fully traceable and open to discussion through modification histories and public talk pages.

---

[1] https://wikimediafoundation.org/news/2025/04/30/our-new-ai-strategy-puts-wikipedias-humans-first/.

LLM regime is invisible, algorithmic, and non-discursive [2]. It produces plausible text without traceability or a mechanism for debate, requiring users to have specific skills to formulate queries and verify responses [1].

Despite their promise of equal access independent of socio-economic status, both systems tend to reproduce - and sometimes amplify - existing inequalities in access and participation. Effective use of both is socially and cognitively situated. Contributing to Wikipedia requires technical and social skills, which has led to the over-representation of specific demographics (male, highly educated, and politically engaged, particularly with regard to political content) that influences how knowledge is constructed.

The role of generative AI is a subject of ongoing debate within the Wikipedia community [3]. Some contributors are staunchly opposed to its use, arguing that it undermines the core principles of neutrality and sourcing. Others adopt a more nuanced position, suggesting AI could be used to *help to do 'but never for' doing in place of* [11,17], emphasizing that a human is ultimately responsible for the quality of any published.

3.2   Methodology

We present a robust, multi-stage methodology to analyze and visualize the conceptual architecture of expert-defined lexicons within content generated by Large Language Models (LLMs). Our approach begins with an extrinsic evaluation, using average ROUGE scores to benchmark the generated text against reference corpora for topical alignment and factual grounding. Following this validation, we conduct an intrinsic analysis focused on a specialized lexicon, where Latent Dirichlet Allocation (LDA) [8] models the latent thematic structure governing the co-occurrence of these specified terms, effectively smoothing the variance inherent in generated texts. Finally, Latent Semantic Analysis (LSA) is applied to this stable probabilistic model to map and visualize the core correlations between the lexicon terms themselves. The cascaded approach yields a low-dimensional semantic space that is robust to the surface-level noise of the initial text generation. A significant strength of this pipeline is its language independence.

LLM Content Analysis. We are treating the LLM as a text generator and analyzing its output's structure, rather than probing its latent space. To quantify the factual grounding and topical relevance of the LLM's output against Wikipedia content, we first compute average ROUGE. By measuring the lexical overlap with a canonical knowledge source like Wikipedia, we get a metric that approximates how "on-topic" and factually aligned the generated text is.

However, even with identical prompts, the generated texts can have significant surface-level variations due to the inherent variance and stochasticity in LLM outputs, particularly when a generation hyperparameter like `temperature` > 0 is used. This stochasticity introduces noise that obscure the underlying semantic structures. And leads to unstable and poorly interpretable visualization. To tackle this, we leverage Latent Dirichlet Allocation (LDA) to distill the noisy, high-dimensional co-occurrence data from the raw text into a more compact and stable representation of its underlying thematic structure. The key output from this stage is the term-topic probability matrix, commonly denoted as the ϕ (phi) matrix. This matrix represents the probability of each lexicon term given a latent topic: $\phi_{k,v} = P(\text{term}_v | \text{topic}_k)$. This matrix serves as a smoothed, thematically-aware representation of the lexicon. This distribution accurately reflects the term's contextual associations—i.e., the statistical likelihood of co-occurring terms and thematic patterns in the generated text. Unlike internal vector embeddings, this representation is grounded in the empirical statistical properties of the output corpus itself.

We perform SVD on the term-topic probability matrix ϕ to extract the principal components of the latent thematic space. Unlike standard LSA, which operates on term-document frequency matrices, this approach analyzes the variance between LDA-generated topic distributions. This enables us to capture the most significant semantic gradients across a filtered vocabulary of interest.

Lexicon Mapping. Following [7] methodology, we reuse the lexicon introduced in [20][2] that was manually extracted from a large set of official political press releases to serve as an analytical tool for identifying and correlating recurring themes and terms that structure the positions and narratives associated with nationalism in contemporary political discourse. This lexicon of 130 uniterms is organized into 10 thematic categories. It is important to note that certain terms may be classified under multiple categories:

1. Politics, Institutions, and Governance
2. Security and Justice
3. Territory and Nationality
4. Media and Communication
5. Activism and Engagement
6. Economy
7. International and Supranational
8. Religions, Ideologies, Beliefs
9. Environment and Ecology
10. Gender and Sexual Identity

Some of the selected terms might appear overly generic or polysemous (e.g., "liberty," "union", "value", "civilization"). We have intentionally retained these terms because our objective is not to essentialize a word's meaning, but rather to analyze the specific contexts in which it is activated, its co-occurrences with other terms, and the types of argumentation it is embedded within.

Therefore, this lexicon is not intended to be exhaustive or semantically neutral. Instead, it functions as a flexible and evolving analytical framework. By mapping the text generated by LLMs onto this expert political lexicon, we can systematically study and compare the correlations between different concepts and themes present in the content. This approach allows for a qualitative

---

[2] Available at https://pol.termwatch.eu/JADT4.html.

interpretation by guiding the observation of recurring topics and term associations within the context of their usage.

4   Data

To construct a benchmark dataset free from contamination by modern LLM-generated content, we utilized the French Wikipedia dump from March 2022. This snapshot ensures all pages were created before the widespread popularity of generative AI.[3]

To create a specialized subcorpus focused on French politics, we followed a structured approach. The process involved the following steps:

1. (i) **Data Ingestion:** All page abstracts were extracted and indexed in a PostgreSQL database using a Generalized Inverted Index (GIN) to enable efficient text-based queries.
2. (ii) **Subcorpus Selection:** We created a "French politics" subcorpus by executing a boolean query for abstracts containing `politique` AND (`france` OR `français` OR `française`) (politics AND (france OR french)).
3. (iii) **Ranking and Filtering:** This query yielded 4,954 pages. To ensure high relevance, these pages were ranked using the cover density weighting scheme [5], and we proceeded with the top-ranked documents.

Our experimental protocol involves regenerating abstracts for the selected Wikipedia pages and comparing them against the original abstracts, which serve as our reference or "ground truth." The corpus was processed in sequential batches of 300 abstracts. For each batch, we generated a standalone co-occurrence model (following Sect. 3.2) to analyze the output. This batch-based approach allows for iterative analysis and management of computational resources.

5   Experiments

To comprehensively evaluate the LLMs, we introduced several factors of variation:

- **Models:** Four different open-weight foundation models were tested (see Table 1).
- **Model Scale:** For Gemma and Mistral, we experimented with two different model sizes to assess the impact of scale on output structure.
- **Stochasticity:** The `temperature` hyperparameter was varied to control the randomness of the generated text.
- **Prompting:** Two distinct prompts were used, a short prompt (see Fig. 1) was tested across all LLMs and configurations, a longer one (see Fig. 2) was used exclusively with the smaller LLMs for computational workload raisons.

Table 1. Models

Model	Parameters	Size	Context
Gemma3	4.3B (27.4B)	3.3 GB (17 GB)	128K
Mistral	7.25B (23.6B)	4.4 GB (14 GB)	32K
Llama	8.03B	4.7 GB	8K
Qwen	8.19B	5.2 GB	40K

Generation was carried out on a local Ollama server powered by two RTX NVIDIA GPUS with 32 Go of RAM. We carefully limit the number of computations by stopping the iterations over the 300 abstracts pools once we observe non significant gaps between output evaluation measures.

prompt = "Ecrit le résumé d'une note encyclopédique ayant comme entrée :",
(Write a summary of an encyclopedic entry with the following entry:)
system = "Tu es un contributeur du chapitre en français du WikiPedia."
(You are a contributor to the French chapter of Wikipedia.)

Fig. 1. Short prompt

We propose to contextualize a glossary of terms on a set of short texts sourced from Wikipedia or automatically generated by LLMs. More specifically, given a corpus of texts C and a small lexicon L characteristic of a specific theme or type of discourse, we aim to find the most significant associations between the constituent terms of this lexicon. We will base these associations on their direct co-occurrences within the corpus C as well as on Probabilistic Modeling (LDA) of term co-occurrences within the documents of C, without considering word order (i.e., using a bag-of-words approach).

6 Results

6.1 Content Evaluation

We use the ROUGE metric [18] in order to evaluate the AI-generated abstracts compare to the Wikipedia real (human) abstract. Results are reported in table 2 for average scores, Figs. 3 and 4 for values distribution (boxplots) over short and long prompts. Because ROUGE is very sensitive to the difference in size of the text, we truncate the generated texts to the median of the Wikipedia texts (628.5 characters).

Table 2 shows the overall ranking of LMMs based on Rouge1 and Rouge2 F1 scores with no significative difference between them although Gemma slightly

---

[3] The R Markdown (.Rmd) source code, datasets, and generated models are available on https://pol.termwatch.eu.

prompt = "Ecrit le résumé d'une note encyclopédique ayant comme titre : ",
(Write a summary of an encyclopedic entry entitled:)
system = "fais comme si tu étais un contributeur du chapitre en français du WikiPedia, mais donne moi juste le contenu, sans ajouts de dialogue entre nous. Le résumé est un texte qui précède le corps de l'article sur Wikipédia. Le contenu de sa première phrase doit faire l'objet d'une attention particulière. Le résumé doit être autonome et offrir une synthèse des informations de manière à constituer un mini-article de type dictionnaire encyclopédique, fournissant ainsi au lecteur une approche globale et didactique du sujet. Le résumé introductif établit le contexte et présente les points les plus importants en montrant l'intérêt du sujet et en résumant d'éventuelles controverses. De longueur proportionnelle au contenu de l'article, entre deux et quatre paragraphes, il doit être rédigé dans un style accessible et neutre. Contrairement à une introduction classique, le résumé introductif ne soulève pas les problématiques du sujet, mais il les résume et y répond brièvement. Il ne doit pas contenir d'information qui ne soit détaillée et correctement sourcée dans le développement de l'article. Il pourra par exception contenir des références pour sourcer certains points, même si les sources doivent en priorité être placées dans le corps de l'article."
(English translation: Pretend you're a contributor to the French Wikipedia chapter, but just give me the content, without adding any dialogue between us. The summary is a text that precedes the body of the Wikipedia article. The content of its first sentence should be given particular attention. The summary should be self-contained and offer a synthesis of the information in such a way as to constitute a mini-article, like an encyclopedia entry, thus providing the reader with a comprehensive and instructive overview of the topic. The introductory summary establishes the context and presents the most important points, highlighting the relevance of the topic and summarizing any potential controversies. Proportional in length to the article's content, between two and four paragraphs, it should be written in an accessible and neutral style. Unlike a traditional introduction, the introductory summary does not raise the issues of the topic, but rather summarizes and briefly addresses them. It should not contain any information that is not detailed and properly sourced in the body of the article. It may exceptionally contain references to cite certain points, although the sources should primarily be placed in the body of the article.")

Fig. 2. Long prompt

Table 2. Comparison of average ROUGE scores with maximum values highlighted in bold using short prompt.

	ROUGE-1			ROUGE-2		
LLM	Recall	Prec.	F1	Recall	Prec.	F1
Gemma	**1.0000**	0.8122	**0.8964**	**0.6939**	0.3411	**0.4574**
Gemma 27b	0.9699	0.8318	0.8955	0.4491	0.3849	0.4145
Llama	0.9004	**0.8637**	0.8817	0.4651	**0.4461**	0.4554
Mistral	0.8118	0.8604	0.8354	0.4093	0.4339	0.4212
Mistral Small	0.5546	0.8501	0.6713	0.2725	0.4190	0.3302
Qwen	0.2360	0.8456	0.3690	0.1191	0.4328	0.1868

over performing others. About Qwen, the "good" precision comes from the fact that it gives very short summaries. Overall, this is the smallest model and does not seem to be appropriate for this task.

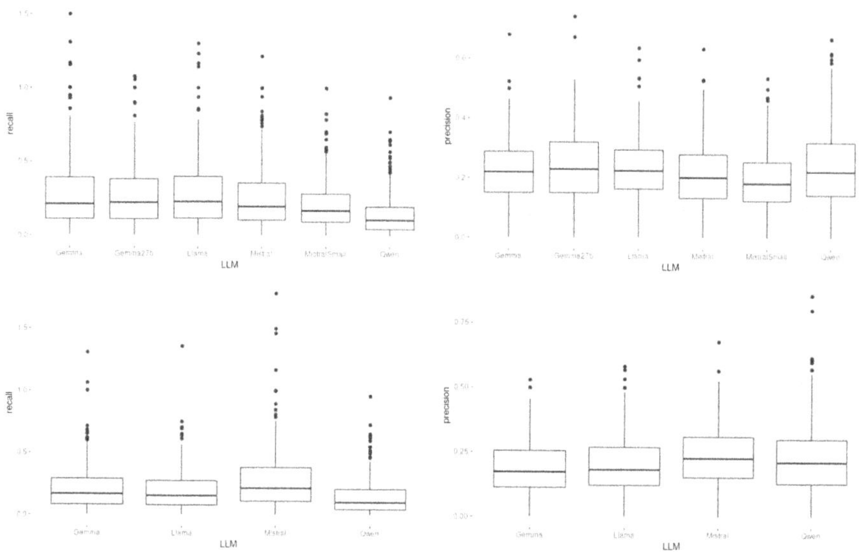

Fig. 3. Rouge1 Recall and Precision for the shortPrompt (up) and LongPrompt

Recall and precision metrics show minimal variation among the LLMs. However, Mistral outperforms the other models in processing long prompts.

6.2 Correlations Analysis

Our primary objective is to quantitatively compare the term correlations within the LLM-generated corpora against those present in the reference Wikipedia corpus. We evaluate this comparison along two key dimensions:

Coverage: The number of statistically significant term associations from the reference corpus that the LLM successfully reproduces.

Accuracy: The degree to which the strength of the reproduced correlations in the LLM corpus matches that of the original correlations.

Table 3 presents the global scores measuring these dimensions, while Fig. 5 offers a qualitative visualization of the most significant correlations using LSA applied to the LDA term-topic matrix. The metrics in the table are defined as follows:

– *Intersect*: This column quantifies coverage. It indicates the number of term-pair correlations found to be statistically significant (Pearson's r, $p < 0.05$ over 20 topics) in both the reference Wikipedia model and the LLM's model.

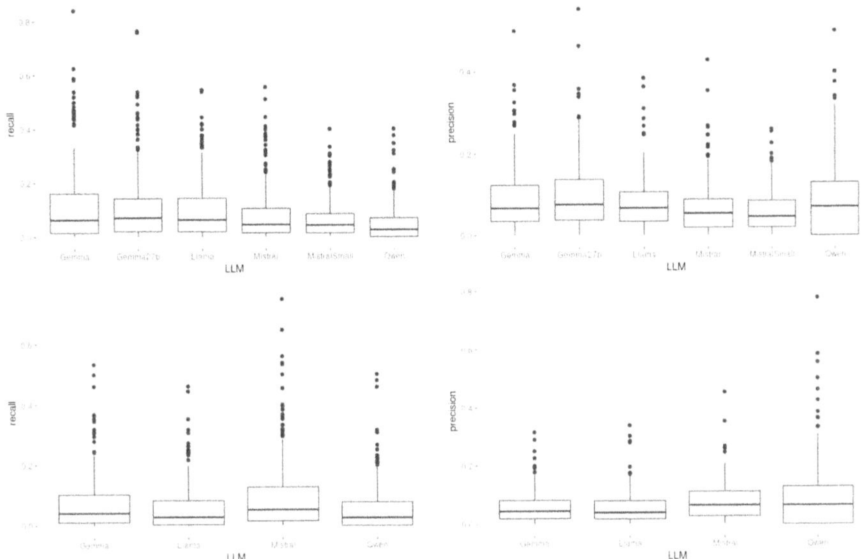

Fig. 4. Rouge2 recall and precision for short prompt (up) and long prompt

- *Dot Product (·)*: This column measures fidelity. It calculates the similarity in the strength of the correlations found in the intersection (a higher value is better).
- *KL Divergence*: This metric provides a global comparison of the two LDA models. It measures the dissimilarity between their term distributions across the entire shared vocabulary, not just the lexicon (a lower value is better).

On *short prompts*, the smaller **Gemma-4B** model achieves the best performance in reproducing lexicon correlations, notably outperforming the much larger Gemma-27B model on our coverage and accuracy metrics.

When evaluating performance on *long prompts in French*, which require a deeper contextual understanding, the Mistral model is the only one to demonstrate improved performance. This result is not surprising and aligns with the model's specific training and optimization. As a foundation model developed by a French company, Mistral has been extensively fine-tuned on high-quality French data, giving it a distinct advantage in processing the language's nuances, syntax, and long-range dependencies.

In contrast, the other models, including Gemma, tend to underperform with the additional context provided in French. This superior capability of Mistral directly corroborates our earlier surface-level observations based on ROUGE-1 scores, where it also proved more adept at leveraging the expanded context of longer prompts.

The KL divergence findings reveal a key distinction, while Mistral may be more effective at using long-prompt context for text generation, Gemma would excel at the more difficult structural task of recreating the specific, fine-grained relationships between our lexicon terms and produces a global topic model that most closely mirrors the human-written reference corpus. This calls for a detailed qualitative analysis, outlined in the next Subsect. 6.3.

To limit GPU usage, we carried out only most informative computations. On short prompts the light Gemma 3B model gets best scores, including against larger Gemma 27B model. On long prompts only Mistral improves while the others under performs, this corroborate previous observation based on Rouge1 directly applied to text before processing LDA model. However, KL divergence between LDA distributions (WikiPedia references content vs Gemma and Mistral outputs) indicates that the Gemma would be closer to WikiPedia reference when considering all vocabulary (not only terms in our lexicon).

Table 3. Lexicon correlations evaluation based on LDA models with twenty 20 topics, over short (S) and long (L) prompts. Intersect shows the number of common correlations. · is the dot product between vector correlations. Only significant correlations (Pearson test with p-value < 0.05) are considered.

LLM	Int. (S)	· (S)	Int. (L)	· (L)	KL div. (L)
Gemma	**9**	**5.9649**	*4*	*2.2360*	**0.019787344**
Llama	*4*	*2.6480*	1	0.5475	0.0945
Gemma27b	3	1.7235	-	-	-
Mistral	3	1.5351	**7**	**3.6051**	*0.0439*
Qwen	0	0	0.3012	0	0

Table 4. Comparison of Lexicon Term Proximity Scores in the reference (WP) and in the corpus generated using Gemma3.

#	Terms	WP	Gemma3
1	autonomie indépendance	0.6178	0.9961
2	autonomie peuple	0.5929	0.9033
3	défense sécurité	0.5821	0.9951
4	démocratique souveraineté	0.6890	0.9899
5	extrême gauche	0.9782	0.9705
6	extrême union	0.6505	0.9012
7	français française	0.5850	0.8845
8	gauche union	0.6633	0.9286
9	indépendance peuple	0.9810	0.9002

6.3   Qualitative Analysis

We do observe in Table 3 that Gemma finds 9 pairs with consistently high scores (often around 0.9). Although it appears to overestimate certain relations (cf. Table 4)- for example, "autonomie-indépendance" scores 0.61 in WP but 0.99 in Gemma - it aligns well with highly correlated pairs, such as "extrême-gauche". It captures the largest number of relations but tends to "believe" too strongly in associations, even when they are not as correlated in the reference corpus.

Gemma 27b retrieves 3 pairs, though also with very high scores. Mistral also has 3 pairs in common but with lower scores. The model overestimates two correlations but remains closer to the WP values on the last one, "gauche-union". However, its associations appear limited. Llama identifies four pairs, with strong correlations in most cases (approximately 0.9), often diverging from the WP corpus values, except for the correlation "extrême-gauche". Finally, Qwen fails to retrieve any pairs, suggesting that this model is not well-suited to the task.

Thus, it appears that some models, such as Gemma, prioritize the coverage of associations but tend to force correlations. Others, such as Mistral, are more conservative, retrieving fewer pairs. Their correlations can be closer to those observed in the Wikipedia corpus, although this is not always systematic. Overall, Fig. 5 analysis reveals that while human-authored Wikipedia content maintains a complex, decentralized web of political terminology, the LLMs tend to over-simplify and over-correlate these terms. They create tighter, more extreme semantic clusters, effectively altering the internal relationships of political concepts and demonstrating their underlying parametric biases.

If we take an ever more qualitative look at the texts generated by the models with respect to the correlations found, we notice that they nonetheless produce numerous hallucinations, even though the text is always clear and plausible in form. For example, regarding the correlation "gauche-union", Mistral notably produces the article on the Union of French Muslim Democrats (UDMF), presented as "a French political party founded in 1990". However, this party was actually founded in 2012. Mistral also describes a very specific ideology, which seems embellished, but does not correspond to the Wikipedia version. The encyclopedia specifically mentions "sever al controversies due to accusations of communitarianism and Islamism made by political and media actors" which are, however, "refuted by several political science and sociology researchers". These details are entirely absent from the text generated by Mistral. The model produces a more structured, easy-to-read text, at the cost of major factual errors. Some information is generalized or invented to make the text coherent but is not verified. Such hallucinations are very recurrent in texts generated by the different models.

For the correlation "défense-sécurité" Gemma, for example, produces the Wikipedia article on the "Fédération nationale des républicains indépendants". The model presents it as "a French political party founded in 1944" that "positions itself as a far-right party, heir to the republican and anti-communist tradition". Gemma provides numerous details about its founders and history. However, the Wikipedia page states that this federation is "a French center-right political movement that existed between 1962 and 1977" and "served as a supporting force for the Gaullist majority". The entire text produced by Gemma, which at first reading seems entirely plausible, is nevertheless completely fabricated. These hallucinations occur across all models and for a very large majority of the texts generated. These examples illustrate what could be called a tendency toward plausible filler, meaning that the generated entries appear credible at first glance but contain inaccuracies and fabrications, which may go even more easily unnoticed when the topics are less familiar to the general public. The models give the illusion of solid information even though the entry is misleading, increasing the risk of acceptance by a non-specialist reader. While their ability to produce a large amount of information is strong, the accuracy and correctness of the reported facts remain low.

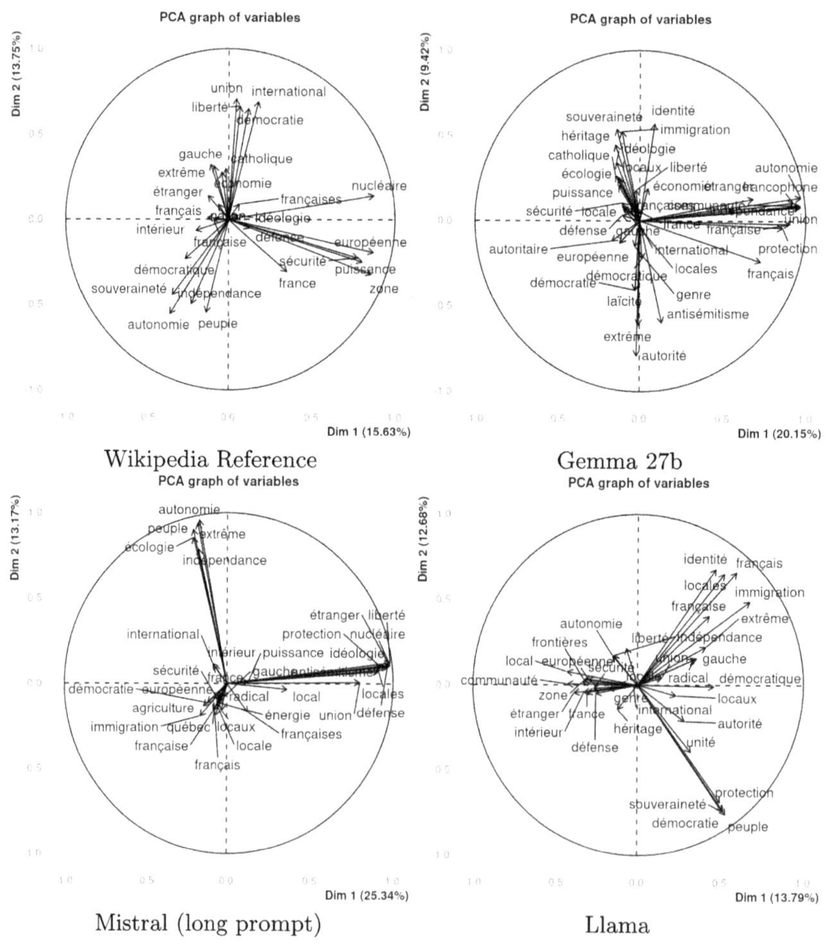

Fig. 5. Significant Lexicon correlations on LDA model

7   Limitations and Generalizability

While this study provides a robust framework for evaluating Large Language Models (LLMs) in a closed-book setting, several limitations regarding its scope and application should be noted.

The methodology is primarily designed as a tool for human analysts to interpret LLM outputs within specific thematic boundaries. The evaluation relies heavily on a pre-defined political lexicon provided by the analyst to identify and correlate recurring themes. Consequently, the depth of the "intrinsic analysis" is constrained by the quality and relevance of the expert-defined terms used to map the latent semantic space.

Our findings are based on using Wikipedia content as the ground truth (specifically the March 2022 French dump to avoid data contamination). The study was conducted using small pools of 300 Wikipedia page, which were selected and ranked based on their overlap with the specialized lexicon. While this batch-based approach allows for iterative analysis and efficient resource management, it represents only a targeted slice of the broader political discourse available on the platform.

Although this specific study focused on the French language, the cascaded pipeline (ROUGE to LDA to LSA) is language-independent. The experimental protocol can be reproduced across other Wikipedia language editions to compare regional parametric biases. Moreover, the framework is not limited to encyclopedic content. The same methodology can be applied to other authoritative sources.

8   Conclusion

Based on this study, several lessons can be drawn for IR, particularly in the context of LLMs. On the one hand, these models reproduce the imbalances and biases present on the web, making it necessary to develop methods to detect and mitigate these biases. On the other hand, although LLMs generate fluent and convincing texts, they may contain inaccurate information and rarely provide explicit and verifiable sources. It is therefore essential to implement provenance and reliability indicators so that users can assess the credibility of the generated responses. Systems should thus allow the identification of responses produced by generative models, monitor biases, and present the corresponding sources. Finally, it is now necessary to train users not only to search for information, but also to critically interpret, verify, and cross-check content in an increasingly automated digital environment.

References

1. Arrieta, A.B., et al.: Explainable artificial intelligence (XAI): concepts, taxonomies, opportunities and challenges toward responsible AI. Inf. Fusion **58**, 82–115 (2020)
2. Bender, E.M., Gebru, T., McMillan-Major, A., Shmitchell, S.: On the dangers of stochastic parrots: can language models be too big? In: Proceedings of the 2021 ACM Conference on Fairness, Accountability, and Transparency, pp. 610–623 (2021)
3. Brooks, C., Eggert, S., Peskoff, D.: The rise of AI-generated content in Wikipedia. arXiv preprint arXiv:2410.08044 (2024)
4. Cardon, D., Levrel, J.: La vigilance participative. Une interprétation de la gouvernance de wikipédia. Réseaux **154**(2), 51–89 (2009)
5. Clarke, C.L., Cormack, G.V., Tudhope, E.A.: Relevance ranking for one to three term queries. Inf. Process. Manage. **36**(2), 291–311 (2000)
6. Dai, S., Xu, C., Xu, S., Pang, L., Dong, Z., Xu, J.: Bias and unfairness in information retrieval systems: new challenges in the LLM era. In: Proceedings of the 30th ACM SIGKDD Conference on Knowledge Discovery and Data Mining, Barcelona Spain, pp. 6437–6447. ACM (2024). https://doi.org/10.1145/3637528.3671458. https://dl.acm.org/doi/10.1145/3637528.3671458
7. Daille, B., Morin, E.: French-English terminology extraction from comparable corpora. In: Dale, R., Wong, K.-F., Su, J., Kwong, O.Y. (eds.) IJCNLP 2005. LNCS (LNAI), vol. 3651, pp. 707–718. Springer, Heidelberg (2005). https://doi.org/10.1007/11562214_62
8. Deveaud, R., SanJuan, E., Bellot, P.: Accurate and effective latent concept modeling for ad hoc information retrieval. Document numérique **17**(1), 61–84 (2014)
9. Dhamala, J., et al.: Bold: dataset and metrics for measuring biases in open-ended language generation. In: Proceedings of the 2021 ACM Conference on Fairness, Accountability, and Transparency, pp. 862–872 (2021)
10. Gao, F., et al.: Evaluating large language models on wikipedia-style survey generation. In: Findings of the Association for Computational Linguistics ACL 2024, pp. 5405–5418 (2024)
11. Grudin, J.: Computer-supported cooperative work: history and focus. Computer **27**(5), 19–26 (2002)
12. Ji, Z., et al.: Survey of hallucination in natural language generation. ACM Comput. Surv. **55**(12), 1–38 (2023)
13. Lewis, P., et al.: Retrieval-augmented generation for knowledge-intensive NLP tasks. Adv. Neural. Inf. Process. Syst. **33**, 9459–9474 (2020)
14. Lin, S., Hilton, J., Evans, O.: TruthfulQA: measuring how models mimic human falsehoods. arXiv preprint arXiv:2109.07958 (2021)
15. Madaan, A., et al.: Self-refine: iterative refinement with self-feedback. Adv. Neural. Inf. Process. Syst. **36**, 46534–46594 (2023)
16. McDowell, Z.J.: Wikipedia and AI: access, representation, and advocacy in the age of large language models. Convergence **30**(2), 751–767 (2024)
17. Park, J.S., O'Brien, J., Cai, C.J., Morris, M.R., Liang, P., Bernstein, M.S.: Generative agents: Interactive simulacra of human behavior. In: Proceedings of the 36th Annual ACM Symposium on User Interface Software and Technology, pp. 1–22 (2023)
18. Petroni, F., et al.: Language models as knowledge bases? arXiv preprint arXiv:1909.01066 (2019)

19. Rettenberger, L., Reischl, M., Schutera, M.: Assessing political bias in large language models. J. Comput. Soc. Sci. **8**(2), 1–17 (2025)
20. Vermeirsche, J., Sanjuan, E., Jiménez, T.: LDApol: vers une méthodologie de contextualisation des discours politiques (LDApol: towards a methodology of political speech contextualisation). In: Moncla, L., Brando, C. (eds.) Actes de la 29e Conférence sur le Traitement Automatique des Langues Naturelles. Atelier TAL et Humanités Numériques (TAL-HN), Avignon, France, pp. 19–27. ATALA (2022). https://aclanthology.org/2022.jeptalnrecital-humanum.3/
21. Vetter, M.A., Jiang, J., McDowell, Z.J.: An endangered species: how LLMs threaten Wikipedia's sustainability. AI & Soc., 1–14 (2025)

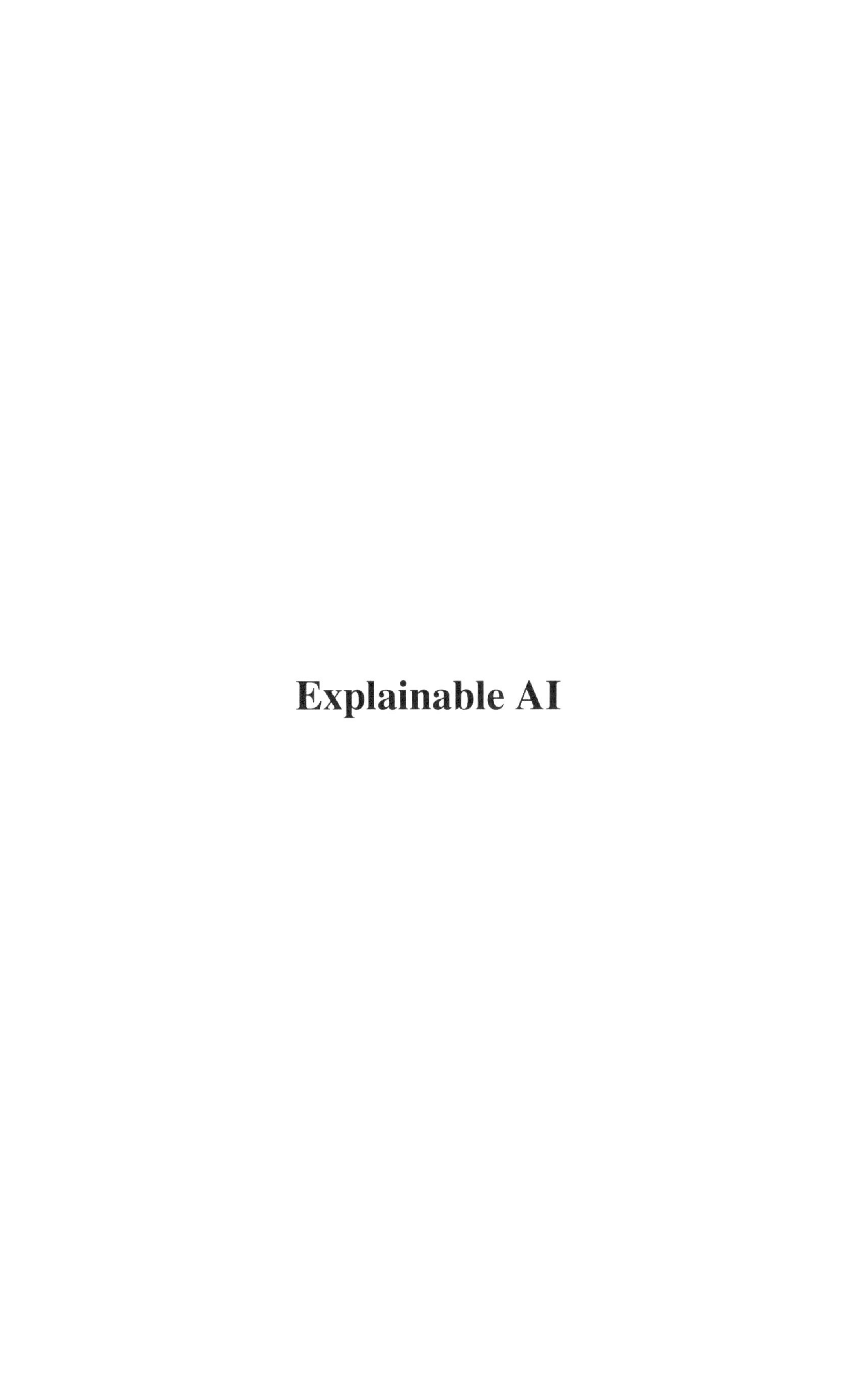

Explainable AI

When Words Move Markets: Interpretable Behavioural and Robustness Analysis of LLMs for Financial Sentiment Reasoning via Local Perturbation Explanations

Sania Verma[1(✉)] , Koorosh Aslansefat[2] , Joyjit Chatterjee[2,3,4] ,
Akash Marar[3] , Anu Mehra[5] , and Aisha Ekundayo[3]

[1] City, St. George's University of London, London, UK
`sania.verma@city.ac.uk`
[2] University of Hull, Hull, UK
`k.aslansefat@hull.ac.uk`, `joyjit_chatterjee@epam.com`
[3] EPAM Systems, London, UK
`akash_marar@epam.com`, `aisha_ekundayo@epam.com`
[4] Loughborough University, Loughborough, UK
[5] Amity University, Noida, India
`amehra@amity.edu`

Abstract. Sentiment analysis plays an integral role in the financial sector towards identifying ongoing and emerging market trends. Whilst LLMs perform efficiently in tasks like sentiment prediction, the token-level and contextual understanding behind their decisions remains under-explored. This thereby limits their adoption in regulated domains. This study aims to decipher the reasoning behind how LLMs judge sentiments by taking predictive stability, token-level evidence and contextual cues into account. We apply Generative Statistical Model-Agnostic Interpretability (GSMILE) technique, to examine how a given sentence influences the model output distributions at the local level. We fine-tuned three open-source models to compare their behaviour in this study – Gemma-3-270M by Google, Mistral-7B-Instructv0.1 and Qwen-2.5-0.5B-Instruct. Our analysis shows that LLM sentiment prediction is shaped by how importance is distributed across tokens and their interactions in a sentence. Moreover, the model predictions are driven more by contextual cues than by lexical sentiment cues. These findings suggest that high efficiency alone is insufficient to enable trust in LLM-based predictions, underscoring the importance of interpretability and transparency when using LLMs in financial analytics.

Keywords: Explainable AI · Large Language Models · Token Attribution · Interpretability

Note that this study was carried out as an independent research project by the authors – views and methodologies presented in the paper are those of the authors and do not represent EPAM Systems.

1   Introduction

Robust sentiment classification of financial text is key to explaining volatile market movements, risk perception, and investor behaviour. However, unlike other kinds of natural language, financial news inherently contains subtle linguistic cues (for instance, terms like *unexpected contraction, easing inflation* etc. This can make sentiment classification both, more challenging as well as ambiguous due to the different possible interpretations of the same text. Whilst in recent times, Large Language Models (LLMs) have showcased their outstanding capabilities in sentiment classification tasks by better inferring complex semantic structures compared to traditional language models [21], their predictions are often black-box, which hinders trust in their real-world adoption within high-stakes financial environments.

Owing to the safety-critical nature of this domain, high predictive accuracy alone is not sufficient for deployment of such models in practice[1]. Furthermore, recent regulations e.g. the EU AI Act have presented increasingly challenging requirements for audibility and explainability in high-risk AI systems [6].

This has led to the growing requirement not just for explainable predictions, but also for deeper, evidence-based insights into the mechanism which LLMs use to infer sentiment based on the varying context, composition and discourse prevalent in financial news. In particular, the insights pertaining to the internal reasoning used by LLMs and the token interactions which influence model predictions can be beneficial for financial practitioners. However, most existing studies focus on token-importance attribution in isolation, without analysing the interaction between multiple cues, which provides limited insight into the predictions [16]. Towards addressing this gap in this paper, we adopt a perspective for behavioral interpretability which empirically analyzes the significance of token-level attributions and contextual reinforcement cues. We are also interested in the distinct behaviours of different LLMs in terms of their reasoning and judgment patterns. Accordingly, this paper addresses the following research questions:

RQ1: What token-level and contextual evidence do LLMs rely on when producing sentiment predictions for financial news text?

RQ2: How stable are sentiment predictions when identical financial news sentences are repeatedly queried to LLMs?

RQ3: Which tokens contributed the most to specific sentiment predictions, and are these contributions consistent across different LLMs?

To investigate these questions and address the interpretability gap in foundational LLMs, we adopt Generative Statistical Model-agnostic Interpretability with Local Explanations (GSMILE) as an analytical probe to examine how LLMs construct sentiment judgments [17]. In comparison to traditional explainability methods which are typically designed for discriminative classifiers, GSMILE

---

[1] It is essential for stakeholders (e.g. investors, analysts, regulatory bodies etc.) to have a nuanced and context-based interpretation of why a model assigns certain labels corresponding to a specific financial news item, as well as the reliability and consistency of the predictions.

is specifically tailored for the generative and auto-regressive nature of LLMs, wherein, it employs perturbation-based analysis and Wasserstein distance metrics for quantifying the contribution of individual tokens to the model's output distribution. We leverage three popular open-source LLMs to validate the efficacy of the proposed approach, and utilize a real-world financial news dataset to show that the models can achieve competitive performance whilst providing transparent decisions.

Beyond this, we also aim to decipher the prediction shifts across LLMs and evaluate the consistency in their sentiment predictions. This helps to uncover both, model-specific as well as generic (shared) strategies in leveraging Generative AI (GenAI) models in the financial domain. We envisage that the proposed framework can help ensure transparent, actionable and behaviourally grounded rationale when adopting LLMs in the financial sector. The paper is organized as follows: Sect. 2 that discusses literature review, Sect. 3 describes the dataset and Pre-processing steps, Sect. 4 presents the methodology, Sect. 5 reports Results and Discussion followed by Sect. 6 Discusses conclusion and outlines future work and References.

2 Literature Review

Explainability in sentiment classification is generally described using three complementary approaches. These include local post-hoc attribution methods, contrastive or counterfactual explanation techniques, and mechanistic interpretability methods[2]. Contrastive or counterfactual explanation techniques highlight how minor linguistic alterations would flip the prediction. On the other hand, mechanistic interpretability methods examine the model's internal reasoning patterns to diagnose systematic behaviours and biases [19]. In financial sentiment analysis, these approaches vary in their fidelity to variations in prompts and their ability to infer evidence from the text. For example, Limonad et al. use LLMs to extract rationale terms for sentiment labels and improve downstream forecasts [10].

A large body of work relies on feature-attribution methods. Classical post-hoc explainability techniques such as LIME and SHAP provide model-agnostic local explanations by estimating which input features drive a prediction and thus struggles to capture non linear behaviour of LLMs [12]. Aslansefat et al. introduced SMILE [2], a statistically sound method that uses distance-based weighting and surrogate models to produce more consistent token-level attributions. GSMILE [3,4] generalises this idea to generative LLMs by incorporating prompt perturbations and tracking distributional shifts in generated outputs. Also, Rule-based methods like LORE [7] miss long-range dependencies, while GSMILE captures input perturbation effects, helping in better explanations for generative LLMsInstead of focusing on predicting the output, GSMILE uses a surrogate model with a different objective. Given a set of perturbed inputs, the

---

[2] Local post-hoc attribution methods explain predictions after they are made by highlighting which word or phrase influenced the outcome.

model does not aim to reproduce the output. Instead, it measures how similar each generated response is to the original output. This allows gSMILE to better reflect how changes in the input affect the behavior of the model. Complementary to post-hoc methods, some recent model architectures embed interpretability. Adhikari et al. present an explainable CNN using hybrid word embeddings and attention for financial news sentiment classification using LIME visualisations to highlight which words most influenced each prediction [1].

Beyond local attribution, contrastive and counterfactual methods have gained attention for their actionable sensitivity analyses. The CELL framework identifies minimal changes to prompts that result in different model responses, helping users understand sensitivity to specific lexical or structural cues [13]. In financial context, sentiment can flip depending on discourse structure (e.g. concessive connectives such as "although" and "despite that"), as well as because of hedging and framing of time. This is the motivation for discourse-aware sentiment models that reassess polarity based on clause roles [8]. Further, Hong et al.'s Query-Guided Dual Attention (QGDA) uses Stock market specific queries to focus on sentiment-relevant clauses and provides concept-level explanations for its predictions [9]. Domain specific adaptation further shapes both sentiment accuracy and explanation relevance. FinBERT, a BERT variant pre-trained on large-scale financial corpora, achieves strong performance gains on financial text mining tasks [11]. However, this strong accuracy may not necessarily reflect financially meaningful reasoning. Mechanistic interpretability complements attribution by tracing systematic biases in how models process prompts i.e. positional bias – where importance is given to whether information appears at the beginning or end of a prompt, hence influencing decisions has been analyzed by Dimino et al. [5].

Finally, explanation quality should be assessed for both stability and faithfulness, particularly because generative LLM inference is inherently stochastic and can yield different outputs across runs. GSMILE addresses this by estimating token influence through controlled perturbations and the resulting distributional changes in model outputs, which makes it well suited for repeated-query robustness evaluation in LLM-based sentiment classification [3]. While the state-of-the-art in financial sentiment classification has leveraged domain-specific pre-training, such as with FinBERT, and local explanation techniques, such as LIME and SHAP to improve accuracy and interpretability, there has been limited research explicitly addressing how generative LLMs utilize token-level evidence and contextual cues to make robust sentiment predictions. We aim to address this gap through the application of GSMILE to capture token-level contributions and contextual cues in financial news sentiment classification in this paper.

3   Data Description and Pre-processing

In this paper, we leverage the **Financial Phrasebank Dataset** [14] wherein news statements were manually collected from financial news sources and official company announcements[3]. The dataset with 75% agreement was chosen to balance the annotation reliability and dataset size.

The dataset with 75% agreement exhibited a significant class imbalance, which could have adversely affected the training of the LLMs. To address this, the training data was balanced using text-based augmentation, where words in a sentence were replaced with their closest synonyms to generate new sentences. Originally, the dataset contained 3,453 sentences, which were expanded to 5,151 after augmentation. The key idea behind this pre-processing was to replace certain words or phrases with their closest synonyms to mitigate class imbalance, maintaining 1717 samples for each sentiment class.

4   Methodology

Our proposed methodology consists of data pre-processing, data augmentation, model fine-tuning and evaluation shown in Fig. 1.

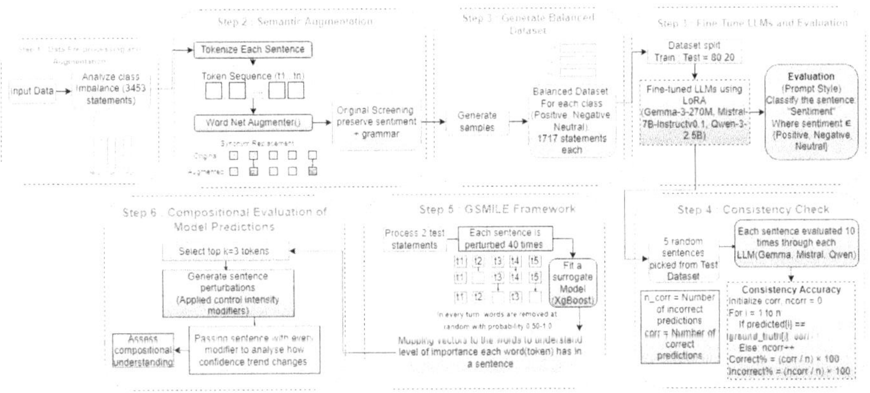

Fig. 1. Overview of the end-to-end workflow pipeline

4.1   Model Selection

We leveraged three foundational LLMs for the implementation of the above methodology: **Gemma-3-270M**, **Mistral7B-Instructv0.1** and **Qwen2.5-0.5B-Instruct**. These models were primarily chosen because they are open-source and feasible to fine-tune within the available computational constraints. The chosen models have shown competitive performance on Natural Language Understanding tasks [8].

---

[3] Sixteen domain experts labeled sentences as positive, negative, or neutral. Four dataset variants (100%, 75%, 66%, 50%) were created based on majority agreement.

4.2 Experimental Setup

Models

Gemma3-270M: It is a lightweight model which was developed by Google [20]. The model's compact size enabled faster inference lower memory use, motivating an assessment of its reasoning capacity.

Mistral 7B-Instruct-v0.1: Mistral is a state-of-the-art model, optimised for efficient reasoning and inference [18]. Since the model size is quite large (nearly 7 billion parameters), the model was loaded using 4-bit Quantization.

Qwen-2.5-0.5B-Instruct: The model is chosen for its optimal balance between parameter scale and computational efficiency and optimised for instruction-following tasks, enabling rapid experimentation on domain-specific datasets.

Data Preparation: The experiments were conducted using the augmented dataset. The dataset was divided into two sets – training and test, in the ratio 80:20. The training data was loaded and prepared for model training using PyTorch's "Data Loader" functionality. The dataset was reformatted into instruction-style prompts to match the generative nature of the models. Each example was converted into a prompt-label pair as follows:

$$p = \mathrm{prompt}(x); \; \mathbf{t} = \mathrm{Tokenizer}(p); \; \mathbf{z} = f_\theta(\mathbf{t}); \; \mathbf{s} = \mathbf{z}_{-1}[\mathcal{L}]; \; P(y_i \mid x) = \frac{\exp(s_i)}{\sum_j \exp(s_j)} \tag{1}$$

Where x is input text; $p = \mathrm{prompt}(x)$; $\mathbf{t} = \mathrm{Tokenizer}(p)$; f_θ the LLM; $\mathbf{z}$ output logits; $\mathbf{z}_{-1}$ final-token logits; L label tokens; s_i logit for $y_i \in L$; $P(y_i \mid x)$ predicted probability.

Fine-Tuning: All the models were fine-tuned using LoRA adapters to reduce computational costs and enable parameter-efficient adaption. Table 1 below summarizes the hyperparameter chosen for each model. Training was performed by employing cross-entropy loss, applied only to the label tokens, whereas prompt tokens were masked. This prevented gradient updates from affecting the instructions and ensured that the model learns only from the target labels. Additionally, the setup included precision optimization (FP16) and gradient accumulation to handle memory constraints for the larger models. Mistral model employed a maximum token length of 128 due to high memory overhead, while other models (Gemma & Qwen) model support a longer context window of nearly 2048 tokens, owing to their compact size and low memory usage.

Evaluation: The models used in this study possess a generative nature, and hence lack a classification head. Therefore, sentiment predication was performed using a prompt-based evaluation strategy. Instead of directly classifying an input sentence, the models were prompted to generate the next token corresponding

Table 1. Fine-tuning Parameters: Mistral 7B, Gemma-3-270M & Qwen2.5-0.5

Parameter	Mistral 7B	Gemma-3	Qwen 2.5
Training Setup			
Per-device train batch size	1	1	2
Per-device eval batch size	1	1	2
Gradient accumulation steps	16	8	4
Optimizer	AdamW	AdamW	AdamW
Number of epochs	15	20	15
Learning rate	3e−4	2e−4	5e−5
Precision & Efficiency			
Precision mode	FP16	FP16	FP16
Logging steps	10	25	50
Fine-tuning Strategy (LoRA/QLoRA)			
Fine-tuning type	QLoRA	LoRA	LoRA
LoRA rank	64	16	8
LoRA alpha	32	16	16
LoRA bias	none	none	none
Learning Control & Regularization			
Maximum input token length	128	2048	2048
Dropout	0.05	0	0.15
Data & Objective			
Training objective/loss	Causal LM	Causal LM	Causal LM
Truncation	Enabled	Enabled	Enabled

to one of the three sentiment labels: positive, negative or neutral. The logits associated with these tokens were extracted and converted into a probabilistic score using a softmax function, assigning a token for a sentence based on highest probability score.

Inference Stability and Consistency Check: We take motivation from the self-verification approach "SelfCheckGPT" proposed by [15], according to which if multiple outputs are generated that disagree with one another, the original output is likely to be hallucinated[4]. Similarly, we evaluated five statements randomly selected from the dataset. Each statement was independently passed to the fine-tuned model 10 times under identical inference conditions. This evaluation was intended to verify the consistency of the model, despite the generative nature of the architecture. The chosen prediction was based on the condition

---

[4] To evaluate a response R, the authors generate N new responses to analyse the consistency of R with respect to the generated responses.

defined in Eq. 2.

$$\text{Consistency Accuracy} = \begin{cases} 100\%, & \text{if all 10 predictions match the ground-truth} \\ 0\%, & \text{otherwise} \end{cases} \tag{2}$$

In the Table 2, in each case the prediction remained consistent (100%), indicating deterministic behaviour. In case of statement 4, wherein the Mistral and Gemma models classified the sentence as neutral in alignment with the ground truth, Qwen consistently predicted a positive sentiment. The indicates a semantic mis-classification, rather than inference variability (Table 4).

4.3   GSMILE Framework

GSMILE is an extended version of SMILE [2] designed for LLMs [3]. It is a local, perturbation-based framework for explaining the predictions from fine-tuned LLMs. It works by generating a perturbed version of a sentence and thereafter fitting a surrogate model to approximate the local decision surface. We used this to identify the most influential words in each sentence. Algorithm 1 illustrates the workflow of the proposed process through pseudocode. In this algorithm, for each modified sample $\tilde{x}_k$, we compute a corresponding representation vector $u_k \in \mathbb{R}^d$. To approximate the local behaviour of the original model, we define an affine surrogate model as

$$g_\beta(u_k) = \beta_0 + \beta^\top u_k, \tag{3}$$

where $\beta_0 \in \mathbb{R}$ denotes the intercept term and $\beta \in \mathbb{R}^d$ is the coefficient vector. The parameters β are estimated by solving the following weighted least-squares problem:

$$\min_\beta \sum_{k=1}^{K} \omega_k \left(g_\beta(u_k) - \delta(x, \tilde{x}_k) \right)^2, \tag{4}$$

where ω_k assigns larger weights to samples closer to the reference input x, and $\delta(x, \tilde{x}_k)$ measures the change in the model output caused by the perturbation. The subtraction inside the squared term is standard in least-squares regression and represents the difference (or error) between the surrogate prediction and the observed change. Even when $\delta(x, \tilde{x}_k)$ is small, this term ensures the surrogate correctly captures these variations.

4.4   Compositional Semantic Probing on Important Tokens

While the tokens that influence a given statement were identified using GSMILE, there was a further need to assess the context-level understanding. We considered the top influential words as output after fitting a surrogate model based on the assigned importance scores. Note that the choice of fewer k words would have failed to present phrase-level sentiment composition, whereas larger k words

Table 2. Prediction consistency across 10 repeated inference runs. All reported predictions were consistent across runs unless otherwise indicated.

Financial Statement	Truth	Mistral	Gemma	Qwen
Validating our fgVoIP client through Symbian Signed represents a significant step forward...	Pos	Pos	Pos	Pos
At end-August, Sampo was Nordea's biggest shareholder with a 20.6% stake...	Neu	Neu	Neu	Neu
The poorest index fig. was given to Finnish power company Fortum, 4.5.	Neg	Neg	Neg	Neg
The share subscription period for C options will commence on 1 Sept 2008...	Neu	Neu	Neu	**Pos**[*]
Kickoff quarter underlying operating profit rose to 41 mln EUR from 33 mln...	Pos	Pos	Pos	Pos

[*]Consistent misclassification across all 10 inference runs (0% agreement with ground truth).

Algorithm 1 Local Explanation – Sentence Perturbation and Surrogate Model

---

Require: Dataset of sentences D
 1: **for** each sentence $s \in D$ **do**
 2:     Compute baseline prediction y_{base} using fine-tuned LLM
 3:     Initialize perturbed set $P \leftarrow \emptyset$
 4:     **for** $i = 1$ to 30 **do**
 5:         Remove words from s with probability $p \in [0.5, 1.0]$
 6:         Let resulting sentence be s_i
 7:         **if** s_i is empty **then**
 8:             Add one random word from s to s_i
 9:         **end if**
10:         Add s_i to P
11:     **end for**
12:     Obtain LLM predictions Y for all sentences in P
13:     Compute TF-IDF representations of P
14:     Train XGBoost surrogate model using TF-IDF(P) and Y
15:     Extract word importance scores from surrogate model
16:     Sort words in s by descending importance
17:     **for** each word w in sorted list **do**
18:         Remove w from s to obtain s'
19:         Compute prediction y' using fine-tuned LLM
20:         **if** $y' \neq y_{base}$ **then**
21:             Record prediction shift; **break**
22:         **end if**
23:     **end for**
24: **end for**

---

would have introduced redundancy. To balance this situation, $k = 3$ was considered. For every statement, controlled perturbations were generated by applying controlled modifiers. This assisted in evaluating how it affects the predicted label confidence.

5 Results and Discussion

5.1 Local Explanation Analysis via Sentence Perturbation

To evaluate the effectiveness of the local-level analysis via sentence perturbation, two financial sentences were considered, which are: **S1: "The company reported increased profits this quarter"** and **S2: "The project failed to meet its targets, yet the team showed remarkable resilience.".** Each sentence was passed to fine-tuned LLMs to get the predicted label, which was compared with the ground truth, followed by implementing Algorithm 1 in Sect. 4.3. Below, we discuss the behaviour of the individual LLMs (Table 3):

Gemma3-270M: For S1 in Fig. 2a, the model predicted the correct sentiment ("Positive"), where the token "increased" received the highest important

Table 3. Token importance levels (scores normalised to max value per sentence)

Col.	Level	Range	Col.	Level	Range
▓	Very High	> 75%		Low	10–25%
▓	High	50–75%	▓	Negligible	< 10%
	Medium	25–50%			

score (0.363), whereas "profits" had an influential impact, nearly (0.201). Other tokens had minimal impact. To understand the role of tokens in a sentence further, the most influential word, "increased", was removed, resulting in the shift of prediction from "Positive" to "Neutral". This behavior highlighted the word's critical role in influencing the behavior of the model towards predicting the sentiment. Similarly, for S2 in Fig. 2b, the predicted sentiment being "Positive", the tokens "remarkable" and "yet" showed notable importance with scores of 0.191 and 0.115, respectively. The word "remarkable", when removed, did not shift the prediction, indicating that "yet" balanced the neutralized negative phrase of the sentence (**"The project failed to meet its targets."**)[5].

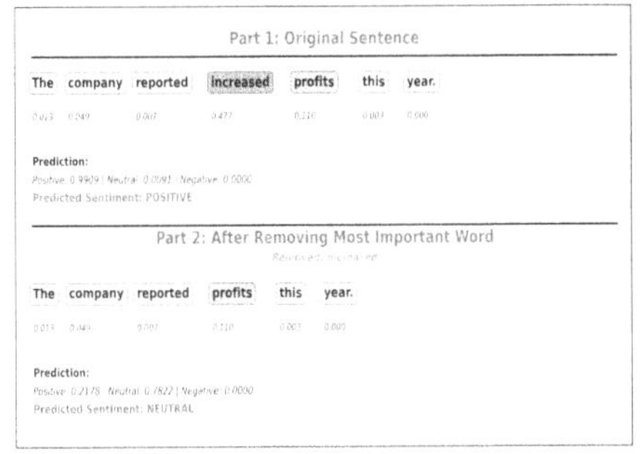

(a) Sentence 1 Analysis

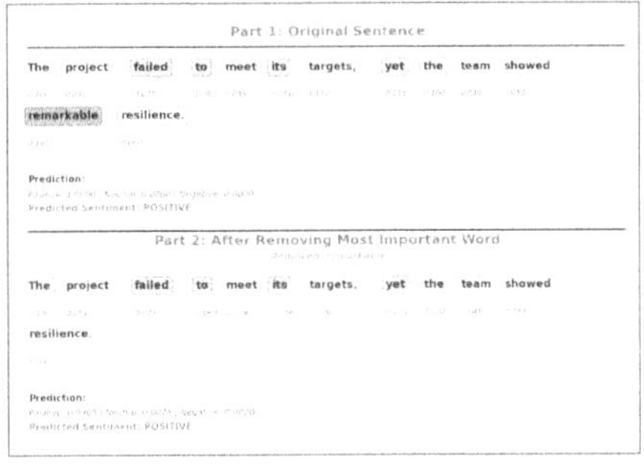

(b) Sentence 2 Analysis

Fig. 2. Gemma-3-270M Sentiment Analysis

Mistral-7B-Instruct-V0.1: The model predicted the sentiment as "Positive" with 100% confidence for S1 in Fig. 3a. The tokens "increased" (0.531) and "this" (0.126) were marked as important tokens, showing reliance on the phrase "Increased profits". The prediction changed to Neutral with confidence (87.84%) when the token "increased" was removed. Even though the remaining sentence "The company indicated profits this year" seemed positive to us, the model

---

[5] This phenomenon suggests the model's sensitivity towards the structural words, rather than lexicon-based sentiment cues, without supporting contextual evidence.

marked it as neutral, demonstrating the significance of contextual cues over isolated sentiment-bearing words. Similarly, for S2 in Fig. 3b, the sentence was initially predicted as "Neutral" with 99.32% confidence, with highlighted tokens like "yet", "failed", "resilience" and "showed". Since "yet" is most influential, it balanced out the negative and positive phrase resulting in a neutral prediction. Upon removal of the token "yet", the prediction remained the same. This uncovers the distributed and context-dependent nature in transformer-based models.

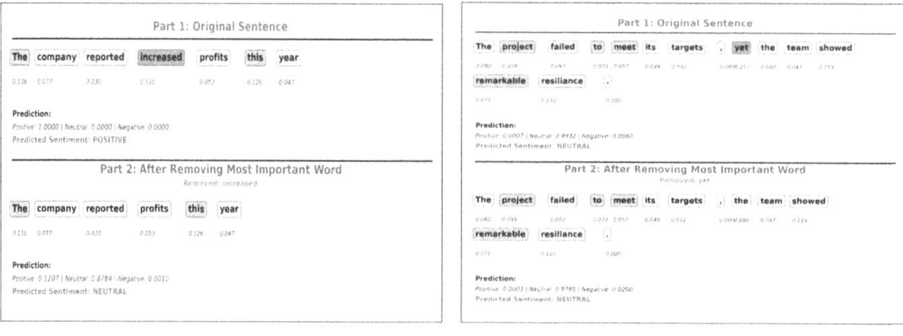

(a) Sentence 1 Analysis   (b) Sentence 2 Analysis

Fig. 3. Mistral-7B-Instructv0.1 Sentiment Analysis

Qwen2.5-0.5B-Instruct: The model predicted the sentiment of the sentence S1 as positive with 53% confidence. The analysis of S1 in Fig. 4a reveals the influential token "increased" (0.305) as the dominating attribute token. It is consistent across all the models. Upon removal of the token "increased", the prediction shifted to "Neutral" with 92.77% confidence. For S2 Fig. 4b The token "yet" received the highest importance in S2, whilst other tokens like "failed", "resilience" etc. also emerged as important with scores of 0.161 and 0.145, respectively. Removing the topmost important token, the new prediction was Negative. Since, the sentence started with a negative clause, it might redistribute importance, preferring its alignment towards negative over the positive, which finally resulted in a negative prediction. These results highlights fragility of the model towards minute lexical changes.

5.2 Compositional Evaluation of Model Predictions

To probe contextual sensitivity, we applied controlled modifier intensifiers to the top 3 influential words identified by GSMILE. For this experiment the sentence S2 was considered. Figure 5a shows the robustness of the performance of the Mistral model in S2. Of the three words – "yet", "showed", "resilience", **"yet"** is highly stable (0.861–0.994), suggesting that the model maintains high confidence regardless of modifier intensity. In contrast, **"showed"** is the most variable

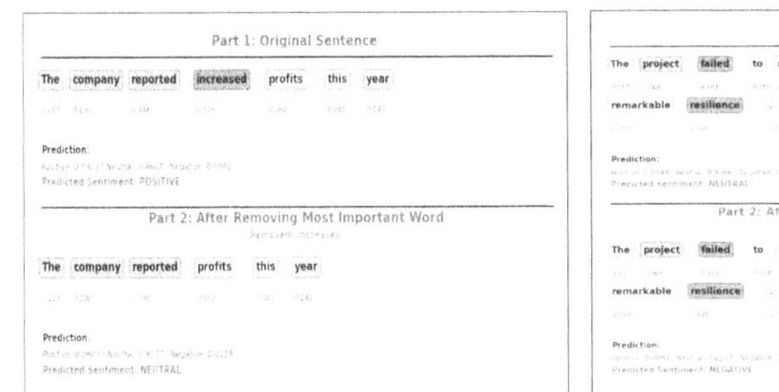

(a) Sentence 1 Analysis

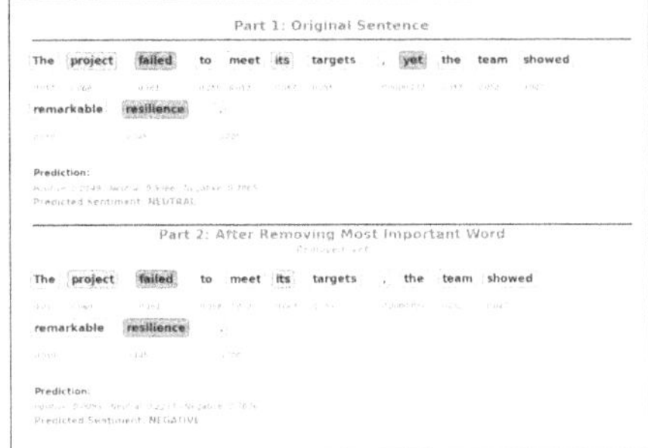

(b) Sentence 2 Analysis

Fig. 4. Qwen-2.5-0.5B-Instruct Sentiment Analysis

Table 4. Prediction Shift Analysis After Removing Most Important Token

	Gemma3-270M	Mistral-7B	Qwen-2.5-0.5B
	Sentence 1		
Prediction Flow	Positive ↓ *remove* increased (0.363) ↓ *Neutral*	Positive ↓ *remove* increased (0.531) ↓ *Neutral*	Positive ↓ *remove* increased (0.305) ↓ *Neutral*
Impact	**SHIFT**	**SHIFT**	**SHIFT**
	Sentence 2		
Prediction Flow	Positive ↓ *remove* remarkable (0.191) ↓ Positive	*Neutral* ↓ *remove* yet (0.212) ↓ *Neutral*	*Neutral* ↓ *remove* yet (0.177) ↓ *Negative*
Impact	NO SHIFT	NO SHIFT	**SHIFT**

(0.802–0.995), with the lowest minimum score, indicating higher sensitivity to perturbations. This indicates that model's behaviour is affected by extreme modifiers on this particular verb. **"Resilience"** remains strong (0.791–0.989) with moderate variability. The heatmap in Fig. 5a reveals the nuanced behaviour of the model, where "yet" showed highest confidence across all modifiers (0.861–0.994). This analysis demonstrates that while the Mistral model exhibits some sensitivity to modifier placement and intensity, it maintains acceptable performance thresholds across all perturbation scenarios, with 87% of predictions exceeding 90% confidence. Figure 5b shows **"Yet"** is highly unstable (0.496–0.932, range 0.436, IQR = 0.159), with the lowest observed score at 0.496.

"Failed" exhibits similarly concerning variance (0.533–0.963), suggesting inconsistent behaviour, while **"resilience"** consistently under performs (0.689–0.785), with a compressed IQR, indicating systematic weakness. The heatmap shows only 40% of conditions exceed 0.90, while another 40% fall below 0.80, indicating highly unreliable predictions. Overall, Qwen exhibits extreme sensitivity to modifier placement and intensity, with systematic under performance on negatively-balanced and contextually critical words. Unlike the other models, Gemma achieved confidence (100%) across all modifiers, suggesting extreme robustness. Raising concerns about whether the model truly captures compositional semantics or simply relies on high-level pattern features. This uniform baseline indicates a complete lack of responsiveness to contextual cues, highlighting a fundamental limitation in the model's ability to capture compositional semantics.

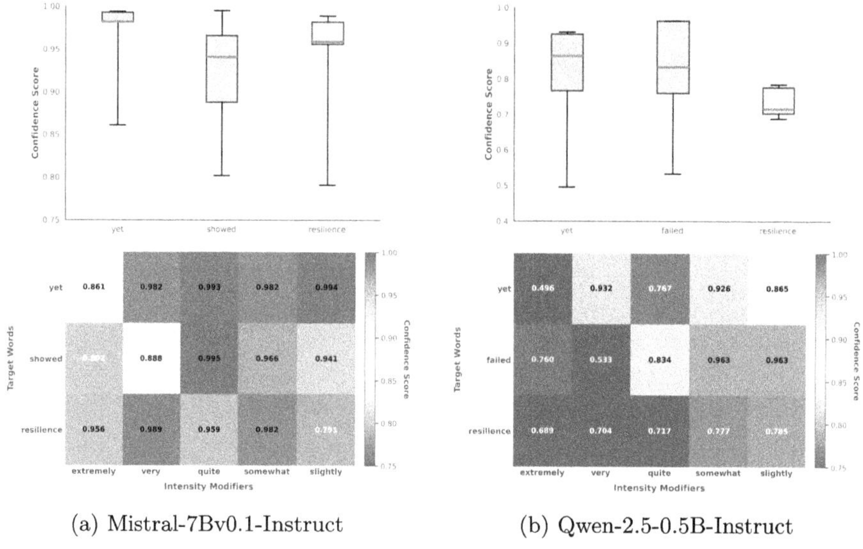

(a) Mistral-7Bv0.1-Instruct   (b) Qwen-2.5-0.5B-Instruct

Fig. 5. Impact of token modifications on model confidence

6   Conclusion and Future Work

This study examines how LLMs predict sentiment in financial news, with a particular focus on interpretability, token-level evidence, and prediction stability. Clearly, individual keywords alone are insufficient to explain sentiment prediction, especially when accounting for volatile market movements, risk perception, and investor behavior. Instead, contextual structure and token interactions play a critical role in shaping model predictions. For instance, the token "increased" is consistently associated with positive sentiment across models; however, its influence is highly context-dependent. Removing it shifted prediction from positive to neutral for all models, illustrating its strong but non-independent contribution to sentiment reasoning.

In terms of sensitivity and robustness of the model, Mistral-7B exhibited the most balanced and stable behaviour by distributing importance across multiple tokens. Gemma-3-270M showed high robustness to perturbations, although this may indicate reliance on coarse-grained patterns rather than fine-grained semantic reasoning. In contrast, Qwen-2.5-0.5B was the most fragile model, with small lexical changes leading to large shifts in sentiment predictions. While all models produced deterministic outputs across repeated inference runs, our analysis shows that inference stability can mask consistent misclassification. Furthermore, adding intensifiers revealed differences in compositional semantic understanding. Mistral maintained high confidence across most perturbations, Qwen displayed extreme sensitivity, and Gemma remained uniformly confident, which may indicate oversmoothing.

Overall, this study demonstrates that high sentiment accuracy alone is insufficient for financial AI systems. The findings highlight that different LLMs exhibit distinct reasoning styles and sensitivities. Future research directions could focus on evaluating the proposed approach with larger and more diverse financial datasets to improve generalization. Additionally, expanding the experimental scope to induce more samples to understand the model behavior in larger LLMs, extending to multi-modal financial analysis, developing adaptive perturbation strategies for improved efficiency, and introducing causal verification techniques to distinguish true causal token contributions from purely correlational attributions.

Code Availability. The code for reproducing the experiments is publicly available at: Code

Disclosure of Interests. All authors have no conflicts of interest.

References

1. Adhikari, S., Thapa, S., Naseem, U., Lu, H.Y., Bharathy, G., Prasad, M.: Explainable hybrid word representations for sentiment analysis of financial news. Neural Netw. **164**, 115–123 (2023). https://doi.org/10.1016/j.neunet.2023.04.011
2. Aslansefat, K., Hashemian, M., Walker, M., Akram, M.N., Sorokos, I., Papadopoulos, Y.: Explaining black boxes with a SMILE: statistical model-agnostic interpretability with local explanations. IEEE Softw. **41**(1), 87–97 (2023)
3. Dehghani, Z., Aslansefat, K., Khan, A., Akram, M.N.: Explainability of large language models using SMILE: statistical model-agnostic interpretability with local explanations. arXiv preprint arXiv:2505.21657 (2025)
4. Dehghani, Z., Aslansefat, K., Khan, A., Rivera, A.R., George, F., Khalid, M.: Mapping the mind of an instruction-based image editing using smile. arXiv preprint arXiv:2412.16277 (2024)

5. Dimino, F., Saxena, K., Sarmah, B., Pasquali, S.: Tracing positional bias in financial decision-making: mechanistic insights from qwen2. 5. In: Proceedings of the 6th ACM International Conference on AI in Finance, pp. 96–104 (2025)
6. Golpayegani, D., et al.: AI cards: towards an applied framework for machine-readable AI and risk documentation inspired by the EU AI Act (2024)
7. Guidotti, R., Monreale, A., Ruggieri, S., Turini, F., Giannotti, F., Pedreschi, D.: Local rule-based explanations of black box decision systems. arXiv preprint arXiv:1805.10820 (2018)
8. Hogenboom, A., Frasincar, F., de Jong, F.M.G., Kaymak, U.: Using rhetorical structure in sentiment analysis. Commun. ACM **58**(7), 69–77 (2015). https://doi.org/10.1145/2699418
9. Hong, C., He, Q.: Integrating financial knowledge for explainable stock market sentiment analysis via query-guided attention. Appl. Sci. **15**(12), 6893 (2025). https://doi.org/10.3390/app15126893
10. Limonad, L., Fournier, F., Vera Díaz, J.M., Skarbovsky, I., Gur, S., Lazcano, R.: Monetizing currency pair sentiments through LLM explainability. arXiv preprint arXiv:2407.19922 (2024). https://doi.org/10.48550/arXiv.2407.19922
11. Liu, Z., Huang, D., Huang, K., Li, Z., Zhao, J.: FinBERT: a pre-trained financial language representation model for financial text mining. In: Proceedings of the Twenty-Ninth International Joint Conference on Artificial Intelligence (IJCAI 2020), pp. 4513–4519 (2020). https://doi.org/10.24963/IJCAI.2020/622
12. Lundberg, S.M., Lee, S.I.: A unified approach to interpreting model predictions. Curran Associates, Inc. (2017). http://papers.nips.cc/paper/7062-a-unified-approach-to-interpreting-model-predictions.pdf
13. Luss, R., Miehling, E., Dhurandhar, A.: CELL your model: contrastive explanations for large language models. arXiv preprint arXiv:2406.11785 (2024)
14. Malo, P., Sinha, A., Korhonen, P., Wallenius, J., Takala, P.: Good debt or bad debt: detecting semantic orientations in economic texts. J. Am. Soc. Inf. Sci. **65**, 782–796 (2014)
15. Manakul, P., Liusie, A., Gales, M.: SelfCheckGPT: zero-resource black-box hallucination detection for generative large language models. In: Proceedings of the 2023 Conference on Empirical Methods in Natural Language Processing (EMNLP), pp. 9004–9017 (2023)
16. Mihaila, G.: Learning to explain: supervised token attribution from transformer attention patterns. arXiv preprint arXiv:2601.14112 (2026)
17. Moghaddam, Z.Z., et al.: Explainable knowledge graph retrieval-augmented generation (KG-RAG) with KG-smile. arXiv preprint arXiv:2509.03626 (2025)
18. Sharma, P., Susan, S.: Holistic evaluation of 7b-scale LLMs for sentiment analysis: accuracy meets explainability, pp. 29–36 (2025)
19. Tatsat, H., Shater, A.: Beyond the black box: interpretability of LLMs in finance. arXiv preprint arXiv:2505.24650 (2025)
20. Team, G., et al.: Gemma 3 technical report (2025)
21. Zhang, W., Deng, Y., Liu, B., Pan, S., Bing, L.: Sentiment analysis in the era of large language models: a reality check, pp. 3881–3906 (2024)

Attention-Pruned SHAP: Accelerating SHAP-Based Explainability with Attention-Guided Feature Pruning

Hamza Shafik, Ahmed Sherif[✉], and Caroline Sabty

German International University, New Administrative Capital, Egypt
`hamza.shafik@student.giu-uni.de`, `ahmed.sherif@giu-uni.de`,
`caroline.sabty@giu-uni.de`

Abstract. Transformer-based models achieve strong predictive performance across natural language processing tasks but remain difficult to interpret. In sentiment analysis and other user-facing applications, understanding token-level contributions is essential for building trust and supporting model debugging. Perturbation-based methods such as SHAP provide theoretically grounded feature attributions; however, their computational cost grows rapidly with sentence length, making token-level explanations expensive in practice. We propose Attention-Pruned SHAP, a hybrid explanation method in which attention scores serve as a prefilter, selecting a subset of candidate tokens on which SHAP is actually computed, assigning zero contribution to pruned tokens. We introduce fixed pruning strategies based on global top-k and top-p thresholds, as well as an adaptive, length-aware variant that adjusts pruning strength according to sentence length, preserving the perturbation-based semantics of SHAP while reducing the effective feature dimensionality. We evaluate raw attention, full KernelSHAP, and the proposed pruning variants on Arabic social media sentiment classification using both rank-based and distributional similarity metrics: Spearman rank correlation, cosine similarity, top-5 token overlap, and Jensen–Shannon divergence, alongside runtime measurements. Results show that the adaptive variant in particular achieves strong agreement with full KernelSHAP while meaningfully reducing computational cost, offering a practical path toward scalable token-level explainability in Transformer-based NLP.

Keywords: Explainable AI · SHAP · Attention Mechanisms · Sentiment Analysis · Arabic NLP · Code-Switching · Token Attribution · Transformer Models

1 Introduction

Transformer-based models have become the dominant architecture for sentiment analysis, particularly in social media settings, and have shown strong performance for morphologically rich and dialectally diverse languages such as Arabic

[1, 12, 13]. Through self-attention, these models capture long-range dependencies and contextual cues such as negation, intensifiers, code-switching, and emojis. Despite their predictive accuracy, they remain difficult to interpret: when a model classifies an Arabic tweet as negative, it is often unclear which tokens drove the decision. Explainable artificial intelligence (XAI) addresses this opacity by producing human-interpretable explanations of model predictions. In sentiment analysis, explanations are typically defined at the token level, assigning each token a contribution score for the predicted label. Such explanations support debugging, detection of spurious correlations, and improved trust in automated systems, especially in user-facing or high-stakes applications [2, 8].

Existing XAI methods for NLP fall into several families. Gradient-based approaches, including Gradient $\times$ Input and Integrated Gradients, compute attributions efficiently through backpropagation, but can be sensitive to nonlinearities in the network and may produce unstable or noisy attributions, particularly in deep Transformer architectures [9]. Perturbation-based methods, such as occlusion and LIME, take a more direct approach by measuring prediction changes under feature removal; however, they require many model evaluations, and their results can depend heavily on the choice of masking strategy [8]. SHapley Additive exPlanations (SHAP) offers a more principled framework, grounded in Shapley values from cooperative game theory, and satisfies desirable axiomatic properties such as local accuracy and consistency [2]. At the token level, however, SHAP scales poorly: the feature space grows with sentence length, and even approximate variants such as KernelSHAP become computationally expensive when applied to Transformer models over longer inputs.

Attention weights are often used as a lightweight proxy for explanations, since they are readily available during the forward pass at negligible additional cost [5–7]. However, attention reflects internal information routing rather than the causal effect of removing a token, and different attention patterns can produce identical predictions [14]. Raw attention, therefore, cannot reliably substitute for perturbation-based explanations, even if it carries useful structural signal about which tokens the model focuses on.

This work combines these perspectives. Instead of treating attention as a final explanation or relying solely on expensive perturbation methods, we use attention as a structural prior to guide where SHAP is applied. We develop a token-level explainability framework for a Transformer-based Arabic sentiment classifier, adopting KernelSHAP as the reference explanation method while extracting aggregated token-level saliency scores from multi-head self-attention.

We introduce Attention-Pruned SHAP, a hybrid explanation method where attention scores are used to select a subset of candidate tokens before running KernelSHAP. SHAP is then computed only within this reduced feature space, and pruned tokens are assigned zero contribution. We explore two fixed pruning strategies based on global top-k and top-p thresholds, as well as an adaptive length-aware strategy that adjusts the pruning strength based on sentence length, ensuring that shorter sentences are not over-pruned while longer ones benefit from greater dimensionality reduction.

We evaluate the proposed methods on Egyptian Arabic–English code-switched social media data [11]. Agreement with full KernelSHAP is measured using Spearman's rank correlation, cosine similarity, Jensen–Shannon divergence, Top-5 token overlap, and runtime per example. Full KernelSHAP requires 13.24 s per instance on average. Raw attention shows only weak alignment with SHAP (Spearman's p = 0.26; JSD = 0.51), confirming that attention alone is not a reliable causal explanation. In contrast, adaptive Attention-Pruned SHAP achieves Spearman correlations up to 0.53 and cosine similarity around 0.81 while reducing total runtime by roughly 18% relative to full SHAP. Fixed pruning strategies show a predictable speed–fidelity trade-off, with higher pruning yielding faster explanations at modest loss in agreement.

These results demonstrate that internal attention signals can be used to make perturbation-based explanations more efficient while maintaining strong fidelity to full SHAP, providing a practical path toward scalable token-level explainability in Transformer-based NLP models.

2   Related Work

This section reviews prior work relevant to XAI in natural language processing, with a particular focus on token-level explanations. We first summarize major families of explanation techniques proposed for neural NLP models. We then review existing work on SHAP-based feature attribution and the use of attention as an explanation mechanism. Finally, we discuss explainability research in Arabic sentiment analysis and highlight gaps that motivate the present study.

2.1   Explainable AI for NLP

Explainability methods for neural NLP models can be grouped into several families. Perturbation-based methods, such as SHAP [2], measure how the output changes when features are removed or masked. Gradient-based methods, including Gradients × Input [10] and Integrated Gradients [9], use information from backpropagation to estimate how sensitive the prediction is to each input. Attention-based methods interpret the model's own attention weights as a form of importance.

In the context of token-level explanations, perturbation-based methods are often considered more faithful, since they directly observe the changes that happen to the prediction when tokens are added or removed. However, they are computationally heavy because they require many forward passes per input. Gradient-based methods are typically very fast, but they may be noisy. Attention-based explanations are attractive because attention is available "for free" after a forward pass, but some might argue whether attention can be interpreted as an explanation or not [24].

2.2 SHAP and Feature Attribution

SHAP is a general framework for feature attribution based on Shapley values from cooperative game theory [2]. Shapley values assign an importance score to each feature by averaging its marginal contribution across all possible subsets of features, resulting in explanations that satisfy desirable theoretical properties such as local accuracy, missingness, and consistency [15]. In practice, computing Shapley values exactly is infeasible for most real-world models due to the exponential number of feature coalitions. To address this, several approximations have been proposed. One widely used variant is KernelSHAP, a model-agnostic method that treats features as either present or absent and estimates their contributions by sampling binary masks. It is evaluated on these masked inputs, and a weighted linear regression is fitted in the space of coalition indicators to recover approximate Shapley values [2,16,23].

SHAP-based methods have been applied to a variety of machine learning models, including deep neural networks and Transformer architectures, and are often regarded as among the most faithful explanation techniques because they explicitly measure how predictions change under feature perturbations [17,18]. However, prior work consistently highlights their high computational cost, especially in NLP settings. When features correspond to tokens, the dimensionality of the feature space grows with sentence length, leading to a rapid increase in the number of required model evaluations. Even with sampling-based approximations, KernelSHAP can become prohibitively slow for long sequences, motivating research into more efficient variants and acceleration strategies such as amortized or sequence-aware Shapley value estimation [20,21].

2.3 Attention as Explanation

Self-attention provides a natural mechanism for inspecting how neural models distribute focus across tokens during prediction. As a result, several studies have proposed interpreting attention weights directly as importance scores, treating them as explanations for model decisions. Early work demonstrated that attention maps could highlight relevant regions or tokens associated with generated outputs [5]. Subsequent approaches extended this idea to text classification models, where attention weights were used to rank words and sentences by their estimated importance [6,7]. However, attention is a mechanism inside the model and does not define what would happen if a token were removed. For this reason, using raw attention as a causal explanation may be problematic.

2.4 Explainability for Arabic Sentiment Analysis

Arabic sentiment analysis faces additional challenges compared to English: dialectal variation, code-switching, and the noisy nature of written social media content [19]. Recent work on explainable AI for NLP highlights the importance of transparent, token-level explanations for sentiment analysis tasks, emphasizing that post-hoc interpretability methods can reveal which linguistic elements most strongly influence model decisions [22]. Nevertheless, comprehensive evaluations of these methods on Arabic and code-switched sentiment datasets remain scarce, especially for dialectal and noisy social media text. This gap motivates further research into explainability techniques that are better aligned with the linguistic and sociocultural characteristics of Arabic sentiment expression.

3   Transformer-Based Sentiment Classifier

The sentiment classifier used in this work is based on the Transformer architecture [11], which presents an evaluation of several models for Egyptian Arabic–English code-switched sentiment analysis, including a BiLSTM-Attention model, a Hybrid-Transformer model, and large language models. In this work, only the Transformer-based model is adopted, implemented in TensorFlow/Keras as an encoder-only Transformer. The model begins with an embedding layer that maps input token IDs to continuous vector representations, followed by positional encodings to retain information about token order. The core of the architecture is a custom Transformer block that applies multi-head self-attention followed by a position-wise feed-forward network, both wrapped with residual connections and normalization. After this block processes the sequence, a pooling operation aggregates the token representations into a single sentence-level vector. This vector is then passed to a classification head that produces three logits corresponding to positive, neutral, and negative sentiment.

Within the Transformer block, the multi-head attention module exposes the final attention tensor with shape $[B, H, T_q, T_k]$, where B is the batch size, H the number of attention heads, and T_q and T_k the query and key lengths. The module also tracks padding masks for both queries and keys, ensuring that attention scores are computed only for valid tokens and not for padding positions.

4   Attention-Based Token Saliency

The first XAI approach explored in this work relies directly on the model's internal attention patterns. Self-attention provides a structured view of how the model distributes focus across tokens when processing a sentence. Each layer produces attention weights that describe which tokens influence one another and to what extent.

4.1   Extracting Attention Weights

During a forward pass, the multi-head attention module produces an attention tensor

$$A \in \mathbb{R}^{B \times H \times T_q \times T_k} \tag{1}$$

Equation (1) defines the full attention tensor produced by the multi-head attention module. Each entry $A_{b,h,i,j}$ represents how strongly the i-th query token attends to the j-th key token in head h for a given example b. The model also maintains padding masks that distinguish real tokens from padding tokens in both the query and key dimensions. For each example b, the slice $A_b \in \mathbb{R}^{H \times T_q \times T_k}$ is extracted and then reduced to contain only valid (non-padding) positions before computing token-level importance.

4.2   Aggregating Per-Token Scores

The goal is to convert the high-dimensional attention representation into a single importance score for each token. Attention scores in a multi-head self-attention layer are the result of interactions between query and key representations: each entry $A_{b,h,i,j}$ reflects how strongly the i-th query token attends to the j-th key token in head h. To obtain a token-level importance score, we therefore average over query positions, summarizing how collectively attended each key token is across all valid queries in the sequence. Formally, after selecting valid (non-padding) indices from the padding masks, the reduced tensor $A'_b \in \mathbb{R}^{H \times T_q^{\mathrm{valid}} \times T_k^{\mathrm{valid}}}$ is averaged across all valid query positions to obtain a matrix of shape $[H, T_k^{\mathrm{valid}}]$. This captures how strongly the full set of queries, taken together, focuses on each key position. Averaging across attention heads then produces a single vector $a \in \mathbb{R}^{T_k^{\mathrm{valid}}}$, which is normalized to sum to one. This normalized vector represents a probability-like distribution over valid tokens and serves both as an attention-only explanation and as the guiding signal for the pruning strategies described in Sect. 6. Padding positions are assigned zero importance and mapped back to their original locations in the full sequence.

4.3   Attention as a Saliency Signal

The attention-based importance scores are cheap to compute. They basically require only a single forward pass and some tensor operations. However, they should not be interpreted as causal explanations because they do not encode how the prediction changes when a token is removed. In this work, attention is treated as a signal to guide SHAP toward the most promising tokens, rather than as a substitute for SHAP.

5   KernelSHAP as the Reference Method

The second XAI technique is KernelSHAP. We used it as the main baseline for token-level explanations. Each sentence is represented as a sequence of T tokens, including padding, and every non-padding token is treated as an individual feature. A binary mask vector $m \in \{0,1\}^T$ specifies which tokens are considered present and which are masked. Applying a mask simply replaces the embeddings of masked tokens with zero vectors, while the remaining tokens and all model parameters are left unchanged.

The explanation target is defined as the model's predicted sentiment class for the original unmasked input. Given this target, KernelSHAP constructs a local surrogate model around the corresponding prediction. It does so by sampling multiple binary masks in the T-dimensional feature space, evaluating the sentiment classifier on the corresponding masked inputs, and using these evaluations to fit a weighted linear regression that approximates how the model's output varies as a function of the mask. The resulting regression coefficients serve as the SHAP values, giving one importance score per token and indicating how each token contributes—positively or negatively—to the chosen class. This produces a token-level importance vector of length T for every example.

5.1   Baseline Implementation

To apply SHAP over the development set, we implemented a helper function to convert a batch of binary masks into masked token embeddings and run them through the classifier, returning the scalar logit for the predicted class. SHAP was then computed on the first 50 development examples to maintain manageable runtimes during experimentation. All token-level SHAP values were written to CSV, with one row per token containing the example index, token index, and corresponding SHAP value. This full SHAP configuration serves as the reference method against which attention-based and pruned-SHAP explanations are evaluated throughout this work.

6   Attention-Pruned SHAP

Combining the advantages of the first and second XAI techniques, we implemented the third XAI technique, Attention-Pruned SHAP. Full KernelSHAP treats all tokens as potential features. For an input with T tokens, SHAP operates in a T-dimensional feature space and requires sampling many combinations of tokens. This process becomes computationally expensive as T grows. In practice, many tokens (e.g., stopwords, punctuation, and padding artifacts) have almost no impact on the final prediction.

The key idea of Attention-Pruned SHAP is to use attention to select a subset of tokens on which SHAP will operate. We used attention as it may highlight key sentiment words. SHAP is then run in a lower-dimensional space, and its outputs are lifted back to the original token space by assigning zero to pruned tokens. This way, SHAP remains the causal explainer, and attention guides it to the tokens that might matter.

6.1   Formulation

The Attention-Pruned SHAP framework makes token-level explanations more practical by using the model's internal attention signals to simplify the feature attribution process. Initially, the system identifies a subset of influential tokens to keep based on their attention scores, which allows it to filter out low-impact elements like punctuation or padding. Perturbation-based evaluations are then conducted only within this smaller group; binary masks are applied to these "kept" tokens to observe how the model's prediction changes, while all pruned tokens are held at a constant zero-embedding state. After fitting a local surrogate model to these samples, the resulting coefficients are mapped back to the original sequence. Tokens excluded during the initial pruning phase are assigned an importance score of zero. This mechanism is used with two pruning strategies: a fixed strategy that applies global rules to all sentences, and an adaptive strategy that adjusts pruning based on sentence length.

6.2   Fixed Attention-Pruned SHAP

In the fixed setting, the same pruning rule is applied to all sentences, regardless of their length. Two natural strategies are implemented.

Top-k Pruning.

Tokens are sorted in descending order of attention score, and the top k tokens are kept. To prevent degenerate cases—such as keeping too few tokens or exceeding the sentence length—the selected value of k is constrained by lower and upper bounds:

$$k^\star = \min\left(\max(\min\_tokens, k), \max\_tokens, T_{\text{actual}}\right) \tag{2}$$

where T_{actual} is the number of non-padding tokens in the input.

Equation (2) ensures that the pruning rule behaves sensibly across sentences of different lengths. The inner max enforces a minimum number of kept tokens so that pruning never becomes too aggressive, while the outer min guarantees that the algorithm never selects more tokens than the allowed upper bound or more tokens than actually exist in the sentence. After determining $k^\star$, the first $k^\star$ tokens in the attention-ranked list form the kept set used for SHAP.

Top-p Pruning. Tokens are sorted in descending order of attention, and the smallest prefix of tokens whose cumulative attention mass reaches a threshold p is kept. The final number of tokens is bounded as before. This strategy keeps all tokens that together carry at least a fraction p of the attention mass.

In both modes, padding positions are excluded by inspecting the original token sequence length for each example. The output of the selection function for each example is the list of kept indices K.

SHAP in the Reduced Feature Space. Once the influential token subset K is identified, the feature attribution process is restricted to this lower-dimensional space to improve efficiency. The algorithm generates samples by toggling only the retained tokens on or off via binary coalition vectors, while all pruned tokens remain in a constant zero-embedding state. By evaluating the model's predictions across these specific combinations, KernelSHAP fits a weighted linear surrogate model to determine the precise contribution of each kept token. These calculated values are subsequently mapped back to their original positions in the full sequence, with all pruned positions assigned a formal importance score of zero. All the metadata needed for analysis is saved. This includes the number of real tokens per sentence, the number of kept tokens, the pruning ratio, and the runtime per example.

6.3 Adaptive Attention-Pruned SHAP

The fixed pruning strategy treats every sentence the same, regardless of its length. In practice, this creates a mismatch between pruning strength and the actual amount of text available. A sentence of five tokens has almost nothing that can be removed, while a sentence of thirty tokens contains far more redundancy. The adaptive variant addresses this by allowing the pruning behavior to depend on sentence length.

Adaptive pruning addresses the limitations of fixed strategies by adjusting pruning strength based on sentence length. The framework partitions inputs into four distinct length buckets (very short, short, medium, and long), each assigned a specific cumulative attention threshold and a range for allowable token counts. For a given input, tokens are ranked by their attention scores and selected until the threshold is met, after which the count is clamped within the bucket's predefined bounds to prevent overly aggressive pruning in short sentences or insufficient reduction in long ones. This length-aware mechanism ensures that the most informative tokens are prioritized for KernelSHAP analysis, significantly improving the trade-off between computational efficiency and explanation fidelity compared to global fixed rules.

7 Experimental Setup and Results

This section describes the experimental setup, evaluation metrics, and results of comparing the proposed Attention-Pruned SHAP variants against raw attention and full KernelSHAP.

7.1 Dataset and Experimental Setup

The experiments utilize the Egyptian Arabic–English code-switched sentiment dataset, adopting the same preprocessing, normalization, and tokenization pipeline established [11]. The dataset follows the original train–development split, where the training set is used to train the classifier and the development set supports both model selection and explainability analysis. The classifier implements the Hybrid Transformer architecture [11], utilizing cross-entropy loss and the Adam optimizer with hyperparameters mirroring the original configuration. After training, the model parameters are frozen to ensure that all explanation methods are evaluated on the same classifier. The sole modification is to instrument the multi-head attention module to expose attention tensors during the forward pass; all other components remain unchanged.

To keep runtimes manageable, explainability experiments are carried out on a subset of the development set. In this work, the first fifty development examples are used, covering a mix of short and long sentences and a range of code-switched structures typical of social media text. All examples pass through the same preprocessing pipeline as in the original study, ensuring consistency between training and evaluation.

A set of explanation methods is applied to each selected sentence to generate token-level importance scores for the model's predicted class. Full KernelSHAP serves as the reference baseline, evaluated over the entire token sequence, while the Raw Attention method uses normalized importance vectors derived directly from the model's multi-head attention weights. The Fixed Attention-Pruned SHAP variant restricts computation to global sets of high-attention tokens using Top-k ($k \in \{10, 7, 5\}$) and Top-p ($p \in \{0.98, 0.95, 0.90\}$) strategies with global bounds (min tokens $= 3$, max tokens $= 15$). The adaptive pruning framework partitions inputs into four length buckets, each assigned a cumulative attention threshold p and minimum/maximum token-count bounds. The rationale is length-driven: very short sentences (≤ 5 tokens) have negligible redundancy, so p is set close to 1.0 and at most one token is pruned; short sentences (6–10 tokens) permit slightly more pruning while retaining most tokens; medium sentences (11–20 tokens) support moderate reduction with a capped maximum; and long sentences (≥ 21 tokens) benefit most from pruning, with a lower p and tighter bounds to enforce meaningful dimensionality reduction. The Conservative, Medium, and Aggressive configurations vary these parameters uniformly across all buckets, producing a controlled speed–fidelity spectrum. The specific values in Table 1 are heuristically chosen based on the length distribution of the dataset and adjusted empirically to balance pruning strength against explanation fidelity.

Table 1. Parameters for Adaptive Pruning Configurations

Bucket (L)	Conservative			Medium			Aggressive		
	p	min	max	p	min	max	p	min	max
V. Short (≤ 5)	0.99	$L-1$	L	0.99	$L-1$	L	0.98	$L-2$	$L-1$
Short (6–10)	0.98	7	$L-1$	0.97	6	$L-2$	0.95	5	$L-3$
Medium (11–20)	0.97	9	20	0.95	8	18	0.92	7	15
Long (≥ 21)	0.93	12	24	0.90	10	22	0.88	8	18

7.2 Evaluation Metrics

To compare the different explanation methods against full SHAP, several metrics are used. Spearman's rank correlation captures how similarly two methods order tokens by importance, while cosine similarity measures the angular agreement between their importance vectors. The top-5 overlap focuses on the most influential tokens by computing the fraction of positions shared in the top five tokens selected by each method. Jensen-Shannon divergence treats each normalized importance vector as a probability distribution and measures how different these distributions are. Finally, the runtime per example records the wall-clock time required to compute a single explanation, allowing an estimate of the speed gains achieved through pruning. All metrics are computed per-example and then averaged to produce aggregate results. For attention-only explanations, attention scores are substituted for SHAP values in all calculations.

7.3 Results and Analysis

This section evaluates how closely attention-based methods approximate full KernelSHAP and the amount of computation they save. All results are computed on 50 development examples with an average of 13.0 non-padding tokens per sentence. Full KernelSHAP requires 13.24 s per example (around 662 s total) and serves as the reference point for evaluating similarity and runtime. Four families of explanation methods are compared: raw attention, fixed top-k pruning, fixed top-p pruning, and three variants of adaptive pruning. All metrics measure similarity to full SHAP for the model's predicted class.

Raw Attention vs. Full SHAP. Raw attention provides only limited agreement with SHAP. Its Spearman correlation with SHAP is 0.26, cosine similarity is 0.45, the Top-5 overlap is 0.59, and the Jensen–Shannon divergence (JSD) is high at 0.51. The relatively weak alignment confirms that attention alone does not reliably reflect SHAP-style causal importance, justifying the need for SHAP-guided or hybrid approaches. Table 2 summarizes the results.

Table 2. Raw Attention vs. Full KernelSHAP (50 examples).

Metric	Value
Spearman correlation	0.26
Cosine similarity	0.45
Top-5 token overlap	0.59
Jensen–Shannon div.	0.51

Fixed Top-k Pruning. Top-k pruning keeps the k most attended tokens and assigns SHAP only to those. Larger k improves agreement but increases runtime, while smaller k accelerates computation at the expense of fidelity. The trend is monotonic: $k = 10$ achieves the strongest correlation (Spearman 0.52; cosine 0.81) and the lowest JSD (0.24), whereas $k = 5$ provides the fastest runtimes (457 s total) but weaker agreement. These results confirm that controlling k provides a simple and predictable speed–quality trade-off (Table 3).

Fixed Top-p Pruning. Top-p pruning keeps the fewest tokens whose cumulative attention mass exceeds a threshold p. As with Top-k, larger p retains more signal, yields stronger agreement, but reduces pruning. The effect is slightly smoother than in the Top-k case because p adapts to the shape of the attention

Table 3. Agreement and runtime for Fixed Top-k pruning strategies.

Top-k	Spearman	Cosine	Top-5	JSD	Avg. Kept	Total Time (s)
10	0.52	0.81	0.66	0.24	7.7	563.14
7	0.50	0.78	0.63	0.26	6.1	509.45
5	0.49	0.76	0.59	0.30	4.7	457.40

distribution. The highest threshold ($p = 0.98$) provides the strongest correlation (Spearman 0.54) and low divergence (JSD 0.24), although it approaches the computational cost of full SHAP. Lower thresholds, such as $p = 0.90$, reduce runtime but yield weaker alignment (Table 4).

Table 4. Agreement and runtime for Fixed Top-p pruning strategies.

Top-p	Spearman	Cosine	Top-5	JSD	Avg. Kept	Total Time (s)
0.98	0.54	0.81	0.65	0.24	8.9	578.61
0.95	0.51	0.78	0.61	0.27	7.9	553.31
0.90	0.48	0.75	0.55	0.30	6.4	531.49

Adaptive Pruning. Adaptive pruning assigns different $(p, \min, \max)$ values depending on sentence length, allowing shorter sentences to keep nearly all tokens and longer sentences to be pruned more aggressively. This yields the most robust speed–quality trade-off among all techniques. Three adaptive configurations were evaluated: Conservative, Medium, and Aggressive. The medium configuration provides the best balance, achieving Spearman ≈ 0.53, cosine similarity ≈ 0.81, Top-5 overlap ≈ 0.66, and JSD ≈ 0.24, with a total runtime of 542.91 s. This improves fidelity over fixed-top-k and fixed-top-p methods operating at similar cost (Table 5).

Table 5. Agreement and runtime for Adaptive Attention-Pruned SHAP.

Config.	Spearman	Cosine	Top-5	JSD	Avg. Kept	Total Time (s)
Conservative	0.54	0.82	0.64	0.24	9.2	550.53
Medium	0.53	0.81	0.66	0.24	8.2	542.91
Aggressive	0.50	0.78	0.61	0.27	7.1	518.33

8   Discussion

In this section, we discuss the implications of our findings. The experiments confirm that perturbation-based explainability in high-dimensional token spaces is computationally demanding, particularly for morphologically rich and variable-length inputs such as Arabic social media text. While KernelSHAP provides faithful local attributions, its cost scales poorly with sequence length, motivating the need for more efficient alternatives.

A key observation is that attention alone is not a reliable measure of causal token influence. Its weak correlation and high Jensen–Shannon divergence relative to KernelSHAP are consistent with prior findings in the literature [14], reinforcing that attention weights should not be treated as explanations in themselves. However, this does not make attention uninformative; its value lies in capturing where the model focuses its computation, which can be exploited as a structural prior to guide SHAP toward a smaller, more relevant feature space.

The fixed pruning strategies reveal a predictable trade-off: retaining more tokens improves fidelity at the cost of runtime. In our experiments, fixed pruning reduced SHAP runtime by approximately 15–30%, depending on the threshold, but stronger pruning settings led to a noticeable drop in alignment with full SHAP. The adaptive strategy breaks this rigidity by conditioning pruning strength on sentence length, it reduced SHAP runtime by roughly 15–20% while achieving better fidelity at comparable runtimes to the fixed strategy. Together, these results suggest that combining internal model signals with perturbation-based reasoning is a practical and principled direction for scalable token-level explainability.

9   Limitations

Several methodological considerations should be kept in mind when interpreting these findings. As with any explainability study, results are influenced by the underlying model's attention distributions, which may vary across architectures and pretraining objectives. Dataset characteristics such as sentence length, domain, and dialect also shape token importance patterns, and broader evaluation across Arabic varieties remains an open direction.

The pruning hyperparameters, including top-k, top-p, and adaptive bucket boundaries, were selected empirically, and different configurations may shift the speed–fidelity trade-off. KernelSHAP results are sensitive to the number of sampled masks and to the masking baseline, both of which are known sources of variance in perturbation-based explanation methods. Finally, the framework operates at the token level; subword, span, or concept-level explanations may capture complementary aspects of model behavior and are left for future work.

10   Conclusion and Future Work

This work presents a hybrid explainability framework for Transformer-based Arabic sentiment analysis that uses token-level attention to prune the SHAP feature space before computing perturbation-based attributions. The proposed Attention-Pruned SHAP variants reduce computational cost while maintaining strong fidelity to full KernelSHAP, with the adaptive strategy consistently achieving the best balance between runtime and agreement. Experiments on Egyptian Arabic–English code-switched social media data show that adaptive pruning achieves Spearman correlations up to 0.53 and cosine similarity around 0.81 with full KernelSHAP, while reducing runtime by approximately 18%, with fixed pruning strategies offering a predictable speed–fidelity trade-off.

Several directions are worth exploring in future work. The pruning heuristics could be tested on larger or domain-specific Arabic Transformer models to assess their generalizability. Rather than using fixed or heuristic-based pruning, learning the selection policy directly through gating mechanisms, differentiable token selection, or reinforcement learning, could yield further efficiency gains. Incorporating complementary signals such as gradients or morphological features may also improve pruning decisions for morphologically rich languages like Arabic.

References

1. Vaswani, A., et al.: Attention is all you need. In: Advances in Neural Information Processing Systems (NeurIPS) (2017)
2. Lundberg, S.M., Lee, S.-I.: A unified approach to interpreting model predictions. In: Advances in Neural Information Processing Systems (NeurIPS) (2017)
3. Jain, S., Wallace, B.C.: Attention is not explanation. In: Proceedings of the 2019 Conference of the North American Chapter of the Association for Computational Linguistics (NAACL) (2019)
4. Serrano, S., Smith, N.A.: Is attention interpretable? In: Proceedings of the 57th Annual Meeting of the Association for Computational Linguistics (ACL) (2019)
5. Xu, K., et al.: Show, attend and tell: neural image caption generation with visual attention. In: Proceedings of the 32nd International Conference on Machine Learning (ICML) (2015)
6. Yang, Z., Yang, D., Dyer, C., He, X., Smola, A., Hovy, E.: Hierarchical attention networks for document classification. In: Proceedings of the 2016 Conference of the North American Chapter of the Association for Computational Linguistics (NAACL) (2016)
7. Lin, Z., et al.: A structured self-attentive sentence embedding. In: Proceedings of the 5th International Conference on Learning Representations (ICLR) (2017)
8. Ribeiro, M.T., Singh, S., Guestrin, C.: "Why should i trust you?": explaining the predictions of any classifier. In: Proceedings of the 22nd ACM SIGKDD International Conference on Knowledge Discovery and Data Mining (KDD) (2016)
9. Sundararajan, M., Taly, A., Yan, Q.: Axiomatic attribution for deep networks. In: Proceedings of the 34th International Conference on Machine Learning (ICML) (2017)
10. Shrikumar, A., Greenside, P., Kundaje, A.: Learning important features through propagating activation differences. In: Proceedings of the 34th International Conference on Machine Learning (ICML) (2017)
11. Sherif, A., Sabty, C.: Sentiment analysis for Egyptian Arabic-English code-switched data using traditional neural models and advanced language models. In: Speech and Computer (SPECOM), Lecture Notes in Computer Science, vol. 15300. Springer, Cham (2025). https://doi.org/10.1007/978-3-031-78014-1_5

12. Antoun, W., Baly, F., Hajj, H.: AraBERT: transformer-based model for Arabic language understanding. In: Proceedings of the 4th Workshop on Open-Source Arabic Corpora and Processing Tools (2020)
13. Abdul-Mageed, M., Elmadany, A., Nagoudi, E.M.B.: ARBERT & MARBERT: deep bidirectional transformers for Arabic In: Proceedings of the 59th Annual Meeting of the Association for Computational Linguistics and the 11th International Joint Conference on Natural Language Processing (2021)
14. Jain, S., Wallace, B.C.: Attention is not explanation. In: Proceedings of the 2019 Conference of the North American Chapter of the Association for Computational Linguistics, pp. 3543–3556 (2019)
15. Štrumbelj, E., Kononenko, I.: Explaining prediction models and individual predictions with feature contributions. Knowl. Inf. Syst. **41**, 647–665 (2014)
16. Covert, I., Lundberg, S.M., Lee, S.-I.: Understanding global feature contributions through additive importance measures. In Proceedings of the 34th International Conference on Neural Information Processing Systems (2020)
17. Linardatos, P., Papastefanopoulos, V., Kotsiantis, S.: Explainable AI: a review of machine learning interpretability methods. Entropy **23**(1), 18 (2020)
18. Yang, C., et al.: Efficient Shapley values estimation by amortization for text classification. In: Proceedings of the 61st Annual Meeting of the Association for Computational Linguistics (ACL) (2023)
19. Hamed, I., Sabty, C., Abdennadher, S., Vu, N.T., Solorio, T., Habash, N.: A survey of code-switched Arabic NLP: progress, challenges, and future directions. In: Proceedings of the 31st International Conference on Computational Linguistics, pp. 4561–4585 (2025)
20. Pan, D., et al.: Fast explanations via policy gradient-optimized explainer. In: Proceedings of the 34th International Joint Conference on Artificial Intelligence (IJCAI) (2025)
21. Nayebi, A., Tipirneni, S., Reddy, C.K., Foreman, B.: WindowSHAP: an efficient framework for explaining time-series classifiers based on Shapley values. arXiv preprint arXiv:2211.06507 (2022)
22. Elkharrat, F., Ghoniem, M., Sherif, A., Sabty, C.: Explainable AI for NLP: enhancing transparency in sentiment analysis and named entity recognition. In: Natural Language Processing and Information Systems: 30th International Conference on Applications of Natural Language to Information Systems, NLDB 2025, Kanazawa, Japan, July 4–6, 2025, Proceedings, Part II, pp. 116–127. Springer, Berlin, Heidelberg (2025). https://doi.org/10.1007/978-3-031-97144-0_11
23. Lundberg, S.M., et al.: Explainable AI for trees: from local explanations to global understanding. arXiv preprint arXiv:1905.04610 (2019)
24. Bastings, J., Filippova, K.: The Elephant in the interpretability room: why use attention as explanation when we have saliency methods? In: Proceedings of the Third BlackboxNLP Workshop on Analyzing and Interpreting Neural Networks for NLP, pp. 149–155. Association for Computational Linguistics (2020)

Temporal Structure in LLM Reasoning: Analyzing Hidden States and Semantic Embeddings

Kotaro Otomura[✉], Kosuke Nakamura, Katsuki Kobayashi, Mitsuki Nakamura, Ryo Hase, and Jumpei Hato

Mitsubishi Electric Corporation, Tokyo, Japan
otomura.kotaro@df.mitsubishielectric.co.jp,
nakamura.kosuke@ds.mitsubishielectric.co.jp,
kobayashi.katsuki@dh.mitsubishielectric.co.jp,
nakamura.mitsuki@bc.mitsubishielectric.co.jp,
hase.ryo@dc.mitsubishielectric.co.jp,
hato.jumpei@ea.mitsubishielectric.co.jp

Abstract. In this paper, we compare hidden states and embeddings of large language models' output text from the perspective of *temporal structure*, that is, the correspondence between feature space geometry and reasoning progression. Analyzing 5 instruction-tuned models across two reasoning datasets, we apply two complementary analyses: global temporal structure and correct/incorrect path comparison. Our experiments reveal that: (1) hidden states exhibit temporal structure confirmed in the original high-dimensional space, (2) temporal structure in embeddings of LLMs' outputs can attenuate with complex reasoning tasks (GSM8k), while being preserved with simpler reasoning tasks (StrategyQA), (3) the reasoning paths of incorrect answers show longer trajectories than those of correct answers. These results suggest an information asymmetry between internal states and output text, indicating that internal state access may be important for reasoning process analysis.

Keywords: LLM · Reasoning Process · Hidden States · Temporal Structure · Semantic Embedding · Chain-of-Thought

1 Introduction

Chain-of-Thought (CoT) prompting has enabled Large Language Models (LLMs) to generate explicit intermediate reasoning steps, significantly improving performance on complex tasks [1,2]. Understanding these reasoning processes is

---

Supplementary Information The online version contains supplementary material available at https://doi.org/10.1007/978-3-032-29532-3_21.

crucial for model interpretability and reliability assessment. Recent research has raised concerns that CoT outputs may not faithfully reflect the model's internal reasoning [3–5]. These studies focus on the divergence of reasoning *content*, that is, whether the logical steps expressed in text match the internal computation.

The reasoning process is inherently sequential, as each step builds upon previous ones. A statistical physics approach [6] has revealed that hidden state trajectories exhibit structured dynamics during reasoning. Meanwhile, latent space collaboration research [7,8] has demonstrated information loss when internal states are converted to text. Together, these findings raise a key question: *are the temporal dynamics of the reasoning process conserved or lost in text conversion?* Our study addresses this question by analyzing *temporal structure*, that is, the correspondence between feature space geometry and reasoning progression.

In this paper, we address three questions: (1) whether hidden state features exhibit temporal structure corresponding to reasoning progression, (2) whether this structure is preserved or not in output text, and (3) how preservation varies across tasks and models. To tackle these questions, we treat reasoning as a time series of feature vectors, extracting hidden states and semantic embeddings (embeddings of output texts) at each sentence-level step, then applying two complementary analyses: global temporal structure and correct/incorrect path comparison.

Our contributions are: (1) demonstrating that hidden states exhibit temporal structure confirmed in original high-dimensional space (Spearman $\rho = 0.20$–0.53); (2) showing this structure attenuates in text embeddings for complex reasoning (GSM8k: Hidden $\rho = 0.49$ vs Semantic $\rho = 0.07$); (3) identifying task-dependent exceptions where semantic embeddings preserve temporal structure (StrategyQA/Qwen2.5); and (4) quantifying geometric differences between correct and incorrect paths (GSM8k: Cohen's $d = -0.76$ to -1.19). These findings suggest an information asymmetry between internal states and output text, complementing CoT unfaithfulness research from a structural perspective. These insights open pathways toward developing interpretation and verification methods that leverage internal state dynamics rather than relying solely on output text.

2 Related Work

Recent studies have examined whether CoT outputs faithfully reflect internal computation. Chen et al. [3] found that reasoning models do not reliably verbalize hints, while Arcuschin et al. [4] identified implicit post-hoc rationalization in frontier models, and Barez et al. [5] argued that CoT is insufficient for explainability. These works focus on *content* divergence; our work complements this by examining *structural* divergence in temporal information.

Latent space communication research has explored alternatives to text-based inter-agent communication. Zou et al. [7] demonstrated that latent transfer guarantees lossless information exchange (their Theorem 3.3), while Zheng et al. [8] showed that sharing latent thoughts improves multi-agent coordination. Our study provides empirical evidence that temporal structure is one form of information attenuated in text representations.

Carson and Reisizadeh [6] analyzed LLM reasoning through statistical physics, discovering regime structures in hidden state trajectories via Switching Linear Dynamical Systems modeling. However, their analysis is limited to hidden states alone and does not examine whether the discovered structure persists in output text. We address this gap by explicitly comparing hidden states and text embeddings, using simpler correlation-based metrics that enable direct cross-representation comparison.

Probing classifiers [9–11] extract linguistic properties from frozen representations, while mechanistic interpretability [12–14] identifies specific neurons or circuits responsible for behaviors. Both approaches analyze representations at individual time points or layers. Our trajectory-based analysis instead examines how representations evolve across reasoning steps, capturing the dynamic structure that point-wise analyses cannot reveal.

3 Method

3.1 Data Collection

We select two reasoning tasks: GSM8k [15] (grade-school math requiring explicit computational steps) and StrategyQA [16] (multi-hop commonsense reasoning for Yes/No questions). We use five instruction-tuned models in the 4-9B parameter range: Llama-3.1-8B-Instruct [17], Mistral-7B-Instruct-v0.3 [18], Qwen2.5-7B-Instruct [19], Qwen3-4B-Instruct-2507 [20], and Gemma-2-9B-it [21]. Table 1 summarizes dataset statistics; correctness is determined by combining LLM-based judging with regex pattern matching (potential errors are noted as a limitation). Figure 1 provides an overview of our experimental pipeline.

Table 1. Dataset statistics across models. GSM8k uses both train and test splits; StrategyQA uses train split only.

Dataset	Model	Samples	Correct	Accuracy(%)
GSM8k	Llama-3.1-8B	8,692	7,230	83.2
	Gemma-2-9B	8,677	7,543	86.9
	Mistral-7B	8,567	4,798	56.0
	Qwen2.5-7B	8,610	7,474	86.8
	Qwen3-4B	8,392	6,296	75.0
StrategyQA	Llama-3.1-8B	2,290	1,511	66.0
	Gemma-2-9B	2,290	1,608	70.2
	Mistral-7B	2,290	1,426	62.3
	Qwen2.5-7B	2,290	1,419	62.0
	Qwen3-4B	2,290	1,571	68.6

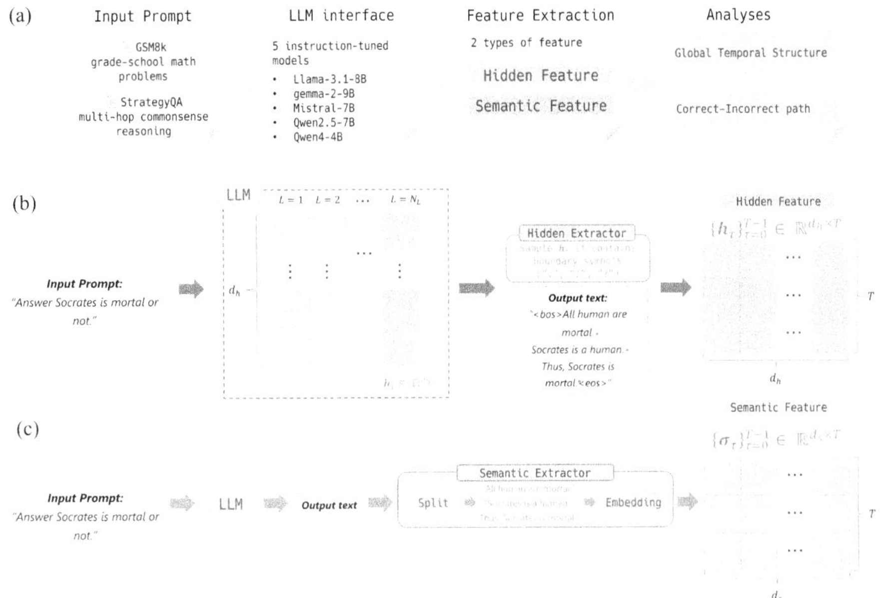

Fig. 1. Experimental pipeline. (a) Workflow from input to feature extraction. (b) Hidden features: final-layer hidden states at sentence boundaries. (c) Semantic features: sentence embeddings via external models.

3.2   Feature Extraction

We segment each reasoning output into sentence-level steps using period-based splitting. Let T denote the total number of steps in a reasoning path. Each step $\tau \in \{0, 1, \ldots, T-1\}$ is assigned a relative time:

$$t_\tau = \frac{\tau}{T-1}, \quad \text{where } t_0 = 0 \text{ (start) and } t_{T-1} = 1 \text{ (end)} \tag{1}$$

Hidden Features: $\boldsymbol{h}_\tau \in \mathbb{R}^{d_h}$ (where d_h: 4096–8192 depending on model) are extracted from the final layer's hidden state at the token that contains a sentence boundary, like ".", "?" or "!" (see Fig. 1(b)). *Semantic features:* $\boldsymbol{\sigma}_\tau \in \mathbb{R}^{d_s}$ are obtained by embedding each step's text using external embedding models (text-embedding-3-small, bge-m3, see Fig. 1(c)). We use $\boldsymbol{x}_\tau$ as generic notation for either $\boldsymbol{h}_\tau$ or $\boldsymbol{\sigma}_\tau$.

3.3   Analysis Methods

Global Temporal Structure Analysis: We quantify global temporal structure through two complementary approaches. First, we project features $\{\boldsymbol{x}_\tau\}$ to 2D using PCA and compute principal component scores:

$$z_k(\tau) = \boldsymbol{w}_k^\top (\boldsymbol{x}_\tau - \bar{\boldsymbol{x}}) \tag{2}$$

where $\boldsymbol{w}_k$ is the k-th eigenvector and $\bar{\boldsymbol{x}} = \frac{1}{T}\sum_\tau \boldsymbol{x}_\tau$.

The maximum absolute Pearson correlation with relative time quantifies temporal structure:

$$\max |r| = \max_{k \in \{1,2,\ldots,k_{\max}\}} |r\left(\{z_k(\tau)\}_\tau, \{t_\tau\}_\tau\right)| \tag{3}$$

We set $k_{\max} = 20$ throughout this paper. We use Pearson correlation because PCA scores are linear transformations that typically follow approximately normal distributions.

Second, we compute pairwise distances in the original high-dimensional space to verify results are not dimensionality reduction artifacts. For all pairs $\tau < \tau'$, we compute distances $D_{\tau,\tau'} = d(\boldsymbol{x}_\tau, \boldsymbol{x}_{\tau'})$ and time differences $\Delta t_{\tau,\tau'} = t_{\tau'} - t_\tau$, then compute Spearman correlation:

$$\rho_{\text{dist-time}} = \rho\left(\{D_{\tau,\tau'}\}_{\tau<\tau'}, \{\Delta t_{\tau,\tau'}\}_{\tau<\tau'}\right). \tag{4}$$

Here, we use two distance functions: cosine distance $d_{\cos}(\boldsymbol{a},\boldsymbol{b}) = 1 - \boldsymbol{a}^\top \boldsymbol{b}/(\|\boldsymbol{a}\|\|\boldsymbol{b}\|)$ and Euclidean distance $d_{\text{euc}}(\boldsymbol{a},\boldsymbol{b}) = \|\boldsymbol{a} - \boldsymbol{b}\|_2$. All features are normalized and standardized before analyzing. We report cosine distance unless noted, since both yield nearly identical results. Positive correlation indicates that temporally distant points are also distant in feature space. We use Spearman (rank) correlation because pairwise distance distributions may be non-linear and contain outliers.

Correct vs. Incorrect Path Analysis: We compare geometric properties of correct (C) and incorrect (I) reasoning paths using five metrics: Step Count T; Path Length $L_{\text{path}} = \sum_{\tau=0}^{T-2} \delta_\tau$; Direct Distance $L_{\text{direct}} = d(\boldsymbol{x}_0, \boldsymbol{x}_{T-1})$; Average Step Distance $\bar{\delta} = L_{\text{path}}/(T-1)$; and Detour Ratio $R_{\text{detour}} = L_{\text{path}}/L_{\text{direct}}$. Effect sizes are quantified using d_{Cohen} (Cohen's d):

$$d_{\text{Cohen}} = \frac{\bar{M}_C - \bar{M}_I}{s_{\text{pooled}}}, \quad s_{\text{pooled}} = \sqrt{\frac{(n_C - 1)s_C^2 + (n_I - 1)s_I^2}{n_C + n_I - 2}}, \tag{5}$$

where $\bar{M}_C$ and $\bar{M}_I$ denote the sample means of correct and incorrect groups, n_C and n_I are the respective sample sizes, and s_C and s_I are the sample standard deviations. Negative d_{Cohen} indicates incorrect paths have larger values. Statistical significance is assessed via permutation tests ($N = 4000$ iterations): we shuffle correctness labels, compute d_{Cohen} for shuffled groups, and build a null distribution; the p-value is the proportion of permuted values as extreme as the observed effect. With $N = 4000$, the minimum reportable p-value is $p < 2.5 \times 10^{-4}$. To control for Step Count confounding, we perform residual analysis: fit $L_{\text{path}} = \beta_0 + \beta_1 T + \epsilon$, then compare residuals between groups using d_{Cohen} and permutation tests.

4   Results

4.1   Global Temporal Structure

Figure 2 shows PCA-projected reasoning trajectories for GSM8k with the Llama model. Each thin line represents an individual sample's path through 2D space, with color indicating relative time. The thick red line shows the mean trajectory. In the hidden feature space, trajectories exhibit clear temporal structure: the color gradient progresses systematically from dark to light, and the mean path traces a coherent arc. In contrast, the semantic feature space shows substantially less temporal organization. This tendency was common across all LLMs in GSM8k. However, this pattern is task-dependent. Figure 3 shows StrategyQA with Qwen2.5, where both hidden and semantic features exhibit strong temporal structure with clear color gradients. Again, this tendency was common among all LLMs in StrategyQA.

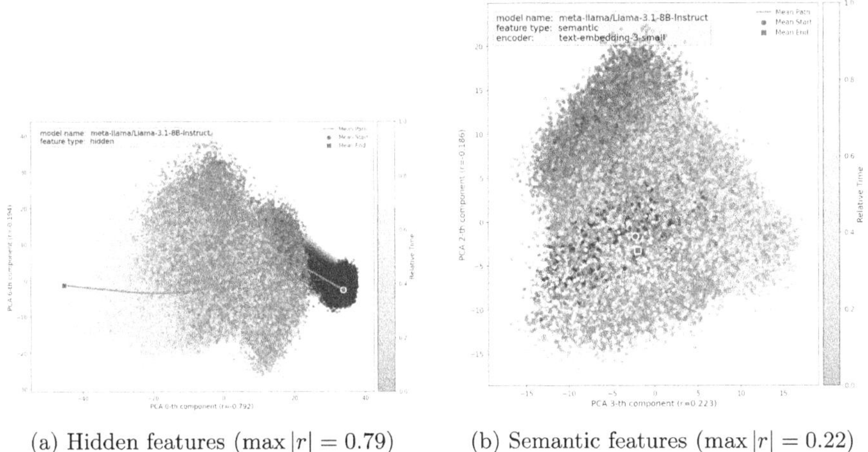

(a) Hidden features (max $|r| = 0.79$)   (b) Semantic features (max $|r| = 0.22$)

Fig. 2. PCA-projected reasoning trajectories for GSM8k/Llama. Each thin line represents one sample's path; color indicates relative time.

Table 2 quantifies these observations. For GSM8k, hidden features consistently show higher correlations than semantic features ($\Delta = 0.04$ to 0.57). For StrategyQA, the pattern is mixed: some models show nearly equal correlations, and semantic embedding of Gemma shows slightly exceeding hidden (bge-m3: $|r| = 0.68$, while $|r| = 0.64$ for hidden embeddings). UMAP and t-SNE analyses confirm these patterns (Appendix B). Table 3 shows Spearman correlations in the original high-dimensional space. The pattern mirrors PCA results: GSM8k shows consistent Hidden > Semantic gaps (e.g., Llama: 0.49 vs. 0.07), while StrategyQA shows exceptions (Qwen2.5: 0.46 vs. 0.44).

In summary, hidden features exhibit temporal structure across most conditions ($|r| = 0.37$–0.94), which is substantially attenuated in semantic features for GSM8k but preserved for certain StrategyQA conditions. See Sect. 5 for interpretation of task dependence.

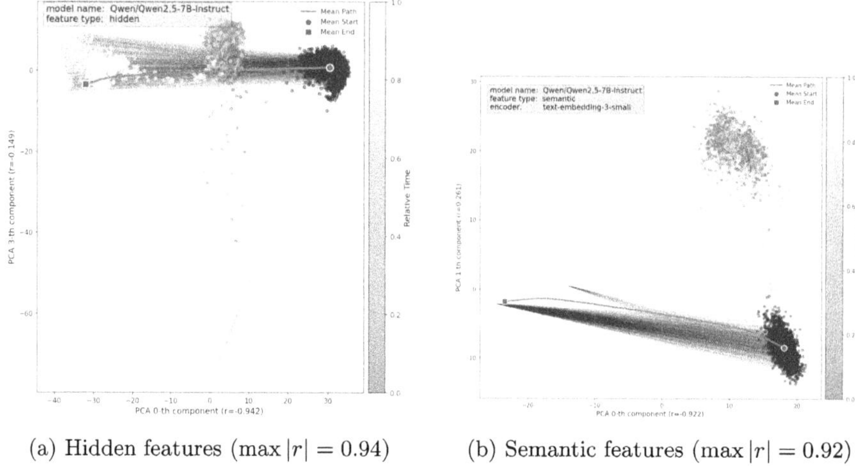

(a) Hidden features (max $|r| = 0.94$)   (b) Semantic features (max $|r| = 0.92$)

Fig. 3. PCA-projected reasoning trajectories for StrategyQA/Qwen2.5 ($\Delta = 0.02$).

4.2   Correct vs. Incorrect Paths

In GSM8k, incorrect paths are consistently longer and more circuitous. Step Count shows $d_{\text{Cohen}} = -0.76$ (Llama) to $d_{\text{Cohen}} = -1.19$ (Qwen3), and Detour Ratio shows $d_{\text{Cohen}} = -0.46$ to -1.02 ($p < 2.5 \times 10^{-4}$ for all). Figure 4 visualizes this: the correct vs. incorrect split shows clearly separated mean paths, while the permutation baseline (Sect. 3) shows overlapping paths.

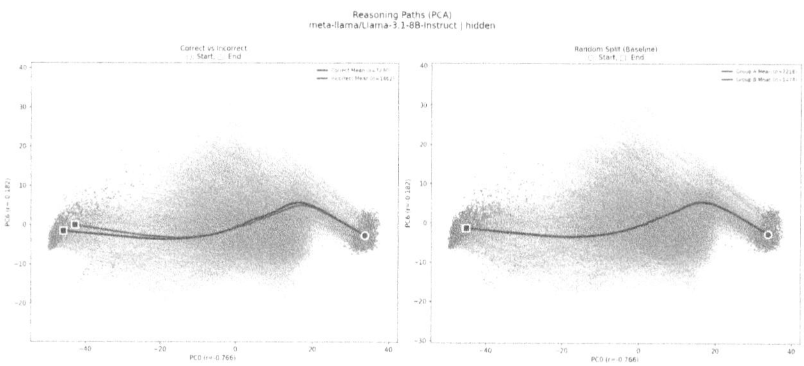

Fig. 4. Correct vs. incorrect path comparison for GSM8k/Llama (hidden features). Left: Mean paths show distinct patterns. Right: Permutation baseline shows overlapping paths.

Residual analysis controlling for Step Count still shows significant differences (Llama: residual $d_{\text{Cohen}} = +0.11$). StrategyQA shows smaller effect sizes

Table 2. Maximum absolute Pearson correlation between PCA components and relative time ($\max |r|$). Sem(text) and Sem(bge) represent semantic embeddings of text-embedding-3-small and bge-m3, respectively. Δ_{text} represents Hidden$-$Sem(text). Bold indicates Semantic $\geq$ Hidden.

Dataset	Model	Hidden	Sem(text)	Sem(bge)	Δ_{text}
GSM8k	Llama	0.79	0.22	0.25	+0.57
	Gemma	0.68	0.37	0.35	+0.31
	Mistral	0.79	0.24	0.22	+0.55
	Qwen2.5	0.55	0.25	0.31	+0.30
	Qwen3	0.37	0.33	0.30	+0.04
StrategyQA	Llama	0.66	0.58	0.65	+0.08
	Gemma	0.64	0.60	**0.68**	+0.04
	Mistral	0.77	0.76	0.75	+0.01
	Qwen2.5	0.94	0.92	0.90	+0.02
	Qwen3	0.62	0.41	0.42	+0.21

Table 3. Spearman correlation ($\rho_{\text{dist-time}}$) in original high-dimensional space (cosine distance).

Dataset	Model	Hidden	Sem(text)	Sem(bge)	Δ_{text}
GSM8k	Llama	0.49	0.07	0.14	+0.42
	Gemma	0.52	0.19	0.25	+0.33
	Mistral	0.37	0.10	0.15	+0.27
	Qwen2.5	0.20	0.08	0.13	+0.12
	Qwen3	0.20	0.09	0.10	+0.11
StrategyQA	Llama	0.45	0.04	0.17	+0.41
	Gemma	0.45	0.07	0.22	+0.38
	Mistral	0.53	0.22	0.25	+0.31
	Qwen2.5	0.44	**0.46**	**0.46**	−0.02
	Qwen3	0.31	0.03	0.11	+0.28

($d_{\text{Cohen}} = -0.16$ to -0.33) with non-significant residual differences ($p = 0.093$). Table 4 compares d_{Cohen} between hidden and semantic features. Unlike temporal structure analysis where hidden features substantially outperform semantic features, correct/incorrect discrimination shows similar effect sizes across both feature types. For Step Count, hidden and semantic features yield nearly identical d_{Cohen} values (e.g., Llama: -0.76 vs. -0.77). Detour Ratio shows modest differences (Llama: -0.74 vs. -0.58), but both remain significant. See Appendix B for complete d_{Cohen} values across all metrics.

Table 4. d_{Cohen} for correct vs. incorrect paths: hidden vs. semantic features on GSM8k. Negative values indicate incorrect paths have larger values.

Model	Step Count			Detour Ratio		
	Hidden	bge-m3	text-emb-3	Hidden	bge-m3	text-emb-3
Llama	−0.76	−0.77	−0.77	−0.74	−0.58	−0.57
Gemma	−0.98	−0.98	−0.98	−0.95	−0.80	−0.80
Mistral	−0.32	−0.32	−0.32	−0.39	−0.14	−0.16
Qwen2.5	−0.51	−0.51	−0.51	−0.46	−0.34	−0.33
Qwen3	−1.19	−1.24	−1.24	−1.02	−0.88	−0.88

5   Discussion

5.1   Information Asymmetry Between Internal States and Output Text

The central finding of this study is that temporal structure in LLM hidden states $\{\boldsymbol{h}_\tau\}$ tends to *attenuate* when reasoning outputs are encoded as text embeddings $\{\boldsymbol{\sigma}_\tau\}$, particularly for complex reasoning tasks. For GSM8k, hidden features show strong temporal correlations ($\max |r| = 0.37$–0.79), while semantic features show substantially weaker correlations ($\max |r| = 0.22$–0.37). This attenuation is confirmed by both complementary approaches: dimensionality reduction (Pearson $\max |r|$) and original-space distance analysis (Spearman $\rho_{\text{dist-time}}$), suggesting it is not a dimensionality reduction artifact. The qualitative visualizations (Figs. 2 and 3) provide intuitive confirmation of these patterns.

These results extend prior work in three ways: First, they complement CoT unfaithfulness research [3–5] by showing that not only reasoning content but also temporal structure diverge between internal states and output text. Second, they provide concrete evidence for the information loss suggested by latent space collaboration research [7,8]. Third, they extend hidden state dynamics analysis [6] by revealing that such structure does not fully transfer to text embeddings, at least for complex reasoning tasks.

5.2   Task Dependence of Temporal Structure Preservation

A critical caveat to our findings is the strong task dependence. For StrategyQA, multiple models show semantic correlations approaching or matching hidden correlations (Qwen2.5: $\max |r| = 0.92$ vs 0.94; Gemma with bge-m3: $\max |r| = 0.68$ vs 0.64). This stands in stark contrast to GSM8k, where hidden features $\{\boldsymbol{h}_\tau\}$ consistently dominate.

We hypothesize this difference arises from how the reasoning structure is encoded in output text (see Appendix B for representative examples). GSM8k requires extended multi-step computation, with each sentence representing a distinct computational step. The semantic content of each step (e.g., "$100/2 = 50$" or "$\$144 + \$54 = \$198$") does not inherently encode its position in the overall reasoning sequence. These arithmetic statements are semantically self-contained units. In contrast, StrategyQA elicits responses with explicit discourse markers that encode reasoning progression. Verbs such as "Determine," "Identify," "Confirm," and "Conclude" indicate distinct stages of reasoning (premise $\rightarrow$ inference $\rightarrow$ conclusion), and this progression structure is preserved in sentence embeddings because the semantic content itself encodes temporal position.

This task dependence implies that our main finding—temporal structure attenuation in text embeddings—should not be overgeneralized. For tasks with structured, stereotyped outputs, text embeddings may sufficiently capture temporal information. Future work should characterize the task properties that predict preservation versus attenuation.

5.3 Correct vs. Incorrect Path Differences

The correct/incorrect path comparison revealed that incorrect reasoning paths in GSM8k are longer and more circuitous than correct paths ($d_{\mathrm{Cohen}} = -0.76$ to -1.19 for Step Count T). The residual analysis showed this is not merely due to length: even controlling for T, incorrect paths show greater detour in L_{path} (residual $d_{\mathrm{Cohen}} = +0.11$, $p < 0.00025$). Figure 4 provides visual confirmation: correct and incorrect paths show distinctly separated mean trajectories, while random label shuffling produces overlapping paths. This suggests that hidden state trajectory geometry reflects reasoning quality. Incorrect paths may indicate exploration, backtracking, or uncertainty manifested as longer, more winding trajectories. However, this discriminative power is task-dependent: StrategyQA shows smaller effect sizes and non-significant residual differences.

Notably, hidden and semantic features show nearly identical effect sizes for correct/incorrect discrimination (e.g., GSM8k/Llama: $d_{\mathrm{Cohen}} = -0.76$ vs. -0.77 for Step Count; -0.74 vs. -0.58 for Detour Ratio). This contrasts with temporal structure, where hidden features substantially outperform semantic features. The finding suggests that the information lost through the hidden-to-semantic transformation pertains specifically to temporal progression, while geometric properties distinguishing correct from incorrect paths are preserved. In other words, semantic embeddings retain path shape information but lose temporal ordering information.

We emphasize that correlation does not imply causation. We cannot determine whether circuitous trajectories *cause* errors or whether incorrect reasoning *leads to* circuitous trajectories. The observed patterns could arise from multiple underlying mechanisms.

5.4 Limitations

All results are correlational. We do not claim that temporal structure *causes* reasoning progress or that its attenuation *causes* information loss. Intervention experiments would be needed to establish causal relationships. Temporal correlations could arise from surface features (sentence length, vocabulary, template structure) rather than "reasoning progress" per se. The causal mechanism underlying temporal structure remains to be investigated. We used text-embedding-3-small and bge-m3 for semantic embeddings. Different embedding models, particularly task-specific fine-tuned models, might show different patterns.

GSM8k uses both train and test splits while StrategyQA uses only train. Direct comparison between datasets should account for potential population differences. The original-space distance analysis computes pairwise distances across all points, mixing within-sample dynamics with between-sample differences. While the dimensionality reduction analysis partially addresses this, the mixing should be noted. Our period-based sentence segmentation may not always align with logical reasoning boundaries, potentially introducing noise in step-level features. Similarly, our LLM-based judge and regex matching may introduce errors in correctness labels, particularly for borderline cases. With $N = 4000$ permutations, $p = 0.0$ means $p < 2.5 \times 10^{-4}$; we cannot report smaller p-values.

5.5 Future Work

Intervention experiments (e.g., manipulating hidden states mid-reasoning) could establish causal relationships between temporal structure and reasoning outcomes. Extending to other tasks (code generation, summarization), larger models, and different architectures would test the generality of our findings. Potential applications include: reasoning progress monitoring using hidden states, early detection of reasoning failures via trajectory geometry, and improved multi-agent communication through latent state sharing. Investigating why temporal structure attenuates—whether due to semantic embedding limitations, text generation processes, or fundamental information bottlenecks—would provide deeper insights.

6 Conclusion

We investigated whether temporal structure in LLM hidden states is preserved when reasoning outputs are encoded as text embeddings. Our experiments confirm that hidden states exhibit temporal structure (Spearman $\rho = 0.20$–0.53), but this structure attenuates in text embeddings for GSM8k (Hidden: $\rho = 0.49$ vs Semantic: $\rho = 0.07$). However, attenuation is task-dependent: StrategyQA shows semantic features approaching hidden features (Qwen2.5: Hidden $\rho = 0.44$ vs Semantic $\rho = 0.46$).

These results provide empirical support for latent space collaboration research [7,8] while specifying *temporal structure* as one form of attenuated information, and complement CoT unfaithfulness research [3–5] by demonstrating structural (not just content) divergence. From a practical perspective, internal state access may be valuable for analyzing reasoning processes, particularly for complex tasks. While our findings are correlational and subject to the limitations discussed in Sect. 5, they provide a new structural perspective on the gap between internal computation and textual output in LLMs.

Disclosure of Interests. All of the authors are employed by Mitsubishi Electric Corporation.

References

1. Wei, J., et al.: Chain-of-thought prompting elicits reasoning in large language models. In: Proceedings of the 36th International Conference on Neural Information Processing Systems, pp. 24824–24837 (2022). https://doi.org/10.52202/068431-1800
2. Kojima, T., et al.: Large language models are zero-shot reasoners. In: Proceedings of the 36th International Conference on Neural Information Processing Systems, pp. 22199–22213 (2022). https://doi.org/10.52202/068431-1613
3. Chen, Y., et al.: Reasoning models don't always say what they think. arXiv preprint arXiv:2505.05410 (2025)
4. Arcuschin, I., et al.: Chain-of-thought reasoning in the wild is not always faithful. arXiv preprint arXiv:2503.08679 (2025)
5. Barez, F., et al.: Chain-of-thought is not explainability. Oxford AI Governance Initiative (AIGI) (2025). https://aigi.ox.ac.uk/wp-content/uploads/2025/07/Cot_Is_Not_Explainability.pdf
6. Carson, J.D., Reisizadeh, A.: A statistical physics of language model reasoning. arXiv preprint arXiv:2506.04374 (2025)
7. Zou, J., et al.: Latent collaboration in multi-agent systems. arXiv preprint arXiv:2511.20639 (2025)
8. Zheng, Y., et al.: Thought communication in multiagent collaboration. arXiv preprint arXiv:2510.20733 (2025)
9. Belinkov, Y.: Probing classifiers: promises, shortcomings, and advances. arXiv preprint arXiv:2102.12452 (2021)
10. Conneau, A., et al.: What you can cram into a single vector: probing sentence embeddings for linguistic properties. arXiv preprint arXiv:1805.01070 (2018)
11. Hewitt, J., Manning, C.D.: A structural probe for finding syntax in word representations. In: NAACL-HLT, pp. 4129–4138 (2019). https://doi.org/10.18653/v1/N19-1419
12. Williams, I., et al.: Mechanistic interpretability needs philosophy. arXiv preprint arXiv:2506.18852 (2025)
13. Geva, M., et al.: Transformer feed-forward layers are key-value memories. In: EMNLP, pp. 5484–5495 (2021). https://doi.org/10.18653/v1/2021.emnlp-main.446
14. Meng, K., et al.: Locating and editing factual associations in gpt. arXiv preprint arXiv:2202.05262 (2023)
15. Cobbe, K., et al.: Training verifiers to solve math word problems. arXiv preprint arXiv:2110.14168 (2021)
16. Geva, M., et al.: Did aristotle use a laptop? A question answering benchmark with implicit reasoning strategies. arXiv preprint arXiv:2101.02235 (2021)
17. Grattafiori, A., et al.: The llama 3 herd of models. arXiv preprint arXiv:2407.21783 (2024)
18. Jiang, A.Q., et al.: Mistral 7b. arXiv preprint arXiv:2310.06825 (2023)
19. Yang, A., et al.: Qwen2 technical report. arXiv preprint arXiv:2407.10671 (2024)
20. Team, Q.: Qwen3 technical report. arXiv preprint arXiv:2505.09388 (2025)
21. Team, G., et al.: Gemma 2: improving open language models at a practical size. arXiv preprint arXiv:2408.00118 (2024)

Interpretability and Models Analysis in NLP

Expansion Is Not Enough: Revisiting Dynamically Expandable Networks for NLP Tasks

M. Uzzwal Vanshik Reddy[1], S. Sowmya Kamath[1(✉)], and Vijayan Sugumaran[2]

[1] Healthcare Analytics and Language Engineering (HALE) Lab, Department of Information Technology, National Institute of Technology Karnataka, Surathkal, Srinivasnagar P.O., Mangaluru 575025, India
`{uzzwalvansh.221it043,sowmyakamath}@nitk.edu.in`
[2] Department of Decision and Information Sciences, School of Business Administration, Oakland University, Rochester, MI, USA
`sugumara@oakland.edu`

Abstract. Continual learning in the NLP domain remains challenging due to catastrophic forgetting, even when leveraging large pretrained language models. This problem is particularly relevant in real-world NLP applications such as evolving text streams, domain adaptation and language understanding systems, where models must continuously incorporate new information without degrading prior knowledge. While architectural approaches such as Dynamically Expandable Networks (DEN) have shown promise in Computer Vision, their effectiveness and computational trade-offs in NLP settings remain unexplored. In this work, we present a systematic empirical study of regularization- and expansion-based continual learning (CL) strategies under a Task-Incremental Learning setting with frozen transformer representations. We evaluate naive sequential fine-tuning, Elastic Weight Consolidation (EWC), SoftDEN variants and DEN on standard datasets, spanning short and long task sequences with increasing semantic diversity. Our goal is to analyze how different CL behave under stable pretrained representations in NLP. Results show that parameter regularization alone mitigates forgetting in short task sequences, while dynamic expansion adds little benefit. For longer or more diverse sequences, regularization is insufficient and neuron-level isolation in DEN maintains higher performance at the cost of increased model size.

Keywords: Continual Learning · Natural Language Processing · Catastrophic Forgetting · Pretrained Language Models

1 Introduction

Continual learning (CL) addresses the challenge of enabling machine learning (ML) models to acquire new tasks over time without forgetting previously learned knowledge. Deep neural networks achieve strong performance across

© The Author(s), under exclusive license to Springer Nature Switzerland AG 2027
E. Cabrio and E. Monteiro (Eds.): NLDB 2026, LNCS 16696, pp. 317–331, 2027.
https://doi.org/10.1007/978-3-032-29532-3_22

many domains, but they are prone to catastrophic forgetting when trained sequentially on multiple tasks. Most research in CL has focused on computer vision, where high representation drift and task interference make forgetting particularly severe [3] [14]. By comparison, CL in NLP has received less attention and studies involving transformer-based models remain limited. This limitation is particularly important in practical NLP scenarios such as continuously evolving text streams, domain adaptation across corpora and lifelong language understanding systems, where models must incorporate new knowledge without degrading previously acquired linguistic or semantic representations. Pretrained language models, such as BERT [4], provide rich and reusable feature representations, which are often frozen during downstream task adaptation. While this can reduce interference between tasks, it also constrains model flexibility and affects the dynamics of forgetting, posing unique challenges for CL in NLP [9] [16].

Architectural techniques such as Dynamically Expandable Networks (DEN) [19] mitigate catastrophic forgetting by selectively isolating important neurons for previous tasks and expanding the network with new neurons for incoming tasks. Existing methods generally preserve previously learned knowledge through mechanisms such as parameter regularization, weight consolidation, or selective retraining, but most have been developed and evaluated in computer vision settings [3]. Their behavior under more stable representation scenarios, such as those found in NLP, remains underexplored. In this work, we consider a Task-Incremental Learning (Task-IL) formulation where each task corresponds to a dataset partition or domain-specific classification problem rather than fundamentally different NLP objectives (e.g., NER vs. sentiment analysis). In Task-IL scenarios for NLP, the task identity is known at inference time and task-specific output heads are used [18]. This setup can produce different patterns of task interference compared with class-incremental learning, highlighting the unique challenges for CL in NLP.

CL approaches can broadly be categorized into three major families: regularization-based methods, replay-based methods and architectural methods. Regularization-based approaches constrain important parameters as they do not diverge from previously learned values, using importance measures derived from Fisher gradients [1]. Replay-based methods preserve knowledge by interleaving previously seen samples or their generated approximations while learning new tasks. Architectural approaches modify the network structure by allocating task-specific components or expanding capacity to reduce interference. Each strategy provides a different trade-off between memory usage, computational cost and plasticity and their effectiveness often depends on the representation stability of the underlying feature extractor. However, to the best of our knowledge, a systematic comparison of these strategies under frozen transformer representations in NLP Task-IL settings has not been explicitly studied. In particular, it remains unclear how architectural expansion methods behave when representation drift is inherently limited due to pretrained language encoders and whether their advantages observed in vision tasks transfer to language tasks.

In this work, we present a systematic evaluation of CL methods in NLP Task-Incremental Learning (Task-IL) using frozen transformer-based representations. The order in which tasks are encountered in CL can also influence the degree of forgetting and transfer, hence tasks are presented sequentially following a fixed ordering defined by dataset construction, to enable analysis of performance under controlled and reproducible task sequences. Rather than proposing a new CL method, our contribution lies in a controlled empirical analysis of how regularization, expansion and isolation mechanisms behave in NLP settings with stable pretrained representations. The rest of the article is structured as follows. Section 2 provides an overview of related work in CL, specifically focusing on regularization and architectural methods, as well as their use in NLP. Section 3 introduces the Task-Incremental Learning scenario, datasets, model architecture and training methods. In Sect. 4, the experimental findings are reported, followed by concluding remarks in Sect. 5.

2   Related Work

CL has been well explored in addressing the problem of catastrophic forgetting in the scenario of learning multiple tasks in succession. The available techniques to address the problem of catastrophic forgetting in CL can be viewed as follows: regularization-based techniques, architectural techniques and the hybrid approach, which combines the above-mentioned techniques. Although the initial work focused mainly on computer vision tasks, recently the focus in CL in NLP tasks has started to gain importance with the availability of transformer models.

Regularization-based methods aim to mitigate catastrophic forgetting by controlling how much parameters critical to previously learned tasks can change during the learning of new tasks. Elastic Weight Consolidation (EWC) penalizes changes to important parameters, with importance estimated using the Fisher Information Matrix, which quantifies each parameter's sensitivity to the loss on previous tasks [10]. Synaptic Intelligence (SI) similarly assigns importance scores to parameters based on their contribution to reducing the training loss over time, allowing the network to selectively protect parameters that are most useful for earlier tasks [20]. Learning Without Forgetting (LwF) approaches take a different perspective by treating previous task outputs as soft targets and incorporating a distillation loss during training on new tasks, thereby preserving functional behavior without explicitly constraining individual parameters [12]. Together, these methods illustrate different strategies for balancing plasticity and stability in CL. These methods are attractive due to their simplicity and low memory footprint, but their effectiveness depends heavily on task similarity and the stability of learned features. For sequences of dissimilar tasks or long task chains, regularization alone can over-constrain learning, limiting adaptability to new tasks. In NLP scenarios with pretrained encoders, the interaction between feature stability and regularization remains an active area of research, as frozen or partially frozen representations can both reduce interference and restrict flexibility.

Architectural strategies mitigate forgetting by modifying the network structure to protect information relevant to previous tasks. Progressive Neural Networks add new network columns for each task while freezing existing parameters, preventing interference between tasks [15]. PathNet uses an evolutionary approach to select task-relevant network pathways, freezing selected paths to preserve previously learned knowledge [5]. PackNet iteratively prunes and reuses weights to accommodate multiple tasks within a single network, ensuring that important parameters for prior tasks are preserved [13]. Thus, architectural changes can explicitly separate task representations and reduce interference, providing a complementary approach to parameter regularization. Dynamically Expandable Networks (DEN) implement a strategy that adapts network capacity when existing parameters are insufficient for learning new tasks [19]. The approach combines selective retraining, neuron addition and neuron-level isolation to preserve knowledge from previous tasks while accommodating new ones. However, in scenarios with low representation drift, such as NLP with frozen pretrained encoders, the benefits of DEN are less pronounced, while the additional complexity in estimating neuron importance and performing isolation for each task increases computational overhead. Soft dynamic expansion variants further relax strict isolation by allowing controlled sharing of neurons, providing a flexible trade-off between stability and adaptability.

Continual learning in NLP has received relatively less attention compared with vision domains, partly due to the effectiveness of strong pretrained models. Early work in NLP-CL focused primarily on regularization and rehearsal-based methods combined with fine-tuning [2]. More recently, adapter-based approaches have gained attention [7]. Moreover, parameter-efficient fine-tuning (PEFT) techniques, including low-rank adaptation (LoRA) [8] and other similar approaches [6], have proved to be successful means of adapting pre-trained language models without adding many extra parameters. These PEFT techniques allow task-based adaptation without making changes to the whole model [17] and recently have gained popularity in the CL paradigm. However, most evaluations have considered either full fine-tuning or class-incremental settings where class identity is unknown during inference. In Task-Incremental Learning (Task-IL) scenarios, where task identity is known at inference, the dynamics of catastrophic forgetting differ significantly from conventional incremental learning. In particular, the role of architectural expansion approaches, especially when using frozen pretrained encoders, has not been thoroughly explored.

Our research complements recent advances in CL for NLP by focusing on a controlled empirical analysis of architectural and regularization-based strategies under frozen transformer representations, rather than introducing new parameter-efficient adaptation mechanisms. Unlike previous DEN-based methods, which rely heavily on neuron-level isolation to preserve prior task knowledge, we evaluate the effectiveness of dynamic expansion and selective retraining under conditions where the feature representations remain stable. By comparing these strategies with standard regularization-based baselines, we aim to identify which components of architectural CL approaches retain their effectiveness in contemporary NLP scenarios. We also aim to highlight the trade-offs between preserving prior knowledge, adapting to new tasks and controlling model complexity, providing practical guidance for designing efficient CL systems for pretrained language models. By examining the influences of expansion, regularization and isolation in an isolated context, our work offers a perspective that is supplementary to the recent parameter-efficient paradigms on CL in NLP.

3   Methodology

In this section, we present the CL setup, task formulation and dataset construction for each experiment. All experiments are designed to follow a Task-Incremental Learning (Task-IL) paradigm and employ frozen transformer representations in order to focus on CL effects in the classifier modules, which means training models using a set of tasks sequentially. In each stage of the training procedure, the data from the concerned task for which the model will be learned is available and data from the previous tasks will not be revisited during each stage. Meanwhile, during inference, the task is already known and the prediction results will be generated using the output head corresponding to that specific task. The objective is to learn each new task without impairing performances on previously learned tasks, without retraining all tasks jointly. Additionally, since task identities are available in test time, there is no class ambiguity between tasks and hence there is no effect of catastrophic forgetting in terms of inter-task classification. However, forgetting can still occur within the shared classifier trunk, as parameters important for previously learned tasks may be overwritten when adapting to new tasks.

Formally, a sequence of tasks $\{\mathcal{T}_1, \mathcal{T}_2, \ldots, \mathcal{T}_K\}$ is presented to the model in order. Each task $\mathcal{T}_k$ consists of an input space $\mathcal{X}_k$ and a task-specific label space $\mathcal{Y}_k$. The training process is independent and sequential for each task. The model is not given data from previous tasks once training on a specific task is completed. In order to make specific predictions on the tasks, a separate classification head is maintained for each task, while the tasks have a common feature extractor and a classifier trunk. The output layer is determined based on the known task identity for the purpose of separate analysis of representational stability and interference with parameters.

Datasets. Two different datasets were used for the experiments - the AG News dataset [21] and the 20 Newsgroups Dataset [11]. Dataset statistics for both AG News and 20 Newsgroups under the Task-IL setup are summarized in Table 1. These are widely adopted text classification benchmark datasets, however, the selection of these benchmark datasets was made to enable an ideal scenario for the application of CL with differing degrees of task difficulty: the AG News dataset is used as a task sequence that is relatively shorter, while 20 Newsgroups was selected due to its higher diversity.

Table 1. Dataset statistics for Task-Incremental Learning experiments.

Dataset	Task	Train	Val	Test
AG News	Task 1	48,000	12,000	3,800
AG News	Task 2	48,000	12,000	3,800
20 Newsgroups	Task 1 (Computer)	1,796	449	1,494
20 Newsgroups	Task 2 (Recreation)	1,880	470	1,566
20 Newsgroups	Task 3 (Science)	1,912	478	1,590
20 Newsgroups	Task 4 (Politics)	1,902	475	1,581
20 Newsgroups	Task 5 (Religion)	1,562	390	1,301

Task Construction. The AG News dataset comprises news articles with four classes: the World, Sports, Business and Science and Technology categories. When used for evaluation in a Task-IL setting, the dataset will be split into two binary classification tasks. The first binary classification task considered articles from the World and Sports categories and the second is based on articles from the Business and Science and Technology categories, with class labels mapped to a binary label space. The original training split is again split into training and validation splits using the ratio 80:20. The standard test split is also retained for evaluation. The two tasks are learned sequentially, where the model is fully trained on the first task before moving on to the second task. This type of task construction helps to maintain semantic coherence within a task while ensuring disjoint label spaces. The choice of splitting AG News into two binary tasks is intended to create a controlled short task sequence with moderate semantic separation, enabling analysis of CL behavior in a simplified setting before extending to more complex scenarios.

The 20 Newsgroups dataset comprises documents from twenty different categories. In order to test CL in longer task sequences, the set is divided into five different tasks based on semantic similarity between categories. Each of these tasks is a four-class classification problem among related newsgroups. The first task includes computer technology-related categories, followed by tasks related to recreational topics, scientific topics, political and general discussion forums and then religion and belief-based categories. Within each of these tasks, new class labels are projected onto a local label space that consists of four classes. Here, for each of the tasks, the training dataset is randomly shuffled, forming an 80:20 split, whereas the testing split remains constant. Tasks are learned sequentially in the above order. The ordering is fixed and follows increasing semantic diversity across tasks, allowing us to study how CL methods behave as task complexity and distributional shift increase. The task grouping brings about varying levels of semantic diversity within tasks, leading to a more difficult Task-IL scenario than that represented by the AG News dataset. This design also allows us to evaluate performance under longer task sequences, complementing the shorter AG News setup and varying levels of semantic diversity within tasks, leading to a more difficult Task-IL scenario than that represented by the AG News dataset.

Model Architectures. All CL experiment codes are implemented on top of a transformer encoder that was pretrained for a CL experiment. More specifically, a BERT-based encoder was used and its parameters were frozen throughout the experiment. This means that there are no gradient updates on the encoder for task-wise learning and all CL phenomena are captured in the classifier parts only. In addition, atop the frozen encoder, a shared multi-layer perceptron (MLP) trunk is used to transform the representations obtained at the sentence level from BERT. It includes two fully connected layers, with each containing 512 and 256 units, respectively, as well as a non-linear activation function. This is a shared unit of all the tasks and it is the most critical part in which representation adaptation or interference may happen. In the case of specific task prediction, a separate linear classifier is maintained for every specific task. Each of the linear classifiers projects the shared trunk representation onto the label space for the specific task. In inference mode, a specific classifier is chosen based on the known task identity.

Model Training. Training proceeds sequentially over tasks, using only data from the current task at each stage. Validation data from the current task is used to monitor learning progress and guide model updates. Across both datasets, the same model architecture and training protocol are applied, enabling consistent comparison of CL behavior across short and long task sequences.

1. Selective Training and Dynamic Expansion Strategy. To control the pattern of model adaptation across tasks, training of each adapted model follows the process of selective retraining and conditional capacity expansion over two stages. The motivation to apply this approach follows the observation that the prevailing classifier weights may already be adequate in the presence of frozen encoder representations. When the new task is presented, the parameters of the whole shared classifier trunk are frozen, but the task-specific output head for the new task is trained. This phase, where the particular outputs are fine-tuned, is referred to as selective retraining. This phase is essential in that the model is able to assess the appropriateness of the learned representations in the preceding tasks for the new task. If the performance is satisfactory, the parameters will not be further adjusted. However, when the performance is still inadequate, the network shifts to a second state wherein the shared classifier trunk is allowed to adapt. In this state, the capacity expansion is achieved by the addition of new neurons to the shared levels of the classifier trunk. At the same time, the newly added parameters are trained alongside the task-specific head, while the rest of the parameters are maintained by the previously learned values. This helps the network to adapt capacity as needed, hence avoiding unnecessary interference.

The validation performance for the current task forms the basis for making the decision on applying the expansion. If the validation loss increases after retraining to a threshold, then the expansion operation is applied to the trunk of the shared classifier. Such a conditional expansion helps the model to balance the trade-offs between adaptability and stability by reusing the pre-existing representations and adding the flexibility when it is needed. Even though this process is motivated by the expansion principle of Dynamically Expandable Networks, the current formulation diverges from the classical formulation of DEN in a series of important aspects. For one, no estimation of the relative importance of each neuron, no masking of parameters, or hard task isolation between neurons occurs. Instead, the entire parameter sharing remains fully trainable after the expansion is triggered. Thus, the proposed methodology effectively provides a softer version of dynamic expansion, wherein capacity expansion is decoupled from task parameter isolation.

Regularization with Elastic Weight Consolidation. Besides architectural adaptation, we assess the impact of regularization-based CL by including in the training procedure EWC. EWC attempts to prevent catastrophic forgetting by penalizing large updates to parameters deemed important for previously learned tasks. The importance of parameters is approximated through the Fisher Information Matrix, representing an estimate of the loss sensitivity w.r.t. each parameter. It computes the Fisher Information Matrix [10] for learnable parameters of classifier components after training on a task. It adds a quadratic penalty term in the loss function for deviations of important parameters from their previously learned values while training on new tasks. This regularization term is only applied to parameters shared across tasks, while task-specific output heads are unconstrained.

In the context of the present study, EWC is restricted to the classifier trunk, since the parameters of the encoder are kept frozen throughout the training process. In the case of selective retraining, the operation of EWC normalization follows the head-only training procedure, to avoid interfering with the initial evaluation of compatibility between the tasks. Finally, in the case of capacity expansion, EWC operates on the existing parameters, while the newly introduced parameters are not subject to normalization constraints. This integration also can be used to explore how this regularization helps cope with dynamic expansion under stable representations. In evaluating the presented extension of EWC as a standalone algorithm and combined with conditional expansion, we seek to understand whether regularization benefits also translate to improved stability.

Experimental Setup and Baselines. Several baseline methods were considered in our evaluation study and implemented within a unified experimental protocol to assess CL behavior in the NLP Task-Incremental Learning setting. All baselines share the same frozen BERT encoder, classifier architecture, task formulation and dataset splits, ensuring that any observed performance differences can be fairly attributed to the CL strategy rather than architectural or data-related factors. This controlled setup is designed to isolate the impact of CL mechanisms, rather than improvements arising from model or data variations. Naive fine-tuning serves as the standard reference baseline. In this setting, the model is trained sequentially on each incoming task without any explicit mechanism to mitigate catastrophic forgetting. When a new task is presented, all trainable parameters of the classifier components are updated using only the data from the current task. No regularization, replay, or architectural adaptation is employed. As a result, this baseline corresponds to standard sequential training and provides a lower bound on CL performance.

We apply EWC as a representative regularization-based CL method. In EWC, parameter importance is estimated after training each task using the Fisher Information Matrix and deviations of important parameters are penalized during subsequent training through a quadratic regularization term. In our setup, EWC is applied only to the shared classifier trunk, since the encoder is frozen and task-specific output heads are independent across tasks. In addition, the original DEN was included as an architectural baseline. DEN supports network growth by adding new neurons when existing capacity is insufficient to learn a new task, while preserving previously acquired knowledge through selective retraining and parameter isolation mechanisms. This baseline represents a fully specified expansion-based CL approach and serves as a point of comparison for analyzing the impact of dynamic capacity growth in NLP settings.

In addition to the use of DEN, the effectiveness of the soft dynamic expansion variant of the method is evaluated. The soft dynamic expansion method parallels the previously mentioned selective retraining and conditional expansion approach but does not incorporate the use of importance estimation at the neuron level, parameter masking, or hard isolation of respective task solutions from the models. Rather, all shared parameters are still trainable after expansion and only focus on validation performance with the use of capacity growth alone, occurring in the corresponding task. All methods are trained sequentially for a set of tasks using the same optimization and evaluation techniques. Performance is evaluated after every set of task on test sets of all previously learned tasks, for assessing both the taskwise and forgetting curve aspects.

4   Results and Discussion

This section presents the experimental results and corresponding analysis for CL in NLP under a Task-Incremental Learning (Task-IL) setting with frozen transformer representations. Experiments are conducted on AG News (2 tasks) and 20 Newsgroups (5 tasks), comparing naive sequential fine-tuning, EWC, SoftDEN variants and the original DEN.

Evaluation Metrics. The performance of CL methods is evaluated using metrics that capture both predictive performance on individual tasks and the extent of forgetting across tasks. Thus, we use the metrics task-wise accuracy, average forgetting, F1-score and AUROC to provide a comprehensive assessment of both classification quality and knowledge retention. Since experiments are conducted under a Task-IL setting with oracle task identity available at inference time, all evaluations are performed using the task-specific output head corresponding to each task. To assess the memory overhead of different CL strategies, the total number of expansions and duplications is reported after training on all tasks. This reflects the degree of capacity expansion in architectural methods.

Task-wise accuracy measures the classification performance of the model on a specific task after sequential training. After training on task k, the accuracy on a previously learned task $\mathcal{T}_i$ is computed as per Eq. (1), where $\mathcal{D}_i^{\text{test}}$ denotes the test set of task $\mathcal{T}_i$, $f_i(\cdot)$ is the task-specific prediction function and $\mathbb{I}(\cdot)$ is the indicator function. To summarize overall performance after training on task k, the average accuracy across all learned tasks is computed as per Eq. (2). The final average accuracy is reported after completion of training on the last task. Catastrophic forgetting is quantified using an average forgetting measure. For a given task $\mathcal{T}_i$, forgetting is defined as the difference between the maximum accuracy achieved on that task during training and its final accuracy after learning all tasks as per Eq. (3), where, K denotes the total number of tasks. The average forgetting across tasks is then computed as per Eq. (4).

$$A_i^{(k)} = \frac{1}{|\mathcal{D}_i^{\text{test}}|} \sum_{(x,y) \in \mathcal{D}_i^{\text{test}}} \mathbb{I}\left[f_i(x) = y\right], \tag{1}$$

$$\bar{A}^{(k)} = \frac{1}{k} \sum_{i=1}^{k} A_i^{(k)}. \tag{2}$$

$$F_i = \max_{k \geq i} A_i^{(k)} - A_i^{(K)}, \tag{3}$$

$$\bar{F} = \frac{1}{K-1} \sum_{i=1}^{K-1} F_i. \tag{4}$$

Continual Learning Performance for AG News Task. Table 2 summarizes performance on the AG News benchmark. Naive sequential fine-tuning exhibits severe catastrophic forgetting, with average accuracy dropping to 0.695 and forgetting reaching 0.473 after learning the second task. This confirms that freezing the encoder and using task-specific heads alone is insufficient to prevent interference in the shared classifier. EWC substantially mitigates forgetting, achieving an average accuracy of 0.896 and reducing forgetting to 0.068. This indicates that, for short task sequences with limited semantic shift, parameter regularization is highly effective. SoftDEN without regularization performs comparably to naive fine-tuning, with both average accuracy and forgetting remaining near baseline levels. This demonstrates that dynamic expansion alone does not prevent catastrophic forgetting when shared parameters remain unconstrained. Combining SoftDEN with EWC yields a modest improvement over EWC alone, while the original DEN achieves the best performance, with an average accuracy of 0.928 and minimal forgetting. However, the gains over EWC are incremental, suggesting diminishing returns from architectural expansion in this setting. The results on AG News indicate that regularization dominates CL performance under frozen representations and short task sequences, while expansion and isolation mechanisms provide limited additional benefit.

Continual Learning Performance for 20 Newsgroups Task. Table 3 reports results on the 20 Newsgroups benchmark, which is a more challenging CL scenario due to a longer task sequence and increasing semantic diversity. Naive

Table 2. Continual Learning Performance on AG News (Task-IL)

Method	Avg Accuracy ↑	Forgetting ↓
Naive	0.6953	0.4726
EWC [10]	0.8963	0.0684
SoftDEN	0.6874	0.4711
SoftDEN + EWC	0.9049	0.0453
DEN [19]	**0.9275**	**0.0255**

Table 3. Continual Learning Performance on 20 Newsgroups (5 Tasks)

Method	Avg Acc. ↑	Forgetting ↓	Expansions	Duplications
Naive	0.3641	0.5077	0	0
EWC [10]	0.4784	0.3474	0	0
SoftDEN	0.3436	0.5455	4	0
SoftDEN + EWC	0.5079	**0.3158**	4	0
DEN [19]	**0.6095**	0.3735	4	247

fine-tuning suffers from pronounced catastrophic forgetting, with final average accuracy decreasing to 0.364 and forgetting exceeding 0.50. EWC improves stability, raising average accuracy to 0.478 and reducing forgetting to 0.347, but performance continues to degrade as additional tasks are learned. SoftDEN without regularization performs poorly in this setting, yielding the lowest average accuracy (0.344) and the highest forgetting (0.546). Despite repeated capacity expansions, the absence of parameter protection leads to severe interference, confirming that expansion alone is insufficient for CL in NLP. SoftDEN combined with EWC improves upon EWC alone, achieving an average accuracy of 0.508 and reducing forgetting to 0.316. While this suggests that expansion can complement regularization, the gains remain limited. The original DEN achieves the highest average accuracy at 0.610, consistently outperforming all other methods. Although forgetting remains non-negligible, DEN was better on earlier tasks across the task sequence.

Performance Evolution and Capacity Trade-offs. Figure 1 illustrates the evolution of average accuracy across tasks on 20 Newsgroups. Naive fine-tuning exhibits rapid performance degradation, while EWC degrades more gradually. SoftDEN combined with EWC closely follows the EWC trajectory, indicating limited additional benefit from expansion alone. In contrast, DEN maintains substantially higher average accuracy throughout the task sequence, particularly in later tasks. Figure 2 shows the corresponding growth in model size. EWC maintains a constant parameter count, while SoftDEN introduces modest growth due to repeated expansions. DEN exhibits substantial parameter growth resulting from both expansion and neuron duplication. These results highlight a clear trade-off between performance and model complexity: DEN provides the strongest protection against forgetting but at the cost of significant architectural growth.

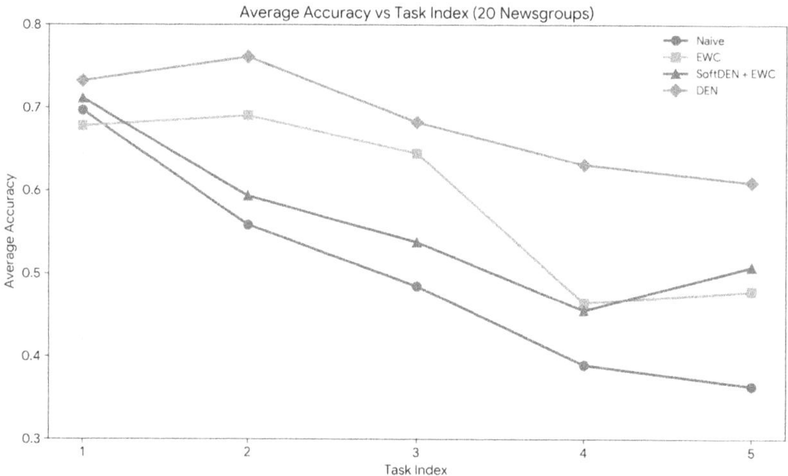

Fig. 1. Average accuracy as a function of task index on 20 Newsgroups benchmark *(Naive fine-tuning degrades rapidly, whereas EWC shows more gradual decline. Soft-DEN + EWC closely tracks EWC, while DEN achieves the highest average accuracy, especially in later tasks).*

Discussion. Taken together, these results highlight the complementary roles of regularization, capacity expansion and parameter isolation in CL for NLP. As shown in Table 4, regularization alone (EWC) substantially improves performance over naive fine-tuning, indicating that constraining updates to important parameters is effective under frozen representations. In contrast, expansion without explicit parameter protection (SoftDEN) fails to mitigate forgetting, performing comparably to or worse than the naive baseline. Combining expansion with regularization (SoftDEN + EWC) yields further gains, suggesting that additional capacity is only beneficial when coupled with mechanisms that preserve previously learned knowledge. The strongest performance is achieved by DEN, which integrates regularization, expansion and explicit parameter isolation, but at the cost of significantly increased model capacity. Overall, these findings suggest that while regularization-based methods are sufficient for moderate task sequences in Task-IL settings, robust performance over longer or more diverse task sequences requires some form of parameter isolation.

While tasks are presented in a fixed order in our experiments, prior work has shown that task ordering can influence CL performance. A systematic analysis of order sensitivity is beyond the scope of this study and is left for future work. Even though this study examines only two benchmark NLP tasks for text

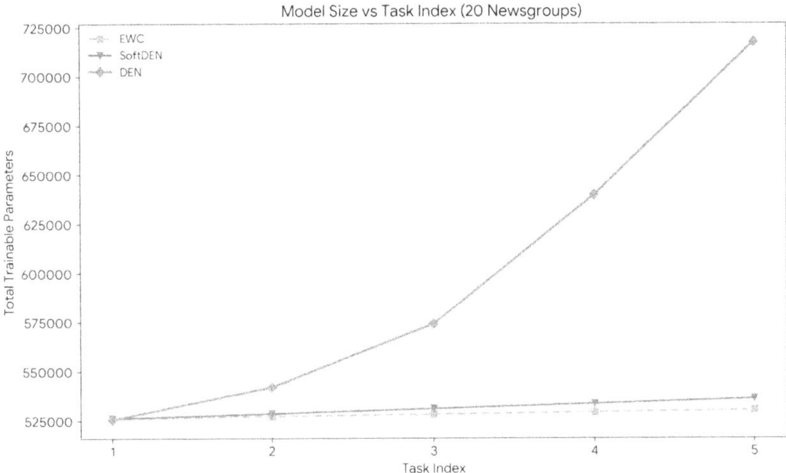

Fig. 2. Increase in number of trainable parameters as tasks are added on the 20 Newsgroups benchmark *(EWC maintains a constant model size, SoftDEN introduces moderate growth through expansion, DEN leads to substantial parameter increase due to both expansion and neuron duplication, reflecting the trade-off between performance and model complexity).*

classification, the findings suggest that similar trends may old but it is left to further studies to be sure, in which the underlying pretrained representations do not change and the nature of the task is clearly specified. Extending this line of investigation to more diverse datasets and task formulations should be considered for further research. Parameter-Efficient Fine-Tuning (PEFT), which encompasses adapters and low-rank adaptations, is another approach that was recently proposed to prevent forgetting through the addition of smaller sets of parameters to pre-trained language models. Although not considered in this work, our observations on parameter isolation and controlled model growth would prove useful when evaluating the benefits of such approaches. Finally, in scenarios of CL where new tasks can arrive over time, finding the right balance between growth and model stability becomes more crucial. Our experimental results indicate that methods that include such balance would prove more efficient. This, in turn, motivates future work on parameter-efficient isolation strategies that can better align with the scalability constraints of modern pretrained language models.

5   Conclusion and Future Work

In this work, we presented a systematic empirical study of architectural and regularization-based continual learning strategies under a Task-Incremental Learning setting with frozen transformer representations. By evaluating naive fine-tuning, Elastic Weight Consolidation (EWC), SoftDEN variants and Dynamically Expandable Network (DEN) on AG News and 20 Newsgroups, we

Table 4. Comparison of Continual Learning Mechanisms

Method	Regularization	Expansion	Isolation
Naive	×	×	×
EWC	✓	×	×
SoftDEN	×	✓	×
SoftDEN + EWC	✓	✓	×
DEN	✓	✓	✓

examined how different mechanisms address catastrophic forgetting across varying task sequence lengths and semantic diversity. The results show that parameter regularization can mitigate forgetting for short task sequences with limited distributional shift. On AG News, EWC underperforms, while dynamic expansion without parameter protection gains an upper hand. In this setting, architectural expansion offers only marginal gains, indicating diminishing returns when representations are frozen and task interference is limited. In contrast, longer and more diverse task sequences expose the limitations of regularization alone. On 20 Newsgroups, EWC slows but does not prevent performance degradation as tasks accumulate and expansion without regularization remains ineffective. The original DEN achieves the best performance by combining expansion, regularization and neuron-level isolation, maintaining higher accuracy across tasks at the cost of increased model capacity.

Our study revealed several interesting observations. Neuron-level isolation reduces interference when learning long or highly diverse task sequences, but this comes with a substantial increase in model size and computational cost. In our experiments, the benefits of architectural isolation are not consistent across settings and tend to appear only once regularization-based methods are no longer sufficient. This suggests that isolation should not be applied by default, but rather introduced when task interference becomes significant. Although the experiments in this paper are performed on two representative data sets in the realm of text classification, this is an environment that allows a controlled investigation into the behaviors associated with CL across different lengths and levels of semantic dissimilarity in tasks. However, there are several areas in which further investigations are needed. First, recent developments in PEFT and their variants such as adapters and low-rank adaptation can prove beneficial in avoiding forgetting in less computationally expensive ways. Future work will focus on developing more parameter-efficient isolation mechanisms that retain the advantages of DEN while limiting capacity growth, as well as adaptive strategies that trigger architectural expansion only when interference is observed.

References

1. Amari, S.I.: Natural gradient works efficiently in learning. Neural Comput. **10**(2), 251–276 (1998)

2. Dai, X., Huang, P.S., Chen, Y., Le, Q.: Continual learning for natural language processing. In: Proceedings of the 1st Workshop on Continual Learning for Natural Language Processing. EMNLP-IJCNLP Workshop (2019)
3. De Lange, M., Aljundi, R., Masana, M., et al.: A continual learning survey: defying forgetting in classification tasks. IEEE Trans. Pattern Anal. Mach. Intell. **44**(7), 3366–3385 (2021)
4. Devlin, J., Chang, M.W., Lee, K., et al.: BERT: pre-training of deep bidirectional transformers for language understanding. In: Proceedings of NAACL-HLT (2019)
5. Fernando, C., Banarse, D., Blundell, C., et al.: PathNet: evolution channels gradient descent in super neural networks. In: Genetic and Evolutionary Computation Conference. GECCO (2017)
6. He, J., Zhou, C., Ma, X., Berg-Kirkpatrick, T., Neubig, G.: Towards a unified view of parameter-efficient transfer learning. In: International Conference on Learning Representations (ICLR) (2022)
7. Houlsby, N., Giurgiu, A., Jastrzebski, S., et al.: Parameter-efficient transfer learning for NLP. In: 36th International Conference on Machine Learning. ICML (2019)
8. Hu, E.J., Shen, Y., Wallis, P., et al.: Lora: low-rank adaptation of large language models. In: International Conference on Learning Representations (ICLR) (2022)
9. Ke, Z., Liu, B.: Continual learning of natural language processing tasks: a survey. arXiv preprint arXiv:2211.05273 (2022)
10. Kirkpatrick, J., Pascanu, R., Rabinowitz, N., et al.: Overcoming catastrophic forgetting in neural networks. Proc. Natl. Acad. Sci. **114**(13), 3521–3526 (2017)
11. Lang, K.: NewsWeeder: learning to filter netnews. In: International Conference on Machine Learning (ICML) (1995)
12. Li, Z., Hoiem, D.: Learning without forgetting. In: Proceedings of the European Conference on Computer Vision, pp. 614–629. ECCV (2016)
13. Mallya, A., Lazebnik, S.: Packnet: adding multiple tasks to a single network by iterative pruning. In: Proceedings of the IEEE Conference on Computer Vision and Pattern Recognition, pp. 7765–7773. CVPR (2018)
14. Parisi, G.I., Kemker, R., Part, J.L., Kanan, C., Wermter, S.: Continual lifelong learning with neural networks: a review. Neural Netw. **113**, 54–71 (2019)
15. Rusu, A.A., Rabinowitz, N.C., Desjardins, G., et al.: Progressive neural networks. Neural Netw. **88** (2016)
16. Sun, F.K., Ho, C.H., Lee, H.Y.: LAMOL: language modeling for lifelong language learning. In: International Conference on Learning Representations (ICLR) (2020)
17. U, R., Kamath, S.S., Ananthanarayana, V.: Parameter-efficient tuned longformer for diagnostic code classification based on unstructured clinical reports. In: International Conference on WorldS4, pp. 166–175. Springer, Cham (2025). https://doi.org/10.1007/978-3-032-11509-6_16
18. van de Ven, G.M., Tolias, A.S.: Three scenarios for continual learning. arXiv preprint arXiv:1904.07734 (2019)
19. Yoon, J., Yang, E., Lee, J., Hwang, S.J.: Lifelong learning with dynamically expandable networks. In: International Conference on Learning Representations (ICLR) (2018)
20. Zenke, F., Poole, B., Ganguli, S.: Continual learning through synaptic intelligence. In: Proceedings of the 34th International Conference on Machine Learning, pp. 3987–3995. ICML (2017)
21. Zhang, X., Zhao, J., LeCun, Y.: Character-level convolutional networks for text classification. In: Advances in Neural Information Processing Systems 28 (NIPS 2015), pp. 649–657 (2015)

Automated ICD-10 Coding Approaches with UMLS Integration and Model Interpretability Support

Ritik Mahajan[1], S. Sowmya Kamath[1(✉)], Vijayan Sugumaran[2], and V. Geetha[1]

[1] Healthcare Analytics and Language Engineering (HALE) Lab, Department of Information Technology, National Institute of Technology Karnataka, Surathkal, Srinivasnagar P.O., Mangaluru 575025, India
`{ritikmahajan.232it026,sowmyakamath,geethav}@nitk.edu.in`
[2] Department of Decision and Information Sciences, School of Business Administration, Oakland University, Rochester, MI, USA
`sugumara@oakland.edu`

Abstract. Accurate disease coding is essential for healthcare management, reimbursement and medical research. However, manual coding is labor-intensive, error-prone and inadequate for handling the increasing volume and complexity of clinical data. In this article, an automated coding approach leveraging deep learning and natural language processing (NLP), enhanced by the Unified Medical Language System (UMLS) as an external knowledge base is presented. The integration of UMLS facilitates the standardization of clinical terminology and improves semantic understanding, leading to more accurate and efficient ICD code assignment. The proposed system automates the classification of discharge summaries into appropriate ICD codes, addressing limitations of manual methods while enhancing operational efficiency and data-driven decision-making. To ensure transparency and interpretability, model explainability techniques like Local Interpretable Model-agnostic Explanations and SHapley Additive exPlanations, are applied to analyze prediction performance. Experimental evaluation highlighted the effectiveness of the G-Attn model trained on C2V embeddings in comparison to other approaches.

Keywords: ICD coding · Medical record management · Model explainability · Clinical Natural Language Processing

1 Introduction

Medical records, which document a patient's episode of care, are essential for clinical decision making as they contain vital information such as clinical findings, diagnoses, interventions, laboratory test results and medication details. To ensure meaningful analysis and facilitate efficient healthcare processes, these

© The Author(s), under exclusive license to Springer Nature Switzerland AG 2027
E. Cabrio and E. Monteiro (Eds.): NLDB 2026, LNCS 16696, pp. 332–347, 2027.
https://doi.org/10.1007/978-3-032-29532-3_23

medical records are annotated with clinical codes, which provide a standardized way of representing medical information. The International Classification of Diseases (ICD) [27] is one such coding system, providing a comprehensive taxonomy of disease classes, each identified by a unique code. In many countries, these codes are used for multiple purposes, including communication between healthcare providers, insurance companies and government agencies, ensuring consistency in reporting medical services and tracking health trends.

The International Classification of Diseases, Tenth Revision (ICD-10) [5] is a standardized WHO system for coding diseases, symptoms and health conditions using alphanumeric codes (up to 7 characters). Organized into 21 clinically-relevant chapters each representing a broad category of conditions or external factors. For instance, Chapter I covers infectious and parasitic diseases (codes A00-B99), while Chapter IX is dedicated to diseases of the circulatory system (codes I00-I99). Within each chapter, ICD-10 codes follow a structured alphanumeric format, beginning with an alphabetical character that signifies the overarching category, such as 'C' for neoplasms or 'S' for injuries. The chapter-based organization and detailed structure of ICD-10 codes are crucial for healthcare systems worldwide, enabling seamless data sharing and in-depth analysis across different medical settings. This hierarchical arrangement not only facilitates efficient diagnosis and treatment recording but also allows researchers, policymakers and health agencies to systematically analyze health data.

Clinical coding is typically performed by trained professionals known as clinical coders. These experts are responsible for assigning appropriate ICD codes to a patient's medical records, based on their deep understanding of medical terminology, clinical classification systems and coding rules. However, the current process of assigning clinical codes is manual, making it time-consuming, expensive and prone to errors [29]. Mistakes in code assignment can lead to significant issues, including financial losses, increased labor costs, the need to review entire processes and delays in reimbursement. Inaccuracies in coding can also affect the broader healthcare ecosystem, as coded data is used not only for reimbursement but also by government agencies and policymakers for analyzing healthcare systems, justifying investments and planning future initiatives. Given the importance of accurate and efficient ICD coding, automating this process has the potential to significantly reduce errors, improve workflow efficiency and save costs. Automated ICD coding systems can enhance consistency, eliminate human variability and ensure faster processing of patient records. This is particularly important as the healthcare industry generates ever-increasing volumes of data, making manual coding unsustainable.

In this article, an automated ICD coding framework that integrates deep learning and NLP techniques with the Unified Medical Language System (UMLS) as an external knowledge base. By incorporating UMLS, the system enhances the standardization of clinical terminology and improves semantic representation, enabling more accurate and efficient ICD code assignment. The remainder of this article is organized as follows: Sect. 2 reviews related work and highlights the challenges of automated ICD coding. Section 3 describes the dataset, preprocessing steps and methodology employed in our approach. Section 4 presents the experimental setup and evaluation metrics, and a discussion of results. Section 5 concludes with a summary of findings and potential future directions.

2   Related Work

Automated ICD coding has gained significant attention due to its potential to enhance efficiency, accuracy and scalability in medical coding processes. Traditional manual coding is often labor-intensive and prone to errors, making it inadequate for the increasing volume and complexity of clinical documentation. Recent advancements in deep learning and NLP have led to the development of automated ICD coding models, leveraging pretrained language models (PLMs), external medical knowledge bases and transformer-based architectures. These approaches aim to improve coding accuracy while addressing challenges such as large label spaces, domain adaptation and the computational demands of processing lengthy clinical texts.

The automated ICD coding process includes several distinct task formulations [30], each addressing different practical needs in clinical settings. The most comprehensive approach is full-code prediction, where models attempt to assign the exact ICD code from the complete classification system - an exceptionally challenging task given the thousands of possible codes and their imbalanced distribution. For many practical applications, researchers often focus on simplified variants like ICD code group prediction, where models identify broader disease categories (e.g., "cardiovascular diseases" rather than specific cardiac conditions), making the problem more tractable while still providing clinically useful information. Another prevalent task involves predicting the top-N most frequent ICD codes, such as the top-10 or top-50 codes [7,17]. In these scenarios, models are trained to focus on a subset of the most commonly occurring codes, which enhances predictive performance and is particularly useful in clinical settings where certain diagnoses are more prevalent. These task-specific approaches enable the development of models that are both efficient and effective, catering to the diverse requirements of automated ICD coding in healthcare applications such as patient phenotyping [20,21], patient data aggregation [24,25], and multilingual medical record coding [15,16].

Zhang et al. [34] proposed BERT-XML for large-scale ICD coding using multi-label attention and a BERT model trained on millions of EHRs. Their approach outperformed baselines, setting a benchmark for large-scale ICD classification. However, the model's performance was constrained by its inability to effectively handle the long-tail distribution of rare codes and its high computational requirements for training. Huang et al. [10] introduced PLM-ICD, a framework for ICD coding using PLMs. Their approach addressed challenges such as large label spaces and domain mismatches through hierarchical and label-wise attention mechanisms. Experiments on the MIMIC dataset achieved state-of-the-art results but required significant computational resources. Yang et al.

[31] presented a knowledge-enhanced Longformer for few-shot ICD coding. They incorporated domain-specific knowledge and prompt-based fine-tuning to tackle label sparsity. Their method excelled in rare disease coding but relied heavily on high-quality knowledge resources. Yuan et al. [32] proposed a multiple synonyms matching network, leveraging UMLS ICD code synonyms for enhanced representation learning. Their method outperformed state-of-the-art approaches on MIMIC-III but introduced computational complexity. Al-Bashabsheh et al. [2] implemented a pipeline with two BERT models for ICD-10 coding. Their system achieved high F1 scores but faced challenges with class imbalance and annotation quality. Gomes et al. [8] developed a Transformer-based ICD coding model, using Longformer or chunked text processing to manage lengthy inputs. Label embeddings incorporating synonyms improved performance on MIMIC-III, though handling long texts remained computationally intensive.

Klotzman et al. [12] evaluated embedding models for mapping ICD-10-CM codes to semantic descriptions. Text-embedding-3-large excelled in semantic similarity, while voyage-large-2-instruct showed superior code retrieval performance. Williamson et al. [28] used NLP++ for low-resource ICD coding, mapping entities to UMLS concepts from hospital discharge summaries. While effective, their approach relied on quality entity extraction and lacked labeled data for rare codes. Aden et al. [1] combined ClinicalBERT with deep learning models to predict ICD codes on MIMIC-III. Their approach achieved top accuracy for predicting the top 10 and 50 ICD codes. While effective, their approach faced challenges in model interpretability for clinical decision-making and required substantial computational resources for training, limiting its practical deployment in resource-constrained settings.

Automated ICD coding has been extensively explored in recent years, revealing several critical challenges that hinder optimal performance. A primary issue is the handling of long and complex clinical documents, as models like BERT are typically limited to processing 512 tokens, whereas clinical notes often exceed this length, necessitating effective strategies for long-text processing. Additionally, the vast and imbalanced label space of ICD codes presents difficulties, with many codes being infrequent or unseen during training, leading to poor generalization. Furthermore, the lack of interpretability in deep learning models raises concerns about their reliability in clinical settings, as these models often function as "black boxes" without providing clear reasoning for their predictions. In our work, we address these gaps by integrating the UMLS to enhance semantic understanding and standardization of clinical terminology, implementing attention mechanisms to manage long-text inputs effectively and incorporating model reasoning/explainability techniques to provide transparent and interpretable predictions.

3   Proposed Methodology

The methodology in this study leverages NLP and deep learning techniques to automate the classification of multiple ICD-10 codes from discharge summaries and clinical notes. The overall workflow is shown in Fig. 1.

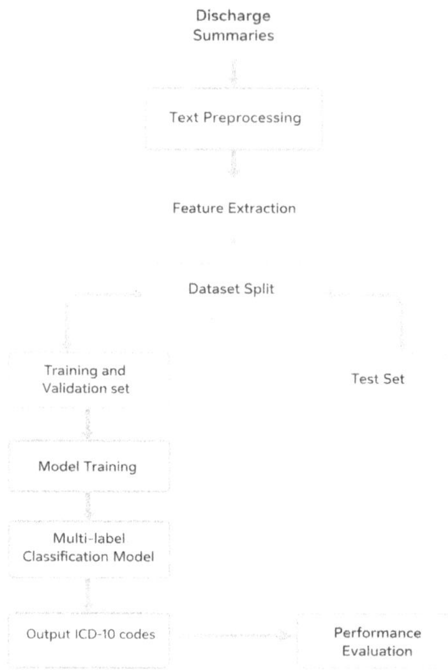

Fig. 1. Proposed Workflow.

Dataset Specifics. In this study, we focus on classifying the top 50 ICD-10 codes using the MIMIC-IV-ICD [19] dataset for experimental validation. MIMIC-IV-ICD is a public benchmark suite for ICD-10 coding, derived from the MIMIC-IV (Medical Information Mart for Intensive Care IV) [11], the most recent publicly available electronic health record (EHR) dataset. It contains 122,317 de-identified hospital admission entries with 26,096 unique ICD-10 codes. As shown in Table 1, for the top 50 ICD-10 codes, we split the dataset into training, validation and test sets, consisting of 104077, 3805 and 7368 documents, respectively.

Table 1. Statistics of the Top-50 ICD-10 Codes Dataset.

Dataset	#EHRs	Avg. Words	Avg. ICD-10
Training	104,077	1,687	5.4
Validation	3,805	1,695	5.4
Testing	7,368	1,669	5.3

Data Preprocessing. The preprocessing begins with the removal of redundant components, including extra whitespaces and newline characters, while discarding non-essential phrases such as "Name:," "Unit No:," and "Admission Date:." Additionally, repeated underscores (e.g., "__," "____") are eliminated to improve text consistency. Algorithm 1 details the text processing phase.

Algorithm 1: Text Preprocessing of Clinical Discharge Summaries

1: **Input:** Raw discharge summary corpus $\mathcal{D} = \{d_1, d_2, \ldots, d_n\}$
2: **Output:** Preprocessed and tokenized document set $\mathcal{D}^*$
3: $\mathcal{D}^* \leftarrow \emptyset$
4: **for** each document $d_i \in \mathcal{D}$ **do**
5:　　Remove extra whitespace and newline characters from d_i
6:　　Replace multiple consecutive spaces with a single space
7:　　Remove non-essential field headers
8:　　Eliminate repeated underscore patterns
9:　　Extract medical terms from d_i using *QuickUMLS*
10:　　**for** each extracted term w **do**
11:　　　Retrieve CUI(w) from UMLS
12:　　　Replace w with its canonical UMLS concept
13:　　**end for**
14:　　Convert d_i to lowercase
15:　　Tokenize d_i into $T_i = \langle t_1, t_2, \ldots, t_m \rangle$
16:　　$\mathcal{D}^* \leftarrow \mathcal{D}^* \cup \{T_i\}$
17: **end for**
18: **return** $\mathcal{D}^*$

A key aspect of this process is the standardization of medical terms using the UMLS, which maintains a comprehensive repository of medical vocabularies [4]. UMLS serves as a platform for integrating medical terminology by using Concept Unique Identifiers (CUIs) to unify distinct medical concepts and terms across Systematized Nomenclature of Medicine – Clinical Terms (SNOMED CT), ICD and Logical Observation Identifiers Names and Codes (LOINC) terminologies. Standardization is essential for ensuring interoperability within healthcare systems, enhance dataset consistency, improve data quality and reliability for downstream tasks. Through UMLS, the system consolidates multiple terms, including synonyms and abbreviations, into a single standardized framework. Medical terms are extracted and normalized using QuickUMLS, which employs CUIs to link clinical terms and create consistent medical data representations. For instance, abbreviations like "HTN" (Hypertension) and synonyms like "heart attack" (Myocardial Infarction) are mapped to their respective CUIs. After standardization, the text is converted to lowercase to prevent processing inconsistencies in subsequent stages. Finally, word tokenization is applied, segmenting the text into individual tokens (words), preparing it for NLP models. These preprocessing steps are essential for transforming raw clinical text into a clean and standardized format, ensuring optimal feature extraction and model training.

Feature Extraction. After completing the text preprocessing steps, we proceed to the feature extraction stage, where the cleaned clinical text is transformed into numerical representations using BioWordVec [33] and CUI2Vec [3] for word embedding generation. In this stage, each token from the preprocessed clinical text is converted into a dense vector of fixed dimensions, ensuring that similar terms or concepts are positioned close together in high-dimensional space. BioWordVec is a pre-trained word embedding model specifically designed for biomedical and clinical text, making it well-suited for capturing the domain-specific semantics of medical terminology. CUI2Vec is also a pre-trained vector embedding model designed to represent medical concepts while capturing semantic relationships relevant to clinical and biomedical contexts. Developed using a large corpus of biomedical and clinical texts, CUI2Vec encodes concepts from UMLS, each mapped to a unique CUI. These embeddings are particularly beneficial for medical NLP tasks, as they effectively capture relationships between medical terms, such as diagnoses, treatments and symptoms, that general-purpose embeddings often fail to distinguish, ultimately improving predictive performance.

Code Prediction Models. To predict ICD codes from clinical text, several advanced deep learning models were employed based on their ability to handle long, complex clinical sequences. These models include Bidirectional LSTM (BiLSTM) [9], Bidirectional GRU (BiGRU) [6], Clinical Longformer [13] and Qwen3 [23]. The BiLSTM processes text in both forward and backward directions, allowing it to leverage contextual information from both preceding and succeeding tokens. This bidirectional structure enhances the model's ability to capture long-range dependencies, making it well suited for clinical text classification. For BiLSTM, three types of embeddings were evaluated: BioWordVec, Cui2Vec and a combination of both to improve medical term representation. Attention mechanisms were also incorporated to assess their impact on performance. The BiGRU architecture extends the standard GRU by introducing bidirectional sequence processing. By using separate forward and backward GRU layers and concatenating their outputs, BiGRU captures contextual information from both past and future tokens, resulting in a richer sequence representation while maintaining computational efficiency.

The Clinical Longformer is specifically designed for long clinical documents and employs a sparse attention mechanism that combines local and global attention, enabling it to process sequences of up to 4,096 tokens. Pre-trained on biomedical corpora such as PubMed and MIMIC-III, it provides efficient and accurate representations of clinical language and medical terminology. Qwen3 is a transformer-based model optimized for long-context processing through advanced attention mechanisms and adaptive computation strategies. Pre-trained on diverse large-scale datasets including web text, academic literature and technical documents, Qwen3 offers strong general linguistic and factual knowledge, enabling effective modeling of complex clinical narratives. All models were trained using the Adam optimizer with binary cross-entropy loss. Hyperparameters such as learning rate, batch size and dropout were optimized via grid search. Early stopping was applied to reduce overfitting, with performance monitored on a held-out validation set. All experiments were conducted on GPU-accelerated hardware to efficiently handle long sequences and high-dimensional embeddings.

4   Experiments and Results

The proposed methodology was evaluated on the MIMIC-IV-ICD dataset, focusing on ICD-10 code prediction. The experiments were conducted in a Python-based environment using Jupyter Notebook for streamlined experimentation. The primary frameworks employed were TensorFlow and PyTorch, chosen for their robust deep learning capabilities and GPU optimization. The experiments were performed on a Linux-based system equipped with an NVIDIA Tesla M40 GPU (24 GB memory) and 128 GB RAM to accommodate the high computational and memory requirements of processing long text sequences and large embedding spaces. The dataset was refined to include the top 50 most frequent ICD-10 codes and split into training, validation and test sets. Preprocessing involved standard text cleaning and medical terminology standardization using QuickUMLS to map terms to UMLS CUIs based on cosine similarity, with the highest-scoring CUI selected for consistent terminology mapping. This process reduced vocabulary size and improved model generalization for multi-label classification. Figure 2 shows a sample output after CUIs mapping. Figure 3 presents the distribution of word counts in EHR documents within the training dataset after preprocessing and mapping terms to UMLS CUIs. The analysis revealed that while the highest word count in an EHR document exceeds 7,000 words, approximately 98% of EHRs contain fewer than 3,000 words. This indicates a skewed distribution with a significant concentration of shorter documents.

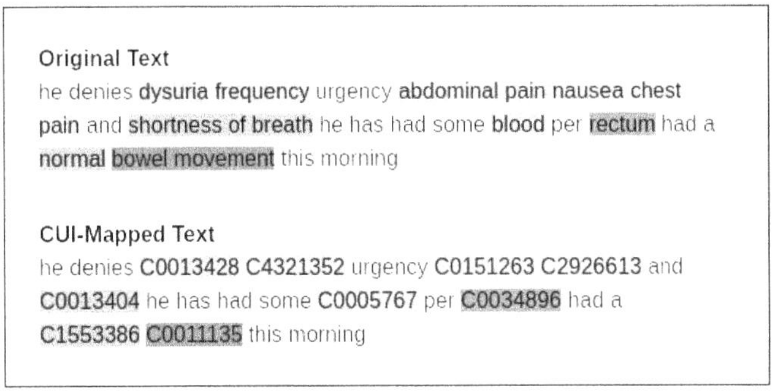

Fig. 2. Sample of CUIs mapping.

Given this observation, a token limit of 3,000 words was strategically applied during model training. This limit minimizes padding for most documents, reducing computational overhead and preventing significant data loss from truncation.

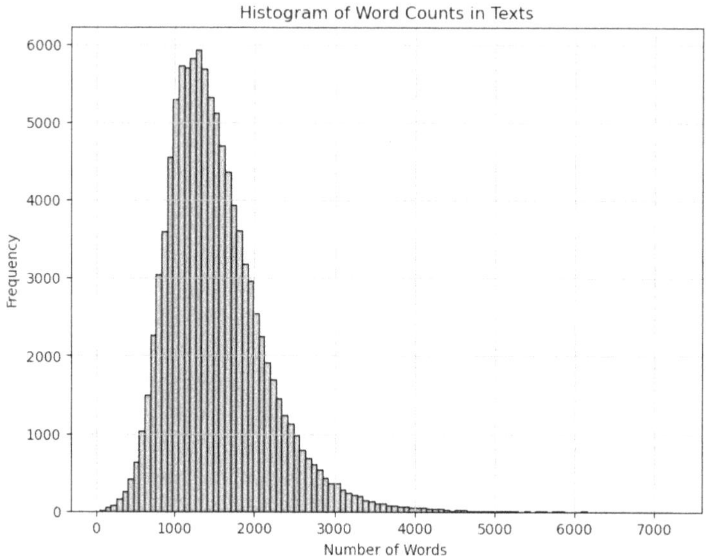

Fig. 3. Number of Words Distribution Over Training Set.

By focusing on a 3,000-word limit, the model's memory and processing requirements are better managed, retaining essential clinical information present in the
majority of EHRs. Additionally, training on a 3,000-word token limit ensures the
model's focus on core clinical content, enabling it to generalize effectively across
records of varying lengths without excessive padding. This strategy enhances
efficiency by avoiding unnecessary computation on padded tokens, resulting in
faster training and improved resource utilization. Converting ICD-10 labels into
binary vectors enabled a multi-label classification setup tailored for efficient and
accurate prediction of the top 50 ICD-10 codes.

We conducted extensive experiments using BiLSTM-based models and the
Clinical-Longformer model. For the BiLSTM models, three embedding strategies
were explored - BioWordVec, which provided word-level biomedical embeddings;
Cui2Vec, which used concept-level embeddings based on UMLS CUIs; and a combination of both to leverage their complementary strengths. We implemented
standard BiLSTM and attention-enhanced BiLSTM variants to capture sequential dependencies and focus on relevant text segments. In parallel, we employed
the Clinical-Longformer model, leveraging its clinical domain pretraining and
specialized tokenizer to process 3,000-token sequences while capturing long-range
dependencies. This systematic comparison of embedding strategies, architectural
variants and model paradigms provided robust insights into ICD-10 classification
performance.

The model performance was evaluated using several standard metrics, including Precision at k (P@k for k = 5), Micro-F1 score, Macro-F1 score, Micro
AUROC and Macro AUROC, to ensure a fair comparison with state-of-the-art

methods and prior research. P@k measures the model's ability to correctly identify relevant codes among its top predictions, while the F1 scores assess classification accuracy through both instance-weighted (Micro) and label-averaged (Macro) perspectives. The AUROC metrics further evaluate ranking performance, with Micro AUROC reflecting overall discriminative ability and Macro AUROC providing equal consideration to all codes regardless of frequency. This comprehensive suite of metrics enables thorough assessment across different aspects of multi-label classification performance, from precise code ranking to balanced evaluation of both common and rare codes.

The effectiveness of different model architectures and embedding techniques in ICD code classification was evaluated by considering different model variants – BiLSTM (B-Std), BiLSTM with Attention (B-Attn), BiLSTM with Differential Attention (B-DiffAt), BiGRU with Attention (G-Attn), BiGRU with Differential Attention (G-DiffAt), Qwen3-4B and Clinical-Longformer (CLF). Each variant is designed to capture varying levels of contextual and hierarchical information from the clinical text. To enhance the semantic representation of medical terminology, three embedding strategies are explored – BioWordVec (BWV), CUI2Vec (C2V) and Combined (BWV+C2V). The objective is to evaluate how different model-embedding combinations impact classification performance and select the most effective approach for automated ICD coding.

Table 2 presents the results of our proposed methodology, comparing the performance of different models using various embeddings. From the results, it is observed that the GRU with Attention (G-Attn) model, when combined with Cui2Vec embeddings (C2V), achieved the highest Macro and Micro F1 scores. This model also performs well in terms of Macro AUROC and Micro AUROC. The P@5 score for this combination is 0.63, indicating strong precision at the top 5 predictions. The Cui2Vec embeddings (C2V) generally outperform BioWordVec (BWV) across most models, particularly in the BiGRU with Attention (G-Attn) and BiGRU with Differential Attention (G-DiffAt) configurations. This superior performance can be attributed to the fact that Cui2Vec embeddings are explicitly trained on UMLS CUIs, which capture structured medical knowledge from sources like PubMed, clinical notes and other biomedical datasets. This makes Cui2Vec embeddings particularly rich in medical semantics, enhancing the model's ability to understand and process biomedical text.

Table 3 compares Precision at k (P@k) scores across different models and embeddings. BiGRU with Attention (G-Attn) model, especially when using the embeddings C2V, consistently achieves higher P@k scores across most values of k (from 1 to 10). This indicates that the model maintains high precision even as the number of considered predictions increases. Combining BiLSTM with Attention and using Cui2Vec embeddings, either alone or in combination with BioWordVec, yields the best performance across multiple evaluation metrics. This underscores the importance of leveraging domain-specific embeddings like Cui2Vec for tasks in the biomedical domain, where capturing precise medical semantics is crucial for accurate predictions. The standardization of medical terminology using UMLS CUIs during preprocessing further enhances the model's

Table 2. ICD-10 code prediction performance *(Abbreviations: B-Std - Standard BiL-STM, B-Attn - BiLSTM with attention, B-DiffAt - BiLSTM with differential attention, BWV - BioWordVec embeddings, C2V - Cui2Vec embeddings, CLF - Clinical-Longformer).*

Model	Embedding	Macro F1	Micro F1	Macro AUROC	Micro AUROC	P@5
B-Std	BWV	0.44	0.49	0.82	0.88	0.47
B-Std	C2V	0.54	0.57	0.86	0.90	0.54
B-Std	BWV+C2V	0.53	0.58	0.87	0.90	0.55
B-Attn	BWV	0.60	0.60	0.90	0.93	0.59
B-Attn	C2V	0.58	0.59	0.88	0.91	0.56
B-Attn	BWV+C2V	0.60	0.66	0.91	0.94	0.60
B-DiffAt	BWV	0.57	0.59	0.89	0.91	0.56
B-DiffAt	C2V	0.54	0.57	0.86	0.89	0.53
B-DiffAt	BWV+C2V	0.59	0.65	0.90	0.93	0.58
CLF	–	0.60	0.61	0.88	0.92	0.58
G-Attn	**C2V**	**0.65**	**0.69**	**0.92**	**0.95**	**0.63**
G-DiffAt	C2V	0.61	0.68	0.91	0.94	0.61
Qwen3-4B	–	0.54	0.57	0.84	0.86	–

effectiveness by ensuring that the input data is well-aligned with the semantic knowledge captured by Cui2Vec.

Table 4 provides a comparative analysis of the proposed methodology against several existing benchmark models for ICD-10 code classification. The evaluation is based on widely used metrics, including Macro F1, Micro F1, Macro AUROC, Micro AUROC and Precision at 5 (P5). Among the benchmarks, PLM-ICD and MSMN demonstrate the highest overall performance, with both achieving strong Macro F1 and AUROC scores, as well as a P5 of 0.65. CAML, an earlier model, shows lower performance across all metrics, particularly in Macro F1 and AUROC. LAAT and Joint LAAT achieve similar results, indicating their robustness in multi-label classification tasks, with slight differences in Micro F1 and AUROC scores.

4.1   Model Interpretation

To enhance transparency and interpretability, we employed Local Interpretable Model-agnostic Explanations (LIME) [22] and SHapley Additive exPlanations (SHAP) [14] to analyze the predictions of our model. LIME identifies influential terms through local text perturbations, revealing key clinical indicators in EHRs that drive specific code assignments. SHAP provides quantitative feature importance measures using game-theoretic principles, offering precise contributions of each term to the prediction. By leveraging these interpretability techniques, we

Table 3. Comparison of P@k Scores Across Models *(Abbreviations: B-Std - Standard BiLSTM, B-Attn - BiLSTM with Attention, B-DiffAt - BiLSTM with Differential Attention, BWV - BioWordVec Embeddings, C2V - Cui2Vec Embeddings)*

Model	Embedding	1	2	3	4	5	6	7	8	9	10
B-Std	BWV	0.67	0.63	0.58	0.51	0.47	0.45	0.42	0.39	0.37	0.33
B-Std	C2V	0.70	0.67	0.63	0.59	0.54	0.51	0.47	0.42	0.39	0.37
B-Std	BWV+C2V	0.71	0.67	0.65	0.61	0.55	0.53	0.47	0.45	0.40	0.38
B-Attn	BWV	0.83	0.77	0.70	0.64	0.59	0.55	0.51	0.47	0.44	0.41
B-Attn	C2V	0.79	0.74	0.67	0.61	0.56	0.52	0.48	0.45	0.42	0.39
B-Attn	BWV+C2V	0.83	0.80	0.74	0.66	0.60	0.57	0.53	0.49	0.47	0.43
B-DiffAt	BWV	0.78	0.74	0.66	0.61	0.56	0.50	0.47	0.45	0.40	0.38
B-DiffAt	C2V	0.70	0.66	0.63	0.57	0.53	0.51	0.46	0.40	0.38	0.35
B-DiffAt	BWV+C2V	0.81	0.77	0.68	0.61	0.58	0.55	0.49	0.47	0.44	0.40
G-Attn	**C2V**	**0.84**	**0.78**	**0.71**	**0.67**	**0.63**	**0.57**	**0.53**	**0.49**	**0.45**	**0.42**
G-DiffAt	C2V	0.84	0.79	0.72	0.66	0.61	0.56	0.52	0.48	0.45	0.42

Table 4. Benchmarking best performing approach with SOTA works

Model	Macro F1	Micro F1	Macro AUROC	Micro AUROC	P@5
PLM-ICD [10]	0.69	0.73	0.93	0.96	0.65
MSMN [32]	0.70	0.74	0.94	0.96	0.65
CAML [18]	0.64	0.67	0.91	0.93	0.60
LAAT [26]	0.68	0.72	0.93	0.95	0.64
Joint LAAT [26]	0.68	0.73	0.93	0.96	0.64
Our Model	0.65	0.69	0.92	0.95	0.63

ensure that the model's predictions are not only accurate but also understandable to healthcare professionals, facilitating clinical validation and adoption in real-world settings.

Figure 4 shows the LIME analysis of our model, where for given EHR it shows 94% confidence prediction of G4733 (Obstructive Sleep Apnea), with key terms color-coded by their influence: "osa" (red) strongly supports the diagnosis due to its direct relevance to obstructive sleep apnea, while "C0009253" (green) reduces confidence due to irrelevance. Figure 5 quantifies feature contributions using SHAP values, providing a more granular understanding of how individual terms influence the model's prediction for G4733 (Obstructive Sleep Apnea). The base probability of predicting G4733 is 0.27331, which increases significantly to 0.987141 due to the contributions of key terms such as "osa" and "C0277786", both of which have the highest positive SHAP values, reinforcing their clinical relevance, whereas "C0150312" negatively impacts the result. Both

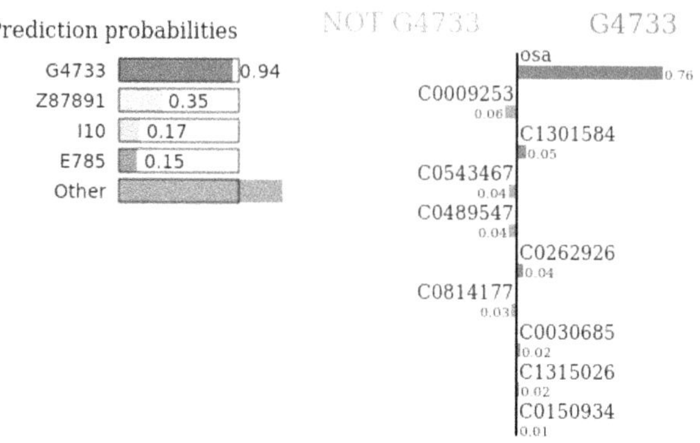

Text with highlighted words

C0009253 f service C0150934 C1717415 tree nut coconut peanut attending C0277786 osa major C0543467 or C0814177 s p C0040423 C0262926 of C0150312 C0221423 pt with osa C1554180 for bilateral C0040423 uncomplicated past C0455458 osa C0018681   C1301584 C0262926 n a C1315026 gen aao C0027270 pulm no C1441722 issues heent C0543467 site without C0019080 cv wwp brief C0489547 pt was C0809949 for C0150369 after her C0040423 she did well with no issues overnight on pod1 she was C0030685d tolerating a diet and C0042034 without concerns C0030685 C0013227 C0173449 C1304698 5mg q4h for C0278140 C0721362 15ml q6h swish and C0232515 for C0242429 C0030685 C0012655 home C1555319 s p C0040423 C0030685 C0009647 C0488569 clear and C0542044 C0751054 C0718338 and interactive C3890554 status C1547135 C0439857 C0030685 C3263700 C0871893 for C0173449 and C0721362 in C0684240 please watch for serious C0019080 if you have any serious C0019080 call or return to your C0013956 department you can advance to a C0301569

Fig. 4. LIME Analysis of Best-performing Model on sample text.

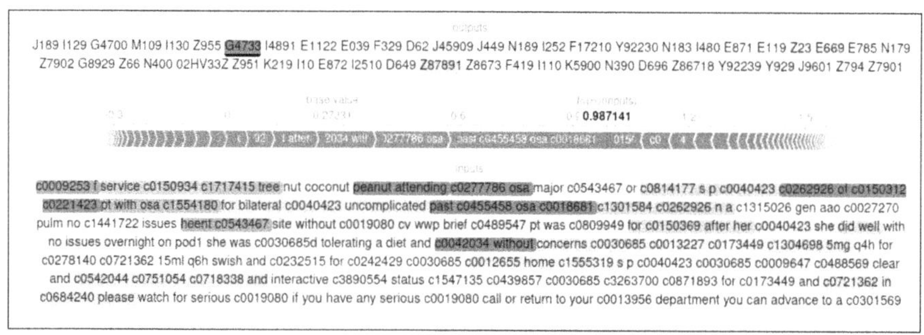

Fig. 5. SHAP Analysis for BiLSTM with attention Model with BWV+C2V embeddings on Sample Text.

methods reveal the model's focus on clinically relevant features while identifying noise, validating its decision-making process for healthcare practitioners. This dual interpretability approach enhances trust in the automated coding system by making its reasoning transparent and clinically meaningful.

In Fig. 5, SHAP values quantify the influence of individual words (features) on the model's output for the G4733 class. The bar at the top represents the model's base value and the contribution of individual features toward the predicted probability. A higher contribution (moving to the right) corresponds to stronger support for the prediction, while a lower contribution (moving to the left) detracts from the prediction. The base value (0.27331) represents the model's average probability of predicting G4733 without considering any specific features. The model's predicted probability for G4733 in this instance is 0.987141, a significant increase from the base value, indicating strong confidence in the prediction.

5   Conclusion and Future Work

In this article, a methodology for automating ICD coding by leveraging deep learning and NLP techniques has been presented. By integrating UMLS, the proposed approach ensures the standardization of medical terminology, with a systematic preprocessing pipeline including text cleaning, normalization, tokenization and UMLS concept mapping aligns medical terms with standardized concepts. We focused on automating the assignment of the top 50 ICD-10 codes, demonstrating high performance in experimental evaluations. Beyond predictive accuracy, interpretability techniques such as SHAP and LIME provided deeper insights into the model's decision-making process, by identifying key phrases and medical concepts that influence ICD code assignments, enhancing model transparency and facilitating validation by healthcare professionals.

As part of future work, we plan to expand this approach to include all ICD-10 codes, enabling comprehensive coding across a broader spectrum of medical conditions. We also plan to enhance the system through iterative evaluation and refinement, improving its scalability, robustness and overall performance. By optimizing both model architecture and preprocessing strategies, we seek to further reduce computational complexity while maintaining high accuracy. These advancements will contribute to the development of a fully automated, reliable and efficient ICD coding system, ready for real-world deployment.

References

1. Aden, I., Child, C.H., Reyes-Aldasoro, C.C.: ICD prediction from MIMIC-III clinical text using pre-trained ClinicalBERT and NLP deep learning models. Big Data Cogn. Comput. **8**(5), 47 (2024)
2. Al-Bashabsheh, E., Alaiad, A., Al-Ayyoub, M., et al.: Improving clinical documentation: automatic inference of ICD-10 codes from patient notes using BERT model. J. Supercomput. **79**(11) (2023)
3. Beam, A.L., Kompa, B., Schmaltz, A., et al.: Clinical concept embeddings learned from massive sources of multimodal medical data. In: Pacific Symposium on Biocomputing. Pacific Symposium on Biocomputing, vol. 25, p. 295 (2020)
4. Bodenreider, O.: The unified medical language system (UMLS): integrating biomedical terminology. Nucleic Acids Res. **32** (2004)
5. Brämer, G.R.: International statistical classification of diseases and related health problems. Tenth revision. World Health Stat. Q. **41**(1), 32–36 (1988)
6. Chung, J., Gulcehre, C., Cho, K., Bengio, Y.: Empirical evaluation of gated recurrent neural networks on sequence modeling (2014)

7. Gangavarapu, T., Jayasimha, A., Krishnan, G.S., Kamath, S.: Predicting ICD-9 code groups with fuzzy similarity based supervised multi-label classification of unstructured clinical nursing notes. Knowl.-Based Syst. **190**, 105321 (2020)
8. Gomes, G., Coutinho, I., Martins, B.: Accurate and well-calibrated ICD code assignment through attention over diverse label embeddings. arXiv preprint arXiv:2402.03172 (2024)
9. Hochreiter, S., Schmidhuber, J.: Long short-term memory. Neural Comput. **9**(8), 1735–1780 (1997)
10. Huang, C.W., Tsai, S.C., Chen, Y.N.: PLM-ICD: automatic ICD coding with pretrained language models. arXiv preprint arXiv:2207.05289 (2022)
11. Johnson, A., Bulgarelli, L., Pollard, T., Horng, S., Celi, L.A., Mark, R.: Mimic-IV. PhysioNet 49–55 (2020)
12. Klotzman, V.: Enhancing automated medical coding: evaluating embedding models for ICD-10-cm code mapping. medRxiv (2024)
13. Li, Y., Wehbe, R.M., Ahmad, S., et al.: Clinical-longformer and clinical-bigbird: transformers for long clinical sequences. arXiv preprint arXiv:2201.11838 (2022)
14. Lundberg, S.M., Lee, S.I.: A unified approach to interpreting model predictions. In: Advances in Neural Information Processing Systems, vol. 30 (2017)
15. Mayya, V., Kamath, S.S., Sugumaran, V.: LATA - label attention transformer architectures for ICD-10 coding of unstructured clinical notes. In: IEEE Conference on Computational Intelligence in Bioinformatics and Computational Biology (2021)
16. Mayya, V., Kamath, S.: Multi-channel, convolutional attention based neural model for automated diagnostic coding of unstructured patient discharge summaries. Futur. Gener. Comput. Syst. **118**, 374–391 (2021)
17. Merchant, A., Shenoy, N., Kamath, S.: Ensemble neural models for ICD code prediction using unstructured and structured healthcare data. Heliyon **10**(17) (2024)
18. Mullenbach, J., Wiegreffe, S., Duke, J., et al.: Explainable prediction of medical codes from clinical text. In: 2018 conference of the North American chapter of ACL (2018)
19. Nguyen, T.T., Schlegel, V., Kashyap, A., et al.: Mimic-IV-ICD: a new benchmark for extreme multilabel classification. arXiv preprint arXiv:2304.13998 (2023)
20. Prabhakar, A., Shidharth, S., Kamath, S.S.: Neural language modeling of unstructured clinical notes for automated patient phenotyping. In: 2022 56th Annual Conference on Information Sciences and Systems (CISS), pp. 142–147. IEEE (2022)
21. Prabhakar, A., Srinivasan, S., Krishnan, G.S., Kamath, S.S.: Diagnostic code group prediction by integrating structured and unstructured clinical data. In: Srirama, S.N., Lin, J.C.-W., Bhatnagar, R., Agarwal, S., Reddy, P.K. (eds.) BDA 2021. LNCS, vol. 13147, pp. 197–210. Springer, Cham (2021). https://doi.org/10.1007/978-3-030-93620-4_15
22. Ribeiro, M.T., Singh, S., Guestrin, C.: "Why should i trust you?" Explaining the predictions of any classifier. In: Proceedings of the 22nd ACM SIGKDD International Conference on Knowledge Discovery and Data Mining, pp. 1135–1144 (2016)
23. Team, Q.: Qwen3 technical report (2025). https://arxiv.org/abs/2505.09388
24. Unnikrishnan, R., Kamath, S.S., Ananthanarayana, V.: Parameter-efficient tuned LongFormer for diagnostic code classification based on unstructured clinical reports. In: International Conference on WorldS4, pp. 166–175. Springer, Cham (2025). https://doi.org/10.1007/978-3-032-11509-6_16
25. Unnikrishnan, R., Kamath, S., et al.: Sensefusion: a unified framework for multimodal and temporal clinical data modeling for predictive analytics applications. Inf. Fusion 104021 (2025)

26. Vu, T., Nguyen, D.Q., Nguyen, A.: A label attention model for ICD coding from clinical text. arXiv preprint arXiv:2007.06351 (2020)
27. WHO: International classification of diseases (2025). https://www.who.int/standards/classifications/. Accessed Apr 2026
28. Williamson, A., de Hilster, D., Meyers, A., Hubig, N., Apon, A.: Low resource ICD coding of hospital discharge summaries. In: Proceedings of the 23rd Workshop on Biomedical Natural Language Processing, pp. 548–558 (2024)
29. Xie, P., Xing, E.: A neural architecture for automated ICD coding. In: Gurevych, I., Miyao, Y. (eds.) 56th Annual Meeting of the ACL (2018)
30. Yan, C., Fu, X., Liu, X., et al.: A survey of automated ICD coding: development, challenges, and applications. Intell. Med. **2**(3) (2022)
31. Yang, Z., Wang, S., Rawat, B.P.S., Mitra, A., Yu, H.: Knowledge injected prompt based fine-tuning for multi-label few-shot ICD coding. In: Conference on Empirical Methods in Natural Language Processing, vol. 2022 (2022)
32. Yuan, Z., Tan, C., Huang, S.: Code synonyms do matter: multiple synonyms matching network for automatic ICD coding. arXiv preprint arXiv:2203.01515 (2022)
33. Zhang, Y., Chen, Q., Yang, Z., et al.: Biowordvec, improving biomedical word embeddings with subword information and mesh. Sci. Data **6**(1) (2019)
34. Zhang, Z., Liu, J., Razavian, N.: BERT-XML: large scale automated ICD coding using BERT pretraining. arXiv preprint arXiv:2006.03685 (2020)

Author Index

GPSR Compliance
The European Union's (EU) General Product Safety Regulation (GPSR) is a set
of rules that requires consumer products to be safe and our obligations to
ensure this.

If you have any concerns about our products, you can contact us on

ProductSafety@springernature.com

In case Publisher is established outside the EU, the EU authorized
representative is:

Springer Nature Customer Service Center GmbH
Europaplatz 3
69115 Heidelberg, Germany